The *Sams Teach Yourself in 24 Hours* Series

Sams Teach Yourself in 24 Hours books provide quick and easy answers in a proven step-by-step approach that works for you. In just 24 sessions of one hour or less, you will tackle every task you need to get the results you want. Let our experienced authors present the most accurate information to get you reliable answers—fast!

IDE Hotkeys

GENERAL IDE HOTKEYS

F1	Context-sensitive help
Ctrl+S	Save the current file or form
Ctrl+F	Find text
Ctrl+R	Find and replace text
F3	Repeat find or replace
F11	Show Object Inspector
F12	Switch between a form and the form's code
Ctrl+F9	Make a project
Ctrl+Shift+F11	Display the Project Options dialog
F9	Compile and run the program

EDITOR HOTKEYS

Ctrl+S	Save the current file
Ctrl+C	Copy highlighted text
Ctrl+X	Cut highlighted text
Ctrl+V	Paste text at the cursor
Ctrl+Z	Undo the last operation
Ctrl+Shift+Z	Redo the last operation
Ctrl+F4	Close the current file
Ctrl+Enter	Open the file under the cursor
F1	Context-sensitive help

DEBUGGER HOTKEYS

F9	Run the program in the debugger
F8	Step over a function
F7	Trace into a function
F5	Toggle breakpoint
Shift+F5	Add a variable to the watch window
Alt+F5	Inspect an object with the Debug Inspector

Teach Yourself

Borland C++Builder 4

®

in 24 Hours

Important C++Builder 4 Toolbars

C++Builder 4 provides Rapid Application Development in a Visual Environment.

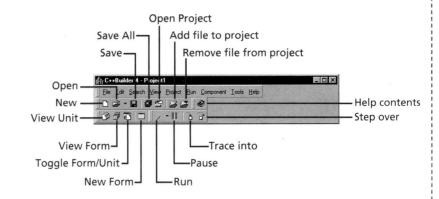

Feel free to customize the C++Builder 4 IDE any way you want. It's your development environment, so make it work for you.

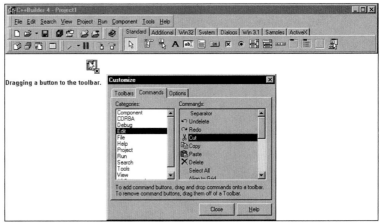

Customizing a toolbar.

The C++Builder 4 Component palette is a multipage window that enables you to place components or other controls on forms. Click the tabs to navigate between the pages and to display the available components or controls.

The Component palette scroll buttons.

Kent Reisdorph

SAMS
Teach Yourself
Borland
C++Builder® 4
in 24 Hours

SAMS

A Division of Macmillan Computer Publishing
201 West 103rd Street, Indianapolis, Indiana 46290

Sams Teach Yourself Borland C++Builder® 4 in 24 Hours

Copyright © 1999 by Sams Publishing

International Standard Book Number: 0-672-31626-9

Library of Congress Catalog Card Number: 98-83060

Printed in the United States of America

First Printing: April 1999

01   00   4

Trademarks

All terms mentioned in this book that are known to be trademarks or service marks have been appropriately capitalized. Sams Publishing cannot attest to the accuracy of this information. Use of a term in this book should not be regarded as affecting the validity of any trademark or service mark.

C++Builder is a registered trademark of Inprise Corporation.

Warning and Disclaimer

Every effort has been made to make this book as complete and as accurate as possible, but no warranty or fitness is implied. The information provided is on an "as is" basis. The authors and the publisher shall have neither liability nor responsibility to any person or entity with respect to any loss or damages arising from the information contained in this book or from the use of the CD or programs accompanying it.

EXECUTIVE EDITOR
Brian Gill

ACQUISITIONS EDITOR
Brian Gill

DEVELOPMENT EDITOR
Gus A. Miklos

TECHNICAL EDITOR
Ellie Peters

MANAGING EDITOR
Jodi Jensen

PROJECT EDITOR
Tonya Simpson

COPY EDITOR
Rhonda Tinch-Mize

INDEXER
Cheryl Landes

PROOFREADER
Mona Brown

SOFTWARE DEVELOPMENT SPECIALIST
Dan Scherf

TEAM COORDINATOR
Carol Ackerman

INTERIOR DESIGN
Gary Adair

COVER DESIGN
Aren Howell

LAYOUT TECHNICIANS
Brandon Allen
Stacey Richwine-DeRome
Timothy Osborn
Staci Somers

Contents at a Glance

Contents

Hour 18 Adding Functions, Data Members, and Resources 317

Hour 19 Managing Projects with C++Builder 335

About the Author

Kent Reisdorph is a senior software engineer at TurboPower Software Co. He also has his own consulting and training business. Kent is a contributing editor for The Cobb Group's *C++Builder Developer's Journal*. He is also a member of TeamB, Borland's online volunteer support group. As a member of TeamB, Kent puts in many hours each week on the Borland newsgroups, answering questions on C++Builder and Windows programming in general. Kent lives in Colorado Springs, Colorado, with his wife Jennifer and their six children, James, Mason, Mallory, Jenna, Marshall, and Joshua.

Dedication

For me, book dedications are easy. There is only one person in the world that deserves the dedication and that person is my wife, Jennifer. Jennifer suffers more than just a little hardship while I'm busy working on my books. She always manages to keep things going while I'm immersed in my writing. Thanks one more time, Jen.

Acknowledgments

First I want to thank Brian Gill of Macmillan Computer Publishing. Brian is unlike any other executive editor I have ever dealt with. He is honest, always helpful, and looks after my interests as much as he looks after those of Macmillan (at least he appears to!). Character like Brian's is rare in this business. I also want to thank Gus Miklos, the development editor for this book. Rather than taking this opportunity to rib Gus (something I'm very tempted to do!), let me instead say that he did a great job on this book. I am very appreciative of his hard work and his influence on the finished product. I enjoyed working with Gus and look forward to working with him in the future.

I would also like to thank Tonya Simpson, Rhonda Tinch-Mize, Cheryl Landes, and Mona Brown of Macmillan for their work on this book.

People at Inprise whom I want to thank include David Kipping, Michael Swindell, and, as always, Nan Borreson. One person at Inprise that deserves special mention is Ellie Peters. Ellie is a good friend and one heck of a technical editor. It's a luxury to be able to turn tech editing over to Ellie and not give it a second thought after that. Bruneau Babet and George Cross of Inprise had absolutely nothing to do with this book, but they know how to show me a good time when I'm in Scotts Valley so they deserve some credit!

Last but certainly not least, I want to thank my wife Jennifer. Jennifer is my guiding light during my book projects. She sits quietly by while I work hour after hour, day after day, week after week. When I need a break from writing, she's always there to listen to my complaints, my uncertainties, and, best of all, my dreams. Thanks as always, Jen.

Tell Us What You Think!

As the reader of this book, *you* are our most important critic and commentator. We value your opinion and want to know what we're doing right, what we could do better, what areas you'd like to see us publish in, and any other words of wisdom you're willing to pass our way.

As the executive editor for the Programming and Borland Press team at Sams Publishing, I welcome your comments. You can fax, email, or write me directly to let me know what you did or didn't like about this book   as well as what we can do to make our books stronger.

Please note that I cannot help you with technical problems related to the topic of this book, and that due to the high volume of mail I receive, I might not be able to reply to every message.

When you write, please be sure to include this book's title and author, as well as your name and phone or fax number. I will carefully review your comments and share them with the author and editors who worked on the book.

Fax: 317-817-7070
Email: prog@mcp.com
Mail: Brian Gill
         Executive Editor
         Programming and Borland Press Team
         Sams Publishing
         201 West 103rd Street
         Indianapolis, IN 46290 USA

Introduction

Welcome to C++Builder! C++Builder easily offers the fastest route to writing real-world Windows applications in C++. With C++Builder, you can prototype applications in hours instead of weeks or months as with other C++ programming environments. Don't let anyone tell you that you have to buy that "other" C++ development environment in order to learn C++. I am certain beyond doubt that writing Windows GUI applications is much faster and much easier with C++Builder than with any other Windows C++ programming environment available today.

This book is accompanied by a CD-ROM containing the Standard version of C++Builder. The Standard version provides an inexpensive way to learn the C++ language and a way to learn what C++Builder is all about. For the early stages of your involvement with C++Builder, the Standard version will do just fine. Inprise Corporation (formerly Borland) sells Professional and Enterprise versions of C++Builder. These versions provide more functionality than the Standard version does. In particular, these versions provide a powerful combination of database components that make writing database applications a breeze. They also include Internet components, a charting component, report writing components, and much more. These versions also allow you to write CORBA, COM, and MTS objects for distributed computing. The Enterprise goes beyond the Professional version to give you full client/server database and distributed application capabilities. If you like what you see in C++Builder Standard, I strongly urge you to purchase either the Professional or Enterprise version of C++Builder. You won't be sorry you did.

I encourage you to experiment as you read this book. Putting the book down and playing around for a while can prove more valuable than the best teacher. I also want to encourage you to explore the various online resources at your disposal. In particular, be sure to check out the Inprise newsgroups at forums.inprise.com. There you will find members of Inprise's TeamB (a volunteer group) and fellow C++Builder users answering questions for beginning and experienced users alike. Also, be sure to check the Inprise Web site at www.inprise.com, where you will find additional information on C++Builder as well as available updates.

In addition to this book, you should consider other Macmillan books on C++Builder. My book, *Teach Yourself Borland C++Builder 3 in 21 Days* (ISBN 0-672-31266-2) provides much of what is contained in this book, plus an additional 400 pages or so. Even though the book was written for C++Builder 3, you'll find the information presented there completely valid for C++Builder 4. Other books I heartily recommend include *C++Builder 4 Unleashed* (available Summer, 1999) and *Borland C++Builder How-To*. You should get any and all these books as your budget allows.

Another great source of information on C++Builder is Ziff-Davis Journals' *C++Builder Developer's Journal*. Each monthly issue contains 16 full pages of C++Builder-specific articles. I write regularly for this journal and as such can attest to its value. You can find out more about the journal at `http://www.zdjournals.com/cpb`. The Web site contains several free articles, so be sure to check it out.

Finally, be sure to visit my Web site at `http://www.reisdorph.com/bcb`. This site contains some articles I have written and, most importantly, errata pages and updated information on my books.

Have fun learning to program with C++Builder! Before long you'll be writing real-world Windows programs in C++.

Hour 1

Getting Started with C++Builder

Congratulations—you've chosen one of today's hottest new programming tools! Before you get started using all that C++Builder has to offer, though, you first need to learn a little about C++. Today, you will find

- A quick tour of C++Builder
- How to write a 32-bit Windows console application
- An introduction to the C++ language
- Facts about C++ variables and data types

Introducing C++Builder

NEW TERM *Win32* is commonly used to describe a 32-bit Windows program. A Win32 application is designed to run on Windows 95, Windows 98, or Windows NT. C++Builder produces only 32-bit programs.

C++Builder is Inprise's rapid application development (RAD) product for writing Windows applications in C++. With C++Builder you can create Win32 console applications or Win32 graphical user interface (GUI) programs. When creating Win32 GUI applications with C++Builder, you have all the power of C++ wrapped up in a RAD environment. This means you can create the user interface to a program using drag-and-drop techniques for true rapid application development. You can also drop ActiveX controls on forms to create specialized programs, such as Web browsers, in a matter of minutes. C++Builder gives you all this, but doesn't sacrifice program execution speed because you still have the power that the C++ language offers.

NEW TERM The *user interface* (UI) of a program means the menus, dialog boxes, main window, and so on. The UI is the part of the program that the user can interact with in order to operate the program. *Graphical user interface* (GUI) is also used to describe the UI in a traditional windows program. GUI is synonymous with UI in nearly all cases.

NEW TERM An *ActiveX control* is a pre-packaged piece of software that can be used in a wide variety of programming environments such as C++Builder, Delphi, Visual C++, Visual Basic, PowerBuilder, and so on. C++Builder ships with several sample ActiveX controls.

I must point out that the C++ language is not easy to conquer. I don't want you to think that you can buy a program like C++Builder and be a master Windows programmer overnight. C++Builder does a good job of hiding some of the low-level details that make up the guts of a Windows program, but it cannot write programs for you. Although you'll have to learn some programming, the good news is that C++Builder can make your trek fairly painless and even fun. Yes, you can work and have fun doing it! C++Builder *is* a great product, so have fun learning Windows programming.

Launching C++Builder

NEW TERM *Integrated Development Environment* (IDE) refers to all of the parts of C++Builder that work together to help you create programs. Some of the elements of the IDE are visible. For example, the C++Builder main window, Form Designer, Object Inspector, and Code Editor are visible elements of the IDE. Other aspects of the IDE—such as the actual C++ compiler—are not visible to the user. All elements of the IDE work together to make your job as a programmer easier.

This section contains a quick look at the C++Builder IDE. I'll give the IDE a once-over now, examining it in more detail in Hour 10, "Exploring the C++Builder IDE." When you first start C++Builder, you are presented with both a blank form and the IDE, as shown in Figure 1.1.

FIGURE 1.1

Starting C++Builder brings up the IDE and an initial blank form.

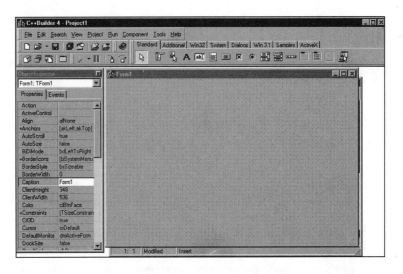

A *component* is a self-contained piece of software that performs some specific predefined function, such as a text label, an edit control, or a list box.

The C++Builder IDE is divided into three parts. The top window can be considered the main window. It contains the toolbar on the left and the Component palette on the right. The toolbar gives you one-click access to tasks such as opening, saving, and compiling projects. The Component palette contains a wide array of components that you can drop onto your forms. For convenience, the components are divided into groups. Did you notice the tabs along the top of the Component palette? Click on the tabs to explore the different components available to you. To place a component on your form, simply click the component's button in the Component palette and then click on your form where you want the component to appear. Don't worry about the fact that you don't yet know how to use components. You'll get to that in due time. When you are done exploring, click on the tab labeled Standard because you'll need it in a moment.

A *property* determines the operation of a component.

Below the toolbar and Component palette and on the left side of the screen is the Object Inspector. It is through the Object Inspector that you modify a component's properties and events. You will use the Object Inspector constantly as you work with C++Builder. The Object Inspector has two tabs. The Properties tab gives you access to a component's *properties*. Properties control how a particular component operates. For example, changing the Color property of a component changes the background color of that component. The list of properties available varies from component to component, although components usually have several common elements (Width and Height properties, for example).

An *event* is something that occurs as a result of a component's interaction with the user or with Windows.

 An *event handler* is a method that is invoked in your application in response to an event.

The second tab on the Object Inspector is the Events tab. Events occur as the user interacts with a component. For example, when a component is clicked, an event is generated that tells you the component was clicked. You can write code that responds to these events, performing specific actions when an event occurs. As with properties, the events that you can respond to vary from component to component.

Each page of the Object Inspector has two columns. The left-hand column shows the property or event name. The right-hand column is where you change a property or event's value (throughout this book I will refer the right-hand column of the Object Inspector as the Value column). A vertical scrollbar appears on the Object Inspector if the number of properties for a particular component exceeds that which the Object Inspector can display. Properties and events are listed in the Object Inspector in alphabetical order.

To the right of the Object Inspector is the C++Builder workspace. The workspace initially displays the Form Designer. It should come as no surprise that the Form Designer enables you to create forms. In C++Builder, a form represents a window in your program. The form might be the program's main window, a dialog box, or any other type of window. You use the Form Designer to place, move, and size components as part of the form creation process.

Hiding behind the Form Designer is the Code Editor (see Figure 1.2). The Code Editor is where you type code when writing your programs. The Object Inspector, Form Designer, Code Editor, and Component palette work interactively as you build applications.

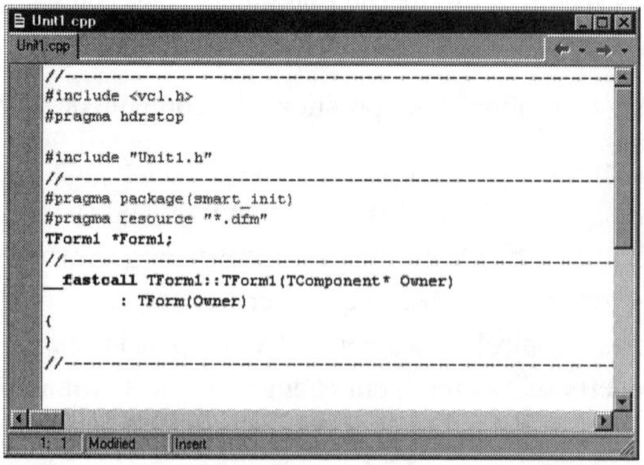

FIGURE 1.2

The C++Builder Code Editor as it appears after creating a new project.

```
//---------------------------------------------------
#include <vcl.h>
#pragma hdrstop

#include "Unit1.h"
//---------------------------------------------------
#pragma package(smart_init)
#pragma resource "*.dfm"
TForm1 *Form1;
//---------------------------------------------------
__fastcall TForm1::TForm1(TComponent* Owner)
        : TForm(Owner)
{
}
//---------------------------------------------------
```

1

Now that you've had a look at what makes up the C++Builder IDE, let's actually create our first program.

Writing a Simple Program with C++Builder

It's tradition. Almost all programming books start you off by having you create a program that displays "Hello World" on the screen. I'm tempted to do something else, but tradition is a force to be reckoned with, so "Hello World" it is. You've got some work ahead of you in the next few hours, so I thought I'd give you a taste of C++Builder's goodies before putting you to work learning the seemingly less glamorous basics of C++.

Right now you should have C++Builder running, and you should be looking at a blank form. By default, the form is named Form1. Locate the Caption property in the Object Inspector. Note that it currently has a value of Form1 (a default value provided by C++Builder). Click the Value column next to the Caption property and type Hello World! to change the form's caption.

As you modify properties, C++Builder immediately displays the results of the property change when appropriate. As you type the new caption, notice that the window caption of the form is changing to reflect the text you are typing.

Now click the Run button on the toolbar (the one with the green arrow). C++Builder begins to build the program. The compiler status dialog box, shown in Figure 1.3, is displayed, and you can watch as C++Builder races through the files necessary to build your program. After a brief wait, the compiler status box disappears, the form is displayed, and the caption shows Hello World!. In this case, the running program looks almost identical to the blank form. You might scarcely have noticed when the program was displayed because it is displayed in the exact location of the form in the Form Designer. (There is a difference, though, because the Form Designer displays small dots representing the Form Designer's alignment grid and the running program does not.)

FIGURE 1.3

Clicking the Run button displays the compiler status dialog box and runs the program.

Congratulations—you've just written your first C++ Windows program with C++Builder.

"But what is it?" you ask. It's not a lot, I agree, but it is a true Windows program nonetheless. It can be moved by dragging the title bar, it can be sized, it can be minimized, it can be maximized, and it can be closed by clicking the Close button. You can even locate the program in Windows Explorer (it should be in your \CBuilder4\Projects directory as Project1.exe) and double-click it to run it.

Okay, so maybe displaying "Hello World!" just in the caption was cheating a little. Let's spruce it up a bit. If you still have the Hello World program running, close it by clicking its Close button. The Form Designer is displayed again, and you are ready to modify the form (and, as a result, the program).

To make the program more viable, you're going to add text to the center of the window itself. To do this, you'll add a text label to the form.

Click on the Standard tab of the Component palette. The third component button on the palette has an *A* on it. If you put your mouse cursor over that button, the ToolTip displays Label. Click the label button and then click anywhere on the form. A label component is placed on the form with a default caption of Label1. Black sizing handles appear around the label to indicate that it is the selected component. The Object Inspector now displays the properties for the label (remember that previously it was showing the properties for the form). Click the Value column to the right of the Caption property and type Hello World!. Notice that the label on the form now shows "Hello World!." As long as you're at it, change the size of the label's text as well. Double-click on the Font property name in the Object Inspector. The property expands to show the additional font attributes below it. Locate the Size property under Font and change the font size to 24 (it is currently set to 8). As soon as you press Enter or click on the form, the label instantly changes to the new size.

Because the label is probably not centered on the form, you might want to move it. To move a component, simply click on it and drag it to the position you want it to occupy. When you have the label where you want it, you're ready to recompile and run the program. Click the Run button again. C++Builder compiles the program again and, after a moment (shorter this time), the program runs. Now you see "Hello World!" displayed in the center of the form as well as in the caption. Figure 1.4 shows the Hello World program running.

With this little taste of C++Builder, you can see that writing C++ Windows programs with C++Builder is going to be an interesting endeavor. To prepare for what you are going to do next, you need to close the current project in the C++Builder IDE. Choose File, Close All from the main menu. Click on No when prompted to save changes to Project1, or save the project as HelloWorld if you are fond of your new creation.

FIGURE 1.4

The Hello World program is easily modified to display text.

Building a Win32 Console Application

In the next few hours you are going to learn the basics of the C++ language. Along the way you will write some simple test programs.

NEW TERM A *console application* is a 32-bit program that runs in an MS-DOS Prompt box under Windows 95 and Windows 98, or a Command Prompt box under Windows NT.

These test programs work best as console applications. For all intents and purposes, these programs look like DOS programs when they run. There are some major differences between a Win32 console application and a DOS program, but you need not be concerned about that right now. So, without further ado, let's create Hello World as a Win32 console program with C++Builder.

From the main menu, choose File, New. C++Builder displays the Object Repository as shown in Figure 1.5. Curiously enough, the Object Repository's title bar says New Items, but don't be thrown by that. The Object Repository contains prebuilt projects, forms, dialog boxes, and other objects you can add to your applications or use to begin a new project. I will discuss the Object Repository in detail in Hour 17, "Common Dialogs and the Object Repository." For now, click on the New tab in the Object Repository and double-click the Console Wizard icon. Click the Finish button in the Console Application Wizard dialog box to create a new console application project. C++Builder creates the project and displays the Code Editor so that you can enter code for the program. Don't worry that you might not yet know what to do with the Code Editor. I'll show you how to enter code in just a bit. I discuss the Code Editor in detail in Hour 20, "Using the Code Editor."

Notice a couple of differences between the C++Builder IDE now and how it looked earlier when you created a GUI application. First, there is no Form Designer. That's because a console application, being a text-mode application, doesn't have a main form. Second, notice that the Object Inspector is blank. You can only place components on a form, thus the Object Inspector is useless in a console application.

FIGURE 1.5

The Object Repository allows you to create a new project, form, or other program element.

When writing console applications, you can close the Object Inspector to make more room for the Code Editor window. Close the Object Inspector by clicking the Close button on the Object Inspector's title bar. To bring back the Object Inspector, press F11 or choose View, Object Inspector from the main menu.

When you examine the Code Editor, you will see the following lines of code displayed in the editor window:

```
#pragma hdrstop
#include <condefs.h>


//----------------------------------------------------------
#pragma argsused
int main(int argc, char* argv[])
{
        return 0;
}
```

Don't be concerned if the console application code generated for you by C++Builder doesn't exactly match the code snippet. Products like C++Builder have been known to change late in the development cycle.

ANALYSIS This is a do-nothing C++ program, but a valid C++ program nonetheless. You'll modify the code in just a moment to make this program actually do something, but first I want you to notice the line that begins with `//`. This is a `comment line`. Programmers typically add comments to their code to help document the code. Commenting code helps others reading your code understand what the code does. In addition, comments in your code will benefit you when you come back to a program that you haven't worked on for a period of time. In this program the comment serves no purpose other than to divide the program's code visually. C++Builder adds these comment lines automatically when a new console application is first created. (In future code listings I won't include the comment lines, to save space.) Notice also that the single statement in this code ends in a semicolon. (I know it doesn't make sense right now, but the fact is that there is only one actual executable statement in this program.) The semicolon is used at the end of each statement in a C++ program.

Also notice the opening and closing braces in the program. In C++ a block of code begins with the opening brace ({) and ends with the closing brace (}). The braces are used to delineate the beginning and end of code blocks associated with loops, functions, and `if` statements, and in other cases as well. In this program there is only one set of braces because it is a simple program.

NEW TERM *Functions* are sections of code, separate from the main program, that perform a single, well-defined service.

NEW TERM A *class* is a collection of data members and functions that work together to accomplish a specific programming task. You use a class by assigning values to its data members and by calling its functions.

To display "Hello World!" on the screen, you need to make use of a C++ class called `iostream`, so a quick tutorial on that class is needed. (You don't know about classes yet, but don't worry about that right now.) The `iostream` class uses *streams* to perform basic input and output, such as printing text on the screen or getting input from the user. The `cout` stream is used to send data to the standard output stream. In a console application, the standard output stream means the console, or the screen. The `cin` stream is used to get data from the console, such as user input. `iostream` implements two special operators to place information on a stream or to extract information from a stream. The *insertion operator* (`<<`) is used to insert data into an output stream, and the *extraction operator* (`>>`) is used to extract data from an input stream. To output information to the console, you would use

```
cout << "Do something!";
```

This tells the program to insert the text `Do something!` into the standard output stream. When this line in the program executes, the text is displayed on the screen.

> cout is for use in console-mode applications only. A Windows GUI applica-
> tion does not have a standard output stream, so the output from cout goes
> nowhere in a Windows GUI program. The easiest way to display text in a
> GUI program is by using a Label component, as you saw earlier.

Before you can use cout, you need to tell the compiler where to find the description
(called the *declaration*) of the iostream class. The declaration for iostream is located in
a file called IOSTREAM.H. This file is called a header file.

 A *header file* (or just *header* for short) contains function and/or class
declarations.

 A *declaration* is a section of code that describes a function or class. The
definition is the actual code for the function or class. In C and C++, the distinction between these two separate states is very important. In general, a declaration is
stored in a header file, and a definition is contained in a source code file.

For example, suppose you were writing a function called "Multiply." The declaration for
the function would look like this:

```
int Multiply(int Number1, int Number2);
```

A declaration is followed by a semicolon. Note that the declaration simply describes the
function but doesn't contain any executable code. The definition for the function, on the
other hand, contains the code for the function:

```
int Multiply(int Number1, int Number2)
{
   return Number1 * Number2;
}
```

In this case the function is very simple, containing just a single line of code. I'll talk
more about function declarations and definitions in Hour 4, "Scope, Structures, and
Functions in C++."

To tell the compiler to look in IOSTREAM.H for the declaration of the iostream class, use
the #include directive as follows (see Listing 1.1, line 5):

```
#include <iostream.h>
```

Now the compiler will be able to find the declaration for the iostream class and will
understand what to do when it encounters the cout statement.

If you forget to include the header file for a class or a function your program references, you will get a compiler error. The compiler error will say something to the effect of `Undefined symbol 'cout'`. If you see this error message, you should immediately check to be sure that you have included all the headers your program needs. To find out what header file a class or function's declaration is in, click on the function or class name and press F1. The Windows help system is invoked, and the help topic for the item under the cursor will be displayed. Toward the top of the help topic, you will see a reference to the header file in which the function or class is declared.

There's one more thing I'll mention before you write the console version of Hello World. The `iostream` class contains special *manipulators* that can be used to control how streams are handled. The only one you are concerned with right now is the `endl` (end line) manipulator, which is used to insert a new line in the output stream. You'll use `endl` to insert a new line after you output text to the screen. Note that the final character in `endl` is the letter "l" and not the number "1."

Now that you have some understanding of the `iostream` class, you can proceed to write Hello World as a console application. Edit the program until it looks like Listing 1.1. Each of the lines has a number that I've put there for identification and to help you follow along as I walk through the code.

C++ doesn't use line numbers, so be sure to omit the line numbers when you type in the lines. Otherwise, your program won't compile.

LISTING 1.1 HELLO.CPP

```
 1:
 2: #pragma hdrstop
 3: #include <condefs.h>
 4: #include <conio.h>        // add this line
 5: #include <iostream.h>     // add this line
 6:
 7:
 8: //---------------------------------------------
 9: #pragma argsused
10: int main(int argc, char* argv[])
11: {
12:    // add the following two lines
```

continues

LISTING 1.1   CONTINUED

```
13:   cout << "Hello World!" << endl;
14:   cout << "Press any key to continue...";
15:   getch();
16:   return 0;
17: }
```

In C++, whitespace is ignored. For the most part, it doesn't matter where you put spaces or new lines. You cannot insert spaces in the middle of keywords or variable names, but other than that just about anything goes. For example, the following lines of code are equivalent:

```
int main(int argc, char* argv[])
{
cout << "Hello World!";
return 0;
}
```

This is the same as

```
int main(int argc,char* argv[])
{cout<<"Hello World!";return 0;}
```

Obviously, the first form is more readable and is much more preferable. Although coding styles vary, if you adopt the coding conventions you see in this book, you will be okay when it comes to programming in the real world.

ANALYSIS   Now click the Run button on the toolbar. The program compiles and runs. When the program runs, you will see a console window pop up and the words "Hello World!" displayed on the screen. Notice line 15 in Listing 1.1. You will add this line to most of the console applications you will write in the next few hours. The getch() function (declared in CONIO.H) is used to get a keystroke from the keyboard. This prevents the application from terminating until a key on the keyboard is pressed. This is necessary because a console window immediately closes at program termination (when the return statement is executed). By delaying program termination until a key is pressed, you get a chance to see the results of your handiwork. To end the program and close the console window, press any key on the keyboard.

I want you to be aware of how C++Builder saves console applications in case you decide to save the program in Listing 1.1. When you save the project, C++Builder creates two files. The project file has a .BPR extension and contains the information C++Builder needs to build the project. The source file has a .CPP extension and contains the actual program code. For example, if you saved the project with a name of HELLO, your hard disk will have two files; HELLO.BPR and HELLO.CPP. To reopen the project you open HELLO.BPR, but the Code Editor window will show HELLO.CPP. It's sort of confusing at first, but after the first couple of times you will understand what is happening.

The programs listed in the text are on the book's CD. The examples need to be installed on your hard drive before they can be compiled. Although it's good practice early on to enter short programs by hand, you might want to load the longer sample programs from your hard drive to avoid inevitable typing errors and the compiler errors that are sure to follow.

That's all there is to it. The console version of Hello World isn't too exciting, but you'll make good use of console-mode applications as you explore the C++ language. That's why it is necessary for you to understand how to create and run a console-mode application. Now let's move on to the basics of the C++ language.

C++ Language Primer

C++ is a powerful language. As is true in most of life, that kind of power doesn't come without responsibility. The C++ language can be unforgiving of programmer errors. I'll show you what programming pitfalls you are likely to encounter and how to avoid them in your programs.

I strongly suggest that after reading this book and experimenting with C++Builder for a period of time, you buy a book that explains C++ in greater detail.

 An *object*, like components described earlier, is a piece of software that performs a specific programming task.

The term *object* describes a piece of software at the lowest level. Components are objects but not all objects are components. Take the C++Builder Label component, for example. It is a component by virtue of the fact that it appears on the Component palette. It also appears on your form at design time. The `iostream` class discussed earlier is not a component. It doesn't appear on the Component palette nor on your forms. It is, however, an object. It provides a specific service. Granted, this can be confusing at first. In time, though, you'll come to understand the difference between a component and an object.

C++ enables you to take advantage of object-oriented programming (OOP) to its fullest. OOP is not just a buzzword. It has real benefits because it enables you to create objects that can be used in your current program and reused in future programs.

An object reveals to the user (the programmer using the object) only as much of itself as needed to simplify its use. All internal mechanisms that the user doesn't need to know about are hidden from sight. All this is included in the concept of object-oriented programming. OOP enables you to take a modular approach to programming, thus keeping you from constantly re-inventing the wheel. C++Builder GUI programs are OOP-oriented because of C++Builder's heavy use of components. After a component is created (either one of your own or one of the built-in C++Builder components), it can be reused in any C++Builder program. Best of all, components hide their internal details and let the programmer concentrate on getting the most out of the component. Objects and C++ classes are discussed in detail in Hours 6 and 7, "C++ Classes and Object-Oriented Programming."

The next few hours focus primarily on the part of the C++ language that has its roots in C. C++ is built on the C programming language. It has been described as "C with classes." This foundation in C is still very prevalent in C++ programs written today. It's not as if C++ were written to replace C, but rather to augment it. Beginning in Hour 4, "Scope, Structures, and Functions in C++," you will start to encounter language elements specific to C++. You don't have to be concerned with recognizing what information is from C and what is from C++ because it's all part of the language called C++.

It would be nice if presenting the C++ language could be handled sequentially. That's not the case, though, because all the features we will be discussing are intertwined. I'll take the individual puzzle pieces one at a time and start fitting them together. By the end of Hour 7, you'll have a complete picture of the C++ language. Don't be concerned if you don't instantly grasp every concept presented. Some of what is required to fully understand C++ can only come with real-world experience.

Variables and Identifiers

Well, we have to start somewhere, so let's take a look at variables. Before we do, however, I want to talk for just a moment about *identifiers*.

NEW TERM An *identifier* is a name given to a variable, structure, class, function, or other C++ language element.

Identifiers can mix uppercase and lowercase letters and can include numbers and the underscore (_), but they cannot contain spaces or other special characters. The identifier must start with a character or the underscore. The maximum allowable length of an identifier varies from compiler to compiler. If you keep your identifiers to 31 characters or less, you'll be safe. In reality, anything more than about 20 characters is too long to be useful anyway. The following are examples of valid identifiers with comments describing them:

```
int aVeryLongVariableName;  // a long variable name
int my_variable;            // a variable with an underscore
int _x;                     // OK, but not advised
int X;                      // uppercase variable name
int Label2;                 // a variable name containing a number
int GetItemsInContainer();  // a function name
```

> Identifiers in C++ are case sensitive. The following are two distinct variables:
> ```
> int xPos;
> int xpos;
> ```
> If you are coming from a language where case doesn't matter (Pascal, for example), the case-sensitive nature of C++ might cause you some trouble until you get used to it.

NEW TERM A *variable* is a location set aside in computer memory to contain some value.

A variable is essentially a name assigned to a memory location. After you have declared a variable, you can then use it to manipulate data in memory. That probably doesn't make much sense to you, so let me give you a few examples. The following code snippet uses two variables. At the end of each line of code is a comment that describes what happens when that line executes:

```
int x;         // variable declared as an integer variable
x = 100;       // 'x' now contains the value 100
x += 50;       // 'x' now contains the value 150
int y = 150;   // 'y' declared and initialized to 150
x += y;        // 'x' now contains the value 300
x++;           // 'x' now contains the value 301
```

Notice that the value of x changes as the variable is manipulated through the use of operators (=, +=, and ++ in this example). A little later I'll discuss the C++ operators used to manipulate variables.

> Variables that are declared but are not initialized contain random values. Because the memory to which the variable points has not been initialized, there is no telling what that memory location contains. For example, look at the following code:
>
> ```
> int x;
> int y;
> x = y + 10;  // oops!
> ```
>
> In this example the variable x could contain any value because y was not initialized prior to use.

Data Types

 In C++ a *data type* defines the way the compiler stores and operates on information in memory.

In some programming languages you can get by with assigning any type of value to a variable. For example, look at the following examples of BASIC code:

```
x = -1;
x = 1000;
x = 3.14
x = 457000;
```

In BASIC, the interpreter takes care of allocating enough storage to fit any size or type of number. In C++, however, you must declare a variable's type before you can use the variable:

```
int x1 = -1;
int x = 1000;
float y = 3.14;
long z = 457000;
```

This enables the compiler to do type-checking and to make sure that things are kept straight when the program runs. Improper use of a data type results in a compiler error or warning that can be analyzed and corrected so that you can head off a problem before it starts. Some data types can have both signed and unsigned versions.

 A *signed* data type can contain both negative and positive numbers, whereas an *unsigned* data type can contain only positive numbers. Table 1.1 shows the basic data types in C++, the amount of memory they require, and the range of values possible for each data type.

TABLE 1.1 DATA TYPES USED IN C++ (32-BIT PROGRAMS)

Data Type	Size in Bytes	Possible Range of Values
char	1	–128 to 127
unsigned char	1	0 to 255
short	2	–32,768 to 32,767
unsigned short	2	0 to 65,535
long	4	–2,147,483,648 to 2,147,483,647
unsigned long	4	0 to 4,294,967,295
int	4	Same as long
unsigned int	4	Same as unsigned int
enum	4	–2,147,483,648 to 2,147,483,647
int64	8	9,223,372,036,854,775,807 to –9,223,372,036,854,775,808
float	4	1.18E-38 to 3.40E38[1]
double	8	2.23E-308 to 1.79E308[2]
bool	1	true or false

In Table 1.1, you might notice that an int is the same as a long. So why does C++ have two different named data types that are exactly the same? Essentially, it's a holdover from days gone by. In a 16-bit programming environment, an int requires 2 bytes of storage and a long requires 4 bytes of storage. In a 32-bit programming environment, however, both require 4 bytes of storage and have the same range of values. C++Builder produces only 32-bit programs, so an int and a long are identical.

Only the double and float data types use floating-point numbers (numbers with decimal places). The other data types deal only with integer values. Although it's legal to assign a value containing a decimal fraction to an integer data type, the fractional amount is discarded and only the whole-number portion is assigned to the integer variable. The expression

```
int x = 3.75;
```

results in x containing a value of 3. Note that the resulting integer value is not rounded to the nearest whole number; rather, the decimal fraction is discarded altogether.

C++ performs conversion between different data types when possible. Take the following code snippet, for example:

```
short result;
long num1 = 200;
long num2 = 200;
result = num1 * num2;
```

In this case I am trying to assign the result of multiplying two long integers to a short integer. Even though this formula mixes two data types, C++ is able to perform a conversion. Would you like to take a guess at the result of this calculation? You might be surprised to find out that the result is -25,536. This is because of *wrapping* (also called *overflow*). If you look at Table 1.1, you'll see that a short can have a maximum value of 32,767. What happens if you take a short with a value of 32,767 and add 1 to it? You will get a value of -32,768. This is essentially the same as the odometer on a car turning over from 99,999 to 00,000 when you drive that last mile. To illustrate, type in and run the program contained in Listing 1.2.

 Some of the listings you will see over the next several hours don't have this statement:

```
#include <condefs.h>
```

This statement is automatically added when C++Builder creates a new console application. It isn't strictly necessary for the programs you will be working on, so I have eliminated it from the code listings. Your application will run the same, regardless of whether this statement is included.

LISTING 1.2   WRAPME.CPP

```
1: #include <iostream.h>
2: #include <conio.h>
3: #pragma hdrstop
4:
5: int main(int argc, char* argv[])
6: {
7:    short x = 32767;
8:    cout << "x = " << x << endl;
9:    x++;
10:   cout << "x = " << x << endl;
11:   getch();
12:   return 0;
13: }
```

ANALYSIS After compiling and running the program in Listing 1.2, the output is

```
x = 32767
x = -32768
```

In general, you won't go too far wrong if you use the int data type as your data type of choice. A range of -2 billion to +2 billion is sufficient for most programming needs.

Okay, where was I? Oh, yes, I was talking about automatic type conversion. In some cases, C++ cannot perform a conversion. If that is the case, you will get a compiler error that says

```
Cannot convert from datatype1 to datatype2
```

You might also get a compiler warning that says

```
Conversion might lose significant digits
```

> Learn to treat compiler warnings as errors because the compiler is trying to tell you that something is not quite right. Ultimately, you should strive for warning-free compiles. In some cases a warning cannot be avoided, but be sure to examine all warnings closely. Do your best to understand the reason for the warning and correct it if possible.

Operators

Operators are used to manipulate data. Operators perform calculations, check for equality, make assignments, manipulate variables, and perform other more esoteric duties most programmers never use in real-world applications. There are a lot of operators in C++. Rather than present them all here, I will list only those most commonly used. Table 1.2 contains a list of those operators.

TABLE 1.2 COMMONLY USED C++ OPERATORS

Operator	Description	Example
Mathematical Operators		
+	Addition	x = y + z;
-	Subtraction	x = y - z;
*	Multiplication	x = y * z;
/	Division	x = y / z;

continues

TABLE 1.2   CONTINUED

Operator	Description	Example
Assignment Operators		
=	Assignment	x = 10;
+=	Assign and sum	x += 10; (same as x = x + 10;)
-=	Assign and subtract	x -= 10;
*=	Assign and multiply	x *= 10;
\=	Assign and divide	x \= 10;
&=	Assign bitwise AND	x &= 0x02;
¦=	Assign bitwise OR	x ¦= 0x02;
Logical Operators		
&&	Logical AND	if (x && 0xFF) {...}
¦¦	Logical OR	if (x ¦¦ 0xFF) {...}
Equality Operators		
==	Equal to	if (x == 10) {...}
!=	Not equal to	if (x != 10) {...}
<	Less than	if (x < 10) {...}
>	Greater than	if (x > 10) {...}
<=	Less than or equal to	if (x <= 10) {...}
>=	Greater than or equal to	if (x >= 10) {...}
Unary Operators		
*	Indirection operator	int x = *y;
&	Address of operator	int* x = &y;
~	Bitwise NOT	x &= ~0x02;
!	Logical NOT	if (!valid) {...}
++	Increment operator	x++; (same as x = x + 1;)
--	Decrement operator	x--;
Class and Structure Operators		
::	Scope resolution	MyClass::SomeFunction();
->	Indirect membership	myClass->SomeFunction();
.	Direct membership	myClass.SomeFunction();

The list of C++ operators can be a bit overwhelming, so don't worry about trying to memorize each one. As you work with C++, you will gradually learn how to use all the operators.

It should be noted that the increment operator can be used either pre-increment (++x) or post-increment (x++). A *pre-increment* operator tells the compiler, "Increment the variable's value and then use the variable." A *post-increment* operator tells the compiler, "Use the variable first and then increment its value." For example, this code

```
int x = 10;
cout << "x = " << x++ << endl;
cout << "x = " << x << endl;
cout << "x = " << ++x << endl;
cout << "x = " x << endl;
```

results in the following output:

```
x = 10
x = 11
x = 12
x = 12
```

The same is true of the decrement operator (--). A lot of this won't make sense until you've worked with C++ for a while, but be patient and it will eventually come to you. As Pontius said to Augustus, "Relax, Augie. Rome wasn't built in a day, ya know."

Notice that some of the operators use the same symbol. The meaning of the symbol is different depending on the context. For example, the asterisk (*) can be used to perform multiplication, declare a pointer, or dereference a pointer. This can be confusing at first, and to be honest, it can be confusing at times no matter how long you've been programming in C++. Just keep working away and eventually you will begin to learn it.

You will see many examples of these operators as you go through this book. Rather than try to memorize the function of each operator, try instead to learn through careful study of the sample programs and code snippets.

Summary

In this first hour, you scratched the surface of Windows programming with C++Builder. You got to tinker with the C++Builder IDE by creating a GUI Hello World program. Following that, you were introduced to console-mode applications, where you created Hello World, II. After the initial playing around, you were put to work learning the basics of the C++ language. You have learned about C++ features such as variables, operators, and data types. Don't feel bad if you can't remember everything presented in this and upcoming hours. You might have to go back occasionally and review material you have previously read.

Workshop

The Workshop contains quiz questions to help you solidify your understanding of the material covered and exercises to provide you with experience in using what you have learned. The answers to the Quiz questions are provided following the questions. The Exercises are given for you to work out and code on your own.

Q&A

Q What's the difference between a Win32 GUI application and a Win32 console-mode application?

A A GUI application is a traditional Windows program. It usually has a title bar, menu, and window area. A console-mode application is a 32-bit character-mode application that runs in an MS-DOS Prompt box in Windows. The console application looks like a DOS program.

Q Can I assign a number containing decimal places to an integer data type variable?

A Yes, but the decimal fraction will be dropped (not rounded) and only the whole number portion will be assigned to the integer variable.

Quiz

1. What component is used to display text in a standard Windows (GUI) program?
2. What value does a variable have when it is initially declared?
3. What does the ++ operator do?
4. What is the difference between signed and unsigned data types?

Answers

1. The Label component is used to display text on a form (in a GUI application).
2. An uninitialized variable contains random data. When a variable is declared, it can contain any value until an explicit value is assigned to it.
3. The ++ operator increments a variable's value by 1.
4. Signed data types can have both negative and positive values. Unsigned data types only have positive values.

Exercises

1. Write a Windows GUI program that displays the words `Welcome to C++Builder!` on the window when the program runs.

2. Write a Windows console-mode application that outputs `This is a test` to the screen.

3. Write a Windows console-mode application. In the program, declare two variables and assign values to those variables. Multiply the two numbers together and display the result on the screen.

1

Hour **2**

Functions, Arrays, and Strings

In this hour you learn about functions and arrays in C++. As part of our discussion on arrays, you learn about how strings are handled in C++.

Functions

This section deals with functions primarily as they exist in the C language. I'll discuss the aspects of functions specific to C++ in Hour 4, "Scope, Structures, and Functions in C++." I have broken the discussion of functions into these two groups so that you can absorb the concepts of functions a little at a time.

 Functions are sections of code, separate from the main program, that perform a single, well-defined service.

These code sections are executed (called) in order to perform specific actions in a program. For example, you might have a function that takes two values, performs a complex mathematical calculation on those two values, and returns the result.

 A *parameter* is a value passed to a function that is used to alter its operation or indicate the extent of its operation.

Functions are an important part of any programming language. The simplest type of function takes no parameters and returns void (meaning it returns nothing at all). Other functions might take one or more *parameters* and might return a value. Rules for naming functions are the same as those discussed for variables in Hour 1. Figure 2.1 shows the anatomy of a function.

FIGURE 2.1

The anatomy of a function.

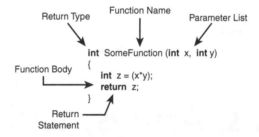

 A *declaration* or *prototype* describes a function's parameters and return value.

Before a function can be used, it must have first been declared. The *function declaration*, also called the *prototype*, tells the compiler how many parameters the function takes, the data type of each parameter, and the data type of the return value for the function. Listing 2.1 illustrates this concept.

LISTING 2.1   MULTIPLY.CPP

```
 1: #include <iostream.h>
 2: #include <conio.h>
 3: #pragma hdrstop
 4:
 5: int multiply(int, int);
 6: void showResult(int);
 7:
 8: int main(int argc, char* argv[])
 9: {
10:    int x, y, result;
11:    cout << endl << "Enter the first value: ";
12:    cin >> x;
13:    cout << "Enter the second value: ";
```

```
14:    cin >> y;
15:    result = multiply(x, y);
16:    showResult(result);
17:    cout << endl << endl << "Press any key to continue...";
18:    getch();
19:    return 0;
20: }
21:
22: int multiply(int x, int y)
23: {
24:    return x * y;
25: }
26:
27: void showResult(int res)
28: {
29:    cout << "The result is: " << res << endl;
30: }
```

2

ANALYSIS This program asks for two numbers from the user (using the standard input stream, cin) in lines 11–14, calls the multiply() function to multiply the two numbers together (line 15), and then calls the showResult() function to display the result (line 16). Notice the function prototypes for the multiply() and showResult() functions on lines 5 and 6, just above the main program. The prototypes list only the return type, the function name, and the data type of the function's parameters. That is the minimum requirement for a function declaration.

If desired, the function prototype can contain variable names that can be used to document what the function does. For example, the function declaration for the multiply() function could have been written like this:

```
int multiply(int firstNumber, int secondNumber);
```

In this case it's fairly obvious what the multiply() function does, but it can't hurt to document your code both through comments and through the code itself.

Look again at Listing 2.1. Notice that the function definition for the multiply() function (lines 22–25) is outside the block of code defining the main function (lines 8–20). The function definition contains the actual body of the function. In this case the body of the function is minimal because the function simply multiplies the two function parameters together and returns the result. The return statement tells the compiler to exit the function and return a value. Note that there is no return statement for the showResult() function. This function doesn't return a value, so the return statement isn't required.

The `multiply()` function in Listing 2.1 can be called in one of several ways. You can pass variables, literal values, or even the results of other function calls:

```
result = multiply(2, 5);        // passing literal values
result = multiply(x, y);        // passing variables
showResult(multiply(x,y));      // return value used as a
                                // parameter for another function
multiply(x, y);                 // return value ignored
```

Notice in the last example that the return value isn't used. In this case it doesn't make much sense to call the `multiply()` function and ignore the return value, but ignoring the return value is something that is done frequently in C++ programming. There are many functions that perform a specific action and then return a value indicating the status of the function call. In some cases the return value is not relevant to your program, so you can just ignore it. If you don't do anything with the return value, it is simply discarded and no harm is done. For example, we have been ignoring the return value of the `getch()` function (which returns the ASCII value of the key that was pressed) in our sample programs.

NEW TERM *Recursion* is the process by which a function calls itself.

Functions can (and frequently do) call other functions. Functions can even call themselves. This is called *recursion* and is one way to get into trouble in C++ programming. Recursion is best left alone until you've put in some time with the C++ language.

HOUSE RULES FOR FUNCTIONS IN C++

- A function can take any number of parameters or no parameters at all.
- A function can be written to return a value, but it isn't mandatory that a function return a value.
- If a function has a return type of `void`, it cannot return a value. If you attempt to return a value from a function with a return type of `void`, a compiler error is issued. A function that returns `void` need not contain a `return` statement at all. If no `return` statement is provided, the function returns automatically when it gets to the end of the function block (the closing brace).
- If the function prototype indicates that the function returns a value, the function body should contain a `return` statement that returns a value. If the function doesn't return a value, a compiler warning is issued.
- Functions can take any number of parameters but can return only one value.

SYNTAX

The function statement, in declaration (prototype) format is

```
ret_type function_name(argtype_1 arg_1, argtype_2 arg_2, ...,
➥argtype_n arg_n);
```

The function declaration identifies a function that is included in the code. It shows the return data type (*ret_type*) of the function and the name of the function (*function_name*) and identifies the order (*arg_1*, *arg_2*, ..., *arg_n*) and types (*argtype_1*, *argtype_2*, ..., *argtype_n*) of data arguments (if any) the function will expect.

The function statement, in definition format is

```
ret_type function_name(argtype_1 arg_1, argtype_2 arg_2,
➥..., argtype_n arg_n)
{
statements;
return ret_type;
}
```

The function definition identifies the code block (*statements*) that makes up the function and shows the return data type (*ret_type*) of the function. *function_name* identifies the function. The parameters (if any) supplied to the function (*arg_1*, *arg_2*, ..., *arg_n*) and their types (*argtype_1*, *argtype_2*, ..., *argtype_n*) are included.

Some functions do not take parameters. When declaring, defining, or calling a function with no parameters, the parentheses are still required. For example, here's a declaration for a function that takes no parameters:

```
void MyFunction();
```

The code to call this function, then, would look like this:

```
MyFunction();
```

Failure to add the parentheses results in a compiler error.

The `main()` Function

A C++ program must have a `main()` function. This function serves as the entry point to the program. You have seen this in each of the sample programs thus far. Not all C++ programs have a traditional `main()` function, however. Windows programs written in C and C++ have an entry-point function called `WinMain()` rather than the traditional `main()` function.

A C++Builder GUI application has a WinMain(), but it is placed in the project source file where you typically never see it. C++Builder frees you from having to worry about the low-level details of a Windows program and enables you to concentrate on creating the user interface and the remainder of the program.

main() is a function like any other function. That is, it has the same basic anatomy. You already saw that for 32-bit console applications, C++Builder creates a default main() function with the following prototype:

```
int main(int argc, char* argv[]);
```

This form of main() takes two parameters and returns an integer value. As you learned earlier, you pass values to a function when you call the function. In the case of main(), though, you never call the function directly—it's automatically executed when the program runs. So how does the main() function get its parameters? The answer: from the command line. Let me illustrate.

Let's assume that you have a Win32 console application that you execute from a DOS prompt with the following command line:

```
grep WM_KILLFOCUS -d -i
```

In this case you are starting a program called grep with command-line arguments of WM_KILLFOCUS, -d, and -i. Given that example, I will show you how that translates to argc and argv inside the main() function. First, the integer variable argc contains the number of parameters passed in the command line. This is always at least 1 because the program name counts as a parameter. The variable argv is an array of pointers to strings. This array contains each string passed in the command line. For this code example, the following are true:

argc	Contains 4
argv[0]	Contains c:\cbuilder\bin\grep.exe
argv[1]	Contains WM_KILLFOCUS
argv[2]	Contains -d
argv[3]	Contains -i

Let's prove that this works with a little sample program. Create a new console application in C++Builder and enter the program shown in Listing 2.2.

LISTING 2.2   ARGSTEST.CPP

```
 1: #include <iostream.h>
 2: #include <conio.h>
 3: #pragma hdrstop
 4:
 5: int main(int argc, char **argv)
 6: {
 7:   cout << "argc = " << argc << endl;
 8:   for (int i=0;i<argc;i++)
 9:     cout << "Parameter " << i << ": " << argv[i] << endl;
10:   cout << endl << "Press any key to continue...";
11:   getch();
12:   return 0;
13: }
```

Save the project as ARGSTEST. Rather than click the Run button, choose Project, Build All from the main menu. This builds the project but won't execute the program. When the project has finished building, choose Run, Parameters from the main menu. Type the following in the Parameters field of the Run Parameters dialog box and click OK:

one two three "four five" six

Now click the Run button. The program runs and outputs the command-line parameters you specified.

OUTPUT

```
argc = 6
Parameter 0: E:\TYBCPP\HOUR02\ArgsTest.exe
Parameter 1: one
Parameter 2: two
Parameter 3: three
Parameter 4: four five
Parameter 5: six

Press any key to continue...
```

An alternative is to run the program from a command prompt by using the following command line:

argstest one two three "four five" six

In most programs the value returned from main() is irrelevant because the return value is not typically used. In fact, you don't need your main() function to return a value at all.

Arrays

You can place any of the intrinsic C++ data types into an array. This includes pointers, which allow you to store objects of any type in an array. An *array* is simply a collection of values. For example, let's say you want to keep an array of ints that holds five integer values. You would declare the array as follows:

```
int myArray[5];
```

In this case the compiler allocates memory for the array, as illustrated in Figure 2.2. Because each int requires 4 bytes of storage, the entire array takes up 20 bytes in memory.

FIGURE 2.2

Memory allocation for an array of five ints.

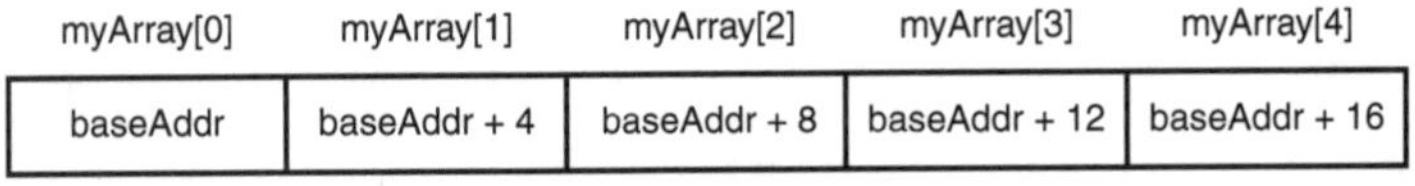

myArray[0]	myArray[1]	myArray[2]	myArray[3]	myArray[4]
baseAddr	baseAddr + 4	baseAddr + 8	baseAddr + 12	baseAddr + 16

In Figures 2.2, and later in 2.3, *baseAddr* refers to the base address of the array in memory. Windows assigns the memory address when the array is created.

Now that you have the array declared, you can fill it with values, using the *subscript operator* ([ ]) as follows:

```
myArray[0] = -200;
myArray[1] = -100;
myArray[2] = 0;
myArray[3] = 100;
myArray[4] = 200;
```

As you can see from this code, arrays in C++ are zero-based. Later in your program, you can access the individual elements of the array again by using the subscript operator:

```
int result = myArray[3] + myArray[4];   // result will be 300
```

There is a shortcut method for declaring and filling an array all at one time. It looks like this:

```
int myArray[5] = { -200, -100, 0, 100, 200 };
```

To take this one step further: If you know exactly how many elements your array will have, and if you fill the array when you declare it, you can even leave out the array size when you declare the array. In that case you would use the following:

```
int myArray[] = { -200, -100, 0, 100, 200 };
```

This works because the compiler can figure out from the list of values being assigned how many elements are in the array and how much memory to allocate for the array.

Arrays can be multidimensional. To create a two-dimensional array of integers, you would use code like this:

```
int mdArray[3][5];
```

This allocates storage for 15 ints (a total of 60 bytes, if you're keeping score). You access elements of the array like you do a simple array, with the obvious difference that you must supply two subscript operators:

```
int x = mdArray[1][1] + mdArray[2][1];
```

Figure 2.3 illustrates how a two-dimensional array might look in memory.

FIGURE 2.3

A two-dimensional array in memory.

	mdArray[ ][0]	mdArray[ ][1]	mdArray[ ][2]	mdArray[ ][3]	mdArray[ ][4]
mdArray[0][ ]	baseAddr	baseAddr + 4	baseAddr + 8	baseAddr + 12	baseAddr + 16
mdArray[1][ ]	baseAddr + 20	baseAddr + 24	baseAddr + 28	baseAddr + 32	baseAddr + 36
mdArray[2][ ]	baseAddr + 40	baseAddr + 44	baseAddr + 48	baseAddr + 52	baseAddr + 56

You must be careful not to overwrite the end of an array. One powerful feature of C++ is direct access to memory. Because of this feature, C++ won't prevent you from writing to a particular memory location, even if that location is memory your program isn't supposed to have access to. The following code is legal but results in a crash in your program (or in Windows):

```
int array[5];
array[5] = 10;
```

This is a common error to make because arrays are 0 based. You might think that the last element of this array is at array index 5 when it is really at array index 4. If you overwrite the end of an array, you have no idea what memory you are overwriting. The results are unpredictable at best. At worst, you will crash your program and maybe even crash Windows, too. This type of problem can be difficult to diagnose because often the affected memory is not accessed until much later, and the crash occurs at that time (leaving you wondering what happened). Be careful when writing to an array.

HOUSE RULES FOR ARRAYS IN C++

- Arrays are 0 based. The first element in the array is 0, the second element is 1, the third element is 2, and so on.
- Array sizes must be compile-time constants. The compiler must know at compile time how much space to allocate for the array. You cannot use a variable to assign an array size, so the following is not legal and results in a compiler error:

```
int x = 10;
int myArray[x];    // compiler error here
```

- Be careful not to overwrite the end of an array.
- Allocate large arrays from the heap rather than from the stack. (You'll learn more on this in Hour 15, "VCL Components," when I discuss pointers.)
- Arrays allocated from the heap *can* use a variable to specify the array size:

```
int x = 10;
int* myArray = new int[x];   // this is OK
```

Character Arrays

Odd as it might seem, there is no support in C++ for a *string* variable (a variable that holds text). Instead, strings in C++ programs are represented by arrays of the char data type. For instance, you could assign a string to a char array as follows:

```
char text[] = "This is a string.";
```

 The *terminating null* is a special character that is represented with \0, which equates to a numerical 0.

This allocates 18 bytes of storage in memory and stores the string in that memory location. You might have noticed that there are only 17 characters in this string. The reason that 18 bytes are allocated is that at the end of the string is a terminating null, and C++ accounts for the terminating null when allocating storage.

When the program encounters a 0 in the character array, it interprets that location as the end of the string. To see how this is done, enter and run Listing 2.3 as a console application.

LISTING 2.3   NULLTEST.CPP

```
 1: #include <iostream.h>
 2: #include <conio.h>
 3: #pragma hdrstop
 4:
 5: int main(int argc, char **argv)
 6: {
 7:   char str[] = "This is a string.";
 8:   cout << str << endl;
 9:   str[7] = '\0';
10:   cout << str << endl;
11:   cout << endl << "Press any key to continue...";
12:   getch();
13:   return 0;
14: }
```

OUTPUT
```
This is a string.
This is
```
```
Press any key to continue...
```

ANALYSIS   Initially, the character array contains the characters This is a string. followed by the terminating null. That string is sent to the screen via cout. The next line assigns the seventh element of the array to \0, which is, of course, the terminating null. The string is again sent to the screen, but this time only This is is displayed. Why? Because as far as the computer is concerned, the string ends at element 7 in the array. The rest of the characters are still in storage but can't be displayed because of the terminating null at index 7. Figure 2.4 illustrates how the character array looks before and after the line that changes element 7 to the terminating null.

FIGURE 2.4

The contents of a character array with the terminating null.

I could have simply assigned a 0 in place of '\0' in Listing 2.3. Either is acceptable because a numerical 0 and the char data type version, '\0', are equivalent. For example, the following two lines of code are equivalent:

```
str[7] = '\0';
str[7] = 0;
```

Note that '\0' and '0' are two separate representations of data. The single backslash is an escape character that tells the compiler a special value follows. To store the number 0 as part of the string you would do one of the following:

```
str[7] = '0'; // a zero character
str[7] = 48;  // the ASCII value of the zero character
```

There is a difference between single and double quotes in a C++ program. When assigning a value to an element of a character array, you must use single quotes. The single quotes effectively turn the character within the quotes into an integer value (the ASCII value of the character). This value is then stored in the memory location. When assigning strings to character arrays, you must use double quotes. If you get it wrong in either case, the compiler lets you know by issuing a compiler error.

String-Manipulation Functions

If you are coming from a programming language that has a string data type, all this might seem a pain. The truth is, it takes very little time to get used to. To aid in string operations, the standard C library has several functions for string manipulation. Table 2.1 lists the most frequently used string-manipulation functions and a description of each. For a complete description of each of these functions and examples of their use, see the C++Builder online help.

TABLE 2.1 STRING-MANIPULATION FUNCTIONS

Function	Description
strcat()	Concatenates (adds) a string to the end of the target string
strcmp()	Compares two strings for equality
strcmpi()	Compares two strings for equality without case sensitivity
strcpy()	Copies the contents of one string to the target string
strstr()	Scans a string for the first occurrence of a substring
strlen()	Returns the length of the string
strupr()	Converts all characters in a string to uppercase
strlwr()	Converts all characters in a string to lowercase
sprintf()	Builds a string based on a variable number of parameters

The string operations discussed here are how strings are handled in C. Most C++ compilers provide a class that simplifies the difficulties inherent in the C way of handling strings. C++Builder provides two such string classes. The Standard Template Library (STL) includes a class called basic_string, and the Visual Component Library (VCL) contains a class called AnsiString (I discuss AnsiString in Hour 9, "Exploring the VCL"). Check the C++Builder online help for more information on basic_string and AnsiString. Although the C way of handling strings is a little quirky, it is by no means obsolete. C++ programmers use C-style string operations as well as string classes like basic_string and AnsiString.

I won't go into examples of all the string-manipulation functions listed in the table, but I'll hit on a couple of the more widely used ones.

The strcpy() function is used to copy one string to another. The source string can be a variable or a string literal. Take the following code, for example:

```
// set up a string to hold 30 characters
// (29 characters plus the terminating null)
char buff[30];
// copy a string literal to the buffer
strcpy(buff, "This is a test.");
// initialize a second string buffer
char buff2[] = "A second string.";
// copy the contents of this string to the first buffer
strcpy(buff, buff2);
```

Accidentally overwriting the end of a character array is even easier to do than with the numeric arrays discussed earlier. For instance, imagine you had done the following:

```
char buff[10] = "A string";
// later....
strcpy(buff, "This is a test.");   // oops!
```

Here we set up a character array to hold 10 characters and initially assigned a string that requires 9 bytes (don't forget about the terminating null). Later on, possibly forgetting how large the array was, we copied a string to the buffer that requires 16 bytes, overwriting the array by 6 bytes. Six bytes of memory somewhere were just erased by our little mistake. Be careful when copying data to character arrays.

Another frequently used string function is sprintf(). This function enables you to build a formatted string by mixing text and numbers together. Here is an example that multiplies two numbers and then uses sprintf() to build a string to report the result:

```
char buff[20];
int x = 10 * 20;
sprintf(buff, "The result is: %d", x);
cout << buff;
```

When this section of code executes, the program displays this:

```
The result is: 200
```

In this example, the %d tells the sprintf() function, "An integer value will go here." At the end of the format string the variable x is inserted to tell sprintf() what value to put at that location in the string (the contents of the variable x). sprintf() is a unique function in that it can take a variable number of arguments. You must supply the destination buffer and the format string, but the number of arguments that come after the format string is variable. Here is an example of sprintf() that uses three additional arguments:

```
int x = 20;
int y = 5;
sprintf(buff, "%d + %d = %d", x, y, x + y);
cout << buff;
```

When this piece of code executes, the result displayed on the screen is this:

```
20 + 5 = 25
```

The single backslash is used in C++ strings to indicate special characters. For example '\n' is for a new line, and '\t' represents a tab character. To put an actual backslash character into a string, you must use a double backslash thus:

```
strcpy(fileName, "c:\\windows\\system\\win.ini");
```

Forgetting this simple fact has caused many programmers sleepless nights trying to find a bug in their program. This is a very common mistake to make. Don't say I didn't tell you!

sprintf() has a cousin called wsprintf() that is a Windows version of sprintf(). You might see either of these two functions used in Windows programs. wsprintf() is functionally the same as sprintf(), with one major difference: It does not enable you to put floating-point numbers in the formatted string. You can use either function in your C++Builder programs, but sprintf() is preferred because it has full floating-point support (and it's one less character to type!). To get a real appreciation of what sprintf() can do for you, consult the C++Builder online help.

Arrays of Strings

Not only can you have character arrays, but also you can have an array of character arrays (effectively, an array of strings). That might sound complicated, but you have already seen this type of array in the ARGSTEST program earlier. You can allocate this kind of array as follows:

```
char strings[][20] = {
  "This is string 1",
  "This is string 2",
  "This is string 3",
  "This is string 4"
};
```

This code creates an array of four strings, each of which can contain up to 19 characters. Although you can use this type of string array, there are much easier ways to handle arrays of strings in C++Builder. In Hour 15, "VCL Components," I'll show you one of those methods when I discuss the TStrings class.

Summary

This hour you learned about functions, arrays, and strings. These are basic elements of the C++ language. As you begin writing programs with C++Builder, you will find that these language elements are used in just about every real-world program you write.

Workshop

The Workshop contains quiz questions to help you solidify your understanding of the material covered and exercises to provide you with experience in using what you have learned. The answers to the quiz questions are provided following the questions. The exercises are given for you to work out and code on your own.

Q&A

Q Do my functions have to take parameters and return values?

A Functions you write can take parameters and can return a value, but they are not required to do either. After a function has been written to return a value, you must provide a return statement that returns a value, or the compiler issues a warning.

Q Will C++ make sure I don't overwrite memory somewhere if I accidentally write past the end of an array?

A No. One of the strengths of C++ is that it gives you the power to access memory directly. With that power comes responsibility. It's up to you, the programmer, to be sure that the memory you are accessing is memory that your program owns. If you accidentally overwrite memory that you are not supposed to have access to, Windows issues an access-violation error. The access violation might come immediately, or it might not come until later when the overwritten memory is used by another part of your program, by another program, or by Windows itself.

Quiz

1. How many return values can a function return?
2. What does the `strcpy()` function do?
3. Can a function call another function?
4. What is the index number of the first element of an array, 0 or 1?

Answers

1. A function can return only one value.
2. The `strcpy()` function copies one character array (string) to another.
3. Yes. Functions frequently call other functions, which call other functions, which call other functions…
4. The index number of the first element of an array is always 0.

Exercises

1. Write a console-mode application that calls a function to display A message from a function. on the screen.
2. Enter and compile the following program. What does the program do?

```
#include <iostream.h>
#include <conio.h>
#include <math.h>
#include <stdio.h>
#pragma hdrstop

void getSqrRoot(char* buff, int x);
```

```cpp
int main(int argc, char** argv)
{
  int x;
  char buff[30];
  cout << "Enter a number: ";
  cin >> x;
  getSqrRoot(buff, x);
  cout << buff;
  getch();
}

void getSqrRoot(char* buff, int x)
{
  sprintf(buff, "The square root is: %f", sqrt(x));
}
```

2

Hour 3

Conditionals, Loops, and Switches

You now have a good start on learning C++. In this hour you will continue to learn about the C++ language by examining more of the fundamentals of C++ that have their roots in C. This hour you will learn about

- The `if` and `else` keywords
- The `for`, `while`, and `do-while` loops
- The `switch` statement

Controlling Program Flow with `if`

Some aspects of programming are common to all programming languages. One such item that C++ has in common with other programming languages is the `if` statement. The `if` statement is used to test for a condition and then execute sections of code based on whether that condition is `true` or `false`. Here's an example:

```
int x;
cout << "Enter a number: ";
cin >> x;
if (x > 10)
  cout << "You entered a number greater than 10." << endl;
```

This code asks for input from the user. If the user enters a number greater than 10, the expression x > 10 evaluates to true and the message is displayed; otherwise, nothing is displayed. Note that when the conditional expression evaluates to true, the statement immediately following the if expression is executed.

Be sure not to follow the if expression with a semicolon. A semicolon by itself represents a blank statement in code. If you accidentally follow your if expression with a semicolon, the compiler will interpret the blank statement as the statement to execute when the expression evaluates to true.

```
if (x == 10);        // Warning! Extra semi-colon!
  DoSomething(x);
```

In this case, the DoSomething() function will always be executed because the compiler does not see it as being the first statement following the if expression. Because this code is perfectly legal (albeit useless), the compiler won't warn you that anything is amiss.

Suppose you have multiple lines of code that should be executed when the conditional expression is true. In that case you would need braces to block those lines:

```
if (x > 10) {
  cout << "The number is greater than 10" << endl;
  DoSomethingWithNumber(x);
}
```

If the conditional expression evaluates to true, the code block (all the code contained within the braces) is executed and the program continues to the next statement following the closing brace. When the conditional expression evaluates to false, the code block associated with the if expression is ignored, and program execution continues with the first statement following the code block.

C++ contains a lot of shortcuts. One of those shortcuts involves using just the variable name to test for true. Look at this code:

```
if (fileGood) ReadData();
```

This method is a shortcut for the longer form, which is illustrated with this line:

```
if (fileGood == true) ReadData();
```

This example uses a bool variable, but any data type will do. The expression evaluates to true as long as the variable contains any non-zero value. You can test for false by applying the logical NOT (!) operator to a variable name:

```
bool fileGood = OpenSomeFile();
if (!fileGood) ReportError();
```

Learning the C++ shortcuts helps you write code that contains a degree of elegance. Knowing the shortcuts will also help you understand C++ code that you read in examples and sample listings.

Remember that uninitialized variables will contain random values. Be sure to initialize your variables before using them in an if statement.

In some cases you want to perform an action when the conditional expression evaluates to true and perform some other action when the conditional expression evaluates to false. In this case you can implement the else statement:

```
if (x == 20) {
  DoSomething(x);
}
else {
  DoADifferentThing(x);
}
```

In this example, one of the two functions will be called based on the value of x, but not both.

Note that the equality operator is the double equal sign (==) and that the assignment operator is the single equal sign (=). A common coding mistake is to use the assignment operator where you meant to use the equality operator. For instance, if the previous example was inadvertently written like this:

```
if (x = 20) {
  DoSomething(x);
}
```

continues

x would be assigned the value of 20. Because this operation would be successful, the expression would evaluate to true. A bug like this, although seemingly obvious, can be hard to spot. Fortunately, the compiler will issue a warning that says Possibly incorrect assignment to alert you to the potential problem.

NEW TERM   You can nest if statements when needed. *Nesting* is nothing more than following an if statement with one or more additional if statements.

```
if (x > 10)
  if (x < 20)
    cout << "X is between 10 and 20" << endl;
```

Keep in mind that these are simplified examples. In the real world you can get lost in the maze of braces that separate one code block from the next. Take a look at this code snippet, for example:

```
if (x > 100) {
  y = 20;
  if (x > 200) {
    y = 40;
    if (x > 400) {
      y = 60;
      DoSomething(y);
    }
  }
}
else if (x < -100) {
  y = -20;
  if (x < -200) {
    y = -40;
    if (x < -400) {
      y = -60;
      DoSomething(y);
    }
  }
}
```

Even this is a fairly simple example, but you get the idea.

When a section of code contains more than two or three consecutive if statements testing for different values of the same variable, the section of code might be a candidate for a switch statement. The switch statement is discussed later in this hour in the section "The switch Statement."

The C++Builder Code Editor allows you to select one of several keystroke mappings: Default, Classic, Brief, Epsilon, or Visual Studio. The initial C++Builder installation sets keystroke mapping to "Default." If you are using the IDE Default keymapping, the C++Builder Code Editor has a handy function to help you find matching braces. Position the cursor on the brace for which you want to find the corresponding brace. Press either the Alt+[or the Alt+] key combination, and the cursor will be positioned at the brace you are looking for. It doesn't matter whether you start on the opening brace or the closing brace. In either case the matching brace will be located.

The `if` statement is heavily used in C++. It's straightforward, so you won't have any trouble with it. The main thing is keeping all the braces straight.

The `if` Statement, Form 1

▼ SYNTAX

```
if (cond_expr) {
    true_statements;
    }
else {
    false_statements;
    }
```

If the conditional expression, *cond_expr*, is `true` (non-zero), the block of code represented by *true_statements* is executed. If the optional `else` clause is specified, the block of code represented by *false_statements* is executed when the conditional expression, *cond_expr*, is `false`.

The `if` Statement, Form 2

```
if (cond_expr_1) {
    true_statements_1;
    }
else if (cond_expr_2) {
    true_statements_2;
    }
else {
    false_statements;
    }
```

If the conditional expression *cond_expr_1* is `true` (non-zero), the block of code represented by *true_statements_1* is executed. If it is `false` and the conditional expression *cond_expr_2* is true, the block of code represented by *true_statements_2* is executed. If both *cond_expr_1* and *cond_expr_2* are `false`, the block of code represented by *false_statements* is executed.

▲

Controlling Program Flow with Loops

The loop is a common element in all programming languages. A loop can be used to iterate through an array, to perform an action a specific number of times, to read a file from disk...the possibilities are endless. In this section I will discuss the `for` loop, the `while` loop, and the `do-while` loop. For the most part they work in very similar ways. All loops have these common elements:

- A starting point
- A body, usually enclosed in braces, that contains the statements to execute on each pass
- An ending point
- A test for a condition that determines when the loop should end
- Optional use of the `break` and `continue` statements

NEW TERM A *loop* is an element in a programming language that is used to perform an action repeatedly until a specific condition is met.

The starting point for the loop is one of the C++ loop statements (`for`, `while`, or `do`) followed by an opening brace. The body contains the statements that execute each time through the loop. The body can contain any valid C++ code. The ending point for the loop is the closing brace. (When the body of a loop is a single line of code, the opening and closing braces are not required.)

Most loops work something like this: The loop is entered and the test condition is evaluated. If the test condition evaluates to `true`, the body of the loop is executed. When program execution reaches the bottom of the loop (usually the closing brace), it jumps back to the top of the loop where the test condition is again evaluated. If the test condition is still `true`, the whole process is repeated. If the test condition is `false`, program execution jumps to the line of code immediately following the loop code block. The exception to this description is the `do-while` loop, which tests for the condition at the bottom of the loop rather than at the top.

The test condition tells the loop when to stop executing. In effect the test condition says, for example, "Keep doing this until x is equal to 10," or "Keep reading the file until the end-of-file is reached." After the loop starts, it continues to execute the body of the loop until the test condition evaluates to `false`.

It's easy to accidentally write a loop so that the test condition never evaluates to `false`. This results in a program that is locked up or hung. Your only recourse at that point is to press Ctrl+Alt+Delete and kill the task. The Windows Close Program box (or the Windows NT Task Manager) comes up and displays the name of your program with `(Not Responding)` next to it. You'll have to select your program from the list and click End Task to terminate the runaway program.

In C++Builder you typically run a program using the Run button on the toolbar or by pressing F9. If you need to kill a runaway program that was run from the IDE, you can choose Run, Program Reset from the main menu or press Ctrl+F2 on the keyboard.

3

Given that general overview, let's take a look at each type of loop individually.

The `for` Loop

The `for` loop is probably the most commonly used type of loop. It takes three parameters: the starting value, the test condition that determines when the loop stops, and the increment expression.

The `for` Loop Statement

```
for (initial; cond_expr; adjust) {
    statements;
    }
```

The `for` loop repeatedly executes the block of code indicated by `statements` as long as the conditional expression, `cond_expr`, is true (non-zero). The state of the loop is initialized by the statement `initial`. After the execution of `statements`, the state is modified using the statement indicated by `adjust`.

That won't make much sense until you see some examples. First take a look at a typical `for` loop:

```
for (int i=0;i<10;i++) {
  cout << "This is iteration " << i << endl;
}
```

This code results in the statement inside the braces being executed 10 times. The first parameter, int i=0, tells the for loop that it is starting with an initial value of 0. (In this case I am declaring and assigning a variable, i, inside the for statement. This is perfectly legal in C++ and is common in for loops.) The second parameter, i<10, tells the loop to keep running as long as the variable i is less than 10. Because I'm starting with 0, I need to stop *before* i is equal to 10 in order to end up with 10 iterations. The last parameter, i++, increments the variable i by one each time through the loop.

> The use of the variable name i has its roots in the FORTRAN language and is traditional in for loops. Naturally, any variable name can be used, but you will often see i used in for loops.

Let's look at a variation of this code. The following code snippet achieves exactly the opposite effect as the first example:

```
for (int i=10;i>0;i--) {
  cout << "This is iteration " << i << endl;
}
```

This time I'm starting with 10, stopping after i is equal to 1, and decrementing i by one on each pass. This is an example of a loop that counts backward.

> In the previous examples, the opening and closing braces are not strictly required. If no opening and closing braces are supplied, the statement immediately following the for statement is considered the body of the loop.

Let's write a little program that illustrates the use of the for loop. You can enter, compile, and run the program found in Listing 3.1. The output from FORLOOP.EXE is shown in Figure 3.1.

LISTING 3.1   FORLOOP.CPP

```
1: #include <iostream.h>
2: #include <conio.h>
3: #pragma hdrstop
4:
5: int main(int argv, char** argc)
6: {
```

```
 7:    cout << endl << "Starting program..." << endl << endl;
 8:    int i;
 9:    for (i=0;i<10;i++) {
10:      cout << "Iteration number " << i << endl;
11:    }
12:    cout << endl;
13:    for (i=10;i>0;i--) {
14:      cout << "Iteration number " << i << endl;
15:    }
16:    getch();
17:    return 0;
18: }
```

FIGURE 3.1

The output from
FORLOOP.EXE.

By now you know that the loop starting number can be any value you like (assuming it fits the range of the data type selected, of course). The test condition can be any C++ expression that eventually evaluates to false. The test value can be a numeric constant, as used in the examples here, a variable, or the return value of a function call. The following are examples of valid test conditions:

```
for (int i=0;i < 100;i++) {...}
for (int i=1;i == numberOfElements;i++) {...}
for (int i=0;i <= GetNumberOfElements();i+=2) {...}
```

Take a closer look at the last example. Notice the last parameter of the for statement. In this case I am incrementing the counter by 2 each time through the loop. The increment parameter can increment (or decrement) by any amount you want.

Now that you've seen the for loop in action, it won't be too difficult to apply the same concepts to the while and do-while loops. Let's take a look at those now.

The while Loop

The while loop differs from the for loop in that it contains only a test condition that is checked at the start of each iteration. As long as the test condition is true, the loop keeps running.

```
int x;
while (x < 1000) {
  x = DoSomeCalculation();
}
```

In this example I am calling a function that I assume will eventually return a value of greater than or equal to 1,000. As long as the return value from this function is less than 1,000, the while loop continues to execute. When the variable x contains a value greater than or equal to 1,000, the test condition yields false, and program execution jumps to the first line following the while loop's ending brace. A common implementation of a while loop uses a bool as a test variable. The state of the test variable can be set somewhere within the body of the loop:

```
bool done = false;
while (!done) {
  // some code here
  done = SomeFunctionReturningABool();
  // more code
}
```

At some point it is expected that the variable done will be true and the loop will terminate. The program in Listing 3.2 illustrates the use of the while loop.

LISTING 3.2   WHILETST.CPP

```
 1: #include <iostream.h>
 2: #include <conio.h>
 3: #pragma hdrstop
 4: int main(int argv, char** argc)
 5: {
 6:   cout << endl << "Starting program..." << endl << endl;
 7:   int i = 6;
 8:   while (i-- > 0) {
 9:     cout << endl << "Today I have " << i;
10:     cout << " problems to worry about.";
11:   }
12:   cout << "\b!\nYipee!";
13:   cout << endl << endl << "Press any key to continue...";
14:   getch();
15:   return 0;
16: }
```

▼ SYNTAX

The while Loop Statement

```
while (cond_expr) {
    statements;
    }
```

The while loop repeatedly executes the block of code indicated by *statements* as long as the conditional expression, *cond_expr*, is true (non-zero). The state of the loop must be initialized prior to the while statement, and modification of the state must be explicit in the block of code. When the conditional expression, *cond_expr*, evaluates to false, the loop terminates.

The do-while Loop

The do-while loop is nearly identical to the while loop. The distinction between the two is important, though. As you can see from Listing 3.2, the while loop checks the conditional expression at the top of the loop. In the case of the do-while loop, the conditional expression is checked at the bottom of the loop:

```
bool done = false;
do {
  // some code
  done = SomeFunctionReturningABool();
  // more code
} while (!done);
```

Whether you use a while or a do-while loop depends on what the loop itself does.

> Because of the way the do-while loop works, the code in the body of the loop will be executed at least once regardless of the value of the test condition (since the condition is evaluated at the bottom of the loop). In the case of the while loop, the test condition is evaluated at the top of the loop, so the body of the loop might never be executed.

▼ SYNTAX

The do-while Loop Statement

```
do {
    statements;
    } while (cond_expr);
```

The do loop repeatedly executes the block of code indicated by *statements* as long as the conditional expression, *cond_expr*, is true (non-zero). The state of the loop must be initialized prior to the do statement, and modification of the state must be explicit in the block of code. When the conditional expression, *cond_expr*, evaluates to false, the loop terminates.

continue and break

Before we leave this discussion of loops, you need to know about two keywords that
help control program execution in a loop. The continue statement is used to force program execution to the bottom of the loop, skipping any statements that come after the
continue statement. For example, you might have part of a loop that you don't want to
execute if a particular test returns true. In that case you would use continue to avoid
execution of any code below the continue statement:

```
bool done = false;
while (!done) {
  // some code
  bool error = SomeFunction();
  if (error) continue;  // jumps to the top of the loop
  // other code that will execute only if no error occurred
}
```

The break statement is used to halt execution of a loop prior to the loop's normal test
condition being met. For example, you might be searching an array of ints for a particular number. By breaking execution of your search loop when the number is found, you
can obtain the array index where the number was located:

```
int index = -1;
int searchNumber = 50;
for (int i=0;i<numElements;i++) {
  if (myArray[i] == searchNumber) {
    index = i;
    break;
  }
}
if (index != -1)
  cout << "Number found at index " << index << endl;
else
  cout << "Number not found in array." << endl;
```

Notice that in this example I initially set index to -1. I used -1 because although the for
loop might set index to some value, it will never set it to -1 (the loop counts from 0 to
some positive value). Following the for loop, I check the value of index. If index is not
-1, I know I have found a match.

There are many situations in which the continue and break statements are useful. As
with most of what I've been talking about, it will take some experience programming in
C++ before you discover all the possible uses for continue and break.

Controlling Program Flow with `switch`

The `switch` statement enables you to execute one of several code blocks based on the result of an expression. The expression might be a variable, the result of a function call, or any valid C++ expression that evaluates to an integral value (such as an integer or a Boolean value). Here is an example of a `switch` statement:

```
switch(amountOverSpeedLimit) {
  case 0  : {
    fine = 0;
    break;
  }
  case 10 : {
    fine = 20;
    break;
  }
  case 15 : {
    fine = 50;
    break;
  }
  case 20 :
  case 25 :
  case 30 : {
    fine = amountOverSpeedLimit * 10;
    break;
  }
  default : {
    fine = GoToCourt();
    jailTime = GetSentence();
  }
}
```

3

Several parts make up a `switch` statement. First, you can see that there is the expression, which in this example is the variable `amountOverSpeedLimit` (remember, I warned you about long variable names!). Next, the `case` statements test the expression for equality. If `amountOverSpeedLimit` equals `0` (case `0` :), the value `0` is assigned to the variable `fine`. If `amountOverSpeedLimit` is equal to `10`, a value of `20` is assigned to `fine`, and so on.

In each of the first three cases, you see a `break` statement. The `break` statement is used to jump out of the `switch` block—it means that a case matching the expression has been found and the rest of the `switch` statement can be ignored. Finally, you see the `default` statement. The code block following the `default` statement will be executed if no matching cases are found.

Notice that cases 20 and 25 have no statements following them. If the expression, amountOverSpeedLimit, evaluates to 20 or 25, those cases fall through and the next code block encountered will be executed. In this situation, values of 20, 25, or 30 will all result in the same code being executed.

Don't forget your break statements! Without break statements the switch continues on even after finding a match and might execute code you didn't intend to be executed. For example:

```
bool AllOK = PerformSomeAction();
switch (AllOK) {
  case true :
    cout << "Success" << endl;
  case false :
    cout << "Failure" << endl;
}
```

In this example, if AllOK is false then "Failure" is displayed on the screen as expected. If AllOK is true, however, both "Success" and "Failure" are displayed because the first case does not have a break statement.

Inclusion of the default statement is not mandatory. You could write a switch without a default statement:

```
switch (x) {
  case 10 : DoSomething(); break;
  case 20 : DoAnotherThing(); break;
  case 30 : DoSomethingElseEntirely();
}
```

Note that there is no break statement following the last case statement. Because this is the last line of the switch, there is no point in including the break statement for this line.

You might want to use a switch if you find that you have several if statements back to back. The switch is a bit clearer to others reading your program.

You can only use the numeric C++ data types (which include char) in the expression portion of a switch statement. The following, for example, is not allowed:

```
switch (someStringVariable) {
  case "One" : // code
  case "Two" : // code
}
```

This code results in a compiler error that says

```
Switch selection expression must be of integral type.
```

▼ SYNTAX

The `switch` Statement

```
switch (expr) {
    case value_1:
        statements_1;
        break;
    case value_2:
        statements_2;
        break;
    .
    .
    .
    case value_n:
        statements_n;
        break;
    default:
        dflt_statements;
}
```

The switch statement offers a way to execute different blocks of code depending on various values of an expression (*expr*). The block of code represented by *statements_1* is executed when *expr* is equal to *value_1*, the block of code represented by *statements_2* when *expr* is equal to *value_2*, and so on through the block of code represented by *statements_n* when *expr* is equal to *value_n*. When *expr* is not equal to any of the *value_1* through *value_n*, the block of code at *dflt_statements* is executed. The break statements are optional.

Summary

In this hour you learned about important C++ language keywords. The keywords discussed here are likely to be needed in any C++ program of any significance. First you learned about checking program conditions with the if and else statements. After that you were introduced to the different types of loops in C++; then, you learned about the switch statement and how to use it.

Workshop

The Workshop contains quiz questions to help you solidify your understanding of the material covered and exercises to provide you with experience in using what you have learned. The answers to the quiz questions are provided following the questions. The exercises are given for you to work out and code on your own.

Q&A

Q How many levels deep can I nest `if` statements?

A There's no limit. There is, however, a practical limit. If you have too many nested `if` statements, it gets very hard to keep all those brackets straight!

Q Will loops automatically terminate if something goes wrong?

A No. If you accidentally write an endless loop, that loop continues to run until you do something to stop it. You can stop a program stuck in an endless loop by bringing up the Windows Task Manager (or the Close Program box) and ending the errant task. If you executed the program via the C++Builder IDE, you can choose Run, Program Reset from the main menu to kill the program.

Quiz

1. What statements are executed in the event an `if` expression evaluates to `true`?
2. What do the three parameters of a `for` statement represent?
3. Besides syntax, what is the difference between a `while` loop and a `do-while` loop?
4. What do the `break` and `continue` statements do?

Answers

1. The statement immediately following the `if` statement is executed when the conditional expression evaluates to `true`. If a code block follows an `if` statement, the entire code block is executed.
2. The first parameter is the starting value, the second parameter is the test expression, and the final parameter is the increment parameter.
3. A `while` loop checks the conditional expression at the beginning of the loop. A `do-while` loop checks the conditional expression at the end of the loop.
4. The `break` statement is used to break out of a loop. The statement following the body of the loop will be executed following a `break` statement. The `continue` statement forces program execution back to the top of the loop.

Exercises

1. Write a program that counts from 200 to 300 by fives and displays the results.
2. Write a program that asks the user to input the day of the week and then displays the name of the day using a `switch` statement.

Hour 4

Scope, Structures, and Functions in C++

In this hour you first learn about scope. Scope is used to differentiate variables based on where they appear in a program. Following that you learn about structures. A structure is a single data element that can hold a number of fields. For example, a structure might be used to store a person's name, address, and phone number. Finally, this hour ends with a discussion on functions in C++ and how they differ from the C-style functions described in Hour 2.

Scope of Variables in C++

 The term *scope* refers to the visibility of variables within different parts of your program.

Most variables have *local scope*. This means that the variable is visible to the compiler only within the code block in which it is declared. Take a look at the program in Listing 4.1.

LISTING 4.1 SCOPE.CPP

```
 1: #include <iostream.h>
 2: #include <conio.h>
 3: #pragma hdrstop
 4: int x = 20;
 5: void CountLoops(int);
 6: int main(int, char**)
 7: {
 8:   int x = 40;
 9:   int i = 0;
10:   cout << "In main program x = " << x << endl;
11:   bool done = false;
12:   while (!done) {
13:     int x;
14:     cout << endl << "Enter a number (-1 to exit): ";
15:     cin >> x;
16:     if (x != -1) {
17:       cout << endl << "In while loop x = " << x;
18:       CountLoops(++i);
19:     }
20:     else
21:       done = true;
22:   }
23:   cout << "Global x = " << ::x << endl;
24:   cout << endl << "Press any key to continue...";
25:   getch();
26:   return 0;
27: }
28: void CountLoops(int x)
29: {
30:   cout << ", While loop has executed "
31:     << x << " times" << endl;
32: }
```

ANALYSIS The first thing you might notice is that the variable x is declared four times. It is declared on line 4 outside the main() function, on line 8 inside the main() function, on line 13 inside the while loop, and in the CountLoops() function on line 28. If you accidentally declare a variable more than once, the compiler spits out an error that says Multiple declaration for 'x', and the compile stops. Yet this program compiles and runs just fine. Why? Because each of the x variables in this program is in a different scope.

Take a closer look at Listing 4.1. The declaration for x on line 13 is inside the body of the `while` loop and is local to that block of code. Effectively, it doesn't exist outside that block. This variable has local scope. Likewise, the declaration for x on line 28 is local to the `CountLoops()` function and doesn't exist outside the function. In this case the declaration for x is less obvious because it's part of the function's parameter list, but it's a variable declaration nonetheless.

Now look at the variables x and i declared inside the `main()` function. These variables are local to the code block in which they are declared, *plus* they are available (in scope) in any code blocks within the code block in which they are declared. In other words, the x and i variables are in scope both in the `main()` function *and* inside the `while` loop. That's easy enough to figure out in the case of i because there is only one variable named i. But what about x? Once inside the `while` loop, there are two variables named x (the one declared in `main()` and the one declared in the `while` loop), and both are in scope. Which one is being used? The answer: the one within the `while` loop because it has the most immediate scope.

Finally, we get to the declaration of the x that falls outside the `main()` function (line 4). Because this variable is declared outside any function, it is called a *global variable* and is said to have *global scope*. This means that the global variable x is available anywhere in the program: inside the `main()` function, inside the `while` block, and inside the `CountLoops()` function.

As mentioned earlier, a local variable has precedence over a global variable. But what if you want to access the global variable x from inside the `main()` function? You use the *scope-resolution operator*, `::`. Line 23 of Listing 4.1 contains this line:

```
cout << "Global x = " << ::x << endl;
```

The scope-resolution operator tells the compiler, "Give me the global variable x and not the local variable x."

Structures in C++

NEW TERM A *structure* is a collection of related data identified as a single storage unit. After a structure is declared, an instance of that structure can be created for use. Each of the elements in a structure is called a *data member*.

For example, suppose you want to keep a mailing list. It would be convenient to use a single data variable to hold all the fields needed in a typical mailing list. A structure enables you to do that. You first declare the structure and then later create an instance of that structure when you want to use the structure. A structure is declared with the `struct` keyword:

```
struct mailingListRecord {
  char firstName[20];
  char lastName[20];
  char address[50];
  char city[20];
  char state[3];
  int zip;
  bool holidayList;
};
```

NEW TERM Each element in a structure is called a *data member*. Notice that each of the data
members must be declared just as if it were a variable in a code block. This
example has five char arrays, one int, and one bool data member. (My apologies to my
friends around the world if this looks like a U.S.-slanted mailing-list record.) Finally,
make note of the semicolon following the closing brace of the structure declaration. This
is a requirement for structure and class declarations.

Now that the structure is declared, it can be put to use. I first need to create an instance
of the structure. Here's how that looks:

```
mailingListRecord record;
```

This statement allocates memory for the structure (118 bytes, give or take) and assigns
that memory to a variable named record. Now that I have an instance of the structure set
up, I can assign values to the data members:

```
strcpy(record.firstName, "Josh");
strcpy(record.lastName, "Burleson");
strcpy(record.address, "1234 Magnolia Ct.");
strcpy(record.city, "Englewood");
strcpy(record.state, "CO");
record.zip = 80111;
record.holidayList = true;
```

This code snippet contains some syntax you haven't seen yet. To access the data members of a structure, you need to employ the dot (.) operator. When used in this context,
the dot operator is sometimes called the *direct membership operator*. The dot operator
enables you to access a particular member of the structure—either to read the value of
the data member or to change the value of the data member.

If you want to, you can instantiate an object and supply its members all at once:

```
mailingListRecord record = {
  "Dave",
  "Dyer",
  "1000 Iron Age Way",
  "Denver",
  "CO",
```

```
    80112,
    false
};
```

This saves you some typing over the first method I showed you but is not always practical in real-world situations. In a real-world application, a structure would likely be filled out as a result of user input or possibly with data read from a file. Assigning data to the structure as you see here is not practical in those situations.

The `struct` Statement

▼ SYNTAX

```
struct name {
    data_member_1;
    data_member_2;
    .
    .
    .
    data_member_n;
    } instance;
```

The `struct` statement declares a grouping of data members (*data_member_1*, *data_member_2*, ..., *data_member_n*) and provides a name for this grouping (*name*). The

▲   optional *instance* statement creates an instance of this grouping.

Arrays of Structures

Just as you can have arrays of `int`s, `char`s, or `long`s, you can also have arrays of structures. Declaring and using an array of structures is not terribly complicated:

```
mailingListRecord listArray[5];
strcpy(listArray[0].firstName, "Georgia");
strcpy(listArray[0].lastName, "Burleson");
// etc.
```

This is only slightly more complicated than using an array of one of the integral data types. You will notice that the subscript operator and the direct membership operator are used together to access a particular data member in a particular record in the array.

Headers and Source Files

NEW TERM   A *source file* is an ASCII text file that contains the program's source code. The compiler takes the source code file, parses it, and produces machine language that the computer can execute.

One of the problems with books on programming is that they use simple examples to communicate concepts and ideas. You will undoubtedly find that in the real world things are never that simple. So far, we have been dealing with very short programs contained in a single source file. In practice, a program of any consequence has several source files.

A program's code is divided up into different source files for a number of reasons. One of the primary reasons is that of organization. By keeping related chunks of code together, you can more easily find a certain section of code when needed.

So how do all the source files get tied together? First, the compiler compiles each source file (.cpp) into an object file (.obj). After each module has been compiled, the linker links all the object files together to make a single executable file (the .exe).

The declarations for classes and structures are often kept in a separate file called a *header file*. Headers have a filename extension of .h or .hpp. A header file should contain only class, structure, and function declarations. You should never put any executable code statements in a header.

> There is an exception to the rule that no code should be placed in headers. You can put *inline functions* in headers. An inline function is a special function in terms of the way the compiler generates code for the function. You'll learn more about inline functions a bit later in this hour.

Use the Object Repository to create a header file from scratch. First, choose File, New from the main menu. When the Object Repository comes up, double-click on the Text icon. C++Builder creates a new text file and displays it in the Code Editor. Enter the code for your header and then save the file with an .h extension.

After you have created a header file for a structure, you can include that header in any source code module that needs to see the structure declaration. To do that, use the #include directive:

```
#include "structur.h"
```

When you use the #include directive, it is as if the contents of the file being included are pasted into the source file at that point. Listing 4.2, in the next section, contains a program that uses the #include directive. The header file referenced in Listing 4.2 is contained in Listing 4.3.

> Header files typically implement a *sentry* to ensure that the header is only included once for a program. A sentry essentially tells the compiler, "I've already been included once, so don't include me again." A sentry looks like this:

```
#ifndef _MYCLASS_H
#define _MYCLASS_H
class MyClass {
  // class declared here
};
#endif
```

C++Builder automatically adds sentries to units that are generated when you create a new form or component. For headers you create from scratch, you need to add the sentry code yourself.

A header file can contain more than one structure declaration. Using a separate header for each structure helps keep your project organized and makes it easier to reuse structures in other programs. Sometimes you will group related structures together in one header. Ultimately, it's up to you how to organize your headers.

Don't be too concerned if this is a little confusing right now. It will probably take some experience writing real programs for all this to come together for you.

An Example Using Structures

Listing 4.2 contains a program that has the user input three names and addresses and stores those records in an array of structures. After the names are input, they are displayed on the screen. The user is then asked to choose one of the records. When the user chooses one of the records, it is displayed on the screen. Listing 4.3 contains the header file for the mailingListRecord structure referenced in the MAILLIST program shown in Listing 4.2.

LISTING 4.2 MAILLIST.CPP

```
 1: #include <iostream.h>
 2: #include <conio.h>
 3: #include <stdlib.h>
 4: #pragma hdrstop
 5: #include "structur.h"
 6: void displayRecord(int, mailingListRecord mlRec);
 7: int main(int, char**)
 8: {
 9:   //
10:   // create an array of mailingListRecord structures
```

continues

LISTING 4.2   CONTINUED

```
11:  //
12:  mailingListRecord listArray[3];
13:  cout << endl;
14:  int index = 0;
15:  // get three records
16:  //
17:  do {
18:    cout << "First Name: ";
19:    cin.getline(listArray[index].firstName,
20:      sizeof(listArray[index].firstName) - 1);
21:    cout << "Last Name: ";
22:    cin.getline(listArray[index].lastName,
23:      sizeof(listArray[index].lastName) - 1);
24:    cout << "Address: ";
25:    cin.getline(listArray[index].address,
26:      sizeof(listArray[index].address) - 1);
27:    cout << "City: ";
28:    cin.getline(listArray[index].city,
29:      sizeof(listArray[index].city) - 1);
30:    cout << "State: ";
31:    cin.getline(listArray[index].state,
32:      sizeof(listArray[index].state) - 1);
33:    char buff[10];
34:    cout << "Zip: ";
35:    cin.getline(buff, sizeof(buff) - 1);
36:    listArray[index].zip = atoi(buff);
37:    index++;
38:    cout << endl;
39:  }
40:  while (index < 3);
41:  //
42:  // clear the screen
43:  //
44:  clrscr();
45:  //
46:  // display the three records
47:  //
48:  for (int i=0;i<3;i++) {
49:    displayRecord(i, listArray[i]);
50:  }
51:  //
52:  // ask the user to choose a record
53:  //
54:  cout << "Choose a record: ";
55:  int rec;
56:  //
57:  // be sure only 1, 2, or 3 was selected
58:  //
```

```
59:    do {
60:       rec = getch();
61:       rec -= 49;
62:    } while (rec < 0 || rec > 2);
63:    //
64:    // assign the selected record to a temporary variable
65:    //
66:    mailingListRecord temp = listArray[rec];
67:    clrscr();
68:    cout << endl;
69:    //
70:    // display the selected recrord
71:    //
72:    displayRecord(rec, temp);
73:    getch();
74:    return 0;
75: }
76: void displayRecord(int num, mailingListRecord mlRec)
77: {
78:    cout << "Record " << (num + 1) << ":" << endl;
79:    cout << "Name:     " << mlRec.firstName << " ";
80:    cout << mlRec.lastName;
81:    cout << endl;
82:    cout << "Address:  " << mlRec.address;
83:    cout << endl << "            ";
84:    cout << mlRec.city << ", ";
85:    cout << mlRec.state << "   ";
86:    cout << mlRec.zip;
87:    cout << endl << endl;
88: }
```

LISTING 4.3   STRUCTUR.H

```
 1: #ifndef _STRUCTUR_H
 2: #define _STRUCTUR.H
 3: struct mailingListRecord {
 4:    char firstName[20];
 5:    char lastName[20];
 6:    char address[50];
 7:    char city[20];
 8:    char state[5];
 9:    int zip;
10: };
11: #endif
```

There are a couple of new things presented in this program and some variations on material we've already covered.

ANALYSIS First, this program uses the `getline()` function of the `cin` class to get input from the user (on line 19, for instance). The second parameter of `getline()` is used to limit the number of characters that are placed into the buffer (in this case the buffer is a data member of the `mailingListRecord` structure). I supply a value here because I don't want to overwrite the end of the arrays in the structure. The `sizeof()` operator is used to determine the size of the destination buffer, so we know how many characters we can safely store in the buffer.

The `atoi()` function on line 36 is also new to you. This function takes a character string and converts it to an integer value. This is necessary to convert the text in the zip code field (which I got from the user as a string) to an integer value that can be stored in the `zip` data member of the `mailingListRecord` structure.

The `displayRecord()` function, which begins on line 76, takes two parameters. The first parameter, `num`, is an `int` that contains the index number of the record to display. On line 78 I add 1 to `num` when I display it because users are accustomed to lists beginning with 1 rather than with 0. The second parameter of the `displayRecord()` function is an instance of the `mailingListRecord` structure. Inside the `displayRecord()` function I use the local instance of the structure passed in (which represents a copy of the structure) to display the contents of the structure.

In this case I am passing the `mailingListRecord` structure *by value*. This means that a copy of the structure is created each time the `displayRecord()` function is called. This isn't very efficient because of the overhead required to pass a structure by value. The overhead comes in the form of the extra time and memory required to make a copy of the structure each time the function is called. It would be better to pass the structure *by reference*, but I haven't talked about that yet so the structure is passed by value in this program. You will learn about passing by reference in Hour 15, "VCL Components."

Note that the `displayRecord()` function is called from both the `for` loop when all the records are displayed (line 49) and again from the main body of the program to display the actual record chosen (line 72). That's precisely why the code to display a record has been placed in a function. By putting it in a function, I only have to write the code once and can avoid duplicating code.

Any time you find yourself repeating code more than a couple times in your programs, think about moving that code to a function. Then you can call the function when you need that code executed.

There is another segment of this program that deserves mention. Look at this do-while loop, which begins on line 59:

```
do {
  rec = getch();
  rec -= 49;
} while (rec < 0 ¦¦ rec > 2);
```

This code first gets a character from the keyboard using the getch() function. As you have seen, I have been using getch() at the end of the sample programs to keep the program from closing prematurely but have been ignoring the return value. The getch() function returns the ASCII value of the key pressed. Because the ASCII value of the 1 key is 49, I want to subtract 49 from the value of the key pressed to obtain the equivalent index number for that record in the records array. If the user presses 1, an ASCII 49 is returned, and 49–49 is 0, which is the first index of the array. If the user presses 2, the calculation yields 1 (50–49), and so on. The do-while loop ensures that the user presses a key between 1 and 3. If a key other than 1, 2, or 3 is pressed, the loop continues to fetch keystrokes until a valid key is pressed.

Finally, look at line 66 of Listing 4.2:

```
mailingListRecord temp = listArray[rec];
```

This code is not necessary in this program, but I included it to illustrate a point. This code creates an instance of the mailingListRecord structure and assigns to it the contents of one of the structures in the array. A simple assignment is possible here because the compiler knows how to copy one structure to another. It does a simple member-to-member copy and copies the values of all structure members to the newly created instance of the structure.

Our discussion of structures up to this point describes how a structure works in C. In C++ a structure operates as it does in C, but C++ extends structures to enable them to contain functions as well as data members. In fact, a structure in C++ is essentially a class where all data members and functions have public access. That won't make sense until later on when I discuss classes in Hours 6 and 7, "C++ Classes and Object-Oriented Programming," but you can file this tidbit away for future reference.

Now you know about structures. Chances are you won't use a lot of structures in your programs. This section is important, though, because it serves as sort of a primer for discussing classes in Hours 6 and 7.

Functions in C++

A function in C++ can do everything that a function can do in C. In addition, C++ functions can do things that functions in C cannot. Specifically, this section looks at the following:

- Function overloading
- Default parameters
- Class member functions
- Inline functions

Function Overloading

C++ enables you to work with functions that have the same name but take different parameters.

NEW TERM *Function overloading* is having two or more functions with the same name but with different parameter lists. Functions that share a common name are called *overloaded functions*.

In Hour 1, I showed you a sample program that contained a function called `multiply()`. The function took two integers, multiplied them, and returned the result. What if you wanted to have the function multiply two floating-point numbers or two `short ints`? In C you would be required to have multiple functions:

```
// declarations for a program written in C
int multiplyInt(int num1, int num2);
float multiplyFloat(float num1, float num2);
short multiplyShort(short num1, short num2);
```

Wouldn't it be a lot easier if you could just have a function called `multiply()` that would be smart enough to know whether you wanted to multiply `shorts`, `ints`, or `floats`? In C++ you can create such a scenario, thanks to function overloading. Here's how the declarations for an overloaded function look:

```
// declarations in C++
int multiply(int num1, int num2);
float multiply(float num1, float num2);
short multiply(short num1, short num2);
```

You still have to write separate functions for each of these declarations, but at least you can use the same function name. The compiler takes care of calling the correct function based on the parameters you pass the function.

```
float x = 1.5;
float y = 10.5;
float result = multiply(x, y);
```

The compiler sees that two `float`s are passed to the function and calls the version of the `multiply()` function that takes two floating-point values for parameters. Likewise, if two `int`s are passed, the compiler calls the version of `multiply()` that takes two integers.

> It is the parameter list that makes overloaded functions work. You can vary either the type or the number of parameters a function takes (or both), but you cannot create an overloaded function by changing just the return value. For example, the following does not constitute an overloaded function:
>
> ```
> int  DoSomething();
> void DoSomething();
> ```
>
> If you try to compile a program containing these lines, you will get a compiler error that says `Type mismatch in redeclaration of 'DoSomething()'`. The two functions need to vary by more than just the return value to qualify as overloaded functions.

4

Let's take a quick detour and talk about something you will need to use on occasion when dealing with overloaded functions.

Casting Variable Types

Using overloaded functions works fine as long as you use the proper data types when calling an overloaded function. What if you mix and match? In this case, you need to cast a variable or literal value.

NEW TERM A *cast* tells the compiler to temporarily treat one data type as if it were another.

A cast looks like this:

```
float x = (float)10 * 5.5;
```

In this case the cast tells the compiler, "Make the number 10 a `float`." (The second number is automatically interpreted as a `float` because it contains a decimal place.) Take a look at the following code snippet:

```
int anInt = 5;
float aFloat = 10.5;
float result = multiply(anInt, aFloat);
```

This code generates a compiler error because there is an ambiguity between the parameters passed and the function declarations. The compiler error, in effect, says, "I can't figure out from the parameters passed which version of multiply() to call." The same error is produced if you use code like this:

```
int result = multiply(10, 10);
// is 10 a float, int or short?
```

Here the compiler cannot figure out whether the numeric constants are to be interpreted as floats, ints, or shorts. When this occurs, you have two choices. First, you can simply avoid using literal values in the function call. If you want to multiply two ints, you can declare two int variables and pass those to the function:

```
int x = 10;
int y = 10;
int result = multiply(x, y);
```

Now there is no ambiguity because x and y are both obviously ints. That's probably overkill for simple situations, though. The other thing you can do is to cast the numeric constants to tell the compiler what type to expect:

```
int result = multiply((int)10, (int)10);
```

Now the compiler knows to treat the literal values as ints. A cast is also used to temporarily force the compiler to treat one data type as if it were something else. Let's go back to the first example in this section and this time cast one of the variables to remove the ambiguity:

```
int x = 5;
float y = 10.5;
float result = multiply((float)x, y);
```

In this case x is an int, but I am casting it to a float, thereby telling the compiler to treat it as a float. The compiler happily calls the float version of multiply() and goes on its way.

Ultimately, you want to write overloaded functions so that ambiguities don't exist and casting isn't necessary. In some cases that isn't possible, and in those cases casting will be required.

Default Parameters for Functions

 A function in C++ can have *default parameters* that, as the name implies, supply a default value for a parameter if no value is specified when the function is called.

A function implementing a default parameter might look like this:

```
// declaration, parameter 'eraseFirst' will be false by default
void Redraw(bool eraseFirst = false);
// definition
void Redraw(bool eraseFirst)
{
  if (eraseFirst) {
    // erase code
  }
  // drawing code
}
```

You can call this function with or without a parameter. If the parameter is supplied at the time the function is called, the function behaves as a regular function would. If the parameter is not supplied when the function is called, the default parameter is used automatically. Given this example, the following two lines of code are identical:

```
Redraw();
Redraw(false);
```

Note that when a parameter has a default value, it can be omitted from the function call altogether. You can mix default and non-default parameters in the same function:

```
int PlaySound(char* name, bool loop = false, int loops = 10);
// call function
int res;
res = PlaySound("chime.wav");           // does not loop sound
res = PlaySound("ding.wav", true);      // plays sound 10 times
res = PlaySound("bell.wave", true, 5);  // plays sound 5 times
```

4

Default parameters are helpful for many reasons. For one thing, they make your life easier. You might have a function that you call with the same parameters 99 percent of the time. By giving it default parameters, you shorten the amount of typing required each time you make a call to the function. Whenever you want to supply parameters other than the defaults, all you have to do is plug in values for the default parameters.

Any default parameters must come at the end of the function's parameter list. The following is not a valid function declaration:

```
int MyFunction(int x, int y = 10, int t = 5, int z);
```

In order for this function declaration to compile, the default parameters must be moved to the end of the function list:

```
int MyFunction(int x, int z, int y = 10, int t = 5);
```

If you don't put the default parameters at the end of the parameter list, the compiler generates an error message.

Class Member Functions

 As you will find out in this section, classes can contain their own functions. Such functions are called *member functions* because they are members of a class.

Class member functions follow the same rules as regular functions: They can be over-loaded, they can have default parameters, they can take any number of parameters, and so on.

Class member functions can be called only through an object of the class to which the function belongs. To call a class member function, use the direct membership operator (in the case of local objects) or the indirect membership operator (for dynamically created objects).

For example, let's say you had a class called `Airplane` that was used to track an airplane for aircraft-control software. That class would probably have the capability to retrieve the current speed of a given aircraft via a function called `GetSpeed()`. The following example illustrates how you would call the `GetSpeed()` function of an `Airplane` object:

```
Airplane plane;   // create a class instance
int speed = plane.GetSpeed();
cout << "The airplane's current speed is " << speed << endl;
```

This code uses the direct membership operator to call the `GetSpeed()` function. Class member functions are defined like regular functions except that the class name and scope-resolution operator precede the function name. For example, the definition of the `GetSpeed()` function might look like this in the source file:

```
int Airplane::GetSpeed()
{
  return speed;   // speed is a class member variable
}
```

Here the scope-resolution operator tells the compiler that the `GetSpeed()` function is a member of the `Airplane` class. I'll talk more about class member functions in Hour 6, so don't worry if it doesn't make complete sense to you right now.

Inline Functions

Normally the machine code for a function appears only once in the compiled executable file. Each section of code that uses the function calls the function. This means that program execution jumps from the point of the function call to the point in the program where the function resides. The statements in the function are executed and then the function returns. When the function returns, program execution jumps back to the statement following the function call.

NEW TERM An *inline function* is placed inline in the compiled code wherever a call to that function occurs.

Inline functions are declared like regular functions but are defined with the `inline` keyword. Each time the compiler encounters a call to an inline function in the source code, it places a separate copy of the function's code in the executable program at that point. Inline functions execute quickly because no actual function call takes place (the code is already "inlined" in the program).

> Inline functions should be reserved for functions that are very small or need to be executed very quickly. Large functions or those that are called from many places in your program should not be inlined because your executable file will be larger as a result.

Inline functions are usually class member functions. Often the inline function definition (the function itself) is placed in the header file following the class declaration. (This is the one time that you can place code in your header files.) Because the `GetSpeed()` function mentioned previously is so small, it can be inlined easily. Here's how it would look:

```
inline int Airplane::GetSpeed() {
  return speed;  // speed is a class member variable
}
```

An inline function can also be defined within a class declaration. Because I haven't talked about classes yet, though, I'll hold that discussion for Hour 6.

Summary

In this hour I talked about scope and what that means to your program's variables. Following that you found out about structures and how they can be used in your programs. We ended the hour with a discussion on how functions in C++ differ from functions in C.

Workshop

The Workshop contains quiz questions to help you solidify your understanding of the material covered and exercises to provide you with experience in using what you have learned. The answers to the quiz questions are provided following the questions. The exercises are given for you to work out and code on your own.

Q&A

Q Can I have more than one variable with the same name?

A Yes, provided they are in different scopes. You cannot have two variables named x that are both declared within a code block. You can, however, have a global variable named x and a local variable with the same name.

Q Can I use a structure by itself, without an object?

A No. Before you can use a structure, you have to create an instance of the structure and access the structure through the instance variable.

Quiz

1. Can a structure contain a mixture of data types (char, int, long, and so on)?

2. How do you access the members of a structure?

3. Is it legal to have arrays of structures?

4. Does the following qualify as an overloaded function? Why or why not?

```
void MyFunction(int x);
long MyFunction(int x);
```

Answers

1. Yes. A structure can contain any valid C++ data type. It can even contain other structures.

2. You access the members of a structure using the direct membership operator (.) or the indirect membership operator (->).

3. Yes. Arrays of structures are commonly used.

4. The function does not qualify as an overloaded function because only the return value is different.

Exercise

1. Write a structure containing data members representing employee information. Include first name, last name, address, hire date, and a data member indicating whether the employee is in the company's insurance plan.

HOUR 5

Pointers, References, and Memory Allocation

The C++ language is often unforgiving because of it's power and flexibility when dealing directly with memory. With the information in this hour, you will be navigating the concepts of C++ that most people trip over. Although I can't address every possible trouble spot you might encounter, I can at least point out some of the common mistakes beginning (and even expert) programmers make. In this hour you will learn about pointers, references, and the `new` and `delete` operators.

Working with Pointers

Pointers are one of the most confusing aspects about the C++ language. They are also one of the most powerful features of C++. This discussion on pointers might very well leave you scratching your head wondering if you'll ever learn to program in C++. My goal in this section is not to teach you the textbook definition of pointers, but rather to teach you pointers in the context of how you will use them in your C++Builder programs.

NEW TERM A *pointer* is a variable that holds the address of a memory location, usually the address of another variable. Because the pointer doesn't have a direct association with the actual data, *indirection* is the term used when referring to this indirect association. tion.

So what is a pointer? It's a variable that holds the address of another variable. There, that wasn't so bad, was it? I wish it were that simple! Because a pointer holds the address of another variable, it is said to "point to" the second variable. This is called indirection because the pointer doesn't have a direct association with the actual data, but rather an indirect association.

Let's look at an example.

Earlier we talked about arrays. Let's say that you had an array of ints. You could access the individual elements of the array using the subscript operator, as I talked about in Hour 4, "Scope, Structures, and Functions in C++":

```
int array[] = { 5, 10, 15, 20, 25 };
int someVariable = array[3];   // the value 20
```

You could also use a pointer to accomplish the same thing:

```
int array[] = { 5, 10, 15, 20, 25 };
int* ptr = array;
int someVariable = ptr[3];
```

In this example, the memory location of the beginning of the array is assigned to the pointer named ptr. Note that the pointer is a pointer of the data type int and that the indirection operator (the * symbol) is used when you declare a pointer. You can declare a pointer to any integral data types (int, char, long, short, and so on) as well as to objects (structures or classes). After the assignment, the pointer contains the memory address of the start of the array and, as such, points to the array. Figure 5.1 shows how the variables from the preceding code might be stored in memory. The Variable row shows the name of the variable, the Address row shows the memory location where that variable is stored, and the Value row shows the value the variable holds.

Look at the members of the array in Figure 5.1. Notice the values of each array element on the Value row. As you can see, they contain the values 5, 10, 15, 20, and 25. These were the values assigned to the array when it was created. Now turn your attention to the ptr variable in this figure. Notice that the ptr variable itself resides at address 00126F28 but that the value it contains is 00126F2C hexadecimal. Not coincidentally, this is the address of the first element of the array. As you can see, the value of the ptr variable is the address of the array variable.

FIGURE 5.1

How the array *and* ptr *variables look in memory.*

Variable	ptr	array[0]	array[1]	array[2]	array[3]	array[4]
Address	0012F628	0012F62C	0012F630	0012F634	0012F638	0012F63E
Value	0012F62C	5	10	15	20	25

> The name of an array variable, when used without the subscript operator, returns the memory address of the first element of the array. Put another way, the variable name of an array is a pointer to the start of the array. That makes it possible to assign an array to a pointer, as in the preceding example.

In this case you can now use the pointer, ptr, just as you would the array name itself. I can hear you wondering, though, "But why would you want to?" The truth is that in this example there is no real benefit to using a pointer. The real benefit of pointers is when you want to create objects dynamically in memory. A pointer is necessary to access the object. I really can't go on with this discussion, though, until I digress a moment and talk about the two ways you can create variables and objects.

Local Versus Dynamic Memory Usage

NEW TERM The *stack* is an area of working memory set aside by the program when the program starts. All the sample programs you have seen thus far use local allocation of objects. That is, the memory required for a variable or object is obtained from the program's stack.

NEW TERM *Local allocation* means that the memory required for a variable or object is obtained from the program's stack.

Any memory the program needs for things like local variables, function calls, and so on is taken from the stack. This memory is allocated as needed and then freed when no longer needed. Usually this happens when the program enters a function or other local code block. Memory for any local variables the function uses is allocated when the function is entered. When the function returns, all the memory allocated for the function's use is freed. It all happens for you automatically; you don't have to give any thought to how or whether the memory is freed.

5

Local allocation has its good points and its bad points. On the plus side, memory can be allocated from the stack very quickly. The downside is that the stack is a fixed size and cannot be changed as the program runs. If your program runs out of stack space, weird things start to happen. Your program might just crash, it might start behaving oddly, or it might seem to perform normally but crash when the program terminates. This is less of a problem in the 32-bit world than in 16-bit programming, but it's still a consideration.

NEW TERM The *heap* in a Windows program refers to all of your computer's virtual memory.

NEW TERM *Dynamic allocation* means that memory required for an object is allocated from the heap.

For things like variables of the built-in data types and small arrays, there is no point in doing anything other than local allocation. But if you are going to be using large arrays, structures, or classes, you will probably want to use dynamic allocation from the heap. The heap amounts to your computer's free physical RAM plus all your free hard disk space. The good news here is that you have virtually unlimited memory available for your programs. The bad news is that memory allocated dynamically requires some additional overhead and, as such, is just a smidgen slower than memory allocated from the stack. In most programs the extra overhead is not noticed in the least. An additional drawback of dynamic allocation is that it requires more from the programmer. Not a lot more, mind you, but a little.

Dynamic Allocation and Pointers

NEW TERM In a C++ program, memory is allocated dynamically by using the new operator.

I'm going to talk about new a little later in the hour, but you need a little sampler as I continue the discussion about pointers. Earlier I talked about structures and used the mailingListRecord structure as an example. Allocating a structure from the stack looks like this:

```
mailingListRecord listArray;
strcpy(listArray.firstName, "John");
strcpy(listArray.lastName, "Leier");
// etc.
```

That's what I did in Hour 4 when I talked about structures. Now I'll create the array dynamically rather than locally:

```
mailingListRecord* listArray;
listArray = new mailingListRecord;
strcpy(listArray->firstName, "John");
strcpy(listArray->lastName, "Leier");
// etc.
```

The first line declares a pointer to a mailingListRecord structure. The next line initializes the pointer by creating a new instance of a mailingListRecord structure dynamically. This is the process by which you dynamically create and access objects in C++.

Now you can begin to see where pointers fit into the scheme of things. When you create an object dynamically, the new operator returns a pointer to the object in memory. You need that pointer to be able to do anything with the object. Figure 5.2 illustrates how the pointer points to the object in memory. Note that although the memory for the dynamically created object is allocated from heap memory, the actual pointer is a local variable and is allocated from the stack (a pointer requires 4 bytes of storage).

FIGURE 5.2

A pointer to an object in memory.

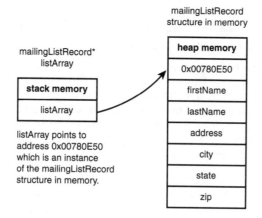

mailingListRecord
structure in memory

mailingListRecord*
listArray

stack memory
listArray

listArray points to
address 0x00780E50
which is an instance
of the mailingListRecord
structure in memory.

heap memory
0x00780E50
firstName
lastName
address
city
state
zip

Let's go back to a code snippet you saw earlier:

```
mailingListRecord* listArray;
listArray = new mailingListRecord;
strcpy(listArray->firstName, "John");
strcpy(listArray->lastName, "Leier");
// etc.
```

On the third line you see that the firstName data member of the structure is accessed using the indirect membership operator (->) rather than the direct membership operator. When you create an object dynamically, you must access the object's data members and functions using this operator.

Creating an array of structures dynamically requires a bit more work. Again, here's the stack-based version:

```
mailingListRecord listArray[3];
listArray[0].zip = 57441;
```

5

And the dynamic version:

```
mailingListRecord* listArray[3];
for (int i=0;i<3;i++)
  listArray[i] = new mailingListRecord;
listArray[0]->zip = 57441;
```

Note that I have to create a new instance of the structure for each element of the array. Notice also that to access a data member of the array, I use the indirect membership operator combined with the subscript operator.

Uninitialized pointers contain random values just like any other uninitialized variable. Attempting to use an uninitialized pointer can wreak havoc on a program. In many cases, a pointer is declared and immediately initialized:

```
MyArray* array = new MyArray;
```

Sometimes, however, you will declare a pointer and then not initialize it until sometime later in the program. If you attempt to use the pointer before initializing it, the pointer will point to some random memory location, and modifying that memory could cause all sorts of nasty problems. Often the problems caused by modifying unknown memory don't show up immediately, making the bug appear to be random. To be safe, you should initialize a pointer to 0 when you declare it:

```
MyArray* array = 0;
```

If you attempt to use a NULL pointer (any pointer set to NULL or 0), you will immediately get an access violation from Windows. Although this might not sound like a good thing, it is certainly the lesser of two evils. It is far better to have an immediate error at the point of the infraction than to have a random problem show up farther down the road.

Dereferencing a Pointer

Frequently you will need to dereference a pointer to retrieve the contents of the memory location (the object) that a pointer points to. Take the following example:

```
int x = 20;
int* ptrx = &x;
// later...
int z = *ptrx;
```

I can just imagine your frustration right now. What a mess! Don't worry, it's not quite as bad as it might appear. The first line in this example declares an int variable called x and assigns it a value of 20. The next line declares a pointer to an int and assigns to the pointer the address of the variable x. This is done by using the address-of operator (&).

In this example, the address-of operator tells the compiler, "Give me the memory address of the variable x, not the value of x itself." After the assignment, ptrx contains the memory address of x.

Later on in the program you might need to get the value of the object pointed to by ptrx. You might think of trying this:

```
int z = ptrx;    // wrong!
```

This won't work because you are trying to assign a memory address to a regular variable. When you try to compile this line, the compiler spits back an error stating Cannot convert int* to int. That makes sense because you are dealing with two different types of variables. So you need to dereference the pointer using the indirection operator:

```
int z = *ptrx;
```

NEW TERM *Dereferencing* a pointer means to retrieve the contents of the memory location that a pointer points to.

This could be considered the opposite of the address-of operator. Here you don't want the actual value of ptrx because the actual value is a memory address. Instead, you want the value of the object pointed to by that memory address. So in this case the indirection operator tells the compiler, "Give me the value of the object that ptrx points to, not the actual value of ptrx." Figure 5.3 shows how the variables from this example appear in memory after this code executes.

FIGURE 5.3

The x, ptrx, and z variables in memory.

Variable	z	ptrx	x
Address	0012F634	0012F638	0012F63C
Value	20	0012F63C	20

5

Note that the ptrx variable contains a memory location, not a value. When you dereference ptrx, you get the value of the memory location ptrx points to (0012F63C), that is, the number 20.

As you can see, the * symbol (an asterisk) is used to declare a pointer (int* x;) and also to dereference a pointer (int z = *x;). The compiler can tell from the context in which the * symbol is used what to do in each case. You don't have to worry that the compiler won't know what you intend.

Let's try to tie together what you have learned in this section. I'll take the MAILLIST program from Hour 4 and modify it so that it uses dynamic memory allocation. This requires a few changes. First take a look at the modified program and then I'll explain the changes. Listing 5.1 contains the modified MAILLIST program, now called POINTER.CPP.

LISTING 5.1   POINTER.CPP

```
 1: #include <iostream.h>
 2: #include <conio.h>
 3: #include <stdlib.h>
 4: #pragma hdrstop
 5: #include "structur.h"
 6: void displayRecord(int, mailingListRecord mlRec);
 7: int main(int, char**)
 8: {
 9:   //
10:   // create an array of pointers to
11:   // the mailingListRecord structure
12:   //
13:   mailingListRecord* listArray[3];
14:   //
15:   // create an object for each element of the array
16:   //
17:   for (int i=0;i<3;i++)
18:     listArray[i] = new mailingListRecord;
19:   cout << endl;
20:   int index = 0;
21:   //
22:   // get three records
23:   //
24:   do {
25:     cout << "First Name: ";
26:     cin.getline(listArray[index]->firstName,
27:       sizeof(listArray[index]->firstName) - 1);
28:     cout << "Last Name: ";
29:     cin.getline(listArray[index]->lastName,
30:       sizeof(listArray[index]->lastName) - 1);
31:     cout << "Address: ";
32:     cin.getline(listArray[index]->address,
33:       sizeof(listArray[index]->address) - 1);
34:     cout << "City: ";
35:     cin.getline(listArray[index]->city,
36:       sizeof(listArray[index]->city) - 1);
37:     cout << "State: ";
38:     cin.getline(listArray[index]->state,
39:       sizeof(listArray[index]->state) - 1);
40:     char buff[10];
41:     cout << "Zip: ";
42:     cin.getline(buff, sizeof(buff) - 1);
```

```
43:    listArray[index]->zip = atoi(buff);
44:    index++;
45:    cout << endl;
46:  }
47:  while (index < 3);
48:  //
49:  // display the three records
50:  //
51:  clrscr();
52:  //
53:  // must dereference the pointer to pass an object
54:  // to the displayRecord function.
55:  //
56:  for (int i=0;i<3;i++) {
57:    displayRecord(i, *listArray[i]);
58:  }
59:  //
60:  // ask the user to choose a record
61:  //
62:  cout << "Choose a record: ";
63:  int rec;
64:  do {
65:    rec = getch();
66:    rec -= 49;
67:  } while (rec < 0 || rec > 2);
68:  //
69:  // assign the selected record to a temporary variable
70:  // must dereference here, too
71:  //
72:  mailingListRecord temp = *listArray[rec];
73:  clrscr();
74:  cout << endl;
75:  //
76:  // display the selected recrord
77:  //
78:  displayRecord(rec, temp);
79:  getch();
80:  return 0;
81: }
82: void displayRecord(int num, mailingListRecord mlRec)
83: {
84:   cout << "Record " << (num + 1) << ":" << endl;
85:   cout << "Name:     " << mlRec.firstName << " ";
86:   cout << mlRec.lastName;
87:   cout << endl;
88:   cout << "Address:  " << mlRec.address;
89:   cout << endl << "           ";
90:   cout << mlRec.city << ", ";
91:   cout << mlRec.state << "  ";
92:   cout << mlRec.zip;
93:   cout << endl << endl;
94: }
```

5

ANALYSIS First, on line 13 I declared the `listArray` array as an array of pointers. Second, I created objects for each element of the array. This takes place in the `for` loop on lines 17 and 18. Third, I changed the direct membership operators (`.`) to indirect membership operators (`->`). Finally, I also had to dereference the pointers on line 57 and again on line 72. This is necessary because an object is expected, and we cannot use a pointer in place of an object.

Notice that the `displayRecord` function (starting on line 82) doesn't change. I haven't changed the fact that the `mailingListRecord` structure is passed to the function by value, so the code in the function doesn't need to be modified.

If you've had previous experience with C++, you might have noticed that this program has a bug in it. I'll let you in on the secret before the end of the hour.

Using References

NEW TERM A *reference* is a special type of pointer that enables you to treat a pointer like a regular object.

References, like pointers, can be confusing. A reference is declared using the reference operator. The symbol for the reference operator is the ampersand (`&`), which is the same symbol used for the address-of operator (don't worry, the compiler knows how to keep it all straight). As I said, a reference enables you to treat a pointer like an object. Here's an example:

```
MyStruct* pStruct = new MyStruct;
MyStruct& ref = *pStruct;
ref.X = 100;
```

Notice that you use the direct membership operator with references rather than the indirect membership operator, as you do with pointers. Now you can get rid of all those pesky `->` operators! Although you won't use references a lot, they can be very handy when you need them.

The book's CD contains a program called `REFERENCE`. It is the `POINTER` example modified to use references instead of pointers. Load the project in C++Builder and compare it to the `POINTER` example to see how references can be used in place of pointers.

Although it might seem that references are preferred over pointers, that is not always the case. References have some peculiarities that make them unsuitable in many cases. For one thing, references cannot be declared and then later assigned a value. They must be initialized when declared. For instance, the following code snippet results in a compiler error:

```
MyStruct* pStruct = new MyStruct;
MyStruct& ref;
ref = *pStruct;
ref.X = 100;
```

Another problem with references is that they cannot be set to 0 or NULL as pointers can. That means you have to take special care to ensure that you do not call delete on a reference twice (I haven't talked about the delete operator yet, but I will do so later in the hour in the section "The new and delete Operators"). References and pointers can often serve the same purpose, but neither is perfect in every programming situation.

Passing Function Parameters by Reference and by Pointer

In Hour 4 I talked about passing objects to functions by value. I said that in the case of structures and classes, it is usually better to pass those objects by reference rather than by value. Any object can be passed by reference. This includes the primitive data types such as int and long, as well as instances of a structure or class.

To review, when you pass function parameters by value, a copy of the object is made and the function works with the copy. When you pass by reference, a pointer to the object is passed and not the object itself. This has two primary implications. First, it means that objects passed by reference can be modified by the function. Second, passing by reference eliminates the overhead of creating a copy of the object each time the function is called.

The fact that an object can be modified by the function is the most important aspect of passing by reference. Take this code, for instance:

```
void IncrementPosition(int& xPos, int& yPos)
{
  xPos++;
  yPos++;
}
int x = 20;
int y = 40;
IncrementPosition(x, y);
// x now equals 21 and y equals 41
```

Notice that when the function returns, both the parameters passed have been incremented by one. This is because the function is modifying the actual object via the pointer (remember that a reference is a type of pointer).

5

Remember that a function can return only one value. By passing parameters by reference, you can achieve the effect of a function returning more than one value. The function still cannot return more than one value, but the objects passed by reference are updated, so the function effectively returns multiple values.

As I said, the other reason to pass parameters by reference is to eliminate the overhead of making a copy of the object each time the function is called. When dealing with primitive data types, there is no real overhead involved in making a copy. When dealing with structures and classes, however, the overhead is something to be considered. You should pass structures of any consequence by reference, as the following code demonstrates:

```
// structure passed by reference
void someFunction(MyStructure& s)
{
  // do some stuff with 's'
  return;
}
MyStructure myStruct;
// do some stuff, then later...
someFunction(myStruct);
```

Notice that the function call looks exactly the same whether the object is being passed by reference or by value.

Do you see a potential problem with passing by reference? If you pass by reference, you avoid the overhead of making a copy of the object, but now the object can be modified by the function. Sometimes you don't want the object to be modified by the function. So what if you want to pass by reference, but make sure the object is not modified? Read on and I'll tell you how.

NEW TERM The const keyword enables you to declare a variable as constant.

After a variable is declared with const, it cannot be changed. The solution, then, is to pass by reference *and* make the object const:

```
void someFunction(const MyStruct& s)
{
  // do some stuff with 's'
  return;
}
MyStructure myStruct;
// later
someFunction(myStruct);
```

Now you are free to pass by reference and not worry that your object might be modified by the function. Note that the function call itself stays the same and that only the function definition (and declaration) is modified with the const keyword.

Note that the object is const only within the function. The object can be modified both before and after the function returns. If you attempt to modify a const value in a function, you get a compiler error that says:

```
Cannot modify a const object.
```

Passing by pointer is essentially the same as passing by reference. Passing by pointer has a couple of syntactical headaches that make it less desirable than passing by reference. Let's take IncrementPosition() function from the first example in this section and modify it to pass by pointer rather than by reference:

```
void IncrementPosition(int* xPos, int* yPos)
{
  *xPos++;    // dereference, then increment
  *yPos++;
}
```

Note that each pointer in the function body must be dereferenced before it can be incremented. Most of the time your needs will be best served by passing by reference, but you can pass by pointer if a situation dictates the need. When passing char arrays, you will usually pass by pointer rather than by reference because you can use a pointer to a char array and the name of the array interchangeably. For example:

```
void ShowString(char* s)
{
  cout << s << endl;
}

int main(int argc, char* argv[])
{
  // declare a character array
  char text[20];
  // give it a value
  strcpy(text, "Hello there.");
  // call ShowString to display the string
  ShowString(text);
  getch();
  return 0;
}
```

In this example, the ShowString() function takes a char* as a parameter. Notice that I simply pass the name of the character array, text, to the ShowString() function. The compiler understands that the name of the array is a pointer to the array itself.

The new and delete Operators

The new and delete operators are two important C++ language features. As mentioned earlier in the hour, memory in a C++ program is allocated dynamically using operator new. You free memory using the delete operator. Unless you have previously programmed in C, you might not appreciate the simplicity of new and delete. In C programs you use malloc(), calloc(), realloc(), and free() to dynamically allocate memory. Windows really complicates things by offering a whole raft of local and global memory-allocation functions. Although this is not exactly difficult, it can be confusing, to say the least. C++ removes those headaches through the use of new and delete.

You've already seen new in action, so let's review. As discussed earlier, you can allocate memory locally (from the stack) or dynamically (from the heap). The following code snippet shows examples of allocating two character arrays. One is allocated from the stack (local allocation), and the other is allocated from the heap (dynamic allocation):

```
char buff[80];
char* bigBuff = new char[4096];
```

In the first case the buffer size is insignificant, so it doesn't really matter whether the stack or the heap is used. In the second case a large char array is needed, so it makes sense to allocate it from the heap rather than the stack. In the case of arrays (remember, a string is just an array of type char), the dynamic and local flavors can be used interchangeably. That is, they use the same syntax:

```
strcpy(buff, "Ricky Rat");
strcpy(bigBuff, "A very long string that goes on and on...");
// later on...
strcpy(bigBuff, buff);
```

Remember that the name of an array when used by itself points to the first memory location of the array. A pointer also points to the first memory location of the array, so that is why the two forms can be used interchangeably.

All memory allocated must be deallocated (released or freed) after you are done with the memory. With local objects this happens for you automatically and you don't have to worry about it. The memory manager allocates the memory your object needs from the stack and then frees that memory when the object goes out of scope (usually when a function returns or when the code block in which the object was declared ends). When using dynamic memory allocation, the programmer must take the responsibility of freeing any memory allocated with the new operator.

NEW TERM   Freeing memory allocated with new is accomplished with the delete operator.

All calls to new should have a matching delete. If you don't free all memory allocated with the new operator, your program might leak memory. I say your program *might* leak memory because 32-bit Windows claims to free all memory allocated by a program when that program terminates. While this is true (at least in theory), I believe it is very bad practice to trust the operating system to clean up after the programmer.

In addition, the memory allocated by the program won't be freed until after the application terminates. If you are allocating large chunks of memory and not freeing that memory when you are done with it, your program will continue to use more and more system memory. This could lead to a situation where your program brings the entire operating system to its knees. Always allocate memory only when needed and free that memory immediately after you are done with it.

Using the delete operator is extremely easy:

```
SomeObject* myObject = new SomeObject;
// do a bunch of stuff with myObject
delete myObject;     // so long!
```

That's all there is to it! There isn't a lot to the delete operator, but there are a couple of things about pointers and delete that you should be aware of. The first is that you must not delete a pointer that has already been deleted, or you will get access violations and all sorts of other problems. Second, it is okay to delete a pointer that has been set to 0. Set any deleted pointers to 0 if there's any chance you might accidentally delete the pointer twice.

Have you figured it out yet? "Huh?" you say? The bug in the POINTER program...have you figured out what it is? You got it! The program leaks memory. I created an array of structures allocated from the heap but never freed the memory. So what I need is a couple of lines to clean up things just before the program ends:

```
getch(); // existing line
for (int i=0;i<3;i++)
  delete listArray[i];
```

There! Now I have a properly behaving program. I just ran through the array of pointers and deleted each one. Nothing to it.

5

When you call new to create an array, you are actually using the new[] version of operator new. It's not important that you know the details of how that works, but you do need to know how to properly delete arrays that are dynamically allocated. Earlier I gave you an example of dynamically creating a character array. Here is the same code snippet except with the delete[] statement added:

```
char buff[80];
char* bigBuff = new char[4096];
strcpy(buff, "Ricky Rat");
strcpy(bigBuff, "Some very long string.");
// later on...
delete[] bigBuff;
```

Notice that the statement calls delete[] and not just plain delete. I won't go into a technical description of what happens here, but this ensures that all elements in the array get properly deleted. Be sure that if you dynamically allocate an array, you call the delete[] operator to free the memory.

Summary

That's a lot to learn! Because you are reading this, you must still be standing. That's good news. In this hour we did the difficult work and took on pointers and references. When you get a handle on pointers, you are well on your way to understanding C++. As part of the discussion on pointers, you learned about local versus dynamic memory allocation, which led to a discussion about the new and delete operators.

Workshop

The Workshop contains quiz questions to help you solidify your understanding of the material covered and exercises to provide you with experience in using what you have learned. The answers to the quiz questions are provided following the questions. The exercises are given for you to work out and code on your own.

Q&A

Q Pointers and references confuse me. Am I alone?

A Absolutely not! Pointers and references are complicated and take some time to fully understand. You will probably have to work with C++ a while before you get a handle on pointers and references.

Q Should I create my objects on the stack or on the heap?

A That depends on the object. Large objects should be created on the heap to preserve stack space. Small objects and primitive data types should be created on the stack for simplicity and speed of execution.

Quiz

1. What is a pointer?
2. What does it mean to dereference a pointer?
3. Should instances of classes and structures be passed to functions by reference or by value?
4. Which is better to use, a reference or a pointer?

Answers

1. A pointer is a variable that holds the address of another variable or an object in memory.
2. To dereference a pointer means to get the value of the variable that the pointer points to and not the value of the pointer itself (which is just a memory location).
3. Usually classes and structures should be passed by reference to eliminate unnecessary overhead.
4. It depends on the situation. No one situation is best every time. This is a trick question.

Exercises

1. Write a program that declares a structure, dynamically creates an instance of the structure, and fills the structure with data.(Hint: Don't forget to delete the pointer.)
2. Explain to a five-year-old the difference between pointers and references.

5

Hour **6**

C++ Classes and Object-Oriented Programming, Part I

In this hour and the next hour, you get to the good stuff—C++ classes. Classes are the heart of C++ and a major part of object-oriented programming. Classes are also the heart of the Visual Component Library (VCL), which you will use when you start writing Windows GUI applications.

First you will find out what a class is and how it's expected to be used. Along the way you will learn the meaning of C++ buzzwords like *inheritance*, *object*, *data hiding*, and *data abstraction*. This hour covers the following features of classes in C++:

- Constructors
- Destructors
- Class data members
- Class member functions

What's a Class?

NEW TERM
A *class*, like a structure, is a collection of data members and functions that work together to accomplish a specific programming task. In this way a class is said to *encapsulate* the task. Encapsulation is also referred to as *data abstraction*. Classes have the following features:

- The capability to control access
- Constructors
- Destructors
- Data members
- Member functions
- A hidden, special pointer called this

Before diving into an explanation of these features, let me give you a quick example of how a class can work. Let's use a typical Windows control as an example—a check box, for instance. A class that represents a check box could have data members for the caption of the check box and for the state (checked or unchecked). This class could also have functions that would enable you to set and query both the check box caption and the check state. These functions might be named GetCheck(), SetCheck(), GetCaption(), and SetCaption(). After the class has been written, you can create an instance of the class to control a check box in Windows. (It's not quite that simple, but this is just an example after all.) If you have three check boxes, you could have three instances of the CheckBox class that could then be used to control each check box individually.

```
MyCheckBox check1(ID_CHECK1);
MyCheckBox check2(ID_CHECK2);
MyCheckBox check3(ID_CHECK3);
check1.SetCaption("Thingamabob Option");
check1.SetCheck(true);
check2.SetCaption("Doohickey Options");
check2.SetCheck(false);
check3.SetCaption("Whatchamacallit Options");
check3.SetCheck(true);
if (check1.GetCheck()) DoThingamabobTask();
if (check2.GetCheck()) DoDoohickeyTask();
// etc.
```

In this example, each instance of the class is a separate object. Each instance has its own data members, and the objects operate independently of one another. They are all objects of the same type but are separate instances in memory. With that brief introduction, let's roll up our sleeves once more and go to work on understanding classes.

Anatomy of a Class

A class, like a structure, has a declaration. The class declaration is usually contained in a header file. In simple cases, both the class declaration and the definition can be contained in a single source file, but you typically won't do that for real applications. Usually you create a class source file with a filename closely matching the class name and with a .CPP extension. Because Windows 95/98 and Windows NT both support long filenames, you can use filenames that exactly match your class name if you want. The header file for the class usually has the same name as the source file but with an extension of .H. For example, if you had a class called MyClass, you would have a source file named MYCLASS.CPP and a header named MYCLASS.H.

Class Access Levels

 Classes can have three levels of access: *private*, *public*, or *protected*. Each of these access levels is defined in this section.

Class access levels control how a class can be used. As a sole programmer, you might be not only the class's creator but also a user of the class. In team programming environments, one programmer might be the creator of the class and other programmers the users of the class.

To understand the role that levels of access play in class operation, you first need to understand how classes are used. In any class there is the *public* part of the class, which the outside world has access to, and there is the private part of a class. The *private* part of a class is the internal implementation of the class—the inner workings, so to speak.

Part of a well-designed class includes hiding anything from public view that the user of the class doesn't need to know.

Data Hiding

 Data hiding is the hiding of internal implementations within the class from outside views.

Data hiding and data abstraction work together to prevent the user from knowing more than he or she needs to know about the class and also prevents the user from messing with things that shouldn't be messed with. For instance, when you get in your car and turn the key to start it, do you want to know every detail about how the car operates? Of course not. You only want to know as much as you need to know to operate the car safely. So in this analogy the steering wheel, pedals, gear shift lever, speedometer, and so on represent the public interface between the car and the driver. The driver knows which of those components to manipulate to make the car perform the way he or she wants.

6

Conversely, the engine, drive train, and electrical system of the car are hidden from public view. The engine is tucked neatly away where you never have to look at it if you don't want to. It's a detail that you don't need to know about, so it is hidden from you—kept private, if you prefer. Imagine how much trouble driving would be if you had to know everything the car was doing at all times: Is the carburetor getting enough gas? Does the differential have enough grease? Is the alternator producing adequate voltage for both the ignition and the radio to operate? Are the intake valves opening properly? Who needs it! In the same way, a class keeps its internal implementation private, so the user of the class doesn't have to worry about what's going on under the hood. The internal workings of the class are kept private, and the user interface is public.

The *protected* access level is a little harder to explain. Protected class members, like private class members, cannot be accessed by users of the class. They can, however, be accessed by classes that are derived from this class. Continuing with the car analogy, let's say you wanted to extend the car (literally) by making it a stretch limousine. To do this, you would need to know something about the underlying structure of the car. You would need to know how to modify the drive shaft and frame of the car at the very minimum. In this case you would need to get your hands dirty and, as a limousine designer, get at the parts of the car that were previously unimportant to you (the protected parts). The internal workings of the engine are still kept private because you don't need to know how the engine works to extend the frame of the car. Similarly, most of the public parts of the car remain the same, but you might add some new public elements, such as the controls for the intercom system. I've strayed a little here and given you a peek into what is called *inheritance*, but I won't go into further details right now. I will talk more about protected access a little later in the section "Class Member Functions," and about inheritance in the next hour in the section "Inheritance."

The C++ language has three keywords that pertain to class access. The keywords are (not surprisingly): `public`, `private`, and `protected`. You specify a class member's access level when you declare the class. A class is declared with the `class` keyword. A class declaration looks like a structure declaration with the access modifiers added:

```
class Vehicle {
  public:
    bool haveKey;
    bool Start();
    void SetGear(int gear);
    void Accelerate(int acceleration);
    void Brake(int factor);
    void Turn(int direction);
    void ShutDown();
  protected:
    void StartupProcedure();
```

```
  private:
    void StartElectricalSystem();
    void StartEngine();
    int currentGear;
    bool started;
    int speed;
};
```

Notice how you break the class organization down into the three access levels. You might not use all three levels of access in a given class. You are not required to use any of the access levels if you don't want, but typically you will have a public and a private section at least.

> Class-member access defaults to private. If you don't add any access key-words, all data and functions in the class will be private. A class where all data members and functions are private isn't very useful in most cases.

Constructors

Classes in C++ have a special function called the constructor.

NEW TERM   The *constructor* is a function that is automatically called when an instance of a class is created.

The constructor is used to initialize any class member variables, allocate memory the class needs, or do any other startup tasks. The Vehicle example you just saw doesn't have a constructor. If you don't provide a constructor, the C++Builder compiler creates a default constructor for you. Whereas this is fine for simple classes, you will almost always provide a constructor for classes of any significance. The constructor must have the same name as the class. This is what distinguishes it as a constructor. Given that, let's add a constructor declaration to the Vehicle class:

```
class Vehicle {
  public:
    Vehicle();        // constructor
    bool haveKey;
    bool Start();
    void SetGear(int gear);
    void Accelerate(int acceleration);
    void Brake(int factor);
    void Turn(int direction);
    void ShutDown();
  protected:
    void StartupProcedure();
  private:
```

6

```
      void StartElectricalSystem();
      void StartEngine();
      int currentGear;
      bool started;
      int speed;
};
```

Notice that the constructor doesn't have a return type. A constructor cannot return a value, so no return type is specified. If you try to add a return type to the constructor declaration, you will get a compiler error.

A class can have more than one constructor. This is possible through function overloading, which I discussed in Hour 4 in the section, "Function Overloading." For instance, a class can have a constructor that takes no parameters (a default constructor) and a constructor that takes one or more parameters to initialize data members to certain values. For example, let's say you have a class called Rect that encapsulates a rectangle (rectangles are frequently used in Windows programming). This class could have several constructors. It could have a default constructor that sets all the data members to 0, and another constructor that enables you to set the class's data members through the constructor. First, let's take a look at how the class declaration might look:

```
class Rect {
  public:
    Rect();
    Rect(int _left, int _top, int _right, int _bottom);
    int GetWidth();
    int GetHeight();
    void SetRect(int _left, int _top, int _right, int _bottom);
  private:
    int left;
    int top;
    int right;
    int bottom;
};
```

The definitions for the constructors would look something like this:

```
Rect::Rect()
{
  left = 0;
  top = 0;
  right = 0;
  bottom = 0;
}
Rect::Rect(int _left, int _top, int _right, int _bottom)
{
  left = _left;
  top = _top;
  right = _right;
  bottom = _bottom;
}
```

The first constructor is a default constructor by virtue of the fact that it takes no parameters. It simply initializes each data member to 0. The second constructor takes the parameters passed and assigns them to the corresponding class data members. The variable names in the parameter list are local to the constructor, so each of the variable names begins with an underscore to differentiate between the local variables and the class data members.

NEW TERM   *Instantiation* is the creation of an object, called an instance, of a class.

It's important to understand that you can't call a constructor directly. So how do you use one of these constructors instead of the other? You do that when you create an instance of a class. The following code snippet creates two instances of the Rect class. The first uses the default constructor, and the second uses the second form of the constructor:

```
Rect rect1;       // object created using default constructor
Rect rect2(0, 0, 100, 100);  // created using 2nd constructor
```

You can have as many constructors as you like, but be sure that your constructors don't have ambiguous parameter lists (as per the rules on function overloading).

> Remember that an uninitialized variable contains random data. This is true for class data members as well as other variables. To be safe, you should set class member variables to some initial value.

NEW TERM   C++ provides a means by which you can initialize class data members in what is called an *initializer list*.

The following is the proper way to initialize data members of a class. Rather than try to explain how to use an initializer list, let me show you an example. Let's take the two constructors for the Rect class and initialize the data members in an initializer list rather than in the body of the function as I did before. It looks like this:

```
Rect::Rect() :
  left(0),
  top(0),
  right(0),
  bottom(0)
{
}

Rect::Rect(int _left, int _top, int _right , int _bottom) :
  left(_left),
  top(_top),
```

6

```
    right(_right),
    bottom(_bottom)
{
}
```

Notice two things in this code snippet. First, notice that the initializer list is preceded by a colon. (The colon is at the end of the function header, so you might not have noticed it.) Notice also that each variable in the initializer list is followed by a comma—except the last variable. Forgetting either of these two things causes compiler errors.

In most cases it doesn't matter whether you initialize your data members in the body of the constructor or the initializer list. I have done it both ways but prefer the initializer list.

Destructors

 The *destructor* is a special function that is automatically called just before the object is destroyed.

The destructor could be considered the opposite of the constructor. It is usually used to free any memory allocated by the class or do any other cleanup chores. A class is not required to have a destructor, but if it does, it can have only one. A destructor has no return value and takes no parameters. The destructor's name must be the name of the class preceded by a tilde (~).

As mentioned, the destructor is called just before the class is destroyed. The class might be destroyed because it was allocated from the stack and is going out of scope, or it might be destroyed as a result of delete being called for the class (if the class was created dynamically). In either case, the destructor will be called just before the class breathes its last breath.

The following shows the updated code for the Rect class:

```
class Rect {
  public:
    Rect();
    Rect(int _left, int _top, int _right, int _bottom);
    ~Rect();          // destructor added
    int GetWidth();
    int GetHeight();
    void SetRect(int _left, int _top, int _right, int _bottom);
  private:
    int left;
    int top;
    int right;
    int bottom;
    char* text;      // new class member added
```

```
};
Rect::Rect() :
  left(0),
  top(0),
  right(0),
  bottom(0)
{
    text = new char[256];
    strcpy(text, "Any Colour You Like");
}
// code omitted
Rect::~Rect()
{
  delete[] text;
}
```

The modified version of the Rect class allocates storage for a char array named text in its constructor and frees that storage in the destructor. (I can't think of a good reason for a class that handles rectangles to have a text data member, but you never know!) Again, use the destructor for any cleanup tasks that need to be done before the instance of the class is destroyed.

Class Data Members

NEW TERM   *Data members* of a class are simply variables that are declared in the class declaration. They could be considered as variables that have class scope.

Data members in classes are essentially the same as data members in structures except that their access can be controlled by declaring them as private, public, or protected. Regardless of a data member's access, it is available for use in all functions of the class. Depending on the data member's access level, it can be visible outside the class as well. Private and protected data members, for instance, are private to the class and cannot be seen outside the class. Public data members, however, can be accessed from outside the class but only through an object. Take the Rect class declared previously, for example. It has no public data members. You could try the following, but you'll get a compiler error:

```
Rect rect(10, 10, 200, 200);
int x = rect.left;  // compiler error!
```

The compiler error will say Rect::left is not accessible. The compiler is telling you that left is a private data member and you can't get to it. If left were in the public section of the class declaration, this code would compile.

6

You can use *getters* and *setters* to change private data members: Getters are functions that get the value of a private data member, and setters are functions that set the value of a private data member. Both getters and setters are public member functions that act on private data members.

To illustrate, let's say that for the `Rect` class you had the following public getters and setters for the `left` data member:

```
int Rect::GetLeft()
{
  return left;
}
void Rect::SetLeft(int newLeft)
{
  left = newLeft;
}
```

Now when you want to obtain the value of the `left` member of the `Rect` class, you can use this:

```
Rect rect;
int x = rect.GetLeft();
```

In some cases this is overkill. Setters have one main advantage, though—they enable you to validate input. By validating input, you can control the values your data members contain.

> Some OOP extremists say that data members should never be public. They would advise you to use getters and setters to access all data members. On the other end of the spectrum is the group that recommends making all your data members public. The truth lies somewhere in between. Some data members are noncritical and can be left public if it is more convenient. Other data members are critical to the way the class operates and should not be made public. If you are going to err, it is better to err on the side of making data members private.

Each instance of your class gets its own copy of the class's data members in memory. The exception to this is that if any class data members are declared with the `static` storage modifier, all instances of the class will share the same copy of that data member in memory. In that case only one copy of that data member will exist in memory. If any one instance of the class changes a static data member, it changes in all the classes. Use of static data members in classes is not common, so don't worry about it if this doesn't make sense right now.

> **HOUSE RULES: CLASS DATA MEMBERS**
> - Use as many data members as you need for vital class operations, but use local variables where possible.
> - Don't make all data members public.
> - Use getters and setters for data members that you want to remain private but need to be able to access.
> - Validate data in your setters to ensure that improper values are not being input.
> - Initialize all data members in either the initializer list or in the body of your constructor.
> - Don't forget to delete any data members that are dynamically allocated.

Class Member Functions

Class member functions are functions that belong to your class. They are local to the class and don't exist outside the class. Class member functions can only be called from within the class itself or through an instance of the class. They have access to all public, protected, and private data members of the class. Member functions can be declared in the `private`, `protected`, or `public` sections of your class. Good class design requires that you think about which of these sections your member functions should go into.

Public member functions represent the user interface to the class. It is through the public member functions that users of the class access it to gain whatever functionality the class provides. For example, let's say you have a class that plays and records wave audio. Public member functions might include functions like `Open()`, `Play()`, `Record()`, `Save()`, `Rewind()`, and so on.

Private member functions are functions that the class uses internally to do its thing. These functions are not intended to be called by users of the class; they are private in order to hide them from the outside world. Frequently a class has startup chores to perform when the class is created. (For example, you have already seen that the constructor is called when a class is created.) In some classes the startup processing might be significant, requiring many lines of code. To remove clutter from the constructor, a class might have an `Init()` function that is called from the constructor to perform those startup tasks. This function would never be called directly by a user of the class. In fact, more than likely bad things would happen if this function were to be called by a user at the wrong time, so the function is private in order to protect both the integrity of the class and the user.

6

Protected member functions are functions that cannot be accessed by the outside world but can be accessed by classes derived from this class. I haven't talked yet about classes being derived from other classes; I'll save that discussion for the next hour in the section, "Inheritance."

In Hour 4 I talked briefly about inline functions in the section, "Inline Functions." There, I said that an inline function is different because the code for the function is placed in the compiled executable each time a call to the inline function appears in the application's code. Inline functions can be declared in one of two ways. Here is the syntax for the first form:

The `inline` Function, Form 1

```
class ClassName {
  public:
    ReturnType FunctionName();
};

inline ReturnType ClassName::FunctionName() {
  statements
}
```

The function *FunctionName* is declared within the body of the class *ClassName*. The function definition (the function itself) is defined outside of the class declaration using the `inline` keyword. *FunctionName* must be preceded by *ClassName* and the scope resolution operator.

In the second form, the function can be defined within the class declaration to which the function belongs:

```
class MyClass {
  public:
    // other stuff
    int GetSomething()
    {
      return Something;
    }
  private:
    int Something;
};
```

Here the function is automatically an inline function by virtue of the fact that the entire function is contained within the class declaration.

▼ SYNTAX ▲

The `inline` Function, Form 2

```
class ClassName {
  public:
    ReturnType FunctionName()
    {
      statements
    }
};
```

The function *FunctionName* is declared and defined entirely within the *ClassName* declaration. The function is an inline function by virtue of the fact that it is contained within the *ClassName* declaration. The `inline` keyword is not required.

HOUSE RULES: CLASS MEMBER FUNCTIONS

- Make public only those functions that users need in order to properly utilize the class.

- Make private any functions that users don't need to know about.

- Make protected any functions that derived classes might need access to but that users don't need to know about.

- Use static member functions only under special circumstances.

- Declare any class member functions that have to be executed quickly as inline functions. Remember to keep inline functions short.

- Place any code duplicated more than twice in a function.

Summary

In this hour you started learning about classes in C++. Early in the hour you learned how a C++ class is designed. You learned about constructors and destructors. Most classes of any significance will have one or more constructors and a destructor. You ended this hour with a look at class data members and class member functions. In the next hour, you will learn more about classes, including more detail on inheritance and virtual functions.

6

Workshop

The Workshop contains quiz questions to help you solidify your understanding of the material covered and exercises to provide you with experience in using what you have learned. The answers to the quiz questions are provided following the questions. The exercises are given for you to work out and code on your own.

Q&A

Q How can I keep a class member function private to the outside world but enable derived classes to call it?

A Make it protected. A protected function is not accessible to users of your class but is accessible to derived classes.

Q What does *data abstraction* mean?

A Data abstraction means hiding the details of the class that the users of the class don't need to see. A class might have dozens of data members and functions, but only a few that the user can see. Only make visible (public) the functions that a user needs to know about to use the class. This process is also included in the term *data abstraction.*

Quiz

1. What is the purpose of having private data members and functions?

2. How can you keep data members private and yet enable users to read and set their values?

3. How and when is a class's destructor called?

4. What does an initializer list do?

Answers

1. Private data members protect data from being modified directly by users of the class. Private data members can be modified through public member functions, but not directly.

2. By using getters and setters, which are public member functions that can be called to change the value of a private data member.

3. The destructor is called when the object is destroyed. For local objects this occurs when the object goes out of scope. For dynamically allocated objects, this occurs when the object is deleted.

4. An initializer list initializes a class's data members and calls any base class constructors prior to the body of the constructor being entered.

Exercise

1. Write a paragraph that explains the purpose of the class constructor and a paragraph explaining the purpose of the destructor.

HOUR 7

C++ Classes and Object-Oriented Programming, Part II

This hour continues the discussion of classes. Specifically, this hour covers the following aspects of C++:

- The this pointer
- Virtual functions
- Inheritance
- Multiple inheritance

The material in this hour will round out your knowledge of C++ classes.

What's this?

NEW TERM   All C++ classes have a hidden data member called this. this is a pointer to the instance of the class in memory. (A discussion on the this pointer quickly starts to sound like a "Who's on First?" comedy sketch, but I'll try anyway.)

Obviously this (pun intended) will require some explanation. First, let's take a look at how the Rect class created in Hour 6 would look if this were not a hidden data member:

```
class Rect {
  public:
    Rect();
    Rect(int _left, int _top, int _bottom, int _right);
    ~Rect();
    int GetWidth();
    int GetHeight();
    void SetRect(int _left, int _top, int _bottom, int _right);
  private:
    Rect* this;        // if 'this' were not invisible
    int left;
    int top;
    int bottom;
    int right;
    char* text;
};
```

This is effectively what the Rect class looks like to the compiler. When a class object is created, the this pointer automatically gets initialized to the address of the class in memory:

```
Rect* rect = new Rect(20, 20, 100, 100);
// now 'rect' and 'rect->this' have the same value
// because both point to the same object in memory
```

"But," you ask, "what does this mean?" Remember that each class instance gets its own copy of the class's data members. But all class instances share the same set of functions for the class (there's no point in duplicating that code for each instance of the class). How does the compiler figure out which instance goes with which function call? Class member functions all have a hidden this parameter that goes with them. To illustrate, let's say you have a function for the Rect class called GetWidth(). It would look like this (no pun intended):

```
int Rect::GetWidth()
{
  return (right - left);
}
```

That's how the function looks to you and me. To the compiler, though, it looks something like this:

```cpp
int Rect::GetWidth(Rect* this)
{
  return (this->right - this->left);
}
```

That's not exactly accurate from a technical perspective, but it's close enough for this discussion. From this code you can see that this is working behind the scenes to keep everything straight for you. You don't have to worry about how that happens, but you need to know that it does happen.

> Never modify the this pointer. You can use it to pass a pointer to your class to other functions or as a parameter in constructing other classes, but don't change its value. Learn to treat this as a read-only variable.

Although this works behind the scenes, it is still a variable that you can access from within the class. As an illustration, let's take a quick peek into the Visual Component Library (VCL).

Most of the time you will create components in VCL by dropping them on the form at design time. When you do that, C++Builder creates a pointer to the component and does all sorts of housekeeping chores on your behalf, saving you from concerning yourself with the technical end of things. Sometimes, however, you will create a component at runtime. VCL insists (as all good frameworks do) on wanting to keep track of which child objects belong to which parent. For instance, let's say you wanted to create a button on a form when another button is clicked. You need to tell VCL what the parent of the new button is. The code would look like this:

```cpp
void _ _fastcall TMyForm::Button1Click(TObject *Sender)
{
  TButton* button = new TButton(this);
  button->Parent = this;
  button->Caption = "New Button";
  button->Left = 100;
  button->Top = 100;
  button->Show();
  // more code
}
```

7

In this code you can see that `this` is used in the constructor (this sets the `Owner` property of the button, but I'll get into that later when I cover VCL components in Hour 15, "VCL Components") and also that it is assigned to the `Parent` property of the newly created button. This is how you will use the `this` pointer the vast majority of the time in your C++Builder applications.

Don't worry too much about this...er, `this` (whatever!). When you begin to use VCL, it will quickly become clear when you are required to use `this` in your C++Builder applications.

An Example Using Classes

Right now it would be nice if you had an example that uses classes. The following listings contain a program that implement a class called `Airplane`. This program enables you to play air traffic controller by issuing commands to three aircraft. Listing 7.1 is the header for the `Airplane` class, Listing 7.2 is the source code for the `Airplane` class, and Listing 7.3 is the main program.

LISTING 7.1   AIRPLANE.H

```
 1: //--------------------------------------------------------
 2: #ifndef airplaneH
 3: #define airplaneH
 4: #define AIRLINER      0
 5: #define COMMUTER      1
 6: #define PRIVATE       2
 7: #define TAKINGOFF     0
 8: #define CRUISING      1
 9: #define LANDING       2
10: #define ONRAMP        3
11: #define MSG_CHANGE    0
12: #define MSG_TAKEOFF   1
13: #define MSG_LAND      2
14: #define MSG_REPORT    3
15: class Airplane {
16:   public:
17:     Airplane(const char* _name, int _type = AIRLINER);
18:     ~Airplane();
19:     virtual int GetStatus(char* statusString);
20:     int GetStatus()
21:     {
22:       return status;
23:     }
24:      int Speed()
25:     {
26:       return speed;
27:     }
```

```
28:     int Heading()
29:     {
30:       return heading;
31:     }
32:     int Altitude()
33:     {
34:       return altitude;
35:     }
36:     void ReportStatus();
37:     bool SendMessage(int msg, char* response,
38:       int spd = -1, int dir = -1, int alt = -1);
39:     char* name;
40:   protected:
41:     virtual void TakeOff(int dir);
42:     virtual void Land();
43:   private:
44:     int speed;
45:     int altitude;
46:     int heading;
47:     int status;
48:     int type;
49:     int ceiling;
50: };
51: #endif
```

LISTING 7.2   AIRPLANE.CPP

```
 1: #include <stdio.h>
 2: #include <iostream.h>
 3: #include "airplane.h"
 4: //
 5: // Constructor performs initialization
 6: //
 7: Airplane::Airplane(const char* _name, int _type) :
 8:   type(_type),
 9:   status(ONRAMP),
10:   speed(0),
11:   altitude(0),
12:   heading(0)
13: {
14:   switch (type) {
15:     case AIRLINER : ceiling = 35000; break;
16:     case COMMUTER : ceiling = 20000; break;
17:     case PRIVATE  : ceiling = 8000;
18:   }
19:   name = new char[50];
20:   strcpy(name, _name);
```

7

continues

LISTING 7.2   CONTINUED

```
21: }
22: //
23: // Destructor performs cleanup.
24: //
25: Airplane::~Airplane()
26: {
27:   delete[] name;
28: }
29: //
30: // Gets a message from the user.
31: //
32: bool
33: Airplane::SendMessage(int msg, char* response,
34:   int spd, int dir, int alt)
35: {
36:   //
37:   // Check for bad commands.
38:   //
39:   if (spd > 500) {
40:     strcpy(response, "Speed cannot be more than 500.");
41:     return false;
42:   }
43:   if (dir > 360) {
44:     strcpy(response, "Heading cannot be over 360 degrees.");
45:     return false;
46:   }
47:   if (alt < 100 && alt != -1) {
48:     strcpy(response, "I'd crash, bonehead!");
49:     return false;
50:   }
51:   if (alt > ceiling) {
52:     strcpy(response, "I can't go that high.");
53:     return false;
54:   }
55:   //
56:   // Do something based on which command was sent.
57:   //
58:   switch (msg) {
59:     case MSG_TAKEOFF : {
60:       // Can't take off if already in the air!
61:       if (status != ONRAMP) {
62:         strcpy(response, "I'm already in the air!");
63:         return false;
64:       }
65:       TakeOff(dir);
66:       break;
67:     }
68:     case MSG_CHANGE : {
69:       // Can't change anything if on the ground.
```

```
70:        if (status == ONRAMP) {
71:          strcpy(response, "I'm on the ground.");
72:          return false;
73:        }
74:        // Only change if a non-negative value was passed.
75:        if (spd != -1) speed = spd;
76:        if (dir != -1) heading = dir;
77:        if (alt != -1) altitude = alt;
78:        status = CRUISING;
79:        break;
80:      }
81:      case MSG_LAND : {
82:        if (status == ONRAMP) {
83:          strcpy(response, "I'm already on the ground.");
84:          return false;
85:        }
86:        Land();
87:        break;
88:      }
89:      case MSG_REPORT : ReportStatus();
90:    }
91:    //
92:    // Standard reponse if all went well.
93:    //
94:    strcpy(response, "Roger.");
95:    return true;
96: }
97: //
98: // Perform takeoff.
99: //
100: void
101: Airplane::TakeOff(int dir)
102: {
103:   heading = dir;
104:   status = TAKINGOFF;
105: }
106: //
107: // Perform landing.
108: //
109: void
110: Airplane::Land()
111: {
112:   speed = heading = altitude = 0;
113:   status = ONRAMP;
114: }
115: //
116: // Build a string to report the airplane's status.
117: //
118: int
```

7

continues

LISTING 7.2   CONTINUED

```
119: Airplane::GetStatus(char* statusString)
120: {
121:   sprintf(statusString, "%s, Altitude: %d, Heading: %d, "
122:     "Speed: %d\n", name, altitude, heading, speed);
123:   return status;
124: }
125: //
126: // Get the status string and output it to the screen.
127: //
128: void
129: Airplane::ReportStatus()
130: {
131:   char buff[100];
132:   GetStatus(buff);
133:   cout << endl << buff << endl;
134: }
```

LISTING 7.3   AIRPORT.CPP

```
 1: //-------------------------------------------------------
 2: #include <condefs.h>
 3: #include <iostream.h>
 4: #include <conio.h>
 5: #pragma hdrstop
 6:
 7: USEUNIT("airplane.cpp");
 8: #include "airplane.h"
 9: int getInput(int max);
10: void getItems(int& speed, int& dir, int& alt);
11: int main(int argc, char* argv[])
12: {
13:   char returnMsg[100];
14:   //
15:   // Set up an array of  Airplanes and create
16:   // three Airplane objects.
17:   //
18:   Airplane* planes[3];
19:   planes[0] = new Airplane("TWA 1040");
20:   planes[1] = new Airplane("United Express 749", COMMUTER);
21:   planes[2] = new Airplane("Cessna 3238T", PRIVATE);
22:   //
23:   // Start the loop.
24:   //
25:   do {
26:     int plane, message, speed, altitude, direction;
27:     speed = altitude = direction = -1;
28:     //
```

```
29:     // Get a plane to whom a message will be sent.
30:     // List all the planes and let the user pick one.
31:     //
32:     cout << endl << "Who do you want to send a message to?";
33:     cout << endl << endl << "0. Quit" <<  endl;
34:     for (int i=0;i<3;i++)
35:       cout << (i + 1) << ". " << planes[i]->name << endl;
36:     //
37:     // Call the getInput() function to get the plane number.
38:     //
39:     plane = getInput(4);
40:     //
41:     // If the user chose item 0, then break out of the loop.
42:     //
43:     if (plane == -1) break;
44:     //
45:     // The plane acknowledges.
46:     //
47:     cout << endl << planes[plane]->name << ", roger.";
48:     cout << endl << endl;
49:     //
50:     // Allow the user to choose a message to send.
51:     //
52:     cout << "What message do you want to send?" << endl;
53:     cout << endl << "0. Quit" << endl;
54:     cout << "1. State Change" << endl;
55:     cout << "2. Take Off" << endl;
56:     cout << "3. Land" << endl;
57:     cout << "4. Report Status" << endl;
58:     message = getInput(5);
59:     //
60:     // Break out of the loop if the user chose 0.
61:     //
62:     if (message == -1) break;
63:     //
64:     // If the user chose item 1, then we need to get input
65:     // for the new speed, direction, and altitude. Call
66:     // the getItems() function to do that.
67:     //
68:     if (message == 0)
69:       getItems(speed, direction, altitude);
70:     //
71:     // Send the plane the message.
72:     //
73:     bool goodMsg = planes[plane]->SendMessage(
74:       message, returnMsg, speed, direction, altitude);
75:     //
76:     // Something was wrong with the message
77:     //
```

7

continues

LISTING 7.3   CONTINUED

```
78:      if (!goodMsg) cout << endl << "Unable to comply.";
79:      //
80:      // Display the plane's response.
81:      //
82:      cout << endl << returnMsg << endl;
83:    } while (1);
84:    //
85:    // Delete the Airplane objects.
86:    //
87:    for (int i=0;i<3;i++) delete planes[i];
88:  }
89:  int getInput(int max)
90:  {
91:    int choice;
92:    do {
93:      choice = getch();
94:      choice -= 49;
95:    } while (choice < -1 ¦¦ choice > max);
96:    return choice;
97:  }
98:  void getItems(int& speed, int& dir, int& alt)
99:  {
100:   cout << endl << "Enter new speed: ";
101:   cin >> speed;
102:   cout << "Enter new heading: ";
103:   cin >> dir;
104:   cout << "Enter new altitude: ";
105:   cin >> alt;
106:   cout << endl;
107: }
```

ANALYSIS   Let's look first at the header file in Listing 7.1. First, notice all the lines that begin with #define. What I am doing here is associating one text string with another. At compile time the compiler just does a search-and-replace and replaces all occurrences of the first string with the second. #defines are used because it's much easier to remember a text string than a number. Which of the following do you prefer?

```
if (type == AIRLINER) ...
// or
if (type == 0) ...
```

Tradition has it that names for #defines be in uppercase, but you can use any mixture of uppercase and lowercase letters. I like all uppercase because it tells me at a glance that this is a defined constant and not a variable.

The next thing to note in the header is that the class includes some inline functions. These functions are so small that it makes sense to inline them. You will also notice that the Airplane class has one overloaded function called GetStatus(). When called with a character array parameter, it returns a status string as well as the status data member. When called without a parameter, it just returns status. Note that there is only one public data member. The rest of the data members are kept private. The only way to access the private data members is via the public functions. For instance, you can change the speed, altitude, and heading of an airplane only by sending it a message. To use an analogy, consider that an air traffic controller cannot physically change an aircraft's heading. The best he can do is send a message to the pilot and tell him to change to a new heading.

Now turn your attention to Listing 7.2. This is the definition of the Airplane class. The constructor performs initialization, including dynamically allocating storage for the char array that holds the name of the airplane. That memory is freed in the destructor. The SendMessage() function does most of the work. A switch statement determines which message was sent and takes the appropriate action. Notice that the TakeOff() and Land() functions cannot be called directly (they are protected), but rather are called through the SendMessage() function. Again, you can't make an aircraft take off or land; you can only send it a message telling it what you want it to do. The ReportStatus() function calls GetStatus() to get a status string, which it outputs.

The main program is shown in Listing 7.3. The program first sets up an array of Airplane pointers and creates three instances of the Airplane class. Then a loop starts. You can send messages to any airplane by calling the object's SendMessage() function. When you send a message, you get a response back from the airplane. The do-while loop cheats a little in this program. Notice that the test condition is simply 1. This means that the loop keeps running indefinitely. In this case it's not a problem because I am using the break statement to break out of the loop rather than relying on the test condition. Run the program and play with it to get a feel for how it works.

Inheritance

One of the most powerful features of classes in C++ is that they can be extended through inheritance.

NEW TERM   *Inheritance* means taking an existing class and adding functionality by deriving a new class from it.

NEW TERM   The class you start with is called the *base class*, and the new class you create is called the *derived class*.

7

Let's take the `Airplane` class as an example. The civilian and military worlds are quite different, as you know. To represent a military aircraft, I can derive a class from `Airplane` and add functionality to it:

```
class MilitaryPlane : public Airplane {
  public:
    MilitaryPlane(char* name, int _type);
    virtual int GetStatus(char* statusString);
  protected:
    virtual void TakeOff();
    virtual void Land()
    virtual void Attack();
    virtual void SetMission();
private:
    Mission* theMission;
};
```

A `MilitaryPlane` has everything an `Airplane` has, plus a few more goodies. Note the first line of the class definition. The colon after the class name is used to tell the compiler that I am inheriting from another class. The class name following the colon is the base class from which I am deriving. The `public` keyword, when used here, means that I am claiming access to all the public functions and data members of the base class.

> When you derive a class from another class, the new class gets all the functionality of the base class plus whatever new features you add. You can add data members and functions to the new class, but you cannot remove anything from what the base class offers.

Notice that in the `private` section there is a line that declares a variable of the `Mission` class. The `Mission` class could encapsulate everything that deals with the mission of a military aircraft: the target, navigation waypoints, ingress and egress altitudes and headings, and so on. This illustrates the use of a data member that is an instance of another class. In fact, you'll see that a lot when programming in C++Builder.

There's something else here that I haven't discussed yet. Note the `virtual` keyword. This specifies that the function is a virtual function. Let me take a moment to discuss virtual functions.

Virtual Functions

 A *virtual function* is a function that is automatically called if a function of that name exists in the derived class.

For example, note that the TakeOff() function is a virtual function in the Airplane class. Refer back to Listing 7.2. Notice that TakeOff() is called by SendMessage() in response to the MSG_TAKEOFF message. If the MilitaryPlane class did not provide its own TakeOff() function, the base class's TakeOff() function would be called. Because the MilitaryPlane class does provide a TakeOff() function, that function is called rather than the function in the base class.

| NEW TERM | Replacing a base class function in a derived class is called *overriding* the function.

In order for overriding to work, the function signature must exactly match that of the function in the base class. In other words, the return type, function name, and parameter list must all be the same as the base class function.

You can override a function with the intention of replacing the base class function, or you can override a function to enhance the base class function. Take the TakeOff() function, for example. If you wanted to completely replace what the TakeOff() function of Airplane does, you would override it and supply whatever code you wanted:

```
void MilitaryPlane::TakeOff(int dir)
{
  // new code goes here
}
```

But if you wanted your function to take the functionality of the base class and add to it, you would first call the base class function and then add new code:

```
void MilitaryPlane::TakeOff(int dir)
{
  Airplane::TakeOff(dir);
  // new code goes here
}
```

By calling the base class function, you get the original behavior of the function as written in the base class. You can then add code before or after the base class call to enhance the function. The scope-resolution operator is used to tell the compiler that you are calling the TakeOff() function of the Airplane class. Note that the TakeOff() function is in the protected section of the Airplane class (see Listing 7.1). If it were in the private section, this would not work because even a derived class cannot access the private members of its ancestor class. By making the TakeOff() function protected in the base class, it is hidden from the outside world but still accessible to derived classes.

7

The scope-resolution operator is required only when you have derived and base class functions with the same name and the same function signature. You can call a public or protected function of the base class at any time without the need for the scope-resolution operator, provided they aren't overridden. For example, if you wanted to check the status of the aircraft prior to takeoff, you could do something like this:

```
void MilitaryPlane::TakeOff(int dir)
{
  if (GetStatus() != ONRAMP) Land(); // gotta land first!
  Airplane::TakeOff(dir);
  // new code goes here
}
```

In this case, the GetStatus() function exists only in the base class, so there is no need for the scope-resolution operator. In the case of the Land() function, the MilitaryPlane version will be called because it has the most immediate scope.

When you derive a class from another class, you must be sure to call the base class's constructor so that all ancestor classes are properly initialized. Calling the base class constructor is done in the initializer list. Here's how the constructor for MilitaryPlane might appear:

```
MilitaryPlane:: MilitaryPlane(char* _name)
  : Airplane(_name, MILITARY)                 // call base class
{
  // body of constructor
}
```

Be sure to call the base class constructor whenever you derive a class from a base class. Figure 7.1 illustrates the concept of inheritance.

You can see from Figure 7.1 that the class called F16 is descended from the class called Fighter. Ultimately, F16 is derived from Airplane because Airplane is the base class for all classes.

FIGURE 7.1

An example of inheritance.

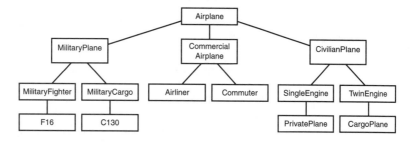

Multiple Inheritance

 The act of deriving a class from two or more base classes is called *multiple inheritance*.

Multiple inheritance isn't used frequently, but it can be very handy when needed. For an example, let's say you had a class called `Armaments` that kept track of the armaments for a particular aircraft. It might look like this:

```
class Armaments {
  public:
    Armaments();
    LoadArms();
  private:
    bool isArmed;
    int numSidewinders;
    int numSparrows;
    // etc.
};
```

Now let's say that you were to create a class to represent a military fighter. You could inherit from both `MilitaryPlane` and `Armaments`:

```
class Fighter : public MilitaryPlane, public Armaments {
  public:
    Fighter(char* name);
  private:
    // other stuff
};
```

Now you have a class that contains all the elements of `MilitaryPlane` and all the elements of `Armaments`. This would enable you to do the following:

```
Fighter fighter("F16");
fighter.LoadArms();
fighter.SendMessage(...);
// etc.
```

The two base classes are blended to form a single class.

7

You should call the base class constructor for all base classes. The following illustrates:

```
Fighter::Fighter(char* _name)
  : MilitaryPlane(_name, Fighter), Armaments()
{
  // body of constructor
}
```

If a class has a default constructor, it isn't strictly necessary to call the base class constructor for that class. In most situations, though, you will call the base class constructor for all ancestor classes.

Let me give you one other example. In the United States, the Military Airlift Command (MAC) is responsible for moving military personnel from place to place. MAC is sort of like the U.S. military's own personal airline. Because personnel are ultimately cargo, this requires a military cargo plane. But because people are special cargo, you can't just throw them in the back of a plane designed to haul freight (not usually, anyway). So what is needed is a military cargo plane with all the amenities of a commercial airliner. Look back to Figure 7.1. It would appear that to get what we want, we can derive from both MilitaryCargo and Airliner—and we can. Figure 7.2 illustrates.

FIGURE 7.2

An example of multiple inheritance.

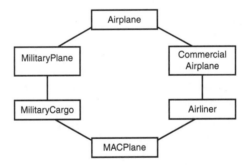

Although you might not use multiple inheritance often, it is a very handy feature to have available when you need it.

VCL is the heart of C++Builder (I'll cover the VCL in Hour 8, "Class Frameworks and the Visual Component Model"). The VCL is written in the Object Pascal language. This makes it possible for Inprise to share the VCL between C++Builder and Delphi. Because Object Pascal does not have multiple inheritance, you cannot use multiple inheritance in classes derived from VCL classes. You can still use multiple inheritance in any C++ classes you write outside the VCL framework.

Summary

In this hour you rounded out your knowledge of classes in C++. A well-designed class is easy to use and saves many programming hours. I'd even go so far as to say a well-designed class is a joy to use—especially when it's your own creation.

The lessons of these first seven hours are important to understand as you progress through this book. If they don't make complete sense to you yet, don't despair. As you continue through the rest of the book, you will see these concepts repeated and put to use in programs that have more practical application than the console applications we've been working with thus far.

Learning C++ can and will lead to brain overload! It's natural and you shouldn't worry about it. You might put down this book for the evening, turn out the lights, and be thinking, "I'll never get it." Trust me, you will.

Sometimes it's necessary to take a couple days off and let it all soak in. Take it a little at a time, and one of these days you'll be just like Archimedes—you'll be running around your office or your house shouting "Eureka!" because the light just came on in your head. But keep track of your clothes, will you? The neighbors could be watching.

Workshop

The Workshop contains quiz questions to help you solidify your understanding of the material covered and exercises to provide you with experience in using what you have learned. The answers to the quiz questions are provided following the questions. The exercises are given for you to work out and code on your own.

Q&A

Q I don't quite understand the `this` pointer. Is that going to be a problem when writing programs with C++Builder?

A Not really, no. There are very few times when you need to use `this` in your day-to-day programming tasks. After you've had some experience writing C++Builder programs, you can review this hour and the discussion of the `this` pointer.

Q I'm trying to use multiple inheritance to derive a class from one of my own classes and from the VCL's `TEdit` class. I keep getting compiler errors. What's wrong?

A You cannot use multiple inheritance with VCL classes. This is because the VCL is written in Object Pascal and Object Pascal doesn't support multiple inheritance. You can use multiple inheritance with any C++ classes, but not with VCL classes.

7

Quiz

1. What does it mean to override a function of the base class?

2. How can you override a base class function and still get the benefit of the operation the base class function performs?

3. How do you call the base class function from an overridden virtual function on the base class?

4. How can you get the functionality of two separate classes all rolled up into a single class?

Answers

1. To override a function means to replace a function in the base class with a function in your derived class. The new function must have the exact same name, parameters, and return type to override the base class function.

2. Call the base class function from within the overridden function:

```
void MyClass::DoIt()
{
  BaseClass::DoIt();
  // do some other stuff
}
```

3. To call the base class function, use the base class name with the scope resolution operator:

```
MyBaseClass::SomeFunction();
```

4. Use multiple inheritance and derive the class from two separate base classes.

Exercises

1. Derive a class from the class you wrote the previous hour (in exercise 1) that also returns the height in meters, centimeters, or millimeters. (Hint: There are 25.4 millimeters in an inch.)

2. Take a day off. You've earned it!

HOUR **8**

Class Frameworks and the Visual Component Model

In this hour, you learn about class frameworks. The C++Builder Visual Component Library (VCL) is a class framework. You'll learn what a framework is and how it helps you as a Windows programmer. After that you'll spend some time learning the visual component model. That section describes how properties, methods, and events work together in the VCL.

Frameworks Fundamentals

"In the beginning there was C…" This applies to both C++ programming and Windows programming. In the beginning, the vast majority of Windows programs were written in C. In fact, the Windows Application Programming Interface (API) is just a huge collection of C functions—hundreds of them. There are still undoubtedly thousands of programmers out there writing Windows programs in C.

Somewhere along the line, folks at Inprise (then called Borland) decided, "There has got to be an easier way." (Actually, the framework revolution might have started on several different fronts, but Inprise was certainly a leader.) It was apparent that Windows programming was very well suited to the C++ language, and vice versa. By creating classes that encapsulate common Windows programming tasks, a programmer could be much more productive. After a class was created to encapsulate a window's various duties, for instance, that class could be used over and over again. The framework revolution began.

But I haven't yet told you what a framework is.

NEW TERM   A *framework* is a collection of classes that simplifies programming in Windows by encapsulating often used programming techniques. Frameworks are also called *class libraries*.

Popular frameworks have classes that encapsulate windows, edit controls, list boxes, graphics operations, bitmaps, scrollbars, dialog boxes, and on and on.

So why should you care? The bottom line is that frameworks make Windows programming much easier than it would be in straight C. Let me give you an example. Listing 8.1 contains a portion of a Windows program written in C. This section of code loads a bitmap file from disk and displays the bitmap in the center of the screen. None of this will make sense to you right now, but be patient.

LISTING 8.1   C CODE TO LOAD AND DISPLAY A BITMAP

```
 1: HPALETTE hPal;
 2: BITMAPFILEHEADER bfh;
 3: BITMAPINFOHEADER bih;
 4: LPBITMAPINFO lpbi = 0;
 5: HFILE hFile;
 6: DWORD nClrUsed, nSize;
 7: HDC hDC;
 8: HBITMAP hBitmap;
 9: void _huge *bits;
10: do
11: {
12:   if ((hFile = _lopen(data.FileName, OF_READ)) == HFILE_ERROR) break;
13:   if (_hread(hFile, &bfh, sizeof(bfh)) != sizeof(bfh)) break;
14:   if (bfh.bfType != 'BM') break;
15:   if (_hread(hFile, &bih, sizeof(bih)) != sizeof(bih)) break;
16:   nClrUsed =
17:     (bih.biClrUsed) ? bih.biClrUsed : 1 << bih.biBitCount;
18:   nSize =
19:     sizeof(BITMAPINFOHEADER) + nClrUsed * sizeof(RGBQUAD);
20:   lpbi = (LPBITMAPINFO) GlobalAllocPtr(GHND, nSize);
21:   if (!lpbi) break;
```

8

```
22:   hmemcpy(lpbi, &bih, sizeof(bih));
23:   nSize = nClrUsed * sizeof(RGBQUAD);
24:   if (_hread(hFile, &lpbi->bmiColors, nSize) != nSize) break;
25:   if (_llseek(hFile, bfh.bfOffBits, 0) == HFILE_ERROR) break;
26:   nSize = bfh.bfSize-bfh.bfOffBits;
27:   if ((bits = GlobalAllocPtr(GHND, nSize)) == NULL) break;
28:   if (_hread(hFile, bits, nSize) != nSize) break;
29:   hDC = GetDC(hWnd);
30:   hBitmap = CreateDIBitmap(hDC, &(lpbi->bmiHeader), CBM_INIT,
31:                       bits, lpbi, DIB_RGB_COLORS);
32:   if (hBitmap) {
33:     LPLOGPALETTE lppal;
34:     DWORD nsize = sizeof(LOGPALETTE)
35:       + (nClrUsed-1) * sizeof(PALETTEENTRY);
36:     lppal = (LPLOGPALETTE)  GlobalAllocPtr(GHND, nSize);
37:     if (lppal) {
38:       lppal->palVersion = 0x0300;
39:       lppal->palNumEntries = (WORD) nClrUsed;
40:       hmemcpy(lppal->palPalEntry, lpbi->bmiColors,
41:       nClrUsed * sizeof(PALETTEENTRY));
42:       hPal = CreatePalette(lppal);
43:       (void) GlobalFreePtr(lppal);
44:     }
45:   }
46: }  while(FALSE);
47: if (hFile != HFILE_ERROR) _lclose(hFile);
48: HPALETTE oldPal = SelectPalette(hDC, hPal, FALSE);
49: RealizePalette(hDC);
50: HDC hMemDC = CreateCompatibleDC(hDC);
51: HBITMAP oldBitmap =(HBITMAP)SelectObject(hMemDC, hBitmap);
52: BitBlt(hDC, 0, 0, (WORD)bih.biWidth, (WORD)bih.biHeight,
53:   hMemDC, 0, 0, SRCCOPY);
54: SelectObject(hMemDC, oldBitmap);
55: DeleteDC(hMemDC);
56: SelectPalette(hDC, oldPal, FALSE);
57: ReleaseDC(hWnd, hDC);
58: if (bits) (void) GlobalFreePtr(bits);
59: if (lpbi) (void) GlobalFreePtr(lpbi);
```

That looks just a little intimidating, doesn't it? Now consider how the same thing would be accomplished using C++Builder's VCL. With C++Builder you simply place a TImage component on a form and set its Picture property as follows:

```
Image->Picture->LoadFromFile("test.bmp");
```

So which would you rather use? This example sums up what frameworks are all about. Frameworks hide details from you that you don't need to know. Everything that is contained in Listing 8.1 is performed behind the scenes in the single line of VCL code that follows it. You don't need to know every detail about what goes on behind the scenes when VCL does its job, and you probably don't want to know. All you want is to take the objects that make up a framework and put them to use in your programs.

A little skeptical, are you? Good. You're bright enough to figure out that if you have all that ease of use, you must be giving up something. Truth is, you are right. You might think that a program written with a framework would be larger and slower than its counterpart written in C. That's partially correct. Applications written with frameworks don't necessarily have to be slower than programs written in C, though. There is some additional overhead inherent in the C++ language, certainly, but for the most part it is not noticeable in a typical Windows program.

The primary trade-off is that Windows programs written in C++ tend to be larger than programs written in straight C. This is because of several factors. One factor is the additional code that makes up the framework itself. Another factor is the additional code C++ includes for language features such as exception handling and runtime type information (RTTI). Personally, I am more than willing to trade some code size for the power that C++ and an application framework give me.

The Visual Component Library

In 1995, Inprise (Borland at that time) introduced a revolutionary new product called Delphi. It was an instant hit. Delphi offered rapid application development (RAD) using something called *components*. Components are objects that can be dropped on a form and manipulated via properties, methods, and events. It's visual programming, if you will.

The concept of form-based programming was first popularized by Microsoft's Visual Basic. Unlike Visual Basic, though, Delphi used a derivative of Pascal as its programming language. This new language, called Object Pascal, introduced object-oriented programming (OOP) to the Pascal language. In a sense, Object Pascal is to Pascal what C++ is to C. Delphi and Object Pascal represented the marriage of object-oriented programming and form-based programming. In addition, Delphi could produce standalone executables. Real programs. Programs that did not require a runtime DLL to run; programs that were compiled, not interpreted; programs that ran tens of times faster than Visual Basic programs. The programming world was impressed.

Delphi also introduced the Visual Component Library (VCL). VCL is an application framework for Windows programming in Object Pascal. Yes, it is a framework, but the core is very different from other C++ frameworks (such as Microsoft's MFC), primarily because it was designed around the concept of properties, methods, and events.

8

You might be wondering why I'm talking about Delphi. The reason is simple—because the very same VCL that is the heart of Delphi is also the heart of C++Builder. That might come as a shock to you. In the end, it doesn't really matter what language the VCL is written in, because it works.

As I talked about in Hour 1, VCL components are objects that perform a specific programming task. Some components are visual components that appear on the form at design time just as they will appear at runtime. Other components are non-visual. Non-visual components are seen on the form at design time as an icon, but do not appear at runtime. VCL components are wrapped up in Object Pascal classes. From now on in this book, we will be encountering components on a regular basis. I won't spend a lot of time explaining every detail of components right now because you will see by example how they work throughout the rest of the book. In Hour 10, "Exploring the C++Builder IDE," I'll explain components in more detail.

In Hour 1, I also gave you a brief introduction to the properties, methods, and events model. These three ingredients make up the public interface of components in VCL (the part of the component the user will see). Let's take a look at these elements one at a time.

Properties

Properties are elements of a component that control how the component operates. Many components have common properties. All visual components, for example, have a Top and a Left property. These two properties control where the component is positioned on a form, both at design time and at runtime. All components have an Owner property, which VCL uses to keep track of the child components a particular parent form or component owns.

A picture is always worth a thousand words, so let's start up C++Builder again and see properties in action. When you start C++Builder, you are greeted with a blank form and the Object Inspector.

The Object Inspector will look something like Figure 8.1. (When C++Builder starts, it sizes the Object Inspector based on your current screen resolution, so your Object Inspector might be taller or shorter than the one shown in Figure 8.1.) If necessary, click on the Properties tab of the Object Inspector window so that the form's properties are displayed. The Object Inspector window can be moved and sized. I like my Object Inspector as tall as my screen permits so that I can see the maximum number of properties at one time. Scroll through the properties until you locate the Left property and then click on it. Change the value for the Left property (any number between 0 and 600 will do) and press Enter on the keyboard. Notice how the form moves as you change the value.

FIGURE 8.1

The Object Inspector.

This illustrates an important aspect of properties—they are more than simple data members of a class. Changing a property often leads to code executed behind the scenes.

Properties are often tied to *access methods* that execute when the property is modified.

> Things start to get confusing at this point. As I said, VCL is written in Pascal. Pascal uses the term *method* whereas C++ uses the term *function*. To further muddy the waters, Pascal uses the term *function* to refer to a method that returns a value, and the term *procedure* to refer to a method that doesn't return a value. I would be happy enough to call all of them functions (being the old C++ hacker that I am), but when discussing the VCL I will use the Pascal parlance. For the most part I will use the generic term *method*.

Properties can be changed at *design time* (when you are designing your form) and at *runtime* (when the program is running through code you write). In either case, if the property has an access method, that access method is called and executed when the property is modified. You already saw an example of changing a property at design time when you changed the Left property and watched the form move on the screen. That is one of the strengths of the VCL: You can instantly see on the screen the result of your design change. Not all properties show a visible change on the form at design time, however, so this doesn't happen in every case. Still, when possible, the results of the new property value are immediately displayed on the form.

To change a property at runtime, you simply make an assignment to the property. When you make an assignment, VCL works behind the scenes to call the access method for that property. To change the Left property at runtime, you use code like this:

```
Label1->Left = 200;
```

In the case of the Left property (as well as the Top property), VCL moves and repaints the component.

> Notice that the previous code line uses the indirect member operator (->) to set the property. All VCL components are allocated from the heap. The indirection operator is always used to access a component's properties and methods. Classes you write for use in your C++Builder applications can be allocated from either the heap or the stack, but all VCL component classes, and all classes derived from them, must be allocated from the heap. In the case of components placed on a form, C++Builder automatically creates dynamic instances of those components for you.

"But why does the form move on the screen when you assign a value to the Left property?" you might be wondering. Some properties make use of read and write methods. Read and write methods are methods that are called when the property is read or written to. In this case, the Left property has a write method called SetLeft. This method is called every time the Left property is assigned a value. As a result the form moves on the screen when the property is assigned a value. If a property includes a write method, that method is called every time the property is written to. If the property includes a read method, that read method is called every time the property's value is read.

The properties of the property (sorry, I couldn't resist) are determined by the writer of the component. A property can be read-only. A read-only property can be read—its value can be retrieved—but not written to. In other words, you can fetch the property's value, but you can't change it.

Properties that appear in the Object Inspector are called *published properties*. Other properties can be specified as runtime-only. A runtime-only property can be accessed only at runtime, not design time. Because a runtime-only property doesn't apply at design time, it isn't displayed in the Object Inspector. A runtime-only property can be declared as read-only, too, which means that it can be accessed only at runtime and can only be read (not written to).

Some properties use an array as the underlying data member. To illustrate, let's put a memo component on our blank form. Go to the C++Builder Component palette, choose the Standard tab, and click the Memo button. (The ToolTip tells when you are over the Memo button.) Now move to the form and click on it where you want the memo's top-left corner to appear. As soon as you place the memo component on the form, the Object Inspector switches to show you the properties of the component just placed on the form, in this case a `TMemo`. Locate the `Lines` property and click on it. Notice that the property value contains the text (`TStrings`) and that there is a little button with an ellipsis (...) to the right of the property value.

> The ellipsis button tells you that this property can be edited by using a property editor. For an array of strings, for instance, a dialog box displays in which you can type the strings. In the case of the `Font` property, clicking the ellipsis button invokes the Choose Font dialog box. The exact type of the property editor is property specific, although certain properties can share a common editor. You can bring up the property editor by clicking the ellipsis button or by double-clicking the property value.

The `Lines` property for a memo component is an array of strings. When you double-click the Value column, the string editor is displayed and you can then type the strings you want displayed in the memo component when the application runs. If you don't want any strings displayed in the memo component, you need to clear the property editor of any strings. Figure 8.2 shows the String list editor as it appears when adding text to a memo at design time.

FIGURE 8.2

The String list editor is used to add strings to a memo component at design time.

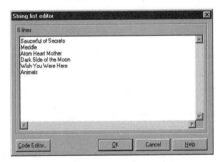

Properties can be instances of other VCL classes. The `Font` property is an obvious example. A font includes things like the typeface, the color, the font size, and so on. Locate the `Font` property in the Object Inspector. (It doesn't matter whether you have selected the memo component or the form.) Notice that there is a plus sign before the property name, *Font*. This tells you that there are individual properties within this property that

8

can be set. If you double-click on the property name, you will see that the Object Inspector expands the property to reveal its individual elements. You can now individually edit the Font property's elements. In the case of the Font property, these same settings can be edited by invoking the Property Editor. You can use either method with the same results.

NEW TERM   A *set* is a collection of possible values for a property.

Some properties are sets. The Style property within the Font object is a good example of a set. Notice that Style has a plus sign in front of it. If you double-click on the Style property, you will see that the Style node expands to reveal the set's contents. In this case the set consists of the various styles available for fonts: bold, italic, underline, and strikeout. By double-clicking the Value column next to a style, you can turn that style on or off. A set can be empty or can contain one or more of the allowed values. I'll talk more about sets in the next hour in the section "Using Sets."

NEW TERM   Some properties can be *enumerations*, a list of possible choices.

When you click on an enumeration property, a drop-down arrow button appears to the right of the value. To see the choices in the enumeration, click the drop-down button to display the list of choices. Alternatively, you can double-click the Value column for the property. As you double-click on the property's value, the Object Inspector cycles through (or enumerates) the choices. The Cursor property gives a good example of an enumerated property. Locate the Cursor property and click the arrow button to expose the list of possible cursors to choose from. Enumerations and sets differ in that with an enumeration property only one of the presented choices can be selected (only one cursor can be in effect at any time).

HOUSE RULES: PROPERTIES

- Properties appear to be class data members and are accessed like class data members.

- Properties are *not* class data members. They are a special category of class element.

- Properties often invoke an access method when they are written to (assigned a value), but not always. It depends on how the particular component is written.

- Published properties usually have default values. The default value is the value that initially shows up in the Object Inspector when a component is first used and is the value that is used if no specific value is assigned.
- Properties can be designed as read-only, write-only, or runtime-only.
- Runtime-only properties don't show up in the Object Inspector and can be modified only at runtime.
- Property types include simple data types, arrays, sets, enumerations, and other VCL classes.

As long as you have C++Builder running and a blank form displayed, you might as well spend some time examining the various components and their properties. Go ahead, I'll wait.

Methods

Methods in VCL components are functions (ahem...*procedures* and functions) that can be called to make the component perform certain actions. For example, all visual components have a method called Show(), which displays the component, and a method called Hide(), which hides the component. Calling these methods is exactly the same as calling class member functions as we did in Hour 7:

```
Label1->Show();
// do some stuff, then later...
Label1->Hide();
```

In C++ parlance, methods are member functions of a component class. Methods in VCL can be declared as public, protected, or private just as functions in C++ can be public, protected, or private. These keywords mean the same thing in Object Pascal classes as they do in C++ classes. Public methods can be accessed by the component's users. In this example, both the Show() and Hide() methods are public. Protected methods cannot be accessed by the component users but can be accessed by classes (components) derived from a component. Of course, private methods can be accessed only within a class itself.

Just like C++ functions, some methods take parameters and return values, and others don't. It depends entirely on how the method was written by the component writer. For example, the GetTextBuf() method retrieves the text of a TEdit component. This method can be used to get the text from an edit control as follows:

```
char buff[256];
int numChars = EditControl->GetTextBuf(buff, sizeof(buff));
```

8

> **HOUSE RULES: METHODS**
>
> - Methods can be private, protected, or public.
> - Methods can take parameters and can return values.
> - Some methods take no parameters and return no values.
> - Only public methods can be called by component users.

As you can see, this particular method takes two parameters and returns an integer. When this method is called, the edit control contents are placed in `buff`, and the return value is the number of characters retrieved from the edit control.

Events

NEW TERM   Windows is said to be an *event-driven* environment. Event-driven means that a program is driven by events that occur within the Windows environment. Events include mouse movements, mouse clicks, and key presses.

Programmers moving from DOS or mainframe programming environments might have some difficulty with the concept of an event-driven architecture. A Windows program continually polls Windows for events. Events in Windows include a menu being activated, a button being clicked, a window being moved, a window needing repainting, a window being activated, and so forth. Windows notifies a program of an event by sending a Windows message. There are somewhere in the neighborhood of 175 possible messages that Windows can send to an application. That's a lot of messages. Fortunately, you don't have to know about each and every one of them to program in C++Builder; there are only a couple dozen that are used frequently.

In VCL, an event is anything that occurs in the component that the user might need to know about. Each component is designed to respond to certain events. Usually this means a Windows event, but it can mean other things as well. For example, a button component is designed to respond to a mouse click, as you would expect. But a nonvisual control such as a database component can generate non-Windows events such as the user reaching the end of the table.

NEW TERM   When you respond to a component event, you are said to *handle* the event. Events are handled through functions called *event handlers*.

A typical Windows program spends most of its time idle, waiting for some event to occur. VCL makes it incredibly easy to handle events. The events that a component has been designed to handle are listed under the Events tab in the Object Inspector window. Event names are descriptive of the event to which they respond. For instance, the event to handle a mouse click is called `OnClick`.

You don't have to handle every event that a component defines. In fact, you rarely do. If you don't respond to a particular event, the event message is either discarded or handled in a default manner as described by either the VCL or the component itself. You can handle any events you have an interest in and ignore the rest.

This will make more sense if you put it into practice. To begin, let's start a new application. Choose File, New Application from the main menu. If you are prompted to save the current project, click No. Now you will again have a blank form. First, let's set up the main form:

1. Change the Name property to PMEForm (PME for properties, methods, and events).

2. Change the Caption property to PME Test Program.

Next, we need to add a memo component to the form:

1. Choose the Standard tab on the Component palette and click the Memo button.

2. Click on the form to place a memo component on the form.

3. Change the Name property to Memo. Be sure the memo component is selected, so you don't accidentally change the form's name instead of the memo component.

4. Double-click on the Lines property in the Value column. The String list editor is displayed.

5. Delete the word Memo and type A test program using properties, methods, and events. Click OK to close the String list editor.

6. Resize the memo component so that it occupies most of the form. Leave room for a button at the bottom.

Your form will now look like the form shown in Figure 8.3.

FIGURE 8.3

The form with a memo component added.

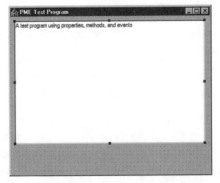

8

Now let's place a button on the form:

1. Choose the Standard tab on the Component palette and select the Button component.

2. Click on the form below the memo component to place the button on the form.

3. Change the Name property for the button to Button.

4. Change the Caption property to Show/Hide.

5. Center the button horizontally on the form.

We will use this button to alternately show and hide the memo component. Now we need to write some code so that the button does something when clicked. Be sure that the button component is selected, and then click on the Events tab in the Object Inspector. A list of the events that a button component is designed to handle is presented. The top event should be the OnClick event. Double-click on the Value column of the OnClick event. What happens next is one of the great things about visual programming. The Code Editor comes to the top and displays the OnClick function ready for you to type code. Figure 8.4 shows the Code Editor with the OnClick handler displayed.

FIGURE 8.4

The C++Builder Code Editor with the OnClick *handler displayed.*

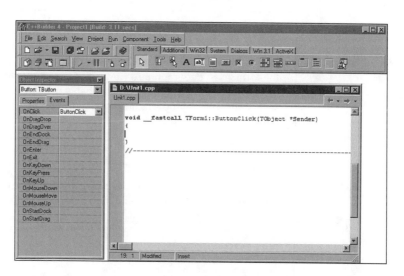

Before you go on, save the project. Choose File, Save All from the main menu. The first thing you are prompted for is the name of the unit (source file). Type PMEMain and click OK. Next, you are prompted for a filename for the project. Type PMETest and press Enter or click OK. Now on to the good stuff...

Notice that the function is already set up for you, and all you have to do is type the code. If you take a good look at the function, you will see that the function is called ButtonClick, that it is a member function of the TPMEForm class, that it returns void, and that it takes a pointer to a TObject called Sender as a parameter. (I'll talk about the Sender parameter in just a bit.) All that is left to do now is type code that shows and hides the button each time the button is clicked. Edit the ButtonClick function until it looks like this:

```
void _ _fastcall TPMEForm::ButtonClick(TObject *Sender)
{
  if (Memo->Visible)
    Memo->Hide();
  else
    Memo->Show();
}
```

This code reads the Visible property of the memo to see if the memo is currently visible. If so, the Hide() method is called to hide the memo. If the memo is not currently visible, the Show() method is called to show the memo.

As soon as you drop a component on a form, C++Builder goes to work behind the scenes. Remember when you dropped a memo component on the form? As soon as you did that, C++Builder created a TMemo* variable in the form's class declaration. At runtime VCL creates a dynamic instance of the TMemo class and assigns it to the variable named Memo. That is why the Show() and Hide() functions and the Visible property are accessed using the indirect member operator.

There is often more than one way to accomplish a given task in C++Builder. The previous event handler could have been written like this:

```
void __fastcall TPMEForm::ButtonClick(TObject *Sender
{
Memo->Visible = !Memo->Visible;
}
```

This code toggles the visible state of the memo by applying the logical not operator (!) to the current value of the Visible property (!true is false, and !false is true).

8

That's all there is to it. But does it work? Let's find out. Click the Run button on the toolbar. After being compiled, the program runs and is displayed. It's the moment of truth. Click the button, and the memo component is hidden. Click the button again, and the memo component is again displayed. It works! After playing with that for a minute, close the program (use the Close Program button in the upper-left corner of the title bar) and you are back to the Code Editor.

Are you getting the fever yet? Hold on because there's much more to come. Oh, and wipe that silly grin off your face...your boss thinks you're working!

The Sender Parameter

As you can see, the ButtonClick() function takes a pointer to a TObject called Sender. Every event-handling function has at least a Sender parameter. Depending on the event being handled, the function might have one or more additional parameters. For instance, the OnMouseDown event handler looks like this:

```
void _ _fastcall TPMEForm::ButtonMouseDown(TObject *Sender,
    TMouseButton Button, TShiftState Shift, int X, int Y)
{
}
```

Here you are getting information on the button that was pressed, which keyboard keys were pressed at the time the mouse was clicked, and the x, y coordinates of the cursor when the mouse button was clicked. The event-handling function contains all the information you need to deal with the particular event the event handler is designed to handle.

So what exactly is Sender? Sender is a pointer to the component that is sending the message to the message handler. In this example, the Sender parameter is extra baggage because we know that the Show/Hide button is the sender. Sender exists to enable you to have more than one component use the same event handler. To illustrate, let's create a new button and make one of our buttons the Show button and the other the Hide button.

1. If the Code Editor is on top, press F12 to switch back to the Form Editor.

2. Click on the Show/Hide button to select it. Change both the Name and Caption properties to Show.

3. Add a new button to the form to the right of the Show button. Arrange the buttons, if you want to give an even look to the form.

4. Change the Name property for the new button to Hide. The Caption property will also change to Hide (you'll have to press Enter before the Caption property will change).

5. Click the Show button and then click on the Events tab in the Object Inspector. Notice that the OnClick event now says ShowClick. Edit it to say ButtonClick again. (The initial event-handler name is a default name. You can change it to any name you like.)

6. Click the Hide button and find the OnClick event in the Object Inspector (it will be selected already). Next to the value is a drop-down arrow button. Click the arrow button and then choose ButtonClick from the list that drops down (there will be only one function name in the list at this point).

7. Double-click on the value ButtonClick. You are presented with the Code Editor with the cursor in the ButtonClick() function. Modify the code so that it reads like this:

```
void _ _fastcall TPMEForm::ButtonClick(TObject *Sender)
{
  if (Sender == Hide)
    Memo->Hide();
  else
    Memo->Show();
}
```

8. Bake at 425 degrees for one hour or until golden brown. (Just checking.)

Your form will look similar to Figure 8.5. Compile and run the program. Click each button to be sure that it functions as advertised.

FIGURE 8.5

The form with all components added.

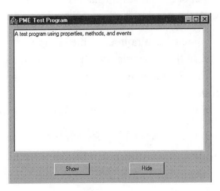

What you have done here is create a single event-handling function that handles the OnClick event of both buttons. We use the Sender parameter to determine which button sent the OnClick event and then either hide or show the memo component as needed. We could have created a separate OnClick handler for each button, but with this method the code is more compact. Besides, it's a good illustration of how Sender can be used.

8

Step 6 in the previous exercise illustrates an important point: After you create an `OnClick` event handler for a particular component, you can attach that same handler to the `OnClick` event of any component on the form. This enables you to use the same event handler for multiple components. I'll discuss events in more detail as we progress through the book.

HOUSE RULES: EVENTS

- You can respond to any of a component's events as needed.
- You are not required to respond to all events a component defines.
- Events are handled by functions called event handlers.
- Several components can share a common event handler.
- Event-handler names produced by C++Builder are default names and can be changed by the programmer.
- Be sure to change an event handler's name only in the Object Inspector.
- An event handler's `Sender` parameter can be used to determine which component generated the event.
- Double-clicking the event handler's name in the Object Inspector displays the Code Editor and takes you to the section of code containing the event handler.
- Each event handler contains the function parameters needed to properly handle that event.

C++Builder and VCL

As I have said, VCL is a library written in Object Pascal. VCL is written in Object Pascal because it was written for Delphi. It made perfect sense for the people at Inprise to take an already existing class library and adapt it for use in C++Builder. There was no point in starting from scratch to build C++Builder when they could hit the ground running by implementing Delphi's VCL. An added benefit is that Delphi users can easily move to C++Builder, and vice versa. Because both use the same VCL, you don't have to learn a new framework when moving around in the Delphi or C++Builder family.

C++Builder is a C++ compiler, and VCL is a library written in Object Pascal. How does that work exactly? Truthfully, you shouldn't be concerned about how it works at the compiler level, but rather how it affects the way you program in C++Builder. Trust me, the fact that the VCL is written in Object Pascal is virtually invisible. Take the following code snippet, for instance:

```
int screenW = GetSystemMetrics(SM_CXSCREEN);
int screenH = GetSystemMetrics(SM_CYSCREEN);
int h = Height;
int w = Width;
Top = (screenH / 2) - (h / 2);
Left = (screenW / 2) - (w / 2);
TPoint cPt;
GetCursorPos((POINT*)&cPt);
h -= 150;
w -= 150;
Height = h;
Width = w;
for (int i=0;i<150;i+=6) {
  Height = h + i;
  Width = w + i;
  SetCursorPos(
    Left + Width,
    Top + Height);
}
SetCursorPos(cPt.x, cPt.y);
```

Now, in this code, which is Object Pascal and which is C++? The fact is, as far as you are concerned, it's all C++. VCL and C++ work together seamlessly to give you rapid application development using C++. VCL gives you RAD through components, and the rest of your code can be written in C++.

 Most VCL components can be created at runtime as well as design time. It's easier to create the components at design time because it is much easier to set the properties using the Object Inspector rather than through code. Still, there are times when you need to create components at runtime, and C++Builder enables you to do that.

Summary

In this hour you learned about frameworks. I explained what the VCL is and how it makes your life as a programmer easier. I discussed properties, methods, and events and gave you some hands-on experience in the process.

Workshop

The Workshop contains quiz questions to help you solidify your understanding of the material covered and exercises to provide you with experience in using what you have learned. The answers to the quiz questions are provided following the questions. The exercises are given for you to work out and code on your own.

8

Q&A

Q Am I supposed to know how to program in Pascal and C++ in order to write Windows programs with C++Builder?

A No. The fact that VCL is written in Pascal is virtually invisible to you. As far as you are concerned, you are just programming in C++. Advanced C++ users might notice some situations where VCL limits their choices, but most users of C++Builder will not.

Q Do I have to respond to each and every event a component defines?

A No. You can respond to as many events as appropriate for your application or not respond to any events at all.

Quiz

1. Are all components visible at runtime?
2. Can VCL objects be allocated locally (from the stack) as well as dynamically?
3. Name two common properties that all visual components share.
4. Can two or more components share the same event-handling function?

Answers

1. No. Only visual components can be seen on the form at runtime. Non-visual components perform behind-the-scenes processing and are not seen at runtime.
2. No. VCL objects must be allocated dynamically (using operator `new`). C++Builder does this for you automatically when you place a component on a form.
3. `Top`, `Left`, `Owner`, `Parent`, `Width`, `Height`, and so on.
4. Yes. Two or more components sharing the same event handler is one of the most powerful aspects of programming in C++Builder.

Exercises

1. Create a C++Builder application that displays a bitmap on the main form when a button is clicked. (Hint: Use a TImage component and toggle its Visible property.)

2. Create a C++Builder application that displays a message box saying Hello, There! when the main form is clicked.

HOUR 9

Exploring the VCL

In this hour, you learn more about the Visual Component Library (VCL).
First you learn some of the C++ classes that C++Builder provides in order
to facilitate interaction with the VCL. These are not VCL classes per se, but
are classes needed when writing VCL programs. After that you learn some
of the standard components available to you as a C++Builder programmer.

VCL String Classes

In Hour 2, in the section "Character Arrays," I talked about how the C
language handles strings. As a language, C++ handles strings the same way
that C does. It must be apparent to you by now, though, that the C++ language enables you to create a class to perform just about any programming
task you can think of. The C++Builder developers developed the
AnsiString class for just this reason. Actually, the AnsiString class was
written to fill another need: a string class that interfaces with the Pascal long
string data type.

Who Needs a String Class?

You might be thinking, "What's so important about a string class? Can't you do anything you want with C character arrays?" Yes, you can, but a class that simplifies C-style character arrays is just plain easier to use. Let me give you an example. First, let's look at the C way of doing things:

```
char buff[20];   // will 20 characters be enough space?
strcpy(buff, "Hello There!");
if (!strcmp(buff, "Hello There!"))
  strcat(buff, " What's up?");
```

Now let's look at how the preceding might be accomplished with a C++ string class:

```
String S = "Hello There!"; // direct assignment
if (S == "Hello There!")   // test for equality
  S += " What's up?";      // concatentation using += operator
```

I don't know about you, but I find the second piece of code more intuitive and much more readable. Notice in particular that with a string class you can use syntax that makes sense. You can assign a string using the = operator, you can test for equality using the == operator, and you can add strings together using the + or += operators. It just makes sense. In addition, string classes dynamically allocate and free memory as needed, freeing you from having to worry about overwriting the end of an array. String classes also have methods. These methods enable you to get the length of a string, search a string for a particular sub-string, delete portions of the string, convert the string to uppercase, and do much more. The bottom line is that string classes give you more flexibility in dealing with strings in C++ than do character arrays.

C++Builder ships with at least three string classes. One string class that you probably won't use very often is a template class called SmallString. This class is provided to interface with the Pascal short string data type. The only time you will use SmallString is when using third-party component libraries that are written using the Pascal short string data type. A second string class is AnsiString. I discuss AnsiString in detail in the next section.

The third string class is the Standard Template Library (STL) class called basic_string. This string class is now part of the C++ standard. I don't use basic_string in my programs simply because I find AnsiString sufficient for my needs. If you are writing applications that don't use the VCL (console applications or Windows NT services, to name two), you might prefer to use the STL string class to keep your code portable.

As I have said, the AnsiString class does what I need so that's the string class I use in my day-to-day C++Builder programming. The following section describes AnsiString.

The AnsiString Class

Before I go into the specifics of the AnsiString class, some background would be helpful.

VCL makes heavy use of the Pascal long string data type—nearly all text-based VCL properties are based on the Pascal long string. For example, the Text, Name, and Caption properties are all Pascal long string properties. VCL also uses this data type in many component methods and event-handling functions.

There are two things to understand about this data type. First, in Pascal the long string is an actual language data type and not just a character array, as in C and C++. Second, C++ has no built-in equivalent for the Pascal long string. Because long string is used so heavily in VCL and because C++Builder uses the Pascal VCL, Inprise created a C++ class to approximate the Pascal long string. This class, AnsiString, can be used wherever a Pascal long string is required.

Let's face it, the name AnsiString is not particularly appealing. Somewhere in SYSMAC.H you will find the following line:

```
typedef AnsiString String;
```

This enables you to use the name String (uppercase S) when declaring an instance of the AnsiString class rather than use the official class name of AnsiString:

```
String s = "This is a test";
```

Because String is the recommended alias for the AnsiString class, there is no reason to use the name AnsiString itself in your C++Builder programs (although you certainly can, if you prefer). For clarity I'll probably refer to the class as AnsiString in the text, but I'll use the short form, String, in code examples.

AnsiString is a very capable string class. The AnsiString class constructors enable you to create an AnsiString object from a char, a char*, an int, or a double. These constructors make it easy to assign a literal string to an AnsiString and convert an integer or floating-point number to a string. All the following examples use the AnsiString constructors, either explicitly or implicitly:

```
String FloatString = 127.123;
String AnotherFloatString(0.999);
String IntString = 49;
String CharString = 'A';
Label1->Caption = "This is a test";
double d = 3.14 * 20;
Edit1->Text = d;
```

You are probably not too interested in the intimate details, but in the cases where a direct assignment is made, the C++ compiler is working behind the scenes to apply the appropriate AnsiString constructor. Take this line, for example:

```
String S = 127.123;   // create an AnsiString from a double
```

Internally the compiler generates something like this:

```
String S = String((double)127.123);
```

So it's the AnsiString constructor that performs the conversion when a direct assignment is made. Another reason the previous code example works is that the AnsiString class has overridden the assignment operator (=). Other operators are overloaded to simplify things like concatenation (using the + operator) and testing for equality (using the == operator).

The AnsiString class, like the other C++ classes, has many methods that make string manipulation easier. Table 9.1 lists a few of the most commonly used AnsiString methods. This is by no means a complete list. Consult the C++Builder online help for a list of all the AnsiString methods.

TABLE 9.1 COMMONLY USED AnsiString METHODS

Method	Description
c_str	Returns a pointer (a char*) to the string's data.
Delete	Deletes part of a string.
Insert	Inserts text into an existing string at the specified location.
Length	Returns the length of the string.This doesn't include a terminating NULL.
LowerCase	Converts the string to lowercase.
Pos	Returns the position of a search string within a string.
sprintf	Allows you to format a string just like the runtime library's sprintf() function does.
SubString	Returns a sub-string within the string starting at a given position within the string and of the given length.
ToDouble	Converts the string to a floating-point number. If the string cannot be converted into a floating-point value, an exception is thrown.
ToInt	Converts the string to an integer. If the string cannot be converted, an exception is thrown.
ToIntDef	Converts the string to an integer and supplies a default value in case the string cannot be converted. No exception is thrown if the string cannot be converted.
Trim	Trims leading and trailing blank space from a string.
UpperCase	Converts a string to uppercase.

A few of these methods deserve special mention. One is the c_str() method. This oddly named method is necessary when you want to get a pointer to the character buffer of an AnsiString. Why would you want to do that? Some Windows API functions require a char* as a parameter. Remember that AnsiString is a class. You can't just pass an AnsiString to a function that is expecting a pointer to a character array. For example, if you were to use the Windows API function DrawText(), you would have to do something like this:

```
RECT R;
Rect(0, 0, 100, 20);
// first, the C way
char buff[] = "This is a test";
DrawText(Canvas->Handle,  buff, -1, &R, DT_SINGLELINE);
// now the VCL way
String S = "This is a test";
DrawText(Canvas->Handle,  S.c_str(), -1, &R, DT_SINGLELINE);
```

The second parameter of the DrawText() function requires a pointer to a character buffer, and the c_str() provides exactly that. This might not make much sense at the moment but file this away in your mind for future reference.

Don't worry too much about understanding the DrawText() function right now. This example does illustrate a point, however. Although VCL insulates you from the Windows API, you can still use the Windows API. As you delve deeper into Windows programming, you will want to use the API occasionally. It's there any time you need it.

Another AnsiString method is ToInt(). This method converts a text string to an integer value. Let's say you have an edit component on a form that will be used to retrieve an integer value from the user. Because an edit component only holds text, you need to convert that text to an integer. You can do it like this:

```
int value = Edit1->Text.ToInt();
```

The ToDouble() method works in exactly the same way. Note that both these methods throw an exception if the conversion cannot be made. If, for example, the user enters S123, an exception would be thrown because the letter S cannot be converted to an integer.

> Several `AnsiString` methods don't operate on the string itself, but instead return a new string. Take the `UpperCase()` method, for example. You might think that the following code would convert the string to all uppercase:
>
> ```
> String FileName = "c:\\mystuff\\mydata.dat";
> FileName.UpperCase();
> ```
>
> This won't work, however, because the `UpperCase()` function returns a new string and doesn't work on the existing string. The proper way to call this function is
>
> ```
> FileName = FileName.UpperCase();
> ```
>
> Before using the `AnsiString` methods, consult the online help to be sure how the method operates. Oh, and lest I forget...don't forget the double backslashes!

`AnsiString`'s `sprintf()` function works just like the like-named function discussed in Hour 2, in the section entitled "String Manipulation Functions." In that hour, I presented an example of using the `sprintf()` function. Here's the same example modified to use an `AnsiString` object:

```
int x = 10 * 20;
String S;
S.sprintf("The result is: %d", x);
```

This code builds a string with the contents The result is: 200. The `sprintf()` function is new to `AnsiString` in C++Builder 4.0. I, for one, am extremely glad to see it added to the `AnsiString` class (thanks, Jeff!).

There is at least one oddity of the `AnsiString` class that I'll mention before we move on. The index operator (`[]`) can be used to reference a particular element of the string, as shown in the following:

```
String S = "Hello World!";
Label1->Caption = S[7];
```

This code assigns the character W to the Caption property of a label component. The important thing to note here is that the string's first element is at array index 1 and not array index 0 as with other C++ arrays. The 1-based index is required for technical reasons, primarily for compatibility with Delphi. Although it's necessary, I suspect that this feature causes grief for some experienced C++ programmers at first. For example, the following code fails silently:

```
String S = "c:\\myprog\\myprog.exe";
int index = S.LastDelimiter("\\");
S.Delete(0, index);
```

When I say this code fails silently, I mean that it compiles without error but won't achieve the desired effect when the code executes. The code fails because 0 is not a valid index number for a string. The correct code is

```
S.Delete(1, index);
```

Remembering that the string is 1-based rather than 0-based will save you a lot of trouble when writing C++Builder applications.

A lot of options are available to you when dealing with strings in your C++Builder applications. For me the choice is easy—I'll use AnsiString for my day-to-day string needs. I rarely need anything else. AnsiString is fast, it has the features I need, and it is designed to integrate seamlessly with VCL.

Using Sets

Certain features of Pascal are not found in C++, and vice versa. One feature that Pascal has, but C++ doesn't, is the set. Sets are used frequently throughout VCL, so you need to know what sets are and how they work.

NEW TERM A *set* is a collection of like objects.

That description doesn't say too much, does it? An example that comes to mind is the TFont class' Style property. This property can include one or more of the following values: fsBold, fsItalic, fsUnderline, and fsStrikeout. Keep that in mind, and we'll get back to it in just a bit.

As I said earlier, there is no built-in support for sets in the C++ language. Fortunately, the C++ language is powerful enough to enable you to do whatever needs to be done. Although there are several ways to solve this particular problem, the folks at Borland decided to implement sets in the form of a template class called, predictably, Set. The good news is that the Set template is very easy to use when you understand it.

So how do you use a set? Let's get back to the font style example from earlier in this section. Typically, you turn the individual Style values for the font on or off at design time. Sometimes, however, you need to set the font's Style property at runtime. For example, let's say that you want to add the bold and italic attributes to the font style. One way is to declare a variable of type TFontStyles and then add the fsBold and fsItalic styles to the set. Here's how it looks:

```
TFontStyles Styles;
Styles << fsBold << fsItalic;
```

Notice the use of the << operator. This operator is overloaded in the Set class to enable you to add elements to a set. Note that this code doesn't actually change a font's style; it just creates a set and adds two elements to it. To change a font's style, you have to assign this newly created set to the Font->Style property of some component:

```
Memo->Font->Style = Styles;
```

Now, let's say that you wanted the font to be bold but not italic. In that case you would have to remove the italic style from the set. To remove an element from a set, you use the >> operator:

```
Styles >> fsItalic;
Memo->Font->Style = Styles;
```

Often you want to know whether a particular item is in a set. Let's say you want to know whether the font is currently set to bold. You can find out whether the fsBold style is in the set by using the Contains() method:

```
bool hasBold = Memo->Font->Style.Contains(fsBold);
if (hasBold) DoSomething();
```

Sometimes you need to make sure you are starting with an empty set. You can clear a set of its contents using the Clear() method—for example:

```
// start with an empty set
Styles.Clear();
// now add the bold and italic styles
Styles << fsBold << fsItalic;
Memo->Font->Style = Styles;
```

Here the font style is cleared of all contents, and then the bold and italic styles are added. If you want, you can create a temporary set and add elements to it all at one time. The previous code snippet could also have been written like this:

```
Font->Style = TFontStyles() << fsBold << fsItalic;
```

This code creates a temporary TFontStyles set, adds the fsBold and fsItalic styles, and then assigns the temporary set to the Style property. Although this looks odd, it is perfectly valid and is a handy way of creating a temporary set on-the-fly.

Because of an oddity in the way Set class works, you should always make an assignment when changing a property that is a set. Take the following code, for example:

```
Font->Style << fsBold << fsItalic;
```

This code compiles but it won't actually change the font style because the write method for the Style property won't be called. To be sure that the Style property is properly updated, use an explicit assignment instead:

```
Font->Style = Font->Style << fsBold << fsItalic;
```

This ensures that the write method for the Style property is called and that the font's style is updated.

9

Sets are easy after you get the hang of them. The Set template in C++Builder is your route to VCL sets. The extraction and insertion operators, although odd looking at first, are a simple way of adding and removing elements from a set.

VCL Classes and Components

The Visual Component Library is a well-designed framework. As with most good frameworks, VCL makes maximum use of inheritance. The bulk of the VCL framework is composed of classes that represent components. Other VCL classes are not related to components. These classes perform housekeeping chores, act as helper classes, and provide some utility services.

The VCL class hierarchy dealing with components is complex. Fortunately, you don't have to know every detail of VCL to begin programming in C++Builder. At the top of the VCL chain you will find TObject. Figure 9.1 shows some of the main base classes and classes derived from them.

FIGURE 9.1

The VCL class hierarchy.

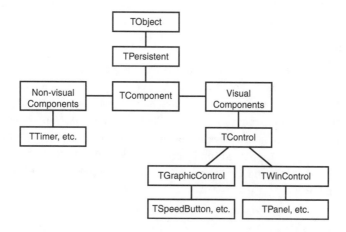

TObject is the granddaddy of all VCL component classes. Below TObject you see TPersistent. This class deals with a component's capability to save itself to files and to memory as well as other messy details we don't need to know about. I'm thankful (and you should be, too) that we don't need to know much about TPersistent to program most applications in C++Builder.

The TComponent class serves as a more direct base class for components. This class provides all the functionality that a basic component requires. Nonvisual components are derived from TComponent itself. Visual components are derived from TControl, which, as you can see from Figure 9.1, is derived from TComponent. TControl provides additional functionality that visual components require. The individual components, then, are derived from either TGraphicControl or TWinControl.

When you drop a component on a form, C++Builder creates a pointer to that component in the form's class declaration so that you can access the component in your code. C++Builder uses the component's Name property for the pointer variable's name. For example, when you place a memo component on a form, C++Builder creates a TMemo* variable and names it Memo1. Similarly, if you drop a button on a form, C++Builder creates a TButton* to represent the button. Before any of that takes place, C++Builder has already derived a new class from TForm and, of course, created an instance of that class to represent the form.

Some understanding of the VCL classes is obviously necessary before working with VCL. Although I cannot review each and every VCL class, I can hit the high points. Let's take a look at some of the classes that you will use most frequently.

Form and Application Classes

Form and application classes represent forms and the Application object in VCL. These classes are derived from TComponent and indeed are components themselves (although they don't appear anywhere on the Component palette). They are listed separately to distinguish them from the controls you drop on a form.

TApplication

The TApplication class encapsulates the basic operations of a Windows program. TApplication takes care of things like managing the application's icon, providing context help, and doing basic message handling. Every C++Builder application has a pointer to the TApplication object called Application. You use the TApplication class primarily to execute message boxes, manage context help, and set hint text for buttons and status bars. TApplication is a bit of an oddity in VCL in that some of its properties (Icon, HelpFile, and Title) can be set via the Application page of the Project Options dialog box.

TForm

The TForm class encapsulates forms in VCL. Forms are used for main windows, dialog boxes, secondary windows, and just about any other window type you can imagine. TForm is a workhorse class in VCL. It can respond to nearly 60 properties, 45 methods, and 20 events. I am going to discuss forms in detail in Hour 11, "C++Builder Forms," so I'll wait to explain each of these methods until that time.

Component Classes

9

This group encompasses a wide range of classes and can be further divided into separate categories, which I've done in the following sections.

Standard Component Classes

The standard components are those that encapsulate the most common Windows controls. The standard component classes include TButton, TLabel, TEdit, TListBox, TMemo, TMainMenu, TPopupMenu, TCheckBox, TRadioButton, TRadioGroup, TGroupBox, TComboBox, TScrollBar, and TPanel.

Most of these classes encapsulate a Windows control. The TMainMenu class encapsulates an application's main menu. At design time, double-clicking the MainMenu component's icon brings up the Menu Designer. TMainMenu has properties that control whether the menu item is grayed out, whether it is checked, the help context ID, the item's hint text, and others. Each menu item has a single event, OnClick, so that you can attach a function to a menu item being selected. I'll discuss menus and the Menu Designer in more detail in Hour 14, "Working with the Menu Designer."

Another standard component of interest is TPanel. A panel represents a rectangular region on a form, usually with its own components, that can be treated as a single unit.

C++Builder has another group of components that I'll throw in with the standard controls. These controls can be found under the Additional tab on the Component palette. The classes representing these components include TBitBtn, TSpeedButton, TMaskEdit, TStringGrid, TDrawGrid, TImage, TShape, TBevel, TscrollBox, TCheckListBox, TSplitter, TStaticText, and TControlBar. The TBitBtn class represents a button that has an image on it. TSpeedButton is also a button with an image, but this component is designed to be used as a speed button on a control bar. A TSpeedButton is not a true button but rather a graphical depiction of a button. This enables you to have a large number of speed buttons and not consume Windows resources for each button. The TImage component enables you to place an image on a form that then can be selected from a file on disk. You can use the TBevel component to create boxes and lines that are raised (bumps) or lowered (dips). Bevels can be used to divide a form into visual regions and to provide an aesthetically pleasing form. The TStringGrid and TDrawGrid classes give you a means of presenting information in a tabular format.

Win32 Custom Control Classes

VCL has component classes that encapsulate many of the Windows 32-bit custom controls. These classes include TListView, TTreeView, TProgressBar, TTabControl, TPageControl, TRichEdit, TImageList, TStatusBar, TAnimate, TToolBar, TCoolBar, and a few others. Some of these controls are, by nature, complicated, and the VCL classes that represent them are complicated as well. Trust me when I say that VCL does much to ease the burden of working with these common controls. You have to spend some time with these classes before you fully understand them.

Common Dialog Classes

As you are no doubt aware, Windows has common dialog boxes for things like opening files, saving files, choosing fonts, and choosing colors. VCL encapsulates these common dialog boxes in classes representing each type. The classes are TOpenDialog, TSaveDialog, TOpenPictureDialog, TSavePictureDialog, TFontDialog, TColorDialog, TPrintDialog, and TPrinterSetupDialog. VCL also adds the TFindDialog and TReplaceDialog classes to this component group. All the components in this group are nonvisual in that they don't have a design-time visual interface. The dialog boxes are visible when displayed at runtime, of course.

System Component Classes

The System tab on the Component palette contains a mixture of visual and nonvisual components. The TTimer class is used to represent a Windows system timer. Its single event is OnTimer, which is called each time the timer fires. The timer interval is set through the Interval property. TTimer is a nonvisual component.

Tucked into this group of classes is the TMediaPlayer class. This class enables you to play media files like wave audio, AVI video, and MIDI audio. The media can be played, stopped, paused, or positioned at a particular point in the file, as well as many other operations. This class has many properties and events that greatly simplify the complex world of the Windows Media Control Interface (MCI).

The TPaintBox component gives you an empty canvas on which you can draw anything you like. This component has many potential uses. The System group includes object linking and embedding (OLE) and dynamic data exchange (DDE) classes as well.

The Win 3.1 Group

Don't make the mistake of automatically discarding this component group just because of the name of the tab on which they reside. This group contains some great components. (The Win 3.1 tab has its roots in Delphi.) In particular, I like the TTabSet and TNotebook components. This group also includes several component classes that enable you to build your own custom File Open or File Save dialog box. The classes are TFileListBox, TDirectoryListBox, TDriveComboBox, and TFilterComboBox.

GDI Classes

The graphics device interface (GDI) classes get a lot of work in Windows GUI applications. These classes encapsulate the use of bitmaps, fonts, device contexts (DCs), brushes, and pens. It is through these GDI objects that graphics and text are displayed on a window. The GDI classes are not associated with a specific component, but many components have instances of these classes as properties. For example, an edit control has a property called Font that is an instance of the TFont class.

The term *device context* is well known by Windows programmers, whether they program in C or with one of the C++ frameworks. In VCL, though, the term is not widely used. This is because VCL encapsulates Windows DCs in the TCanvas class. VCL uses the term *canvas* to refer to a Windows device context. A canvas provides a surface that you can draw on using methods like MoveTo(), LineTo(), and TextOut(). Bitmaps can be displayed on the canvas using the Draw() or StretchDraw() methods. The concept of a canvas that you draw on makes more sense than the archaic term *device context*, don't you think?

The TCanvas class contains instances of the other GDI classes. For example, when you do a MoveTo()/LineTo() sequence, a line is drawn with the current pen color. The Pen property is used to determine the current pen color and is an instance of the TPen class. TPen has properties that determine what type of line to draw: the line width, the line style (solid, dashed, dotted, and so on), and the mode with which to draw the line.

The TBrush class represents a brush used as the fill pattern for canvas operations like FillRect(), Polygon(), and Ellipse(). TBrush properties include Color, Style, and Bitmap. The Style property enables you to set a hatch pattern for the brush. The Bitmap property enables you to specify a bitmap for the fill pattern.

TBitmap encapsulates bitmap operations in VCL. Properties include Palette, Height, Width, and TransparentColor. Methods include LoadFromFile(), LoadFromResourceID(), and SaveToFile(). TBitmap is used by other component classes such as TImage, TBitBtn, and TSpeedButton in addition to TCanvas. An instance of the

9

TBitmap class can also be used as an offscreen bitmap. Offscreen bitmaps are commonly used in graphics-intensive applications to reduce flicker and improve graphics performance.

The TFont class handles font operations. Properties include Color, Height, and Style (bold, italic, normal, and so on). The TFont class is used by all component classes that display text.

In addition to the GDI classes listed here, there are others that either work as helper classes or extend a base class to provide extra functionality. As you work with C++Builder, you will learn more about these classes and how to use them.

Utility Classes

So far I have discussed component classes. VCL also contains utility classes you can use in your applications. A *utility class* simplifies some task in Windows programming. For instance, the TIniFile class eases the use of writing and reading Windows configuration files (.INI files). Conventional wisdom has it that the use of .INI files is out and the Registry is in. To aid in Registry operations, VCL has the TRegistry and TRegkeyInfo classes.

The TStringList class allows for arrays of strings. TStringList is used by many of the component classes to store strings. For instance, the TMemo class uses a TStringList object for its Lines property. TStringList has the capability to save its list of strings to file or load strings from a file using the LoadFromFile() and SaveToFile() methods.

Another useful VCL utility class is the TList class. This class enables you to create arrays of any type of object you want. The TList class simply stores a list of pointers. The main advantage of the TList class is that it provides you with an array that will dynamically grow or shrink as new objects are added or removed.

VCL also includes a set of classes to enable reading and writing of streams. The TFileStream, TMemoryStream, and TResourceStream classes all enable you to read or write data to streams. Of these classes, you're most likely to use the TFileStream class to read and write data files. These classes are for more advanced uses but are invaluable when you need the particular functionality they provide.

And That's Not All...

By no means did I cover all the VCL classes and components here. I did, however, touch on those classes and components that you are most likely to use in your applications.

C++Builder Professional and Enterprise versions come with components not found in the Standard version. The Professional version ships with a wide range of database components that makes C++ database programming a snap. It also ships with a set of Internet components that allow you to easily incorporate FTP, SMTP, POP3, HTML, HTTP, and so on in your C++Builder applications. C++Builder Professional is well worth the money if you plan on doing serious programming with C++Builder. In addition to the components that come with C++Builder Professional, the Enterprise edition of C++Builder add even more components. These primarily come in the form of additional database and Internet tools. The combination of these tools makes creating multitier distributed database applications a joy to write. Another important aspect of C++Builder Enterprise edition is the DCOM, CORBA, and MTS tools and components.

If you like what you see in C++Builder Standard version, I can guarantee that the Professional and Enterprise editions won't disappoint you should you decide to upgrade at a later time.

Summary

Although it might not be immediately apparent, this hour covers some of the most important aspects of writing real-world applications with C++Builder. In particular, the sections describing the AnsiString and Set classes gave you information you'll need as you begin writing applications in C++Builder. We finished the hour by looking at some of the components available to you in C++Builder.

Workshop

The Workshop contains quiz questions to help you solidify your understanding of the material covered and exercises to provide you with experience in using what you have learned. The answers to the quiz questions are provided following the questions. The exercises are given for you to work out and code on your own.

Q&A

Q I am writing a console application that doesn't use the VCL. What string class should I use?

A In this case the STL's basic_string class would probably be the best choice. If you ever find the need to compile your console application with another C++ compiler, you should be able to do so with minimal changes to the code.

Q **There sure are a lot of VCL classes. I thought programming with C++Builder was going to be easy.**

A Programming with C++Builder is much easier than programming Windows in C and easier than programming with a C++ framework like Microsoft's Microsoft Foundation Class Library (MFC). Windows programming, no matter how good the programming tool, requires a lot of experience and knowledge to master. You will master it if you keep at it.

Quiz

1. What does the `sprintf()` function of the `AnsiString` class do?
2. How do you convert a string contained in an `AnsiString` object to an integer?
3. Does the Win 3.1 tab on the Component palette contain only obsolete components?
4. What is the name of the VCL class that encapsulates a Windows device context?

Answers

1. The `sprintf()` function allows you to format a string using program variables.
2. The `ToInt()` method is used to convert an `AnsiString` to an integer value.
3. Absolutely not! The Win 3.1 tab contains many useful components.
4. The `TCanvas` class encapsulates a Windows device context.

Exercise

1. Start C++Builder help and examine the properties and methods of the `TApplication` class.

Hour 10

Exploring the C++Builder IDE

In this hour I explain how to use the C++Builder Integrated Development Environment (IDE). One of the most difficult aspects of learning how to use a new programming environment is finding your way around: getting to know the basic menu structure, what all the options do, and how the environment works as a whole. If you are new to programming, or new to C++, this task is complicated by the fact that you have to learn a new program (the C++Builder IDE) *and* learn a new language at the same time. It can be overwhelming at times. I'll do my best to make learning the C++Builder IDE a painless experience. For the most part you will learn by example, which is more interesting (not to mention more effective). So, without further ado, and referring to Figure 10.1, let's get on with it. Oh, by the way, if you are coming to C++Builder from Delphi, you might find this hour and the one that follows elementary. If that is the case, you might want to at least skim the hours lightly to catch any tidbits that you did not previously know.

FIGURE 10.1

The C++Builder IDE.

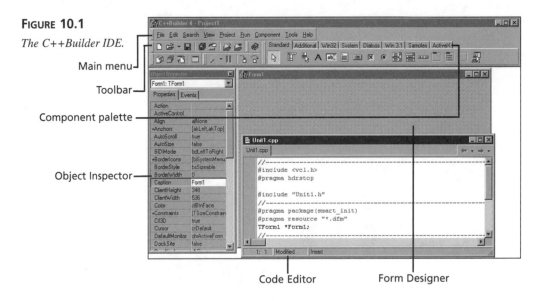

Main menu

Toolbar

Component palette

Object Inspector

Code Editor　　　　Form Designer

The C++Builder IDE consists of these main parts:

- The main menu and toolbars
- The component palette
- The Form Designer
- The Code Editor
- The Object Inspector
- The Project Manager

I can't cover all these in a single session, so over the next several hours I will show you around the C++Builder IDE and examine each of these features in detail. I'll start this hour by discussing projects and how they are used in writing C++Builder applications. After that we'll look at the C++Builder toolbar and the Component palette. For starters, let's look at the way C++Builder views applications and how it has simplified the process of creating programs.

Projects in C++Builder

As you know by now, a lot goes on behind the scenes as you write a C++Builder application. In fact, more goes on than I have told you about up to this point. It's not vital that you know every detail about what happens behind the scenes as you write a C++Builder application, but it is a good idea to have a general overview.

New Term A *project* is a collection of files that work together to create a standalone executable file.

New Term In addition to a single project, C++Builder allows you to create what is known as a project group. A *project group* is a collection of C++Builder projects.

A project group is used to manage a group of C++Builder projects that work together to form a complete software product. I'm going to give you an introduction to projects in this session because projects are a vital part of working with the IDE. I'll talk about project groups in more detail in Hour 19, "More on Projects." For now, you only need to understand that C++Builder creates a new, unnamed project group for you each time you start C++Builder. Any new projects you create will go into that project group. You can save the project group if you like, or you can treat the default project group as temporary.

Files Used in C++Builder Projects

10

C++Builder manages a project through the use of several support files. To illustrate, let's create a simple application to get a look at some of what goes on when C++Builder builds an executable file for your program. Do the following:

1. Before you begin, create a fresh directory (folder) called Test on your hard drive. Your CBuilder4 directory has a subdirectory called Projects. A new directory under Projects would be a good place for your new directory.

2. First choose File, Close All from the main menu so you are starting from scratch. Now choose File, New Application from the main menu. A blank form is displayed.

3. Before you do anything else, choose File, Save All from the main menu.

4. First, you will be prompted for the name of the unit file. Be sure to switch to the empty directory you just created.

5. Next, type in the name MyUnit for the unit filename and click the Save Button.

6. Now you are prompted for the project name. Type Test in the File name field and click Save.

7. Now choose Project, Build Test from the main menu. C++Builder displays the compile status box and goes to work compiling the program.

8. After a while the compile status box reports that it is done compiling, and the OK button is enabled. Click OK to close the compile status dialog box.

9. Now choose File, Close All from the main menu. (Yes, this exercise does have a purpose.)

10. Now run Windows Explorer and locate the directory where you saved the project. You will see a number of files.

Wow! All that to create just one little program that does nothing? Yes, it's true. First, let me tell you what happens when C++Builder builds an application; then I'll explain what each of these files is for.

 Files with extensions that begin with a tilde (~) are backup files. C++Builder might create several backup files, depending on the number of source files in the project and the project options you have set. Project options are discussed in Hour 19.

When you first create a project, C++Builder creates a minimum of six files (assuming a typical C++Builder GUI application), as follows:

- The project source file
- The main form source file
- The main form header file
- The main form resource file
- The project resource file
- The project makefile

The *project source file* contains the WinMain() function (the entry point for all Windows GUI applications) and other C++Builder startup code. You can view the project source file by choosing Project, View Source from the main menu.

The *main form source file* and *main form header file* contain the class declaration and definition for the main form's class. C++Builder creates an additional source file and header for each new form you create. The *main form resource file* and *project resource file* are binary files that describe the main form and the application's icon.

Somewhere in this process, C++Builder creates the project *makefile*. The makefile is a text file that contains information about the compiler options you have set, the names of the source files and forms that make up the project, and what library files have to be included.

There are two types of library files. A *static library* contains common code that an application needs in order to run. An *import library* is needed when your application references functions in a dynamic link library (DLL). A DLL is a file that contains compiled sections of code that can be called (executed) from an application. The code in a DLL is accessed through public functions exported from the DLL. An import library provides a binary description of the DLL's exported functions. The application that uses the DLL needs the import library to resolve the location of the DLL's functions referenced in your code. The number and exact filenames of the library files required depend on the features your application uses. Fortunately, you don't have to worry about managing the library files because C++Builder takes care of that detail for you. Library files have a .LIB or .BPI extension and are tucked away in your C++Builder \Lib directory.

10

There are a few more odds and ends, but that's the bulk of what is contained in the makefile. When you tell C++Builder to compile the project, it hands the makefile to the compiler. The compiler reads the makefile and begins compiling all the source files that make up the project.

Several things happen during this process. First, the C++ compiler compiles the C++ source files into binary object files. Then the resource compiler compiles any resources, such as the program's icon and form files, into binary resource files. Next, the linker takes over. The linker takes the binary files the compilers created, adds any library files the project needs, and binds them all together to produce the final executable file. Along the way it produces more files that perform some special operations (I'll get to that in a minute). When it's all over, you have a standalone program that can be run in the usual ways.

Okay, but what are all those files for? Table 10.1 lists the file extensions C++Builder uses with a description of the role that each file type plays.

TABLE 10.1 TYPES OF FILES USED IN C++BUILDER

Extension	Description
.CPP	The C++ source files. There will usually be one for each unit, one for the main project file, as well as any other source files that you add to the project.
.DFM	The form file. This file is actually a binary resource file (.RES) in disguise. It is a description of the form and all its components. Each form has its own .DFM file.

continues

TABLE 10.1 CONTINUED

Extension	Description
.DSK	The desktop file. This file keeps track of the way the desktop appeared when you last saved (or closed) the project. All the open windows' sizes and positions are saved so that when you reopen the project it looks the same as you left it. This file is only created if you turn on the option to save your desktop (Environment Options dialog box).
.EXE	The final executable program.
.H	C++ header files that contain class declarations. These could be C++Builder-generated files or your own class headers.
.HPP	Also C++ headers files. Headers with an .HPP extension are created by C++Builder when you install components. The VCL header files (located in the \CBuilder4\Include\VCL directory) also have an extension of .HPP to distinguish them from the .H files that C++Builder generates for each unit.
.IL?	The four files whose extensions begin with .IL are files created by the incremental linker. The incremental linker saves you time by linking only the parts of the program that have changed since the last build.
.OBJ	The compiled binary object files. These are the files that the compiler produces when it compiles your C++ source files.
.BPR	The project makefile. This is a text file that contains a description of which files C++Builder needs to compile and link. It also contains special flags that tell the compiler and linker which options to apply when building the project.
.RES	A compiled binary resource file produced by the resource compiler.
.TDS	The debugger symbol table. This file is used by the debugger during debugging sessions.

C++Builder has other associated file extensions as well. For example, the .BPG extension is used to denote a project group, the .BPK extension is used to designate a C++Builder package makefile, and the .BPL extension represents a compiled package. Project groups will be discussed in more detail in Hour 19 and packages in Hour 21.

The files that C++Builder produces can be broken down into two categories: files C++Builder relies on to build the project and files that it creates when it compiles and links a project. If you were to move your source files to another computer, for instance, you wouldn't have to move all the files, just the files C++Builder needs to build the application. Conveniently, the source files happen to be the smallest files in the project. It doesn't take a lot of disk space to back up just the project source files.

The minimum set of files consists of the .CPP, .H, DFM, and .BPR files. All other files are files that C++Builder will re-create when you compile the program. The desktop file (.DSK) is one that you might want to hang on to because it keeps track of the state your project was in when you last worked on it.

> In addition to the source files I've mentioned, some applications use a *resource script file*. Resource scripts have an .RC extension. Resource scripts are text files that are used to define resources like bitmaps, icons, or cursors. If you use a resource script, be sure to keep it with the project if you move the project to another location. I discuss resource files in detail in Hour 18 in the section, "Using Resource Files."

10

Figure 10.2 illustrates how C++Builder takes source files and compiles and links them to form the final executable file.

FIGURE 10.2

The C++Builder compile/link process.

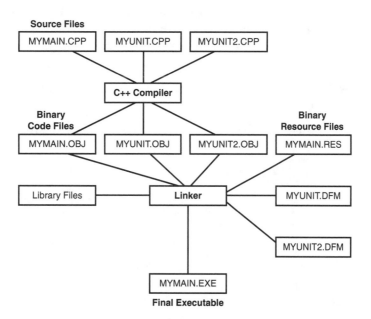

If you find yourself running low on hard disk space, you can delete some of the C++Builder files from projects you aren't currently working on. It is safe to delete the files with the .OBJ, .RES, and .TDS extensions, as well as any files with extensions beginning with .IL. Some of these files can grow quite large, and there is no use in keeping them for non-current projects.

Be careful not to delete any files from the C++Builder directories other than the Examples directory. If in doubt, *don't delete*!

Source Code Units

Earlier I mentioned that most applications of any size have several source files, which are called *units*. The use of the term *unit* in C++Builder is a holdover from Delphi. C++Builder has its roots in the Delphi IDE, and *unit* is used throughout both the Visual Component Library (VCL) and the C++Builder IDE itself. C++ programmers would typically refer to a file containing a program's source as a *module*. Whereas using the term *module* would have been more C++ friendly (and less Pascal-like), replacing the word *unit* with *module* would have required major changes to the C++Builder infrastructure, so the term *unit* was left in. If you are coming from a C++ programming background, it might seem odd to refer to modules as units, but you will get used to it soon enough. In the end, there's no point in getting hung up over terminology.

 C++Builder uses the term *unit* to refer to source files. Most units are a source file/form file pair.

Each time you create a new form, C++Builder does the following:

- Creates a form file (.DFM)
- Derives a class from TForm
- Creates a header (.H file) containing the class declaration
- Creates a unit (.CPP file) for the class definition
- Adds the new form information to the project makefile

Initially C++Builder assigns a default name of Form1 to the form, Unit1.cpp for the associated unit, and Unit1.h for the header. The second form created for the project would have a default name of Form2, and so on. Each time you create a new form C++Builder creates a new unit (.CPP) and header file (.H) for that form.

As soon as you create a new project, you should save it with a meaningful name. Likewise, every time you create a new form, you should save it with a descriptive name. This makes it easier to locate forms and units when you need to make modifications.

I'm going to digress a little bit at this point and talk about the main menu, toolbar, and Component palette. Later we'll get back to how these relate to projects.

The C++Builder Main Menu and Toolbar

The C++Builder main menu has all the choices necessary to make C++Builder work. Because programming in C++Builder is a highly visual operation, you might not use the main menu as much as you might with other programming environments. Still, just about anything you need is available from the main menu if you prefer to work that way. I'm not going to go over every item on the main menu here because you will encounter each item as you work through the next several chapters.

The C++Builder toolbars are a convenient way of accomplishing often-repeated tasks. A button is easier to locate than a menu item, not to mention that it requires less mouse movement. The C++Builder toolbars' default configuration is illustrated in Figure 10.3.

FIGURE 10.3

The C++Builder IDE toolbars.

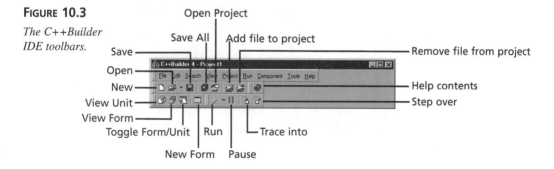

If you are like me, you often forget to use the toolbar. But I'm telling you: Don't forget to learn and use the toolbar. As the old saying goes, "Do as I say, not as I do." If you take the time to learn the toolbar, it will save you time and make you more efficient in the long run. One of the reasons you bought C++Builder was to produce Windows applications quickly, so you might as well make the most of it.

The C++Builder toolbars are fully customizable. As you saw back in Figure 10.1, between the toolbars and the Component palette is a vertical line that acts as a sizing bar. When you place the mouse cursor over the sizing bar, you will see the sizing cursor (a double-headed black arrow). Once you have the sizing cursor, you can drag the sizing bar right or left to make the toolbars take more or less room on the C++Builder main window.

Customizing the toolbars is remarkably easy. C++Builder allows you to add buttons to the toolbars, remove buttons, and rearrange buttons however you see fit. To configure a toolbar, right-click on the toolbar to display the context menu. Choose Customize from the context menu. When you choose this menu item, the Customize dialog box is displayed. The Customize dialog box contains three tabs.

The first tab, Toolbars, shows you the toolbars available with a check mark next to toolbars that are currently visible. You can add or remove toolbars, add new toolbars, or reset the toolbars to their original default settings.

FIGURE 10.4

Customizing the toolbar.

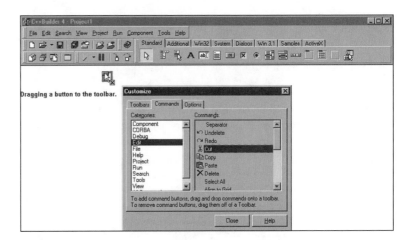

The second tab, labeled Commands, shows all the available toolbar buttons. To add a button to the toolbar, just locate its description in the Commands list box and drag it to the place you want it to occupy on any toolbar. To remove a button from a toolbar, grab it and drag it off the toolbar. It's as simple as that. Figure 10.4 shows the act of adding a button to a toolbar. If you really make a mess of things, simply go back to the Toolbars page and click the Reset button. The toolbar reverts to its default settings.

The third tab is the Options page of the Customize dialog box and it contains options such as whether the ToolTips are displayed, and how they are displayed.

If you want to make room for more buttons, drag the sizing bar to the right to make the toolbar wider. Now just drag any buttons you want from the Toolbar Editor to the toolbar. The toolbar has an invisible grid that aids you when dropping new buttons; just get the buttons close to where you want them and they will snap into place. I happen to like the Make, Compile Unit, and Build buttons on the toolbar, so I have customized my toolbar to include those buttons. Figure 10.4 illustrates the process of dragging a button to the toolbar.

Feel free to customize the C++Builder IDE any way you like. It's your development environment, so make it work for you.

Using the Component Palette

The C++Builder Component palette is used to select a component in order to place that component on a form. The Component palette is a multipage window. Tabs are provided (as shown in Figure 10.5) to allow you to navigate between pages. Clicking on a tab displays the available components or controls on that page.

10

FIGURE 10.5

The Component palette toolbar with scroll buttons.

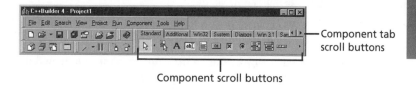

Component tab scroll buttons

Component scroll buttons

Navigating the Component Palette

You can drag the sizing bar, located between the toolbar and the Component palette, to make the Component palette occupy more or less room on the C++Builder main window. If the Component palette is sized small enough so that it cannot display all its tabs, you will see scroll buttons in the upper-right corner of the Component palette. Click these scroll buttons to display tabs not currently in view. Likewise, if a particular page of the Component palette contains more buttons than will fit the width of the display window, scroll buttons will be enabled to allow you to scroll through the available buttons. Figure 10.5 shows the Component palette with both types of scroll buttons enabled.

The Component palette is not terribly complicated, but a basic understanding of its use is vital for programming with C++Builder.

Placing Components on a Form

Placing a component on a form is a two-step process. Go to the Component palette and select the button representing the component you want to use; then click on the form to place the component on the form. The component appears on the form with its upper-left corner placed where you clicked with the mouse. You then simply repeat this process for each component you want to add to the form.

You can also easily place multiple components *of the same type* on a form without re-selecting the component from the Component palette each time.

To place multiple components of the same type on the form, press and hold the Shift key when selecting the component from the Component palette. After you select the component, you can release the Shift key. The component's button on the Component palette appears pressed and is highlighted with a blue border. Click on the form to place the first component. Notice that the button stays pressed in the Component palette. You can click as many times as you like; a new component is placed each time you click the form. To stop placing components, click the selector button on the Component palette (the arrow button). The component button pops up to indicate that you are done placing components.

Seeing is believing, so follow these steps:

1. Create a new project.
2. Press and hold the Shift key on the keyboard and click the Label component button in the Component palette.
3. Click three times on the form, moving the cursor each time to indicate where you want the new component placed.
4. Click the arrow button on the Component palette to end the process. You are then returned to form design mode.

> It's fastest to place all components of a particular type on your form at one time using this technique. Components can always be rearranged and resized at a later time.

> When placing multiple copies of a particular component, it's easy to forget to click the arrow button when you're done. If you accidentally place more components than you intended, you can simply delete any extras. To remove an unwanted component, click on the component to select it and then hit the Delete key on the keyboard.

C++Builder provides a shortcut method of placing a component on a form. Simply double-click the component's button on the Component palette, and the component is placed on the form. The component will be centered on the form both horizontally and vertically. Now you can use your mouse to select and drag the component to any location on the form. After positioning the component, you can double-click another component (or the same one) and repeat the process until you have all the desired components on the form.

> If you repeatedly double-click the same component button, multiple copies of that component are placed in the center of the form and are stacked on top of the previous one. Thus, you might not realize that you have several identical components occupying the same space. If you accidentally place multiple, identical components, just click (select) each of the extra components and delete them from the form.

The Component Palette Context Menu

When you place the mouse cursor over the Component palette and right-click, you will see a menu specific to the Component palette.

The Show Hints item toggles the ToolTips on and off for the component buttons. Unless you really dislike ToolTips, this should be left on.

The Hide item on the context menu hides the Component palette. In order to show the Component palette again, you have to choose View, Toolbars, Component Palette from the main menu.

The Help item on the context menu brings up C++Builder help with the Component Palette page displayed.

The Properties item brings up the Palette page of the Environment Options dialog box, where you can customize the Component palette. Here you can add and remove pages of the Component palette. You can also add, remove, or rearrange the order of components on the individual pages.

Creating a Multiple-Form Application

To illustrate how C++Builder projects work, let's create an application with multiple forms. We'll create a simple application that displays a second form when you click a button:

1. Create a new project by choosing File, New Application from the main menu.

2. Change the Name property to MainForm and the Caption property to Multiple Forms Test Program.

3. Save the project. Save the unit as Main and the project as Multiple.

4. Now place a button on the form. Make the button's Name property ShowForm2 and the Caption property Show Form 2.

5. Choose File, New Form from the main menu (or click the New Form button on the toolbar) to create a new form.

10

At this point, the new form has a name of Form1 and is placed exactly over the main form. We want the new form to be smaller than the main form and more or less centered on the main form.

1. Size and position the new form so that it is about 50 percent of the size of the main form and centered on the main form. Use the title bar to move the new form. Size the form by dragging the lower-right corner.

2. Change the new form's Name property to SecondForm and the form's Caption property to A Second Form.

3. Choose File, Save from the main menu (or click the Save File button on the toolbar) and save the new form with the name Second.

4. Choose a Label component and drop it on the new form. Change the label's Caption property to This is a second form. Change the label's size and color as desired. Center the label on the form.

Your form should now look roughly similar to the one in Figure 10.6.

FIGURE 10.6

*Creating and using
multiple forms.*

Now we'll generate an OnClick event handler for the button. The code in the event handler shows the second form. (I discussed the OnClick event in Hour 8 in the section "Events" if you need to review.)

1. Click on the main form. Notice that the second form is covered by the main form. Double-click the Show Form 2 button. The Code Editor is displayed, and the cursor is placed just where you need it to begin typing code (double-clicking a button is a shortcut way of generating an OnClick event handler).

2. Type in code so that the function looks like this (you only have to type one line of code):

```
void _ _fastcall TMainForm::ShowForm2Click(TObject *Sender)
{
  SecondForm->ShowModal();
}
```

3. Run the program.

At this point you will get a compiler error that says Undefined symbol 'SecondForm'. Hmmm...SecondForm should be a valid symbol because that's the name of the second form we created...I wonder...Aha! Remember, we have two source files with a header for each source file. The problem is that the MainForm unit can't see the declaration for the SecondForm variable (which is a pointer to the TSecondForm class). We have to tell it where to find the class declaration. Switch to the Code Editor and click the Main.cpp tab to display the unit for the main form. Scroll up to the top of the file. The first few lines look like this:

```
//-------------------------------
#include <vcl.h>
#pragma hdrstop

#include "Main.h"
//-------------------------------
```

You can see the #include for Main.h, but there isn't one for Second.h. That's because we haven't yet told C++Builder to add it. Let's do that now:

1. Choose File, Include Unit Hdr from the main menu. The Include Unit dialog box is displayed (see Figure 10.7).

2. You will see a list of available units. In this case, the only unit in the list is Second. Click Second and then click OK to close the dialog box (you could have double-clicked the name of the unit instead).

FIGURE 10.7

The Include Unit dialog box.

10

The Include Unit dialog box shows only those units that exist in the project *and* have not yet been included in this unit. Units that have already been included do not show in the list of available units.

If you blinked, you missed it, but C++Builder added the #include for Second.h when you clicked OK. Now the first few lines of the file show this:

```
//--------------------------------
#include <vcl.h>
#pragma hdrstop
#include "Main.h"
#include "Second.h"
//--------------------------------
```

Now the Main unit can see the class declaration for the Second unit. Click the Run button to run the program. This time the compile goes off without a hitch, and the program runs. When you click the Show Form 2 button on the main form, the second form is displayed. You can close the second form by clicking the system close box on the form's title bar.

As you can see, C++Builder does a good job of managing units for you. You have to be sure that you use the Include Unit Hdr option so that one unit can see the class declarations of other units, but for the most part C++Builder frees you from having to worry about your source files. Later, when your programming needs are more sophisticated, you'll have to do a little more source file management, but at this stage of the game C++Builder does most of the work for you.

Now let's take a moment to look at the different compiling options available to you when writing programs in C++Builder.

Compiling, Building, and Linking

Each time you click the Run button, C++Builder compiles and links your program. But it doesn't necessarily compile every unit in the project. It only compiles any units that have changed since the last compile. This feature saves you time because you don't have to wait for the compiler to compile files that haven't changed. C++Builder keeps track of which files have changed and which haven't, so you don't need to do anything special to use this feature—it's automatic.

Most of the time you want to see in action the results of any changes you have made. In those cases you click the Run button and the program is compiled, linked, and executed.

Sometimes, however, you don't want to run the program. For instance, you might just want to compile the program to see if there are any errors. C++Builder has three menu items in addition to Run that allow you to control the compile/link process. Those menu items are

- Compile Unit—Compiles the unit in the active Code Editor window. The unit is compiled but no link is performed.

- Build—Unconditionally compiles all units in the project and performs a link, producing a final executable.

- Make—Compiles only those units that have changed since the executable was last created and performs a link.

If you choose the Project menu item on the main menu, you will see three menu items called Compile Unit, Make, and Build. The Make and Build menu item's text changes to reflect the name of the active project. For example, when you first start C++Builder these menu items will say Make Project1 and Build Project1. (There are also menu items called Compile All Projects and Build All Projects, but I'll save that discussion for Hour 19 when I discuss project groups.) Let's take these in order of simplest to most complex (from the compiler's perspective).

The Compile Unit option is one I really like. This feature causes C++Builder to compile the current unit in the Code Editor and report any errors and warnings. This is the fastest way to check for errors in your code. C++Builder only compiles the unit—it doesn't perform a link. The purpose of the Compile Unit option is to check your code for syntax errors as quickly as possible. Because the link phase takes extra time, the Compile Unit option skips that step.

The Make option compiles any units that have changed since the last compile just as the Compile Unit options does, but it also links the entire project. Naturally, this takes slightly longer than the Compile Unit option. Use the Make option when you want to be sure the program will compile and link but you don't want to run the program.

> The first time you make or run a project always takes longer than subsequent makes. This is because the incremental linker is building all the files it needs to do its thing. Subsequent links are much faster, usually only taking a second or two.

The keyboard shortcut for Make is Ctrl+F9 and the shortcut for Run is F9. Unfortunately, there are no keyboard shortcuts for Compile Unit and Build. The keyboard shortcuts for the IDE's menu are shown to the right of each menu item. To see the available shortcuts, simply browse the C++Builder main menu.

The Build option takes the longest to perform. This option compiles every unit in the project regardless of whether it has changed since the last build. After compiling all units, C++Builder links the entire project. So far we have been letting C++Builder add units to our projects. Further on down the road you might have to do some hand editing of your source files to add headers and other needed directives. You might even end up editing the makefile. From time to time your project might get goofed up (we all make mistakes). Performing a Build will bring everything up to date so you can better sort out any problems you might be running into. Sometimes a Build resolves compiler and linker errors without the need for you to do anything further. Another thing to remember is that a Build rebuilds all the incremental linker files that results in the build taking longer to complete.

Any time you get unexpected (out of the ordinary) compiler or linker errors, first try a Build. It could just be that something is out of sync, and a Build might cure it. If performing a Build doesn't fix the problem, you'll have to go to work figuring out where the problem lies.

Regardless of the method chosen to compile the project, if errors are detected, the compile status dialog box reports There are errors. and lists the number of errors that were detected as well as any warnings. Figure 10.8 shows the compile status dialog box after detecting errors.

FIGURE 10.8

The Compile Status dialog box shows warnings and errors.

Compiler warnings point out suspicious code that might be incorrect. Take this code, for example:

```
void _ _fastcall TForm1::Button1Click(TObject *Sender)
{
  int x;
  Label1->Caption = "Hello there!";
}
```

When this code compiles, the compiler issues a warning that says:

```
'x' is declared but never used.
```

This warning is telling you that you declared a variable called x but you never actually did anything with the variable. The code isn't quite right from the compiler's perspective so a warning is issued, but the application is not prevented from being compiled.

Compiler errors, on the other hand, indicate problems in your code that are severe enough that the compiler cannot continue compiling the application.

10

The compile status dialog box can be turned off if you don't want to view the compiler progress. You can turn the compile status dialog off through the Environment Options dialog box (Preferences page).

After you click OK to dismiss the compile status dialog box, the Code Editor comes to the top with the first error line highlighted. The message window at the bottom of the Code Editor is displayed, and the errors and warnings are listed there. After a successful Compile Unit, Make, or Build you can immediately run the program via the Run button if you choose.

The Object Inspector

An integral part of the C++Builder IDE is the Object Inspector. This window works in conjunction with the Form Designer to aid in the creation of components. I'm going to discuss the Form Designer in Hour 13, "Working with the Form Designer," but before I do I want to talk a little about the Object Inspector.

The Object Inspector is where you set the design-time properties that affect how the component acts at runtime. The Object Inspector has three main areas:

- The Component Selector
- The Properties page
- The Events page

You have been using the Object Inspector quite a bit up to this point, so I'll review what you already know and show you a few things you don't know.

The Component Selector

The Component Selector is a drop-down combo box that is located at the top of the Object Inspector window. The Component Selector allows you to choose a component to view or modify.

Usually the quickest way to select a component is by clicking the component on the form. Choosing the component from the Component Selector is convenient if the component you are looking for is hidden beneath another component or is off the visible area of the form.

The Component Selector displays the name of the component and the class from which it is derived. For example, a memo component named Memo would appear in the Component Selector as

Memo: TMemo

The class name doesn't show up in the drop-down list of components, but only in the top portion of the Component Selector. To select a component, click the drop-down button to reveal the list of components and then click the one you want to select.

The Component Selector shows only the components available on the current form and the name of the form itself. Other forms and their components aren't displayed until made active in the Form Designer.

After you select a component in the Component Selector, the component is selected on the form as well. The Properties and Events tabs change to display the properties and events for the selected component. (Remember that a form is a component, too.) Figure 10.9 shows the Object Inspector with the Component Selector list displayed.

FIGURE 10.9

The Component Selector list.

The Properties Page

The Properties page of the Object Inspector displays all the design-time properties for the currently selected component. The Properties page has two columns. The Property column is on the left side of the Properties page and shows the property name. The Value column is on the right side of the Properties page and is where you type or select the value for the property.

If the component selected has more properties than will fit in the Object Inspector, a scrollbar is provided so you can scroll up or down to locate other properties.

> If you have multiple components selected on the form, the Object Inspector shows all the properties that those components have in common. You can use this feature to modify the properties of several components at one time. For example, to change the width of several components at one time, you can select all the components and then modify the Width property in the Object Inspector. When you press Enter or move to another property, all the components you selected will have their Width property modified.

Figure 10.10 shows the Object Inspector when a Memo component is selected.

In Hour 8, "Class Frameworks and the Visual Component Model," I discussed how properties can be integer values, enumerations, sets, other objects, strings, and other types. The Object Inspector deals with each property according to the data type of the property. C++Builder has several built-in property editors to handle data input for the property. In the case of complex properties, the property editor might be a dialog that is displayed asking for further input. In the case of simple integer properties, the property editor is contained within the Value column of the Object Inspector for that property. Because you

10

are typing a simple value in the Object Inspector, you don't necessarily even know a property editor is at work. Rest assured that each property knows what it needs to do to present you with the correct property editor. You will see different types of property editors as you are introduced to new components and new properties. For example, the Top property accepts an integer value. Because an int is a basic data type, no special handling is required, so the property editor is fairly basic. The property editor for this type of property allows you to type a value directly in the Value column for integer properties such as Top, Left, Width, and Height.

FIGURE 10.10

The Object Inspector showing Memo *component properties.*

In most cases, the property editor does parameter checking for any properties in which you can enter an integer value. The Width property, for instance, cannot be a negative number. If you attempt to enter a negative number for the Width of a control, C++Builder forces the width to the minimum allowed for that control (usually 0). If you enter a string value for a property that expects an integer value, C++Builder displays an error message. It is the job of the property editor to do parameter checking.

In many cases, the property editor for the property contains a list of items from which you can choose. Properties that have an enumeration or Boolean value as their base data type fall into this category. When you select the property in the Object Inspector, you will see a drop-down button on the right side of the Value column. Clicking this button displays the list of possible values.

If you double-click the Value column for Boolean or enumeration properties, the property editor cycles through the possible choices. To quickly change a `bool` property, for instance, simply double-click its value. Because the only choices are `true` and `false`, double-clicking the value has the effect of toggling the property's value.

If you look closely at the Object Inspector, you will see that some properties have a plus sign preceding the property name. Properties that are sets and properties that are objects (classes) both have the plus sign in front of their name. (I discussed sets in Hour 8 in the section, "Properties.") The plus sign indicates that the property node can be expanded to show the set or, in the case of properties that are objects, the properties of that object. To expand a node, double-click on the Property column for that property (on the property name) or choose Expand from the Object Inspector context menu. To collapse the node, double-click it again or choose Collapse from the Object Inspector context menu.

To see an example of a set, choose a form and then double-click the `BorderIcons` property. The node expands and you see four members of the set. You can turn on or off any of the four members as needed.

In the case of properties that are objects (instances of a VCL class), you have two choices in editing the property. First, you can click the Value column for the property and then click the button to the right side of the value. This button is indicated by an ellipsis (…) on its face. Clicking this button invokes the property editor for that particular control. For example, click the `Font` property and then click the ellipsis button. The Choose Font dialog box is displayed so that you can select the font. The second way you can edit this type of property is by expanding the property node. The property's properties (yes, it's true) are displayed, and you can edit them just like any other property. Again, locate the `Font` property and double-click it. The `TFont` properties are displayed. You can now modify the font's `Height`, `Color`, `Name` or other properties.

The Events Page

The Events page lists all the events that the component is designed to handle. Using the Events page is pretty basic. In order to create an event handler for an event, you simply double-click in the Value column next to the event you want to handle. When you do, C++Builder creates an event-handling function for you with all the parameters needed to handle that event. The Code Editor is displayed, and the cursor is placed in the event

10

handler. All you have to do is start typing code. The name of the function is generated based on the Name property of the component and the event being handled. If, for instance, you had a button named OKBtn and were handling the OnClick event, the function name generated would be OKBtnClick().

You can let C++Builder generate the name of the event-handling function for you or you can provide the function name for C++Builder to use. To provide the function name yourself, type the name in the Value column next to the event and press Enter. The Code Editor is displayed, and so is the event-handling function, complete with the name you supplied.

> C++Builder removes any empty event handlers when you run, compile, or save a unit. For example, let's say you created an event handler for the OnCreate event but didn't type any code. The next time you run, compile, or save the unit C++Builder removes the event handler you just created because it doesn't contain any code. This is the way C++Builder is designed and makes perfect sense, but can be a bit puzzling if you aren't aware of what is going on. If you don't want C++Builder to remove the event handler, either type code right away or type a comment line so that the event handler won't be removed.

After you have created an event-handling function for a component, you can use that event handler for any component that handles the same event. Sometimes it's convenient to have several buttons use the same OnClick event, for instance. To take it a step further, you might have a main menu item, a pop-up menu item, and a toolbar button all use the same OnClick handler. You will learn to appreciate this kind of code reuse as you gain experience with C++Builder. Even though you are dealing with three different components, they can still share a common OnClick handler.

The Value column of the Events page contains a drop-down button that can be used to display a list of all event handlers compatible with the current event. All you have to do is choose an event from the list.

Summary

The C++Builder IDE can be intimidating until you get familiar with it. If you learn it a little at a time, it's not nearly so daunting. In this hour you learned more about the various pieces that make up the C++Builder IDE. You also learned about how projects are used to create an executable file. As you work more with the IDE, the things that seem complex now soon become second nature.

Workshop

The Workshop contains quiz questions to help you solidify your understanding of the material covered and exercises to provide you with experience in using what you have learned. The answers to the quiz questions are provided following the questions. The exercises are given for you to work out and code on your own.

Q&A

Q The C++Builder toolbar doesn't have buttons for the features I use most often. Can I change the toolbar?

A Absolutely. The toolbar is fully customizable. You can add or remove buttons as you see fit.

Q Why does C++Builder use the term *unit* to refer to a source file?

A C++Builder uses the term *unit* because C++Builder was created from Borland's Delphi. Delphi is based on Pascal, and *unit* is a Pascal term for a source file.

Quiz

1. How do you invoke the Toolbar Editor dialog box?
2. How do you remove buttons from the toolbar?
3. What's the easiest way to place a component in the center of the form?
4. When using the Object Inspector, how can you enumerate the choices for a particular property?

Answers

1. Right-click on the toolbar and choose Customize from the toolbar context menu.

2. Drag unwanted buttons off the bottom of the toolbar and drop them.

3. Double-click the component's button in the Component palette.

4. Double-click the value column next to the property name in the Object Inspector.

Exercises

1. Remove the Pause, Step Over, and Trace Into buttons from the C++Builder toolbar. Add Cut, Copy, and Paste buttons to the toolbar.

2. Reset the toolbar to its default settings.

3. Spend some time looking over the components on each page of the Component palette. Place any components you are curious about on a form and experiment with them.

4. Start a new application. Place several components on the form. Click on each component and observe the properties for each component in the Object Inspector.

HOUR 11

C++Builder Forms

In this hour I spend some time explaining C++Builder forms. You have seen several forms in action as you have worked through this book, but you need some more background information on forms, so I'll cover that now.

Main Window Forms

Forms are the main building block of a C++Builder application. Every GUI application has at least one form that serves as the main window. The main window form might be just a blank window, it might have controls on it, or it might have a bitmap displayed on it. In a typical Windows program, your main window would have a menu. It might also have decorations such as a toolbar or a status bar. Just about anything goes when creating the main window of your application. Each application is unique, and each has different requirements.

Dialog Box Forms

Forms are also used where traditional Windows programs use dialog boxes. In fact, to the user there is no difference between a C++Builder form acting as a dialog box and a true dialog box. Dialog boxes usually have several traits that distinguish them from ordinary windows:

- Dialog boxes are not usually resizable. They usually perform a specific function, and sizing of the dialog box is neither useful nor desirable.
- Dialog boxes almost always have an OK button. Some dialog boxes have a button labeled Close that accomplishes the same thing. Simple dialog boxes like an About dialog box typically have only the OK button.
- Dialog boxes might also have a Cancel button and a Help button.
- Dialog boxes typically have only the system close button on the title bar. They do not usually have minimize and maximize buttons.
- Some dialog boxes are *tabbed dialog boxes* that display several tabs from which the user can choose. When a tab is clicked, a different page of the dialog box is displayed.
- The Tab key can be used to move from one control to the next in most dialog boxes.

There are certainly exceptions to every rule. Most dialog boxes have the usual characteristics, but some dialog boxes perform specialty tasks and as such, depart from the norm in one way or another.

Dialog boxes in C++Builder are slightly different from those in other programming environments. First let's take a look at how other programming environments handle dialog boxes; then we'll look at how they are implemented in C++Builder.

Dialog Boxes in Traditional Windows Programs

In a traditional Windows program (one written in C, or with one of the C++ frameworks), a dialog box is created with a dialog box editor. In most cases, the dialog box editor is a visual tool that works somewhat like the C++Builder Form Designer. When the user is done designing the dialog box, the visual representation of the dialog box is converted into a dialog box definition in a resource script file. (A *resource script* is a text file that is later compiled into a binary resource file by the resource compiler.) I discuss resource script files in more detail in Hour 18, "Adding Functions, Data Members, and Resources," in the section "Using Resource Files." I do not, however, discuss dialog resources simply because they are not widely used in C++Builder programming. For a complete discussion of dialog resources, I would recommend *Programming Windows 95* by Charles Petzold (Microsoft Press).

Usually all the application's dialog box definitions are contained in a single resource script file that has a filename extension of .RC. At some point in the program-creation process, the resource script is compiled into a .RES file (the binary resource file), which then gets linked to the .EXE by the resource linker. At runtime the dialog box is displayed either modally or modelessly (see Note box), depending on the dialog box's intended purpose. When the dialog box is executed, Windows loads the dialog box resource from the executable file, builds the dialog box, and displays it.

A *modal* dialog box is one that must be closed before the user can continue using the application. The main window of an application is disabled while this type of dialog box is open. Most dialog boxes are modal. The compile status dialog box in C++Builder is an example of a modal dialog box.

A *modeless* dialog box is one that allows the user to continue to work with the application while the dialog box is displayed. The Find dialog box in some word-processing programs is an example of a modeless dialog box.

11

Now, with that background information on how dialog boxes are handled in a traditional Windows program, let's take a look at how C++Builder handles dialog boxes.

Dialog Boxes in C++Builder

In C++Builder, dialog boxes are simply another form. You create a dialog box just like you do a main window form or any other form. To prevent the dialog box from being sized, you can change the BorderStyle property to bsDialog or bsSingle. If you use bsDialog, your dialog box will have only the close box button on the title bar, which is traditional for dialog boxes. Other than that, you don't have to do anything special to get a form to behave like a dialog box. All C++Builder forms have tabbing support built-in. You can set the tab order by altering the TabOrder property of the individual controls on the dialog box.

C++Builder creates a form file (DFM) for every form you create and places it in your project's directory. The form file is a binary resource file that can't be read by mere humans. When you choose the View as Text context menu item, C++Builder converts the binary resource to readable form. When you switch back to the View as Form option, C++Builder recompiles the form file to implement any changes you have made.

A C++Builder dialog box (any C++Builder form, actually) is modal or modeless depending on how it is displayed. All forms in C++Builder are instances of the Visual Component Library (VCL) TForm class. To execute a modal dialog box, you call the ShowModal() method of TForm. To create a modeless dialog box, you call the Show() method. I'll discuss the TForm class in detail starting with the section, "Key Properties for Forms."

If you need to refresh your memory, methods, properties, and events are discussed in more detail in Hour 8, "Class Frameworks and the Visual Component Model." TForm is covered in Hour 9, "Exploring the VCL."

Let's add an About box to the multiple-forms project we created in Hour 10. If you don't have that project open, choose File, Open from the main menu, or click the Open button on the toolbar and locate the file (you should have saved it with the project name of Multiple).

C++Builder keeps a list of the files and projects you have used most recently. Choose File, Reopen to view the MRU (most recently used) list. The MRU list is divided into two parts. The top part shows the projects you have used most recently, and the bottom part shows the individual files that you have used most recently. Just click one of the items to reopen that project or file.

First you'll add a button to the form that will display the About dialog box:

1. Bring the main form into view. Choose the button component from the Component palette and drop a button on the form.

2. Arrange the two buttons that are now on the form to balance the look of the form.

3. Change the Name property of the new button to AboutButton and the Caption property to About.... An ellipsis following a menu item's text is traditionally used to indicate to the user that selecting the menu item displays a dialog box.

4. Double-click the AboutButton you just created on the form. The Code Editor is displayed with the cursor placed in the event-handler function. Add this line of code at the cursor:

```
AboutBox->ShowModal();
```

You haven't actually created the About box yet, but when you do, name it `AboutBox` so you know enough to type the code that will display the About box.

Now you'll create the dialog box itself:

1. Create a new form (click the New Form button on the toolbar). Size the form to the size of a typical About box (roughly the same size as the form named `SecondForm` that you created in Hour 10, "Exploring the C++Builder IDE").

2. Change the `Name` property to `AboutBox` and change the `Caption` property to `About This Program`.

3. Locate the `BorderStyle` property (it's just above `Caption`) and change it to `bsDialog`.

4. Now add three text labels to the box. Edit the labels so that the About box resembles the one in Figure 11.1. (You can type any text you want, of course.) You can leave the default names C++Builder generates for the text labels' `Name` properties. You aren't actually going to do anything with the `Name` property, so you don't need a descriptive name.

FIGURE 11.1

The About box with text labels added.

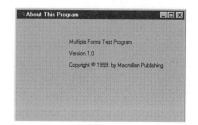

11

 The copyright symbol (©) has an ASCII value of 169 in most typefaces. To create the copyright symbol, press and hold the Alt key and type the numbers `0169` on the numeric keypad (be sure Num Lock is on). When you let go of the Alt key, the copyright symbol appears. You can insert the ASCII value of any character this way. You must type all four numbers, though. For example, the ASCII value of a capital A is 65. To insert an A, you would have to hold down Alt and type `0065` on the numeric keypad.

Next you'll add an icon to the About box:

1. Click the Additional tab on the Component palette and choose the `Image` component. Place the component to the left of the text on the form.

2. Locate the `AutoSize` property for the `Image` component and change it to `true`.

3. Locate the `Picture` property and double-click the Value column. The Picture Editor dialog box is displayed.

4. Click the Load button. In the File Open dialog box, navigate to the `\Borland Shared Files\Images\Icons` directory and choose an icon from the icon files listed. Click Open. The icon you selected is displayed in the Picture Editor window. Click OK to close the Picture Editor. The icon is displayed on the form. Note that the `Image` component has sized itself to the size of the icon.

5. Position the icon as desired.

At this point you need an OK button on the form. Let's branch out a little and take a look at a new component:

1. If you're not already there, click the Additional tab on the Component palette. Select the `BitBtn` component and place a `BitBtn` on the form near the bottom and centered horizontally.

2. Locate the `Kind` property and change it to `bkOK`. Notice that a green check mark has appeared on the button, and the `Caption` property has changed to `OK`. That's all you have to do with the button. The `BitBtn` component already includes code to close the form when the OK button is clicked.

Add one final touch to the About box:

1. Locate the Bevel button (on the Additional tab in the Component palette) and click it.

2. Move to the form, but rather than clicking on the form drag a box around the three text labels. The `Bevel` component appears when you stop dragging. If you didn't get it quite right, you can resize or reposition the component.

3. Locate the `Shape` property and change it to `bsFrame`. You now have a 3D frame around the static text.

Your form should now look something like the one shown in Figure 11.2. Save the unit (File, Save) and give it the name `About`.

Are you ready to compile and run the program? Not yet. You need to tell the main form to `#include` the About unit:

1. Switch to the Code Editor (press F12) and select the `Main.cpp` tab.

2. Choose File, Include Unit Hdr from the main menu.

3. Choose the About unit from the Include Unit dialog box and click OK.

FIGURE 11.2

The finished About box.

Now you're ready to run the program. Click the Run button. When the program runs, click the About button on the main form, and the About dialog box is displayed. Note that the dialog box is modal (you can't go back to the main window while the dialog box is displayed) and that it cannot be sized. The About form behaves in every way like a regular Windows dialog box.

> The common dialog box classes (TOpenDialog, TSaveDialog, TFontDialog, and so on) do not represent dialog boxes created as C++Builder forms. Windows provides these dialog boxes as a set of common dialog boxes that all Windows applications can use (the actual dialog boxes are contained in a file called COMDLG32.DLL). The VCL dialog box classes encapsulate the common dialog boxes to make using them easier.

C++Builder includes several prebuilt forms that you can choose from to help you build dialog boxes as quickly as possible. The Forms tab of the Object Repository contains the prebuilt forms.

Secondary Windows Versus Dialog Boxes

A *secondary window* is a form that you display from your main window. So when is a form a secondary window and when it is a dialog box? When it really comes down to it, there is no difference between a secondary window and a dialog box in C++Builder. You might have windows that resemble dialog boxes, and you might have other windows that resemble a traditional window. In the grand scheme of things, they all are forms and it doesn't make much sense to differentiate between the terms *dialog box* and *secondary form*. It's all the same in the end. In traditional programming environments, you have to specifically create a dialog box or specifically create a secondary window in an application. C++Builder frees you from that restriction and allows you to treat both dialog boxes and windows exactly the same.

The Multiple Document Interface Model

So far you have built only *single document interface* (SDI) applications. An SDI application has a single main window and typically displays dialog boxes as needed, but does not otherwise display child windows. (A main window that displays secondary windows is said to be a *parent window*. A *child window* is a window that is owned by the parent window. If the parent window is destroyed, the child window is also destroyed.)

Some programs follow the *multiple document interface* (MDI) model. MDI applications consist of a main window (the MDI parent) and child windows (the MDI children). Examples of programs that use the MDI model are Windows System Configuration Editor (SYSEDIT) and the Windows 3.1 Program Manager.

One of the most obvious characteristics of the MDI model is that the MDI child windows are confined to the parent. You can drag the child windows within the parent window, but you cannot drag them outside the parent. MDI applications almost always have a Window item on their main menu. This menu usually contains items named Cascade and Tile, which allow you to display the MDI child windows in either a cascaded or tiled arrangement. When an MDI child is minimized, its icon is contained within the MDI parent's frame. When a regular (non-MDI) child window is minimized, its icon is placed on the Windows desktop.

To create an MDI application in C++Builder, you must set the main form's FormStyle property to fsMDIForm. Each of the MDI child windows must have the FormStyle property set to fsMDIChild. Aside from that restriction, there is very little to creating an MDI application in C++Builder. You simply create the main window form and one or more forms to be used as child windows, and you're off and running.

Key Properties for Forms

The TForm class has a lot of properties. Some of these properties are obscure and rarely used; others are widely used. I'll touch on the most widely used properties here. I won't include obvious properties like Color, Left, Top, Width, and Height unless they have a particular feature you should be aware of.

Published Properties

Published properties are displayed in the Object Inspector. They can be set at design time through the Object Inspector and also at runtime (when the program is executing) via code. Let's take the Top property, for example. The following code sets the Top property to the value 20 at runtime:

```
Top = 20;
```

When this code executes, the form will move on the screen because of the change in the value of the Top property.

Properties can be read at runtime as well. Let's say you want to perform some calculation based on the position of the form. In that case you would first read the Top property to retrieve its value:

```
int t = Top;  // 't' now contains the value of the Top property
```

When I say "read the Top property" I mean that the property's value is retrieved, and in this case, stored in a variable.

ActiveControl—This property is used to set the control that will have focus when the form is activated. For instance, you might want a particular edit control to have focus when a dialog box form is displayed. At design time the Value column for the ActiveControl property contains a list of components on the form. You can choose one of the components from this list to make that component the active control when the form is first displayed.

AutoScroll, HorzScrollBar, and VertScrollBar—Together they control the scrollbars for a form. If AutoScroll is set to true (the default), scrollbars automatically appear when the form is too small to display all its components. The HorzScrollBar and VertScrollBar properties each have several properties of their own that control the scrollbar operations.

BorderStyle—This property indicates what type of border the form will have. The default value is bsSizeable, which creates a window that can be sized. Non-sizable styles include bsDialog and bsNone.

ClientWidth and ClientHeight—They specify the client area width and height rather than the full form's width and height when used. (The *client area* of the form is the area inside of the borders and below the title bar and menu bar.) Use these properties when you want the client area to be a specific size and the rest of the window to adjust as necessary. Setting the ClientWidth and ClientHeight properties makes automatic changes to the Width and Height properties.

Constraints—This property is used to set the maximum and minimum width and height of the form. xe "forms:properties:Font" xe "Font property (TForm class)" Simply set the MaxHeight, MaxWidth, MinHeight, and MinWidth values as desired and the form will conform to those constraints.

DefaultMonitor—This property determines which monitor this form will appear on in a multi-monitor environment (such as Windows 98).

11

DockSite—This property determines whether the form will act as a dock site for dockable components.

Font—This property specifies the font that the form uses. The important thing to understand here is that the form's font is inherited by any components placed on the form. This also means that you can change the font used by all components at one time by changing just the form's font. If an individual control's font had been manually changed, that control's font will not be changed when the main form's font changes.

FormStyle—This property is usually set to fsNormal. If you want a form to always be on top, use the fsStayOnTop style. MDI forms should use the fsMDIForm style and MDI child forms should use the fsMDIChild style. MDI forms and MDI child windows are discussed earlier in this chapter, in the section "The Multiple Document Interface Model."

HelpContext and HelpFile—The HelpContext property is used to set the help context ID for a form. If context help is enabled for a form, the Windows Help system will activate when the F1 key is pressed. The context ID is used to tell the Help system which page in the help file to display. The HelpFile property is the name of the help file that will be used when F1 is pressed.

Icon—This property sets the icon that is used on the title bar for the form when the form is displayed at runtime, and also when the form is minimized. In some cases, setting this property has no effect. For instance, when the FormStyle is set to fsDialog, the Icon property is ignored.

KeyPreview—When KeyPreview is True, the form's OnKeyPress and OnKeyDown events will be generated when a key is pressed in any component on the form. Ordinarily, forms don't receive keyboard events when a component on the form has focus.

Menu—Use the Menu property to assign the main menu for the form. You must first have placed a MainMenu component on the form.

PopupMenu—This property is used to specify a popup menu that will be displayed when the user right clicks on the form. You must first have placed a PopupMenu component on the form.

Position—This property determines the size and position of the form when the form is initially displayed. The three basic choices are poDesigned, poDefault, and poScreenCenter. poDesigned causes the form to be displayed in the exact position it was in when it was designed. poDefault allows Windows to set the size and position according to the usual Windows Z-ordering algorithm. (Z-ordering is what Windows uses to decide where it displays a new window on the screen. If the new window does not have specific placement information, it will be displayed just below and to the right of the last window displayed on the screen.) The poScreenCenter option causes the form to be displayed in the center of the screen each time it is shown.

Visible—This property controls whether the form is initially visible. This property is not particularly useful at design time, but at runtime it can be read to determine whether the form is currently visible. It can also be used to hide or display the form.

WindowState—This property can be read to determine the form's current state (maximized, minimized, or normal). It can also be used to indicate how the form should initially be displayed. Choices are wsMinimized, wsMaximized, and wsNormal.

Runtime-Only Properties

Runtime-only properties can be accessed only at runtime through code. Runtime properties, are also called public properties. They are not displayed in the Object Inspector at design time as published properties are. As such, the only way to modify a runtime property is by writing code. The following are the most commonly used TForm runtime properties.

ActiveMDIChild—When read, the ActiveMDIChild property returns a pointer to the currently active MDI child window. This property is read-only. If no MDI child is currently active or if the application is not an MDI application, ActiveMDIChild returns NULL.

Canvas—The form's canvas represents the drawing surface of the form. The Canvas property gives you access to the form's canvas. By using the Canvas property you can draw bitmaps, lines, shapes, or text on the form at runtime. Most of the time you will use a Label component to draw text on a form, an Image component to display graphics, and a Shape component to draw shapes. However, there are times when you need to draw on the canvas at runtime and the Canvas property allows you to do that. The Canvas property can also be used to save an image of the form to disk.

ClientRect—The ClientRect property contains the top, left, right, and bottom coordinates of the client area of the form. This is useful in a variety of programming situations. For instance, you might need to know the client area's width and height in order to place a bitmap on the center of the form.

Handle—This property returns the window handle (HWND) of the form. Use this property when you need the window handle to pass to a Windows API function.

ModalResult—This property is used to indicate how a modal form was closed. If you have a dialog box that has OK and Cancel buttons, you can set ModalResult to mrOK

11

when the user clicks the OK button, and to mrCancel when the user clicks the Cancel button. The calling form can then read ModalResult to see which button was clicked to close the form. Other possibilities include mrYes, mrNo, and mrAbort.

Owner—This property is a pointer to the owner of the form. The owner of the form is the object that is responsible for deleting the form when the form is no longer needed. The parent of a component, on the other hand, is the window (a form or another component) that acts as the container for the component. In the case of a main form, the application object is both the owner of the form and the parent of the form. In the case of components, the owner would be the form, but the parent could be another component, such as a panel.

Parent—This property is a pointer to the parent of the form. See the previous section about Owner for an explanation of Owner versus Parent.

Form Methods

Forms are components, too. As such, forms have many methods in common with components. Common methods include Show(), ShowModal(), and Invalidate(), to name just a few. There are some methods, however, that are specific to forms. As before, I'll only discuss the most commonly used methods.

BringToFront()—This method causes the form to be brought to the top of all other forms in the application.

Close() and CloseQuery()—The Close method closes a form after first calling CloseQuery to ensure that it's okay to close the form. The CloseQuery function in turn calls the OnCloseQuery event handler. If the bool variable passed to the OnCloseQuery handler is set to false, the form is not closed. If it is set to true, the form closes normally. You can use the OnCloseQuery event handler to prompt the user to save a file that needs saving and to control whether a form can close.

Print()—This method prints the contents of the form. Only the client area of the form is printed, not the caption, title bar, or borders. Print() is handy for quick screen dumps of a form.

ScrollInView()—This method scrolls the form so that the specified component is visible on the form.

SetFocus()—This method activates the form and brings it to the top. If the form has components, the component specified in the ActiveControl property will receive input focus (see the ActiveControl property in the section "Published Properties").

Show() and ShowModal()—Both of these methods display the form. The Show() method displays the form as modeless, so other forms can be activated while the form is visible. The ShowModal() method executes the form modally. A modal form must be dismissed before the user can continue to use the application.

MDI Methods

Several form methods deal specifically with MDI operations. The ArrangeIcons() method arranges the icons of any minimized MDI children in an MDI parent window. The Cascade() method cascades all non-minimized MDI child windows. The Tile() method tiles all open MDI child windows. The Next() method activates (brings to the top) the next MDI child in the child list, and the Previous() method activates the previous MDI child in the child list. The MDI methods apply only to MDI parent forms.

Form Events

Forms can respond to a wide variety of events. Some of the most commonly used are listed in the following sections.

OnActivate—This event occurs when the form is initially activated. The form might be activated as a result of its initial creation or when the user switches from one form to another. The Application object also has an OnActivate event that is generated when the user switches from another application to your application.

OnClose and OnCloseQuery—When an application is closed, the OnClose event is sent. OnClose calls the OnCloseQuery event to see if it is okay to close the form. If the OnCloseQuery event's CanClose parameter is false, the form is not closed.

OnCreate—This event occurs when the form is initially created. Only one OnCreate event will occur for any instance of a particular form. Use the OnCreate handler to perform any startup tasks that the form needs in order to operate.

OnDestroy—This event is the opposite of OnCreate. Use this event to clean up any memory a form allocates dynamically or to do other cleanup chores.

OnDragDrop—This event occurs when an object is dropped on the form. Respond to this event if your form supports drag-and-drop.

OnMouseDown, OnMouseMove, and OnMouseUp—Respond to these events in order to respond to mouse clicks and mouse movements on a form.

OnPaint—Occurs whenever the form needs repainting, which could happen for a variety of reasons. Respond to this event to do any painting that your application needs to display at all times. In most cases, individual components will take care of painting themselves, but in some cases you might need to draw on the form itself.

11

`OnResize`—This event is sent every time the form is resized. You might need to respond to this event to adjust components on the form or to repaint the form.

`OnShow`—This event occurs just before the form becomes visible. You could use this event to perform any processing that your form needs to do just before it is shown.

When a form is created, many events are generated. Likewise, when a form is destroyed, several events are generated. But in what order are these events generated? When a form is created, the following events occur in this order (the constructor and `AfterConstruction` virtual methods are listed in addition to the events):

    The form's constructor
    OnCreate event
    AfterConstruction method
    OnShow event
    OnActivate event

When a form is destroyed, the following events are generated in this order:

    OnCloseQuery event
    OnClose event
    BeforeDestruction method
    OnDestroy event
    The form's destructor

In most applications, keeping the order straight generally is not important. In some cases, however, it can be critical. Knowing the order in which the event handlers, the constructor, and the destructor are called can save you some frustration when you really need to know.

Summary

In this hour you learned more about forms. You found out how C++Builder deals with dialog boxes and other child windows. You'll create many forms in your C++Builder programs. Understanding how forms work is vital to programming in C++Builder.

Workshop

The Workshop contains quiz questions to help you solidify your understanding of the material covered and exercises to provide you with experience in using what you have learned.

Q&A

Q What do I need to do in order for my application to be an MDI application?

A Just be sure that the main form has a FormStyle of fsMDIForm and that any MDI child forms have a FormStyle of fsMDIChild.

Q What's the difference between a dialog box and a child window in C++Builder?

A There is no real difference. A dialog box form might have certain traits such as a dialog box border rather than a sizing border; OK, Cancel, and Help buttons; and no minimize or maximize buttons. But a dialog box is still just a form like any other. A form might have the appearance of a dialog box or of a child window, but a form is just a form.

Quiz

11

1. What TForm method do you use to display a form modelessly?
2. What TForm method do you use to display a form modally?
3. What border style do you use to make a form behave as a traditional dialog box behaves?
4. What event do you respond to in order to perform processing before a form is displayed?

Answers

1. The Show() method is used to display a form modelessly.
2. The ShowModal() function is used to display a form modally.
3. To make a form behave as a traditional dialog box set the BorderStyle property to bsDialog.
4. Use the OnCreate event to perform processing before a form is displayed. You could also use the OnShow event.

Exercises

1. Create a new application. Set the main form's `Position` property to `poScreenCenter` and run the application. Note the position of the window. Now set the `Position` property to `poDefault`. Run the program again and note the position of the window on the screen.

2. Create a new application. Place a check box component on the main form. Generate an event handler for the `OnCloseQuery` event and enter this code in the event handler:

```
CanClose = CheckBox1->Checked;
```

   Run the program. Note that the form can only be closed when the check box is checked.

Hour 12

Writing an MDI Application

In this hour you will create your multiple document interface (MDI) application. The purpose of writing this application is to help solidify what you have learned about C++Builder up to this point. The application, called Picture Viewer, allows you to open, view, and save graphics files such as bitmaps, icons, and metafiles.

The Master Plan

Before you dive into creating the application, you need a master plan. Here's what you need to do in order to create the application:

1. Create the main window form (an MDI parent), including a menu.
2. Write code for the File, Open and File, and Save menu selections.
3. Write code for the Cascade, Tile, and Arrange All items on the Window menu.

4. Create the MDI child forms.

5. Create an About box.

6. Create a toolbar for the application.

7. Stand back and admire your work.

 Take time to develop a new application's design before starting the actual work. Taking a few minutes, hours, or even days to plan out your application before writing a line of code can save you time in the long run. There's nothing worse than having to start over on a program because your original design turned out to be flawed.

Step 1: Create the Main Window Form

First you'll create the main window form. The main window for an MDI application must have its `FormStyle` property set to `fsMDIForm`. You will also need to add a menu to the application, as well as File Open and File Save dialog boxes.

1. Start C++Builder and choose File, New Application from the main menu.

2. For the main form, change the `Name` property to `MainForm`.

3. Change the `Caption` property to `Picture Viewer`.

4. Change the `Height` to `450` and the `Width` to `575` (or other suitable values for your display resolution).

5. Change the `FormStyle` to `fsMDIForm`.

Okay, now you've got the main part of the form done. Next you'll add a menu to the form. Because I haven't discussed the Menu Designer yet, you'll take the easy route to creating the menu. To do that, you'll take advantage of a C++Builder feature that allows you to import a predefined menu.

1. Click the Standard tab of the Component palette and click the MainMenu button.

2. Drop a `MainMenu` component on the form. It doesn't matter where you drop it because the icon representing the menu is just a placeholder and won't show on the form at runtime. This is how non-visual components appear on a form (see Figure 12.1).

3. Change the `Name` property to `MainMenu`.

4. Double-click the MainMenu component. The Menu Designer is displayed. (We'll look at the Menu Designer in more detail in Hour 14, "Working with the Menu Designer.")

5. Place your cursor over the Menu Designer and click your right mouse button. Choose Insert from Template from the context menu. The Insert Template dialog box appears. Figure 12.1 shows the Insert Template dialog box with the Menu Designer behind it.

6. Choose MDI Frame Menu and click OK. The menu is displayed in the Menu Designer.

7. Click the system close box on the Menu Designer to close it.

FIGURE 12.1

The Menu Designer with the Insert Template dialog box open.

Now you should be back to the main form. Notice that you have a menu on the form. You can click on the top-level items to see the full menu. Don't click on any submenu items at this point—you'll do that in a minute. Notice that there are a lot of menu items. You won't need all them, but for now just leave the extra items where they are.

Now you need to prepare the File Open and File Save dialog boxes:

1. Click the Dialogs tab on the Component palette. Choose an OpenDialog component and place it on the form. The OpenDialog component's icon can be placed anywhere on the form.

2. Change the Name property of the Open dialog box to OpenDialog.

3. Change the Title property to Open an Image.

4. Add a SaveDialog component.

5. Change the Name property of the component to SaveDialog and the Title property to Save an Image.

Your form should now look like the one in Figure 12.2.

12

FIGURE 12.2

Adding the File Open and File Save dialog boxes to the main form.

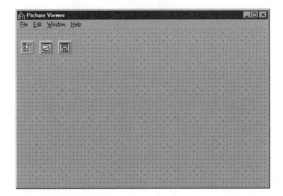

Step 2: Write Code for the File Open and File Save As Menu Items

Now write the code to implement the File, Open and File, and Save As menu items. C++Builder provides a slick way of writing menu handlers with a minimum amount of fuss. You haven't created the MDI child form yet, but you know enough about it to write the code for the menu handlers. Keep in mind that the application won't compile until you get through step 4. Here you go

1. On the main form, choose File, Open from the menu. An event handler is created for that menu item, and the Code Editor is displayed.

2. Type code so that the event handler looks like this:

```
void _ _fastcall TMainForm::Open1Click(TObject *Sender)
{
  if (OpenDialog->Execute())
  {
    TChild* child = new TChild(this);
    child->Image->Picture->LoadFromFile(OpenDialog->FileName);
    child->ClientWidth = child->Image->Picture->Width;
    child->ClientHeight = child->Image->Picture->Height;
    child->Caption = ExtractFileName(OpenDialog->FileName);
    child->Show();
  }
}
```

ANALYSIS This code first executes the File Open dialog box and gets a filename. If the Cancel button on the File Open dialog box is clicked, the function returns without doing anything further. If the OK button on the File Open dialog box is clicked, a new TChild object is created (TChild will be the name of the MDI child class you're going to create later). The image file is loaded into the Image component on the child form; then the MDI child's client area is sized to match the size of the image. Finally, the Caption property is set to the filename selected and the child window is displayed.

In step 2 the ExtractFileName() function is used to extract just the filename from the path and filename contained in the FileName property of the OpenDialog component. Related functions include ExtractFilePath(), ExtractFileDir(), ExtractFileDrive(), and ExtractFileExt(). These functions fall into an odd category. They are not technically part of the Visual Component Library (VCL), yet they come to C++Builder by way of the VCL. These functions are found in a Object Pascal "helper" unit called SysUtils. As I said, this unit is not technically part of the VCL, but it is used by the VCL so it is automatically included in C++Builder. Prior to C++Builder 4, these functions were not in the C++Builder help files. Thankfully, they are included in the help for C++Builder 4.

> Remember our earlier discussion about calling delete for all objects created with new? Notice that I appear to be violating that rule in the preceding code. In reality I am not, because VCL will take the responsibility of freeing the memory allocated for the MDI child windows. Notice that the single parameter in the TChild constructor is this. It tells VCL that the Owner of the MDI child is the MDI form window. When the MDI form is destroyed (when the application closes), it will be sure to delete all its MDI child objects.

Now you'll add the code for the File, Save As menu item. Perform these steps:

1. Press F12 to switch back to the form. Now choose File, Save As from the menu. The File, Save As event handler is displayed.

2. Type code so that the File, Save As event handler looks like this:

```cpp
void _ _fastcall TMainForm::SaveAs1Click(TObject *Sender)
{
  TChild* child = dynamic_cast<TChild*>(ActiveMDIChild);
  if (!child) return;
  if (SaveDialog->Execute())
  {
    child->Image->Picture->SaveToFile(SaveDialog->FileName);
  }
}
```

ANALYSIS The code for the File, Save As menu item is simple. The first two lines check to see whether an MDI child window is active. If, so the File Save dialog box is displayed. If the user clicks OK, the image is saved to disk using the TImage component's SaveToFile() method.

12

In the preceding code you also see a special C++ operator called dynamic_cast. dynamic_cast is used to cast a pointer of a base class to a pointer of a derived class. I discussed casting variables in Hour 4 in the section "Casting Variable Types" and base classes and derived classes in Hour 7, "C++ Classes and Object-Oriented Programming, Part II." Let me explain further. The ActiveMDIChild property returns a pointer to a TForm object. What we actually need in this case is a pointer to a TChild object (our MDI child class, derived from TForm). We need a TChild pointer so that we can access the Image property of the MDI child form.

If dynamic_cast is unable to perform the cast, it returns NULL. For example, you might be trying to cast a pointer you believe to be a TLabel pointer when in fact it is a TEdit pointer. In that case the cast will fail because a TLabel and a TEdit are two distinct types. Attempting to use a NULL pointer will result in an access violation, but the debugger will conveniently point out the offending line so you know exactly where the problem lies. This is much better than the alternative of attempting to use the old-style cast, where a bad cast could result in some random memory location being overwritten.

Before you go on, it would be a good idea to save the project. Choose File, Save All from the main menu. Save Unit1 (the default name C++Builder assigns to a new unit) as PVMain and the project as PictView.

Step 3: Write Code for the Window Menu

Now you'll add code to the Window menu. This part is simple:

1. Switch back to the form by pressing F12. Choose Window, Tile from the form's menu.

2. You only need to enter a single line of code for the event handler. The finished event handler will look like this:
```
void _ _fastcall TMainForm::Tile1Click(TObject *Sender)
{
  Tile();
}
```

3. Switch back to the form and repeat the process for Window, Cascade. The finished function looks like this:
```
void _ _fastcall TMainForm::Cascade1Click(TObject *Sender)
{
  Cascade();
}
```

4. Repeat the steps for the Window, Arrange All menu item. The single line of code to add for the function body is

```
ArrangeIcons();
```

Okay, now you're done with the main form. You can now move on to creating the MDI child form.

Step 4: Create the MDI Child Form

The MDI child form is surprisingly simple. In fact, you don't have to write any code at all.

1. Create a new form using the New Form button on the toolbar or by choosing File, New Form from the main menu.

2. Change the Name property to Child. The Caption property can be ignored because you will be setting the dialog box's caption at runtime (see step 2 under section "Step 2" earlier in the chapter).

3. Change the FormStyle property to fsMDIChild. This is necessary for the form to be treated as an MDI child window.

That's it for the form itself. Now you'll put an Image component on the form. The Image component will display the graphics file selected by the user.

1. Click the Additional tab on the Component palette. Click the Image button and place an Image component anywhere on the form.

2. Change the Name property to Image.

3. Change the Stretch property to true.

4. Change the Align property to alClient. The Image component expands to fill the client area of the form.

5. Choose File, Save and save the form's unit as PVChild.

6. Switch to the Code Editor (press F12 to toggle between the Form Designer and the Code Editor). Click the PVMain.cpp tab. Now choose File, Include Unit Hdr from the main menu, select the PVChild unit, and click OK. This is done so that the compiler is happy when we reference the TChild object.

The form is fairly unimpressive at this point. You should have what looks like an empty form with dashed lines around the perimeter. This is where the graphic image will appear at runtime.

12

You still have to create the About box, but right now you're probably eager to try the program out. Go ahead and click the Run button. After a while, the program is displayed. You can choose File, Open and open any graphics file (any file with a .BMP, a .WMF, or an .ICO extension, that is). Notice that the MDI child window sizes itself to the graphic it contains. Open several files and then try out the Cascade and Tile options under the Window menu. If you want, you can save a file with a different name using the File, Save As menu item.

When typing code described in text, it's almost inevitable that you will eventually mistype a portion of the code. In that case you will get one or more compiler errors. Unless you are an experienced C++ programmer, the cryptic compiler error messages will probably make little sense to you. If you get compiler errors, carefully compare your code to the code in the preceding sections. Some errors you will find immediately. Others can be hard to spot. Eventually, you will discover all the syntax errors and the code will compile. After you have worked with C++Builder a while, the compiler errors will start to make sense and you'll learn how to quickly spot and correct syntax errors in your code.

Step 5: Create the About Box

By now you should know enough about C++Builder to create the About box on your own. Create the About box so that it looks something like Figure 12.3. If you get stuck, you can jump back a few pages and review the steps you took to create the About box for the Multiple program in Hour 11. Feel free to make your About box as personalized as you like.

FIGURE 12.3

The About box for the Image Viewer application.

For applications you write, you can take advantage of long filenames. C++Builder has full support for long filenames. I use the 8.3 file-naming convention in this book for reasons related to electronic publishing.

After you have the box created, you can take these steps to call the dialog box from the menu:

1. Change the `Name` property to `AboutBox`.

2. Save the unit as `PVAbout`.

3. Switch to the `PVMain.cpp` tab in the Code Editor (press F12). Choose File, Include Unit Hdr from the main menu and include the `PVAbout` header.

4. Press F12 to switch back to the main form. Choose Help, About from the menu. You are taken to the Code Editor with the `OnClick` handler for the menu item displayed.

5. Add this line to the event handler:

```
AboutBox->ShowModal();
```

Click the Run button and try out the About item on the Help menu.

Step 6: Add a Toolbar

Next you'll add a toolbar to the application. Adding a toolbar is itself a multi-step process. First, you'll create the basic toolbar. Perform these steps:

1. From the Win32 tab on the Component palette, drop a `ToolBar` component on the form. Notice that the toolbar automatically positions itself at the top of the form. Change its `Name` property to `ToolBar`.

2. Change the `Flat` property to `true`. This gives the toolbar buttons a flat appearance until the cursor passes over them.

3. Change the `AutoSize` property to `true`. By setting this property to `true`, the toolbar will automatically size itself to the size of the toolbar buttons when you add them.

Adding Buttons to the Toolbar

Now you begin adding buttons to the toolbar; you will add several buttons and a few spacers. At first the buttons won't have glyphs on them, but you'll take care of that later. For now, follow these steps:

1. Right-click the toolbar and choose New Button. A button is placed on the toolbar. Change the button's `Name` property to `FileOpenBtn`. Set the `Hint` property to `Open`.

2. Right-click the toolbar again and add another button. Change this button's `Name` property to `FileSaveAsBtn`. Set the `Hint` property to `Save As`.

3. Right-click the toolbar again, but this time choose New Separator. A separator is added to the toolbar.

12

4. Add a button called HelpAboutBtn. Change its Hint property to About Picture Viewer.

5. Select all the toolbar buttons (use Shift+click to select all the buttons). Set the ShowHint property to true. All of the buttons' ShowHint property will be set at one time.

> Buttons and spacers added to the toolbar always appear to the right of the toolbar's last control. You can't insert a button at a specific location in the toolbar, but after a button or spacer is added, you can drag it to a different location on the toolbar. The existing buttons will make room for the new button.

Your form now looks like the one in Figure 12.4.

FIGURE 12.4

The Picture Viewer *main form after adding the toolbar.*

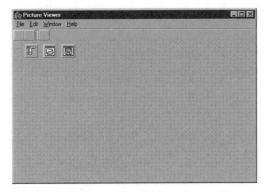

Making the Toolbar Buttons Functional

You now have a good start on the toolbar. The toolbar buttons don't do anything because you haven't assigned any event handlers to their OnClick events. You will do that next.

1. Click the FileOpenBtn (the first button). Select the Events page in the Object Inspector. Click the drop-down arrow next to the OnClick event and choose Open1Click. The button is now hooked up to the Open1Click event handler (the one you created earlier for the File Open menu item).

2. Repeat step 1 for the two remaining buttons, being careful to select the appropriate OnClick handler for each button (SaveAs1Click and About1Click, respectively).

Adding Bitmaps to the Toolbar Buttons

Obviously this toolbar is missing something. You need to add glyphs to the toolbar buttons. To do so, you must add an `ImageList` component to the form, following these steps:

1. Place an `ImageList` component on the form (you'll find it on the Win32 tab of the Component palette). Change the `Name` property to `ImageList`.

2. Right-click the `ImageList` component's icon on your form and choose ImageList Editor. The ImageList Editor is displayed (you can also double-click the ImageList icon on your form to display the ImageList Editor).

3. Click the Add button on the ImageList Editor. Navigate to the `Common Files\Borland Shared\Images\Buttons` directory. Select the `FILEOPEN.BMP` file and click Open.

   A message box appears and asks whether you want to separate the bitmap into two images. What is happening here is that the image list's `Width` and `Height` properties are both set to 16. The bitmap that you have selected is wider than 16 pixels, so it has to be split into two images or shrunk to fit. The button bitmaps that come with C++Builder are a single bitmap with two images. The first image is the normal button bitmap and the second image is for the disabled button. You will have the ImageList Editor split the bitmap into two images, and then you will delete the second part of the image. You delete the second part of the image because the ToolBar component automatically knows how to make a toolbar button look disabled. As such, the disabled button bitmaps are not needed.

4. Click Yes to have the ImageList Editor split the bitmap into two images. The ImageList Editor now shows two images. You need only the first of these images, so click on the second image (the disabled button image) and click the Delete button.

5. Click the Add button again. This time choose the `FILESAVE.BMP` file. Click Yes again when prompted to split the bitmap into two images. Click the disabled image for this bitmap and delete it. Figure 12.5 shows the image editor as it looks just before deleting the second image.

6. Repeat step 5 for the About button. Use any bitmap you like, but make certain you delete the extra bitmap after you add an image to the list. Also make sure that the images in the ImageList editor follow the order of the buttons on the toolbar. When you are done, you will have three images in the image list, numbering from 0 to 2.

7. Click OK to close the ImageList Editor.

12

FIGURE 12.5

The ImageList Editor after adding two images.

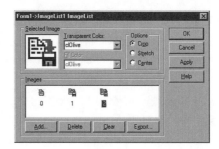

 You can select multiple images in the ImageList Editor's Add Images dialog box and add them all to the ImageList at one time.

Now you are ready to hook the image list to the toolbar. Click on the toolbar. Locate the Images property in the Object Inspector and choose ImageList from the drop-down list. If you did everything right, your buttons now have glyphs. You probably didn't notice, but each time you added a toolbar button, C++Builder automatically incremented the ImageIndex property for the button. Because you created the buttons and images in the same order, the glyphs on the buttons should be correct. If a button is wrong, you can either change the button's ImageIndex property or go back to the ImageList Editor and change the order of the images in the image list.

 To rearrange the images in an image list, drag them to a new position in the ImageList Editor.

Click the Run button and try out the program, especially the toolbar. Note that when you pause your mouse cursor over a toolbar button, that button's hint text is displayed in a ToolTip window. Figure 12.6 shows the Picture Viewer program running with several child windows open.

At this point the program is functional, but it isn't polished by any means. Still, for a 30-minute programming job it's not too bad! There are a few problems with the program as it stands right now. For one thing, you have a lot of extra menu items that you need to get rid of. I'll show you how to do that in Hour 14, "Working with the Menu Designer."

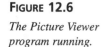

FIGURE 12.6

The Picture Viewer program running.

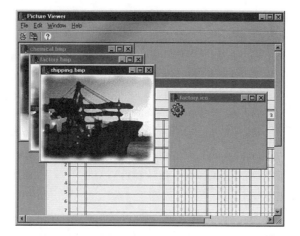

Tying up Loose Ends

There are two problems that I think you should deal with because they are easy to fix. First, did you notice that a blank MDI child window was displayed when the application started? That's because a C++Builder application automatically creates all forms when the application runs. In the case of an MDI child, that means the window is displayed when the application becomes visible. You are creating each MDI child form as needed, so you don't need to have C++Builder auto-create the form for you.

Fortunately, removing the MDI child window form from the auto-create list is easy. Choose Project, Options from the main menu. The Project Options dialog box is displayed. If necessary, click the Forms tab. The list of forms to auto-create is displayed. Click the child form and then click the > button. This removes the child form from the auto-create list and puts it in the Available forms list. Figure 12.7 shows the Project Options dialog box after moving the child form to the Available forms list.

12

FIGURE 12.7

The Project Options dialog box.

Now run the program again. This time the blank MDI child is not displayed.

> If you remove a form from the auto-create list, you must be sure to specifically create the form prior to using it. If you do not create the form, the pointer to the form is uninitialized (remember the pointer is automatically created by C++Builder). Attempting to use the pointer will result in an access violation or erratic program behavior. Once you remove a form from the auto-create list, it is your responsibility to make sure the form has been created before attempting to display it. Here's an example:
>
> ```
> TAboutBox* about = new TAboutBox(this);
> about->ShowModal();
> delete about;
> ```
>
> This code creates a form called TAboutBox dynamically, shows the form, and then deletes it immediately after the user closes the form.

Your application has one other problem you need to address. When you click the close button on one of the MDI windows, you will find that the window minimizes instead of closing. Believe it or not this is the standard behavior as prescribed by Microsoft. Standard behavior or not, it's weird, so you'll fix things so that clicking the close box actually closes the window (as any rational person would expect).

Bring up the child window form in the Form Designer. Be sure the form itself is selected and not the Image component on the form (choose the Child from the Component Selector at the top of the Object Inspector, if necessary). Double-click the Value column next to the OnClose event in the Object Inspector. Add a line of code to the event handler so that it looks like this:

```
void _ _fastcall
TForm1::FormClose(TObject *Sender, TCloseAction &Action)
{
  Action = caFree;
}
```

Setting the close action to caFree tells VCL to close the child window and to free the memory associated with the window. Now the child window will behave as it should when the close box is clicked. Again, run the program to prove that the program behaves as advertised.

Summary

In this hour you got a chance to apply some of what you have learned about C++Builder up to this point. While you didn't write a lot of code to create the Picture Viewer program you got a taste of what writing real-world applications with C++Builder is like. I encourage you to modify the Picture Viewer program in any way you want. You can add functionality, remove functionality, or otherwise modify the program as you see fit. Positively the best way to learn Windows programming with C++Builder is to take time to experiment.

Workshop

The Workshop contains quiz questions to help you solidify your understanding of the material covered and exercises to provide you with experience in using what you have learned.

Q&A

Q MDI apps look pretty cool. Is this the style I should use for my programs?

A That depends on the application. Any application that uses multiple views is a candidate for the MDI model. The MDI model appears to have fallen out of favor in recent years. Still, if your application can benefit from an MDI interface then by all means use MDI.

Q If Picture Viewer is an MDI application why didn't you have us set the About dialog's form style to fsMDIChild?

A Because the About dialog should be displayed as a standard dialog, and not as an MDI child window. An MDI application often displays regular dialog boxes in addition to the MDI child windows.

12

Quiz

1. Is it necessary to delete an MDI child object allocated with new?
2. Can MDI child windows be dragged outside of their parent?
3. What is the purpose of the ImageList component?
4. How do you specify that your program is an MDI application?

Answers

1. It is not necessary to delete MDI child objects created using operator new, provided this is passed in the child's constructor. VCL takes the responsibility for deleting a form's child objects.
2. No. MDI child windows are constrained to their parent's client area.
3. The ImageList component is used to store a list of same-sized images. Several components use image lists (ToolBar, TreeView, ListView, MainMenu, and so on).

4. To create an MDI application, set the main form's `FormStyle` property to `fsMDIForm`. Set the `FormStyle` for any child forms to `fsMDIChild`.

Exercises

1. Run the Picture Viewer program you created in this hour. Open several graphics files. Drag the MDI child windows around in the parent window. Attempt to move a child window outside the parent. What happens?

2. With the Picture Viewer program still running, minimize all windows. Drag the minimized windows to random locations on the screen and then choose Window, Arrange All from the menu.

Hour 13

Working with the Form Designer

As you know by now, C++Builder is heavily form based, a model that takes maximum advantage of the visual programming environment. In this hour you will explore the C++Builder Form Designer. The Form Designer enables you to place, select, move, resize, and align components, and much more. The Form Designer also enables you to size and position the form itself, add menus, and create specialized dialog boxes—everything you need to create the user interface part of a typical Windows program. To illustrate the use of the Form Designer, you will build an application that approximates the Windows Notepad program. Along the way you will gain valuable experience working with the Form Designer.

Placing Components

Placing a component on a form is a trivial act. You simply select the component you want from the Component palette and click on the form to place the component. When you click on the form, the component's upper-left corner is placed at the location you clicked. Notice that when you click a button on the Component palette, the button appears as pressed. When you click on the form to place the component, the button on the Component palette pops up again to indicate that the action is completed.

Most components can be sized. You can place a component on a form and then size it, or you can size the component at the same time you place it on the form. To size while placing the component, click on the form where you want the top-left corner to be placed and then drag with the mouse until the component is the desired size. When you release the mouse, the component will be placed at the size you specified.

Not all components can be sized by dragging. Nonvisual components, for instance, are represented on the form by an icon. Although you can click and drag to place a nonvisual component, the drag size will be ignored. Another example is a single-line edit component. The edit component can be placed by dragging, but only the drag width will be used. The drag height will be ignored because the height of a single-line edit component defaults to the height of a single-line edit control.

> If you change your mind while placing the control via the dragging method, you can press the Esc key on the keyboard before you release the mouse button to cancel the operation. The component's button will still be pressed on the Component palette, however, so you might need to click the Arrow button to return to component-selection mode.

Placing components is simple enough that we don't need to spend much time on the subject, so let's move on to other things.

The Form Designer Grid

The Form Designer has a built-in grid that aids in designing forms. By default, C++Builder shows the grid. The grid size is initially set to eight pixels horizontally and eight pixels vertically. When the Form Designer is set to display the grid, a dot is placed at the intersection of each grid point. Components placed on a form will snap to the nearest grid point. By *snap to* I mean that the component's top-left corner will automatically jump to the nearest grid point. This is an advantage because you frequently want a group of controls to be aligned either on their left, right, top, or bottom edge. When the Snap to Grid option is on, you merely get close enough to the correct location and the Form Designer will automatically place your component at the nearest grid point. This saves you time by sparing you from tweaking the individual component's size or position on the form.

The grid settings can be modified via the Preferences page of the Environment Options dialog box. Here you can change the grid size or turn off the Snap to Grid feature. You can also turn the grid display on or off. When the grid display is off, the grid is still active (assuming Snap to Grid is on), but the dots marking grid points are not drawn on the form.

Selecting Components

After you place a component on a form, you often have to select the component in order to modify it in some way. You might have to select a component to move it, change its properties, delete it, or copy the component to the clipboard.

To select a single component, just click on it. When you select the component, eight black sizing handles appear around the component to indicate that it is selected. (I'll discuss the sizing handles in a moment.) As soon as you select a component, the Object Inspector changes to show the properties and events for the control selected. To deselect a control, simply click on the form's background.

> Each component has a default event handler associated with it. When you double-click a component on a form, the Code Editor displays the default event handler for that component, ready for you to type code. In most cases, the default event handler is the OnClick handler. Exactly what happens when the component is double-clicked depends on how the component is designed. For example, in the case of the Image component, double-clicking displays the Picture Editor dialog box.

Selecting Multiple Components

A common practice in C++Builder programming is to select multiple components so that you can act on them as a group. This is accomplished in one of three ways:

- Shift+click with the keyboard and mouse.
- Drag with the mouse.
- Choose Edit, Select All from the main menu.

To select all components on the form, choose Edit, Select All from the main menu.

To use the Shift+click sequence, first select one control. Then press and hold the Shift key on the keyboard and click any other controls you want to include in the selection. Each control you click is bound by four gray boxes to indicate that it is part of the selection.

13

You can remove a control from the selection by continuing to hold the Shift key and again clicking on the component. In other words, the Shift+click sequence toggles a component's inclusion in the selection. To see how this works, place several components on a form, hold down the Shift key on the keyboard, and click several of the components. Each component you click will be added to the selection. If the component was already part of the selection, when you click on it, it will be removed from the selection.

If you click on a component that is part of a selection, nothing will happen. To select a single control that is currently part of a group selection, you need to first click on the form's background or press the Esc key to remove the group selection. Then you can click on the individual control you want to select.

Selecting Groups of Components

You can also select multiple controls by dragging a bounding rectangle around the controls to be selected. In fact, you don't have to drag the bounding rectangle completely around the components. You only have to touch a component with the bounding rectangle in order for it to be included in the selection.

When you have selected a group of controls, you can use the Shift+click technique explained earlier to add other controls from the selection or to remove controls from the selection. For example, you might want to select all controls in one area of your form except for one. Surround the controls and then deselect the control you want to exclude from the selection.

> You can use Shift+drag to select non-adjacent groups of controls. If, for instance, you had two separate groups of controls in different areas on your form, you could drag around the first set and then hold the Shift key down and drag around the second set. Both groups would be selected.

Selecting Components Within Components

Frequently you will have components placed within other components. The Panel component is often used as a container for other components. To select a group of components on a panel, you have to hold down the Ctrl key on the keyboard while you drag to select the components. (Try it without holding down the Ctrl key and see what happens!)

To illustrate, first start with a blank form. Then do the following:

1. Select a Panel component from the Component palette and place it on the form using the drag method. Drag it so that it occupies most of the form.

2. Now select a `Button` component and place six buttons on the form. Your form will look something like Figure 13.1.

FIGURE 13.1

Selecting components on a form with a panel and six buttons.

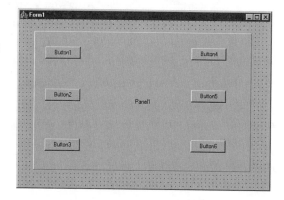

3. Drag a bounding rectangle around Button1, Button2, and Button3. Notice that you moved the panel, which is not what you expected (and not what you wanted). Move the panel back to where it was.

4. Hold down the Ctrl key and drag a rectangle around Button1, Button2, and Button3. The buttons are selected.

5. Now hold down both the Ctrl and Shift keys and drag the bounding rectangle around Button5 and Button6. Now all buttons are selected except Button4.

Using the Ctrl+drag sequence is the only way to select a group of components contained within another component if you are using the drag method. You can use the Shift+click method to select components contained within another component just as you do when selecting components on a form.

Moving Components

Moving components is a common and simple task. To move an individual component, place the mouse cursor over the component and drag. As you drag, a rectangle that represents the component moves with the mouse cursor. When you have the rectangle where you want it, let go of the mouse button, and the component is moved to that location. When you move a control via drag and drop, the control's `Left` and `Top` properties are automatically updated.

It's easiest to move a component by drag and drop. If you need finer control, you can modify the component's `Left` and `Top` properties. You can also use various alignment options, which I'll discuss in a later section, on "Aligning Components."

13

If you have the Snap to Grid option on, the dragging rectangle snaps to the nearest grid point as you drag.

Dragging a group of controls works the same way. After you have a group of components selected, place the mouse cursor over any one of the controls and begin dragging. The dragging rectangle is displayed for each control in the group. This enables you to visualize where the group will be placed when you release the mouse button.

When you have selected a control, you can nudge it by holding down the Ctrl key while using the arrow keys on the keyboard. This enables you to move the control one pixel at a time. This technique works for both groups of controls and individual controls. The Snap to Grid feature is overridden when using this technique.

Ordering, Cutting, Copying, and Pasting Components

You will place some components on top of one another to achieve a visual effect. For example, a shadowed box can be created by placing a white box over a black box (both would be Shape components). Obviously you can't have the shadow on top of the box, so you have to have some way of ordering the controls to tell C++Builder which controls go on top and which go on the bottom. Let's do a simple exercise that illustrates this. Along the way you will also see how you can use Copy and Paste with components. First, start with a blank form (you know the drill by now). Now do this:

1. Click the Additional tab on the Component palette and choose the Shape component. Click on the form to place the shape. A white square appears on the form.

2. Size the shape as desired (mine ended up being 209 pixels by 129 pixels).

3. Be sure the Shape component is selected. Choose Edit, Copy from the main menu.

4. Choose Edit, Paste from the main menu. A copy of the shape is placed below and to the right of the original shape. Conveniently, this is exactly where you want it.

5. Double-click the Brush property and change its Color property to clBlack. The new shape is now black, but it is on top of the original shape. Can't have that!

6. Right-click on the black Shape and choose Send to Back from the context menu (you could also choose Edit, Send to Back from the main menu). The black shape is moved behind the white shape. You now have a box with a shadow. (As an alternative, you could have clicked on the white shape and used Bring to Front to move it on top of the black shape.)

This exercise illustrates two features of the Form Designer. It shows how you can change the stacking order of controls and how you can use Copy and Paste to copy components. The original component's properties are copied exactly and pasted in as part of the pasting process. Each time you paste a component, it is placed below and to the right of the previous component pasted.

> If a component that can serve as a container is selected when you perform Paste, the component in the Clipboard is pasted as the container component's child. For instance, you might want to move a button from the main form to a panel. You could select the button and then choose Edit, Cut from the main menu to remove the button from the form and place it in the Clipboard. Then you could select the panel and choose Edit, Paste from the main menu to paste the button onto the panel.

When you cut a component to the clipboard, the component disappears from the form and is placed in the Clipboard. Later you can paste the component onto the form or onto another component, such as a `Panel` component.

Sizing Components

With some components, you drop them on a form and accept the default size. Buttons are a good example. A standard button has a height of 25 pixels and a width of 75 pixels. For many situations, the default button size is exactly what you want. With some components, however, the default size is rarely exactly what you need. A `Memo` component, for example, nearly always has to be sized to fit the specific form on which you are working. The most basic way of sizing a component is by modifying its `Width` and `Height` properties in the Object Inspector.

When you select a control, eight black sizing handles appear around the control. When you place the mouse cursor over one of the sizing handles, the cursor changes to a double-headed arrow known as the *sizing cursor*. When you see the sizing cursor, you can begin dragging to size the control. How the component is sized depends on which sizing handles you grab.

The sizing handles centered at the top and bottom of the component size it vertically (taller or shorter). Likewise, the right and left sizing handles size the component horizontally (wider or narrower). If you grab one of the sizing handles in the component's corners, you can size both horizontally and vertically at the same time. As with moving a component, a sizing rectangle appears as you drag. When you have the sizing rectangle at the desired size, let go of the mouse button and the component will be resized.

13

To size all the components in a group at one time, modify the Width or Height property in the Object Inspector. All components in the selection will take on the new values.

To size a control or group of controls by one pixel at a time, hold down the Shift key and press any arrow key on the keyboard. The up and down arrows size the control vertically, and the right and left arrows size it horizontally. Only the component's Width and Height properties are affected. The Top and Left properties are not modified.

Aligning Components

Regardless of whether you have the Snap to Grid option turned on, you sometimes need to align components after placing them. Aligning components could mean aligning several components along a common edge, centering components on the form, or spacing components. There are two different ways to go about aligning components:

- Use the Alignment palette and Alignment dialog box.
- Modify a component's Align property.

The following sections explain these two methods.

You might have noticed the Alignment property for some components. This property pertains only to the way the component's text is aligned (centered, right-justified, or left-justified) and has nothing to do with aligning components on a form.

The Alignment Palette and the Alignment Dialog Box

It is often necessary to move or size components relative to the form or relative to one another. The Alignment palette contains several buttons that aid in that task. The Alignment dialog box performs the same operations as the Alignment palette but in a different format. To display the Alignment palette, choose View, Alignment Palette from the main menu. Figure 13.2 shows the Alignment palette and describes each button.

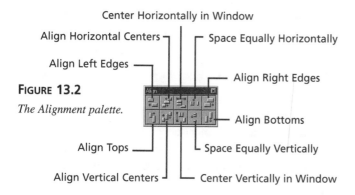

Center Horizontally in Window

Align Horizontal Centers ┐   ┌ Space Equally Horizontally

Align Left Edges ────┐

┌──── Align Right Edges

FIGURE 13.2

The Alignment palette.

Align Bottoms

Align Tops ──┘   └ Space Equally Vertically

Align Vertical Centers ┘   └── Center Vertically in Window

> The Alignment palette can save you a lot of work. Don't spend too much time trying to get controls to line up exactly. Place the components on the form and then use the Alignment palette to position them.

The Align Left Edges button is used to line up components on their left edges. Start with a blank form and then do the following:

1. Place five button components vertically on the form without regard to their left edges.

2. Select the buttons by dragging a bounding rectangle around them (or just touching them). The selection indicators show that all the buttons are selected. The form will look something like the one in Figure 13.3.

FIGURE 13.3

Aligning randomly placed buttons on a form using the Alignment palette.

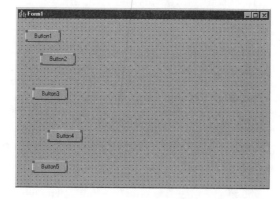

13

3. Choose View, Alignment Palette from the main menu. The Alignment palette is displayed. Move the Alignment palette, if necessary, so that it doesn't obscure the form.

4. Click the Align Left Edges button on the Alignment palette. The buttons are all lined up.

See how easy that is? As long as you have the buttons selected, let's look at another alignment option. The Space Equally Vertically alignment option can now be used to space the buttons evenly. The buttons should still be selected, so all you have to do is click the Space Equally Vertically button on the Alignment palette, and voilà! The buttons are perfectly spaced.

The Space Equally Vertically alignment option spaces the components equally between the first component in the column (the top component) and the last component in the column (the bottom component). Be sure to set the first and last components where you want them before choosing the Space Equally Vertically alignment option. This is true of the Space Equally Horizontally alignment option as well.

The Center Horizontally in Window and Center Vertically in Window alignment options do exactly as their names indicate. These options are convenient for centering a single control, such as a button, on the form or for centering a group of controls. As long as you still have the group of buttons selected, click both the Center Horizontally in Window and Center Vertically in Window buttons on the Alignment palette. The buttons are centered on the form both horizontally and vertically.

When you select a group of controls and click one of the centering buttons, the controls are treated *as a group*. If you choose each control individually and center it both horizontally and vertically on the form, all the controls are stacked on top of one another in the middle of the form. By selecting the group and then centering, you will get the entire group centered as you intended.

The Align Tops, Align Bottoms, and Align Right Edges options work just like the Align Left Edges option you used earlier. Their use is intuitive enough that there's not much point in going over all the possibilities that exist for their use.

The first component selected is the anchor point when using any edge-alignment option. When you chose Align Left Edges, the first component selected remains where it was originally placed and all other selected components line up with the anchor component's left edge.

The Alignment dialog box performs the same actions as the Alignment palette. To bring up the Alignment dialog box, choose Edit, Align from the main menu or Align from the Form Designer's context menu. Figure 13.4 shows the Alignment dialog box.

FIGURE 13.4

The Alignment dialog box.

The `Align` Property

Another type of alignment can be set using the `Align` property. This property controls how a component is aligned with its parent. The possible values for the `Align` property and a description of each are listed in Table 13.1.

TABLE 13.1 POSSIBLE VALUES FOR THE `Align` PROPERTY

Value	Description
alBottom	The component is aligned at the bottom of the parent window. A status bar is an example of a component aligned along the bottom of a main form.
alClient	The component expands to fill the parent window's client area. If other components occupy part of the client area, the component fills what client area remains. Examples include Memo components, Image components, and RichEdit components.
alLeft	The component is aligned along the parent window's left edge. A vertical toolbar is an example of a left-aligned component.
alNone	The component is placed as designed with no special relationship to the parent. This is the default for most components.
alRight	The component is aligned along the parent's right edge.
alTop	The component is aligned along the top of the parent's window. A toolbar is an example of this type of alignment.

13

An illustration will help explain alignment. Start with a blank form. Then perform these steps:

1. Click the Standard tab on the Component palette and choose a `Panel` component. Place the panel anywhere on the form.

2. Locate the `Align` property in the Object Inspector (it's at the top of the list). Notice that it is set on `alNone`. Change the `Align` property to `alTop`. The panel is aligned at the top of the form, and it expands to fill the form's width.

3. Try to move the panel back to the middle of the form. The panel snaps back to the top.

4. Try to make the panel narrower. Notice that the panel retains its width.

5. Change the panel's height. Note that the panel's height can be changed (the width cannot).

6. Change the `Align` to `alBottom`. Now the panel is glued to the bottom of the form.

7. Change the `Align` to `alRight` and then `alLeft`. The width is now the same as the height was before. In effect, the panel is rotated. Again, attempts to move or size the panel vertically fail.

8. Change the `Align` property to `alClient`. The panel expands to fill the form's entire client area. The panel cannot be resized in any dimension.

9. Change the `Align` property to `alNone`. The panel can again be sized and moved.

As you see, changing `Align` to anything other than `alNone` effectively glues the panel to one edge of the form. In the case of `alClient`, the panel is glued to all four edges.

Setting the Tab Order

NEW TERM The *tab order* refers to the order in which components receive input focus when the user presses the Tab key on the keyboard.

C++Builder forms automatically support component navigation using the Tab key. You can move forward from component to component using the Tab key and tab backwards using Shift+Tab.

NEW TERM *Windowed* components are components that accept focus. Windowed components include the `Edit`, `Memo`, `ListBox`, `ComboBox`, and `Button` components, as well as many more.

NEW TERM *Non-windowed* components are components that don't accept keyboard focus. Components such as `Image`, `SpeedButton`, `Label`, `Shape`, and many others are non-windowed components.

The tab order only applies to windowed components. Non-windowed components are excluded from the tab order. There are two types of visual components.

The tab order is initially set based on the order the components were placed on the form when the form was designed. You can modify the tab order by changing the TabOrder property for each control in the Object Inspector. That method is tedious because you have to go to each control individually. The Edit Tab Order dialog box provides an easier way (see Figure 13.5).

FIGURE 13.5

The Edit Tab Order dialog box.

The Edit Tab Order dialog box is invoked by choosing Edit, Tab Order from the main menu. This dialog box displays all windowed components currently on the form. Non-windowed components are not displayed. To change the tab order, click the name of the component you want to move in the tab order and then click the up or down buttons as needed. You can also drag the component to its new position in the tab order. After you get the tab order the way you want it, click OK and the tab order is set. You can confirm the new settings by viewing each control's TabOrder property.

> The tab order starts with 0. The first component in the tab order is 0, the second is 1, and so on.

13

Building a Sample Application

To illustrate how different components work together, build a prototype of an application that resembles Windows Notepad.

Building a text editor probably doesn't sound too glamorous. To be honest, it's not. What building a text editor will do for you, however, is teach you how to conquer many of the real-world problems you will encounter when programming in C++Builder. It might not be glamorous, but it will almost certainly teach you more than building Snazzy Gadgets 1.0.

A *prototype* is an application that has the appearance of a working application but lacks full functionality, usually because it's in the early stages of design.

C++Builder is perfect for quick prototyping of an application. You can have the main screens and dialog boxes designed and displayed in much less time than it would take with traditional Windows programming tools. That is not, however, to say that C++Builder is just for prototyping. C++Builder is fully capable of handling all your 32-bit Windows programming needs.

Step 1: Start a New Application

1. Choose File, New Application from the main menu. If prompted to save the current project, click No.

2. The form is selected, so change the Name property to ScratchPad.

3. Change the Caption to ScratchPad 1.0.

4. Choose Project, Options from the main menu. Click the Application tab and enter ScratchPad 1.0 for the application's title. Click OK to close the Project Options dialog box.

Step 2: Add a Toolbar

You added a toolbar to the Picture Viewer program in Hour 12, so I'm not going to explain each step required to build a toolbar here. Add a toolbar to the application and add buttons for the following operations: File Open, File Save, Cut, Copy, Paste, and About. Use any glyphs you like for the toolbar buttons. Don't forget you'll have to add an ImageList component for the button glyphs. When you set the hint text for the toolbar buttons, use this convention:

Open¦Open a file.

This sets the ToolTip for the button to "Open" and the status bar text to "Open a file." The first part of the string, up to the pipe character (¦), is the short hint. The second part (after the pipe character) is the long hint. Don't worry too much about the distinction between the long and short hint text for right now. I discuss long and short hint text in detail in Hour 15, "VCL Components" in the section describing the Hint property.

The form now looks something like Figure 13.6.

FIGURE 13.6

The ScratchPad form showing the toolbar buttons.

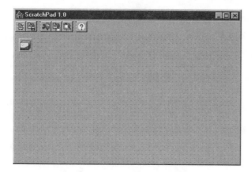

Step 3: Add a Status Bar

Okay, so far, so good. Windows Notepad doesn't have a status bar (or a toolbar, for that matter), but you'll put one in your application:

1. Click the Win32 tab on the Component palette and choose the StatusBar component.

2. Click anywhere on the form. The status bar is automatically placed at the bottom of the form. The status bar has a default Align value of alBottom.

3. Change the Name property to StatusBar.

4. Set the AutoHint property to True.

Setting the AutoHint property to True allows the status bar to automatically display hint text for any component with its ShowHint property set to True.

Step 4: Add the Memo Component

You need some component in which to type text, so use a memo component (believe it or not, you're almost done with your prototype):

1. Click the Standard tab on the Component palette and choose a Memo component. Place the memo anywhere on the form's client area.

2. Change the Name property to Memo.

3. Double-click the Value column next to the Lines property. The String List Editor is displayed. Delete the word Memo and click OK.

4. Change the Scrollbar property to ssVertical. (Initially, you only want a vertical scrollbar on the memo.)

5. Change the Name property of the Font property to Fixedsys. (Because this is a Notepad copycat, you'll use the system font.)

6. Change the Align property to alClient. The memo expands to fill the client area between the toolbar and the status bar.

13

Stand back and admire your work. This is starting to look like a real application! If the form looks too large or too small, resize it by dragging the lower-right corner. It's your program so make it look the way you want it to look.

> Pressing the Esc key selects the parent of the control that currently has the selection. For example, your form's client area is covered by components, making it impossible to select the form itself. To make the form the active component in the Object Inspector, select the memo component and then press the Esc key on the keyboard. You can also choose the form from the Component Selector combo box on the Object Inspector.

Notice that all the controls automatically resize themselves to retain their relationship with the parent window—the form, in this case. That is one of the main advantages to the Align property. The form now looks like the one in Figure 13.7.

Figure 13.7

A C++Builder prototype for the ScratchPad *application.*

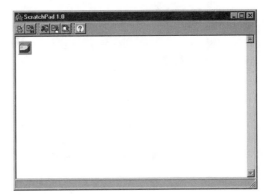

Run the Program

You can now click the Run button to run the program. You can type text in the window's client area, and you can press the toolbar buttons (although they don't do anything at this point). Keep in mind that this is a prototype and is mostly for show right now. You'll add more to the program in upcoming sessions.

You better save the project because you're going to use it later in the book. Choose File, Save All from the main menu. Save the main form's source unit as SPMain and the project as Scratch.

Summary

Congratulations! You have just covered the bulk of the C++Builder visual programming features. I hope it was enjoyable as well as educational. The Form Designer is a powerful tool that enables you to do as much programming as possible visually. If you haven't had to place controls on a window or dialog in a traditional C++ environment, you might not fully appreciate that advantage. Trust me, it's significant.

Workshop

The Workshop contains quiz questions to help you solidify your understanding of the material covered and exercises to provide you with experience in using what you have learned.

Q&A

Q **I'm using the Alignment palette a lot, and every time I switch from the Code Editor back to the Form Designer, the Alignment palette gets lost somewhere. Is there anything I can do about that?**

A Locate the Alignment palette (it's there somewhere!) and right-click it to bring up the Alignment palette's context menu. Choose the Stay on Top item from the context menu. Now the Alignment palette is always on top where you can find it.

Q **I am trying to select a group of components on a panel by dragging the selection rectangle around them, but I keep moving the panel. What's wrong?**

A You need to hold down the Ctrl key while dragging when you are selecting components contained on a panel.

Quiz

1. When do you use Ctrl+drag in selecting components?
2. What significance does the first component selected have when aligning a group of components?
3. What is the quickest method to select a group of components?
4. What does the Align property's alClient option do?

13

Answers

1. Use Ctrl+drag when selecting a group of components that are children of another component (components on a panel, for example).

2. The first component selected servers as the anchor component when aligning a group of components. It retains its position, and all other components are aligned to it.

3. To quickly select a group of components, drag a bounding rectangle around (or just touching) them.

4. The alClient option forces the component to fill the entire client area of its parent, regardless of how the parent (a form usually) is sized.

Exercises

1. Place five edit components on a form and arrange them so that they are stacked vertically with their left edges aligned.

2. Place a ListBox component on a blank form and modify it so that it always occupies the form's entire client area.

3. Add an About box to the ScratchPad program. Use the Alignment palette to quickly align the text labels.

4. Start a new application. Place six edit components on a form in random fashion. Now arrange the tab order so that tabbing proceeds from top to bottom. Run the program to test the tabbing order.

HOUR 14

Working with the Menu Designer

In this hour you learn how to use the C++Builder menu designer. Menus are a big part of most Windows applications. Some Windows programs don't have menus, but the vast majority do. C++Builder makes creating menus (both main menus and pop-up menus) easy with the Menu Designer. The Menu Designer's commands are accessed via the Menu Designer context menu or by interacting with the Object Inspector.

Creating a Main Menu

The Menu Designer enables you to quickly build any menu. The menu structure for a main menu consists of a MainMenu component, which is represented by the Visual Component Library (VCL) class TMainMenu. Each item on the menu is a MenuItem component that is encapsulated in the TMenuItem class. You don't need to be too concerned about the intricacies of how these classes work together because the Menu Designer makes creating menus easy. With that brief overview, let's add a main menu to the ScratchPad application.

Adding a Main Menu to the Form

The first thing you must do is add a MainMenu component to your form.

 By now you have had some experience with C++Builder. From this point on I will abbreviate some steps that you need to take to perform certain actions. For example, from here on I'll say, "Place a MainMenu component on the form" rather than "Click on the Standard tab on the Component palette. Click the MainMenu button and click on the form to place the component." Don't worry, I'll still give plenty of details when new operations are introduced.

1. Open the ScratchPad project you created in the previous hour.

2. Place a MainMenu component on the form and change its Name property to MainMenu. Notice that a MainMenu component has very few properties and no events. All the menu's work is done by the individual menu items.

3. Double-click on the MainMenu icon. The Menu Designer is displayed.

The Menu Designer looks like a blank form without grid points. The Menu Designer can be sized in any way you want. The size is just for your convenience and has no bearing on how the menu operates at runtime. At this point, the Menu Designer is waiting for you to begin building the menu. After you have created your first menu, you will find that menu creation is easy and intuitive.

Creating a Menu by Hand

Many Windows applications have a File menu, and in this section you will create one. Although there are easier ways to create a File menu, you will create your first menu by hand. The Menu Designer always has a blank menu item that acts as a placeholder for any new menu items you will create. When you first start the Menu Designer, the blank item is selected.

1. Change the Name property to FileMenu.

2. Click on the Caption property in the Object Inspector, type &File, and press Enter.

The ampersand (&) is used to create the underlined character for a menu item. The underlined character is the *accelerator* the user can type, in combination with the Alt key, to navigate a menu using the keyboard. You can put ampersands anywhere in the menu item's text. For instance, the customary text string for the Exit menu item would be E&xit. All you have to do is provide the ampersands where appropriate, and Windows will take it from there.

At this point, several things happen. First, the File menu shows up in the Menu Designer. It also shows on the main form behind the Menu Designer. The other thing that happens is that a new, blank placeholder is added below the File menu you just created (you'll have to click on the File menu in the Menu Designer to see the placeholder). In addition, a new pop-up placeholder is created to the right of the File menu. The Object Inspector is displaying a blank MenuItem component, waiting for you to enter the Caption and Name property values. Figure 14.1 shows the Menu Designer as it appears at this point.

FIGURE 14.1

The Menu Designer and Object Inspector after creating the File menu.

Let's continue with the creation of the menu using the following steps:

1. Change the Name property for the new item to FileNew.

2. Change the Caption property to &New and press Enter. Again, a blank item is created in the Menu Designer.

3. Repeat steps 1 and 2 and create menu items for Open, Save, and Save As. If you need help on where to place the ampersand, refer to Figure 14.2. Don't worry that you might not get it exactly right. You can always go back later and fix any errors.

14

Make your menus as standard as possible. Be sure that your accelerators (the underlined characters) are the same as in other Windows programs. Also, remember that an ellipsis (...) following a menu item's text is a visual cue to the user that choosing the menu item will invoke a dialog box.

At this point, we need a menu separator.

A *separator* is the horizontal line on a menu that separates groups of menu items.

Adding a separator is easy with the C++Builder Menu Designer. All you have to do is put in a hyphen for the Caption property. Select the blank menu item under Save As, type a hyphen for the Caption, and press Enter. A separator is placed in the menu. Continue adding menu items until your menu looks like the one in Figure 14.2. If you need to modify a menu item, just click on it and change properties in the Object Inspector as needed.

FIGURE 14.2

The Menu Designer with the finished File menu showing menu separators.

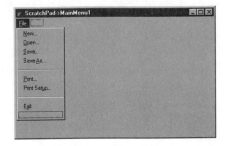

The Menu Designer always provides a blank menu item at the bottom of each pop-up menu and on the menu bar's right side. You cannot delete these blank items, but there's no need to—they are used only in the Menu Designer and won't show on the menu when your program runs.

Now that the File menu is done, you need to create an Edit menu and a Help menu for the ScratchPad application.

Inserting a Menu from a Template

This time take the easy approach. First, click on the blank pop-up menu placeholder to the right of the File menu. Right-click and choose Insert From Template from the context menu. The Insert Template dialog box is displayed. This dialog box shows a list of templates from which you can choose. You can use the predefined templates or create your own. In this case you are only interested in adding an Edit menu, so choose Edit Menu and click OK. A full Edit menu is immediately inserted into the Menu Designer. In fact, it's a little too full. You'll deal with that in a moment.

As long as you're here, add the Help menu too. Click on the placeholder to the right of the Edit menu. Choose Insert From Template again, and this time insert a Help menu. (Don't choose the Expanded Help menu, though.) You'll tidy up both the Edit and Help menus in the next section. Notice that the main form has been updating to show the new menu items as they are placed.

Yes, inserting a menu from a template is really that easy. After using C++Builder for a while, you will no doubt have your own custom templates to choose from for building menus quickly and easily.

Deleting Menu Items

The process of creating a Windows application is a living, breathing thing. Rarely will you get everything exactly right the first time. Users will request new features, the boss will come up with a few of his own, and some features will even be dropped. You will often need to update your application's menus as these changes occur. For example, the Edit menu inserted earlier is a little verbose for your needs; there are several items that you just don't need. No problem—just delete them:

1. Click on the Edit menu.
2. Click on the item called Repeat <command>.
3. Press Delete on the keyboard or choose Delete from the Menu Designer context menu to delete the item. The item disappears and the remaining items move up.
4. Delete the Paste Special menu item as well.

There, that was easy! You're not quite done with the Edit menu, but before we go on I want to mention a very useful feature of the Menu Designer. You are probably familiar with using Shift+click and Ctrl+click when selecting items in other Windows programs. These techniques can be used in Windows Explorer to select files, for instance. The Menu Designer supports Shift+click and Ctrl+click with one qualification—you can use these to select multiple menu items but not to deselect an item. As always, an exercise will illustrate better than I can explain.

1. The Edit menu should still be displayed. If not, click on Edit to reveal the Edit menu.
2. Click on the menu item called Goto.

14

3. Hold down the Shift key and click on the menu item called Object. All items between those two points are selected.

4. Press Delete on the keyboard to delete all the items at one time.

5. Move to the Help menu and delete the first three items. Only the About menu item remains.

As you can see, the Shift+click technique can be used to quickly delete unwanted menu items. Now you have the menus trimmed back to the way you want them to appear in the ScratchPad application.

Inserting Menu Items

Inserting menu items is pretty straightforward. Just click on the menu item above which you want to insert a new item and press the Insert key on the keyboard (or choose Insert from the Menu Designer's context menu). A blank menu item is inserted, and you can now modify the Name and Caption properties just as you did earlier. Let's insert an item into the Edit menu:

1. Click on Edit to display the Edit menu.

2. Click on the Find menu item.

3. Press the Insert key on the keyboard. A new menu item is provided, and all other menu items below the new item move down.

4. Change the Name property to EditSelectAll and change the Caption property to Se&lect All.

5. Click on the empty placeholder at the bottom of the Edit menu. Add a menu separator (remember, just enter a hyphen for the Caption property).

6. Click on the placeholder again and add a new item. Make the Name property EditWordWrap and the Caption property &Word Wrap.

Moving Menu Items

You can easily move menu items as needed. You can move them up or down within the pop-up menu they are already in, or you can move them across pop-ups. There are two ways to move a menu item. The first is by using Cut and Paste. Cut and Paste work as you would expect, so there's no need to go over that. The second way to move a menu item is just by dragging it to a new location and dropping it. Let's try it. You really want the Select All menu item just below the Undo item. No problem—just move it:

1. Click on Edit to display the Edit menu.
2. Click on the Select All item and drag it up until the separator under the Undo item is highlighted.
3. Let go of the mouse, and the menu item is moved.

Too easy, right? Yes, but that's what C++Builder is all about.

Modifying Properties in Batches

Sometimes you want to modify several menu items' properties at once. For example, you have a few menu items in the ScratchPad application that you are not ready to implement at this time. You aren't ready for printing support, for instance, nor are you ready to implement the help system. You need to gray out (disable) those menu items using the following steps:

1. Click on the File menu.
2. Click on the Print menu item, hold the Shift key down, and click on the Print Setup menu item. Both items are selected.
3. In the Object Inspector, change the Enabled property to false. Both menu items are disabled.
4. Repeat steps 4 and 5 to disable the Find and Replace items on the Edit menu.

You can modify a group of menu items at one time with this method. Simply select the items you want to modify and then change the property you want to modify. All menu items currently selected will have the new property value.

Creating Submenus

There's nothing special or tricky about creating submenus.

 A *submenu* is a menu item that, when clicked, expands to show more menu choices.

A submenu is denoted by a right-pointing arrow next to the menu item text. You can create a submenu by choosing Create Submenu from the Menu Designer context menu or by holding down the Ctrl key and pressing the right-arrow key. When you create a submenu, a blank menu item is placed to the right of the menu item. You can add menu

14

items to the submenu just as you did when creating the main menu. You can create a sub-menu by inserting a menu template as well.

Adding Shortcuts

You can easily add a keyboard shortcut to a menu item by changing its ShortCut prop-erty in the Object Inspector. The Edit menu that you inserted earlier already had key-board shortcuts built-in. For instance, the customary shortcut for Cut is Ctrl+X. If you look at the Edit menu, you will see Ctrl+X listed next to the Cut item. Click on the Cut menu item and you will see that the ShortCut property says Ctrl+X. Click on the Value column next to the ShortCut property. On the Value column's right side, you will see a drop-down button. Click on the button to display the list of available shortcuts. The list you see there contains just about any keyboard shortcut you need. To set the keyboard shortcut for a menu item, simply pick a shortcut from the list.

The standard shortcut for Select All is Ctrl+A, so let's add that as a shortcut for your Select All menu item:

1. Choose Edit, Select All from your menu in the Menu Designer.
2. Click on the ShortCut property in the Object Inspector.
3. Choose Ctrl+A from the list of available shortcuts. Now the Select All menu item shows Ctrl+A next to it.

That's all you have to do; C++Builder takes care of it from there. The shortcuts will function without you having to write any code.

Finishing Touches

Let's finish off your menu. First, you'll make the Word Wrap menu item on by default. This menu item is going to be used to turn word wrapping on or off. When word wrap-ping is on, the Word Wrap menu item will have a check mark next to it. When word wrapping is off it will not have a check mark next to it. Click on the Word Wrap menu item and then change the Checked property to true. A check mark shows up to indicate that the word wrap feature is on.

Another thing you need to do is to change the Name property on all of the menu items that you inserted from a template. They were given default names, and you want to change them to more meaningful names. Click on the Edit, Undo menu item. Change the Name property from Undo1 to EditUndo. Notice that you add the pop-up menu name, Edit, to the front of the menu item name and remove the 1 at the end. You can use any naming convention you like, but be consistent. Repeat the process for the Cut, Copy, Paste, Find, and Replace menu items. Now move to the Help menu and modify the Name property of the About menu item to HelpAbout.

That just about finishes your menu. Run through the menu to check it once more. If you find any errors, make the necessary changes. When you are satisfied that the menu is correct, click the close box to close the Menu Designer.

> You can access the Code Editor directly from the Menu Designer by double-clicking any menu item. When you double-click a menu item, the Code Editor displays the OnClick event for that item, and you can start typing code. In this case, you are going to go back to the main form and do your code editing there.

Writing the Code

Okay, so you have all these menu items but no code to make them work. It's going to be a lot of work implementing all these, right? Actually, it's easy. Most of the required code is already part of the Memo component. All you have to do is call the appropriate TMemo methods in your menu handlers. You'll have to do a few other things, but most of what you will add is code you have seen before.

Before writing the code, you need to add the usual OpenDialog and SaveDialog components to the form using the following steps:

1. Place an OpenDialog component on the form.

2. Change the Name property to OpenDialog.

3. Place a SaveDialog component on the form.

4. Change the Name property to SaveDialog.

5. Line up the MainMenu, OpenDialog, and SaveDialog icons on the form.

Okay, that was easy enough. Now let's get on with writing the code for the menu items. You'll start with the File Exit menu item (hey, it's the easiest!). Be sure that the Menu Designer is closed so you don't confuse the Menu Designer with the Form Designer.

1. Choose File, Exit from the main menu. The Code Editor comes to the top, and the FileExitClick() event handler is displayed.

2. The cursor is positioned and ready to go. Type the following at the cursor:

```
Close();
```

14

That's it. I told you it was the easiest. Let's do one more; then I'm going to turn you loose to finish the rest on your own.

1. Choose Edit, Cut from the main menu. The Code Editor comes to the top, and the `EditCutClick()` event handler is displayed.

2. Type the following at the cursor:

   `Memo->CutToClipboard();`

And that's all there is to that particular menu item. You might not fully realize it, but VCL does a lot for you behind the scenes. The whole idea of a framework is to take the burden of the low-level details off the programmer's back. Life is good.

One of the interesting aspects of a program like C++Builder is that you rarely view your program as a whole. C++Builder conveniently takes you to the section of code you need to work on to deal with a particular event, so you usually only see your program in small chunks.

Listing 14.1 contains the header for the ScratchPad program up to this point. The header is entirely C++Builder generated. The entire Scratch.cpp program is shown in Listing 14.2. Follow the examples you've just worked through to write code for each of the remaining menu items. Copy the code for each of the menu `OnClick` handlers from Listing 14.2. (The comment lines are there to explain to you what the code is doing. You don't have to include them when you type the code.)

 The event handlers appear in the source file in the order in which they were created. Don't be concerned if the order of the event handlers in your source file doesn't exactly match Listing 14.2. The order in which the functions appear makes no difference to the compiler.

LISTING 14.1   SPMAIN.H, THE HEADER PORTION OF THE CODE FOR THE SCRATCHPAD APPLICATION

```
 1: //-----------------------------------------------------------------
 2: #ifndef SPMainH
 3: #define SPMainH
 4: //-----------------------------------------------------------------
 5: #include <Classes.hpp>
 6: #include <Controls.hpp>
 7: #include <StdCtrls.hpp>
 8: #include <Forms.hpp>
 9: #include <ComCtrls.hpp>
10: #include <ImgList.hpp>
```

```
11: #include <ToolWin.hpp>
12: #include <Dialogs.hpp>
13: #include <Menus.hpp>
14: //-----------------------------------------------------------
15: class TScratchPad : public TForm
16: {
17: __published:     // IDE-managed Components
18:         TToolBar *ToolBar;
19:         TToolButton *FileOpenBtn;
20:         TToolButton *FileSaveBtn;
21:         TToolButton *ToolButton3;
22:         TToolButton *EditCutBtn;
23:         TToolButton *EditCopyBtn;
24:         TToolButton *EditPasteBtn;
25:         TToolButton *ToolButton7;
26:         TToolButton *ToolButton8;
27:         TImageList *ImageList1;
28:         TStatusBar *StatusBar;
29:         TMemo *Memo;
30:         TMainMenu *MainMenu;
31:         TMenuItem *FileMenu;
32:         TMenuItem *FileNew;
33:         TMenuItem *FileOpen;
34:         TMenuItem *FileSave;
35:         TMenuItem *FileSaveAs;
36:         TMenuItem *N1;
37:         TMenuItem *FilePrintSetup;
38:         TMenuItem *FilePrint;
39:         TMenuItem *N2;
40:         TMenuItem *FileExit;
41:         TMenuItem *EditMenu;
42:         TMenuItem *EditReplace;
43:         TMenuItem *EditFind;
44:         TMenuItem *N4;
45:         TMenuItem *EditPaste;
46:         TMenuItem *EditCopy;
47:         TMenuItem *EditCut;
48:         TMenuItem *N5;
49:         TMenuItem *Undo1;
50:         TMenuItem *HelpMenu;
51:         TMenuItem *HelpAbout;
52:         TMenuItem *EditSelectAll;
53:         TMenuItem *N3;
54:         TMenuItem *EditWordWrap;
55:         TOpenDialog *OpenDialog;
56:         TSaveDialog *SaveDialog;
57:         void __fastcall FileOpenClick(TObject *Sender);
58:         void __fastcall FileSaveAsClick(TObject *Sender);
59:         void __fastcall FileSaveClick(TObject *Sender);
```

14

continues

LISTING 14.1   CONTINUED

```
60:           void __fastcall EditPasteClick(TObject *Sender);
61:           void __fastcall FileExitClick(TObject *Sender);
62:           void __fastcall EditCutClick(TObject *Sender);
63:           void __fastcall EditCopyClick(TObject *Sender);
64:           void __fastcall FileNewClick(TObject *Sender);
65:           void __fastcall Undo1Click(TObject *Sender);
66:           void __fastcall EditSelectAllClick(TObject *Sender);
67:           void __fastcall EditWordWrapClick(TObject *Sender);
68: private:    // User declarations
69: public:         // User declarations
70:           __fastcall TScratchPad(TComponent* Owner);
71: };
72: //-----------------------------------------------------------
73: extern PACKAGE TScratchPad *ScratchPad;
74: //-----------------------------------------------------------
75: #endif
```

Listing 14.2 is the main program for the ScratchPad application.

LISTING 14.2   SPMAIN.CPP, THE MAIN PROGRAM FOR THE SCRATCHPAD APPLICATION

```
 1: //-----------------------------------------------------------
 2: #include <vcl.h>
 3: #pragma hdrstop
 4:
 5: #include "SPMain.h"
 6: //-----------------------------------------------------------
 7: #pragma package(smart_init)
 8: #pragma resource "*.dfm"
 9: TScratchPad *ScratchPad;
10: //-----------------------------------------------------------
11: __fastcall TScratchPad::TScratchPad(TComponent* Owner)
12:           : TForm(Owner)
13: {
14: }
15: //-----------------------------------------------------------
16: void __fastcall TScratchPad::FileOpenClick(TObject *Sender)
17: {
18:   //
19:   // Open a file. First check to see if the current file needs
20:   // to be saved. Same logic as in FileNewClick() above.
21:   //
22:   if (Memo->Modified) {
23:     int result = Application->MessageBox(
24:       "The current file has changed. Save changes?",
25:       "ScratchPad Message", MB_YESNOCANCEL);
26:       if (result == IDYES)
```

```
27:        FileSaveClick(0);
28:     if (result == IDCANCEL)
29:       return;
30:   }
31:   //
32:   // Execute the File Open dialog. If OK was pressed then
33:   // open the file using the LoadFromFile() method. First
34:   // clear the FileName property.
35:   //
36:   OpenDialog->FileName = "";
37:   if (OpenDialog->Execute())
38:   {
39:     if (Memo->Lines->Count > 0)
40:       Memo->Clear();
41:     Memo->Lines->LoadFromFile(OpenDialog->FileName);
42:     SaveDialog->FileName = OpenDialog->FileName;
43:   }
44: }
45: //----------------------------------------------------------------
46: void __fastcall TScratchPad::FileSaveAsClick(TObject *Sender)
47: {
48:   //
49:   // If a filename has already been provided then there is
50:   // no need to bring up the File Save dialog. Just save the
51:   // file using SaveToFile().
52:   //
53:   if (SaveDialog->FileName != "")
54:   {
55:     Memo->Lines->SaveToFile(SaveDialog->FileName);
56:     //
57:     // Set Modified to false since we've just saved.
58:     //
59:     Memo->Modified = false;
60:   }
61:   //
62:   // If no filename was set then do a SaveAs().
63:   //
64:   else
65:     FileSaveAsClick(Sender);
66: }
67: //----------------------------------------------------------------
68: void __fastcall TScratchPad::FileSaveClick(TObject *Sender)
69: {
70:   //
71:   // Display the File Save dialog to save the file.
72:   // Set Modified to false since we just saved.
73:   //
74:   SaveDialog->Title = "Save As";
75:   if (SaveDialog->Execute())
76:   {
```

14

continues

LISTING **14.2** CONTINUED

```
77:      Memo->Lines->SaveToFile(SaveDialog->FileName);
78:      Memo->Modified = false;
79:    }
80: }
81: //--------------------------------------------------------------
82: void __fastcall TScratchPad::EditPasteClick(TObject *Sender)
83: {
84:   Memo->PasteFromClipboard();
85: }
86: //--------------------------------------------------------------
87: void __fastcall TScratchPad::FileExitClick(TObject *Sender)
88: {
89:   Close();
90: }
91: //--------------------------------------------------------------
92: void __fastcall TScratchPad::EditCutClick(TObject *Sender)
93: {
94:   Memo->CutToClipboard();
95: }
96: //--------------------------------------------------------------
97: void __fastcall TScratchPad::EditCopyClick(TObject *Sender)
98: {
99:   Memo->CopyToClipboard();
100: }
101: //--------------------------------------------------------------
102: void __fastcall TScratchPad::FileNewClick(TObject *Sender)
103: {
104:   //
105:   // Open a file. First check to see if the current file
106:   // needs to be saved.
107:   //
108:   if (Memo->Modified) {
109:     //
110:     // Display a message box.
111:     //
112:     int result = Application->MessageBox(
113:       "The current file has changed. Save changes?",
114:       "ScratchPad Message", MB_YESNOCANCEL);
115:     //
116:     // If Yes was clicked then save the current file.
117:     //
118:      if (result == IDYES) FileSaveClick(Sender);
119:     //
120:     // If No was clicked then do nothing.
121:     //
122:     if (result == IDCANCEL) return;
123:   }
```

```
124:    //
125:    // Delete the strings in the memo, if any.
126:    //
127:    if (Memo->Lines->Count > 0) Memo->Clear();
128:    //
129:    // Set the FileName property of the Save Dialog to a
130:    // blank string. This lets us know that the file has
131:    // not yet been saved.
132:    //
133:    SaveDialog->FileName = "";
134: }
135: //----------------------------------------------------------------
136: void __fastcall TScratchPad::EditUndoClick(TObject *Sender)
137: {
138:    //
139:    // Call the Undo method of TMemo.
140:    //
141:    Memo->Undo();
142: }
143: //----------------------------------------------------------------
144: void __fastcall TScratchPad::EditSelectAllClick(TObject *Sender)
145: {
146:    //
147:    // Just call TMemo::SelectAll().
148:    //
149:    Memo->SelectAll();
150: }
151: //----------------------------------------------------------------
152: void __fastcall TScratchPad::EditWordWrapClick(TObject *Sender)
153: {
154:    //
155:    // Toggle the TMemo::WordWrap property. Set the Checked
156:    // property of the menu item to the same value as WordWrap.
157:    //
158:    Memo->WordWrap = !Memo->WordWrap;
159:    EditWordWrap->Checked = Memo->WordWrap;
160:    //
161:    // If WordWrap is on then we only need the vertical
162:    // scrollbar. If it's off, then we need both scrollbars.
163:    //
164:    if (Memo->WordWrap)
165:      Memo->ScrollBars = ssVertical;
166:    else
167:      Memo->ScrollBars = ssBoth;
168: }
169: //----------------------------------------------------------------
```

14

Running the Program

And now, the moment you've all been waiting for! After you have created the event handlers for the menu items, you are ready to run the program. Click the Run button and the program should compile and run. If you get compiler errors, carefully compare your source code with the code in Listing 14.2. Make any changes and click the Run button again. You might have to go through this process a few times before the program will compile and run. Eventually, though, it will run (I promise!).

When the program runs, you will find a program that, although not yet 100 percent feature-complete, acts a lot like Windows Notepad. Even though you have a few things to add before you're finished, you have a fairly good start—especially when you consider the actual time involved up to this point. Figure 14.3 shows the ScratchPad program running.

FIGURE 14.3

The ScratchPad program in action.

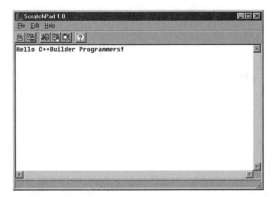

Pop-Up Menus (Context Menus)

I'm not quite finished with my discussion of menus. In C++Builder you can create pop-up menus as easily as you can a main menu. A nice feature of C++Builder is that you can assign a particular pop-up menu to a component via the component's PopupMenu property. When the cursor is placed over the component and the secondary mouse button is clicked, that pop-up will automatically be displayed. Writing event handlers for pop-up menus is exactly the same as writing event handlers for main menus.

A common feature of text-editing programs is to place the Cut, Copy, and Paste operations on a context menu. You'll add that capability to ScratchPad. To create the pop-up, you'll cheat and copy part of the main menu. Here you go:

1. Choose a PopupMenu component from the Component palette and place it on the form.

2. Change the Name property to MemoPopup.

3. Double-click the PopupMenu icon to run the Menu Designer.

4. Right-click to bring up the Menu Designer context menu. Choose Select Menu from the context menu. A dialog box is displayed that shows the menus available for your application. Choose MainMenu and click OK.

5. Click on the Edit menu. Click on the Cut menu item, hold down the Shift key, and click on the Paste menu item. Cut, Copy, and Paste are all now highlighted.

6. To copy the selected items to the Clipboard, choose Edit, Copy from the C++Builder main menu (don't choose Edit, Copy from the menu you are creating in the Menu Designer) or press Ctrl+C.

7. Again, choose Select Menu from the Menu Designer context menu. This time, choose MemoPopup and click OK. The Menu Designer shows a blank pop-up menu.

8. Choose Edit, Paste from the main menu or type Ctrl+V on the keyboard. The Cut, Copy, and Paste menu items are inserted into the pop-up.

Okay, just a few more things and you'll be done. We need to change the Name property for the new menu items:

1. For the Cut menu item, change the Name property to PopupCut.

2. For the Copy menu item, change the Name property to PopupCopy.

3. For the Paste menu item, change the Name property to PopupPaste.

The final step is to write event handlers for the pop-up menu items. Hmmm...we have already written code for the main menu's Cut, Copy, and Paste items. It would be a shame to duplicate that effort (even if it is just a single line in each case). Could you just use the same event handlers that we created earlier? Sure you can. Just follow these steps:

1. Click on the Cut pop-up menu item.

2. Click on the Events tab in the Object Inspector.

3. Click the drop-down arrow button in the Value column next to the OnClick event. A list of event handlers created so far is displayed.

14

4. Choose the `EditCutClick` event handler from the list. Now, when the Cut pop-up menu item is clicked, the Edit, Cut handler will be called. No code duplication is required.

5. Repeat steps 1–4 for the Copy and Paste items on the pop-up menu. When you are done, close the Menu Designer.

6. On the main form, click on the `Memo` component. Change the `PopupMenu` property to `MemoPopup` (by choosing it from the list).

You can attach just about any event to any event handler by using this method. Now run the program again to test the new context menu. Of course it works!

There's one more task to perform before this hour is complete. Your toolbar is not yet functional, so you need to correct that deficiency. Click on each toolbar button and hook its `OnClick` event to the corresponding menu item for that button. When you get done, run the program one more time and ensure that the toolbar buttons function.

Summary

This hour we covered the C++Builder Menu Designer. The Menu Designer is a powerful tool, particularly because of the capability to insert a menu from a template, which makes menu creation easy and actually fun with C++Builder. The Menu Designer also makes updating existing menus a snap. Most of the applications you create with C++Builder will have a menu of some form or another, so understanding how to use the Menu Designer is important.

Workshop

The Workshop contains quiz questions to help you solidify your understanding of the material covered and exercises to provide you with experience in using what you have learned.

Q&A

Q The menu templates provided are nice, but they have so much stuff on them that I don't need. What can I do about that?

A First, you can import a menu and then simply delete the items you don't want. Using the click, Shift+click method you can get rid of unwanted menu items in just a few seconds. Deleting items from a menu inserted from a template has no adverse effects. The second thing you can do is to follow the click, Shift+click method and then, when you have the menu just the way you want it, you can save it as a new template. That way you can keep the original C++Builder-supplied template and have your customized template as well.

Q Can I save my own menus as templates?

A Yes. First create the menu and then choose Save As Template from the Menu Designer context menu. Give the template a name, click OK, and the template is saved. Now all you have to do to reuse the menu later is insert the menu using the Insert From Template feature.

Quiz

1. What does an ellipsis following the text on a menu item mean?
2. What two ways can you move a menu item?
3. How do you add menu accelerators to menu items?
4. How do you initially disable a menu item?

Answers

1. Traditionally, an ellipsis following a menu item means that choosing that menu item will result in a dialog box being displayed.
2. To move a menu item using the Menu Designer, you can drag the menu to a new location or you can use Cut and Paste.
3. When typing the menu item's caption, add the ampersand (&) before the shortcut key you want to be the shortcut for that menu item. For instance, the Caption for the File, Exit menu item would read E&xit.
4. To disable a menu item, set its Enabled property to False in the Menu Designer.

Exercises

1. Add an Undo item and a menu separator to the context menu for the ScratchPad program.
2. Add the Ctrl+S keyboard shortcut to the File, Save menu item in the ScratchPad program.
3. Open the Picture Viewer project you created in Hour 12, "Writing an MDI Application." Remove all unused menu items.

14

HOUR 15

Working with the Visual Component Library (VCL)

As you know by now, components are much of what gives C++Builder its power. Components are designed using the properties, methods, and events model. Using the Form Designer, you can place a component on a form and modify its design-time properties. In some cases, that's all you have to do. If needed, you can also manipulate the component at runtime by changing its properties and calling its methods. Further, each component is designed to respond to certain events. I discussed properties, methods, and events in Hour 8, "Class Frameworks and the Visual Component Model," so I'm not going to go over that again.

In this hour you will find out more about components. You will learn about often-used components and, as a result, learn about the VCL classes that represent those components. As you go through this hour, feel free to experiment. If you read something that you want to test, by all means do so. Learning by experience is as valuable as anything you can do, so don't be afraid to experiment.

Let's review some of what you already know about components. But first, I want to take a moment to explain the differences between a VCL component and a Windows control. Windows controls include things such as edit controls, list boxes, combo boxes, static controls (labels), and buttons, not to mention all the Windows 9x/NT controls. Windows controls, by nature, don't have properties, methods, and events. Instead, messages are used to tell the control what to do or to get information from the control. To say that dealing with controls on this level is tedious and cumbersome would be an understatement.

A VCL component is an object that encapsulates a Windows control (not all VCL components encapsulate controls, though). A VCL component in effect adds properties, methods, and events to a Windows control to make working with the control easier. You might say that VCL takes a fresh approach to working with Windows controls. VCL components work with Windows controls to raise the job of dealing with those controls to a higher level.

Given that discussion, then, I will use the terms *control* and *component* interchangeably when referring to VCL components.

Visual and Nonvisual Components

Visual components include things like edit controls, buttons, list boxes, labels, and so on. Most components you will use in a C++Builder application are visual components. Visual components, as much as possible, show you at design time what the component will look like when the program runs.

 Some components are visual components; others are nonvisual components. A *visual component*, as its name implies, is one that can be seen by the user.

 A *nonvisual component* is one that cannot be seen by the user.

Nonvisual components work behind the scenes to perform specific programming tasks. Examples include system timers, database components, and image lists. Common dialog boxes like File Open, File Save, Font, and so on are considered nonvisual components as well. (They are nonvisual because they don't show themselves at design time. At runtime, they become visible when they are invoked.) When you place a nonvisual component on a form, C++Builder displays an icon representing the component on the form. This icon is used to access the component at design time in order to change the component's properties, but the icon does not show up when the program runs. Nonvisual components have properties, methods, and events just like visual components do.

15

The Name Property

The Name property serves a vital role in components. As soon as you place a component on a form, C++Builder goes to work in the background while you ponder your next move. One thing C++Builder does is create a pointer to the component and assign the Name property as the variable name. For example, let's say you place an Edit component on a form and change the Name property to MyEdit. At that point C++Builder places the following in the header file for the form:

```
TEdit* MyEdit;
```

When the application runs, C++Builder creates an instance of the TEdit class and assigns it to MyEdit. You can use this pointer to access the component at runtime. To set the text for the edit control, you would use

```
MyEdit->Text = "Mallory Kim";
```

C++Builder also uses the Name property when creating event-handler names. Let's say that you wanted to respond to the OnChange event for an Edit component. Normally, you double-click the Value column next to the OnChange event to have C++Builder generate an event handler for the event. C++Builder creates a default function name based on the Name property of the component and the event being handled. In this case, C++Builder would generate a function called MyEditChange().

You can change the Name property at any time provided that you change it *only* via the Object Inspector. When you change a component's Name property at design time, C++Builder goes through all the code that it had previously generated and changes the name of the pointer and all event-handling functions.

> C++Builder will change all the code generated by C++Builder to reflect the new value of the component's Name property, but it will not modify any code you wrote. In other words, C++Builder will take care of modifying the code it wrote, but it is up to you to update and maintain the code you wrote. Generally speaking, you should change the Name property when you initially place the component on the form and leave it alone after that.

Continuing with this example, if you change the Name property of the edit control from MyEdit to FirstName, C++Builder will change the pointer name to FirstName and the OnChange handler name to FirstNameChange(). It's all done automatically; you don't have to do anything but change the Name property and trust that C++Builder will do the rest of the work.

Never change the Name property at runtime. Never manually change a component's name (the name that C++Builder assigned to the component's pointer) or event-handler names in the Code Editor. If you perform either of these actions, C++Builder loses track of components and the results are not good, to say the least. You might even lose the ability to load your form. The only safe way to change the Name property of a component is through the Object Inspector.

C++Builder assigns a default value to the Name property for all components placed on a form. If you place an Edit component, for example, C++Builder assigns Edit1 to the Name property. If you place a second Edit component on the form, C++Builder will assign Edit2 to that component's Name property, and so on. You should give your components meaningful names as soon as possible to avoid confusion and extra work later on.

You can leave the default names for components that will never be referenced in code. For example, if you have several label components that contain static (unchanging) text, you can leave the default names because you won't be accessing the components at runtime.

THE Name PROPERTY
- Change the Name property of a component from the default name to a meaningful name as soon as possible.
- Components not referenced at runtime can be left with the C++Builder-supplied name.
- Never change the Name property of a component in the class header or at runtime.
- Make your component's names meaningful but not overly long.

Important Common Properties

All components have certain properties in common. For instance, all visual components have Left and Top properties that determine where the component is placed on the form. Properties such as Left, Top, Height, and Width are self-explanatory, so I won't go over them. A few of the common properties, however, warrant a closer look.

Align

In Hour 13, "Working with the Form Designer," I discussed the Align and Alignment properties, so I won't go over those again in detail. It should be noted here, however, that not all components expose the Align property at design time. A single-line edit control, for instance, should occupy a standard height, so the features of the Align property do not make sense for that type of component. As you gain experience with C++Builder, and depending on the type of applications you write, you will probably rely heavily on the Align property.

Color

The Color property sets the background color for the component. (The text color is set through the Font property.) Although the Color property is simple to use, there are a few aspects of component colors that should be pointed out.

The way the Color property is handled in the Object Inspector is somewhat unique. If you click the Value column, you will see the drop-down arrow button indicating that you can choose from a list of color values. That is certainly the case, but there's more to it than that. If you double-click the Value column, the Color dialog box will be displayed. This dialog box allows you to choose a color from one of the predefined colors or to create your own colors by clicking the Define Custom Colors button. Figure 15.1 shows the Color dialog box after the Define Custom Colors button has been clicked.

FIGURE 15.1

The Color dialog box.

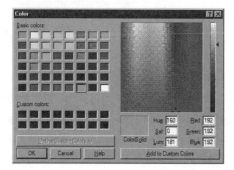

This is the same Color dialog box that is displayed if you implement the ColorDialog component in your application.

If you choose a color from the Color dialog box, you will see that the value of the Color property changes to a hexadecimal string. This string represents the red, green, and blue (RGB) values that make up the color. If you know the exact RGB value of a color, you can type it in (not likely!).

Most of the time you will probably choose a color from the list of color values provided. When you click the drop-down button to display the list of possible values, you will see what essentially amounts to two groups of values. The first group of colors begins with clBlack and ends with clWhite. These are the C++Builder predefined colors; this list represents the most commonly used colors. To choose one of the listed colors, simply click the color in the list. If you can't find a color in the list that suits your needs, you can invoke the Color dialog box as I've discussed.

The second group of colors in the list begins with clScrollBar. This group of colors represents the Windows system colors. If you use colors from this list, your application will automatically adjust its colors when the user changes color schemes in Windows. If you want your application to follow the color scheme the user has chosen for his system, you should choose colors from this list rather than from the first list.

 Remember to keep your users in mind when dealing with colors in your applications. For example, you might be running Windows in 16-, 24-, or 32-bit color mode. On your system your application looks great. That same application run on a machine using 256-color mode will likely look quite different. If Windows cannot find a match for the colors you have used, it will dither colors to approximate the requested color. The result will almost certainly not be what you expected when you wrote the application.

Cursors

The Cursor property controls the cursor that is displayed when the user moves the mouse cursor over the component. Windows automatically changes cursors for some components. For example, Windows changes the cursor to an I-beam when the cursor is moved over an Edit, Memo, or RichEdit component, to name just a few. To let Windows manage the cursor leave the Cursor property set to crDefault. If you have specialized windows (such as a window used as the drawing surface in a paint program), you can specify one of the other cursors. When the mouse is moved over that component, Windows will change the cursor to the one you have specified.

Frequently you will need to change cursors at runtime. A long process, for instance, should be indicated to the user by displaying the hourglass cursor. When you reset the cursor, you need to be sure to set the cursor back to whatever it was originally. The following code snippet illustrates:

```
TCursor oldCursor = Screen->Cursor;
Screen->Cursor = crHourGlass;
// do some stuff which takes a long time
Screen->Cursor = oldCursor;
```

This ensures that the cursor that was originally set for the application is properly restored.

Another cursor property, DragCursor, is used to set the cursor that is used when the mouse cursor is over a component that supports drag-and-drop. As with colors, you should be prudent in your use of cursors. Use custom cursors when needed, but don't overdo it.

Enabled

Components can be enabled or disabled through the Enabled property. When a component is disabled, it cannot accept focus (clicking on it has no effect), and usually it gives some visual cue to indicate that it is disabled. In the case of buttons, for instance, the button text is grayed out as is any bitmap on the button. Enabled is a Boolean property—set it to True to enable the component or set it to False to disable the component. Enabling and disabling windows (remember that windowed components are windows, too) is a feature of Windows itself.

The Enabled property applies mostly to windowed components, but can apply to non-windowed components as well. The Label component is an example of a non-windowed component that can be disabled.

> Modifying the Enabled property for a Panel component has additional implications. Panels are often used as containers for other controls. Therefore, a panel becomes the parent of the controls that are placed on the panel. If you disable a panel, the components on the panel won't show as disabled, but won't function because their parent (the panel) is disabled.

Although components can be disabled at design time, enabling and disabling components is something that is usually done at runtime. Menu items, for instance, should be enabled or disabled according to whether they apply at a given time. The same is true of buttons. There are a variety of reasons why you might want to disable other types of controls as well.

To disable a component at runtime, just assign `False` to its `Enabled` property and to enable a component assign `True` to `Enabled`. The following code snippet enables or disables a menu item based on some condition:

```
if (saveEnabled) FileSave->Enabled = true;
else FileSave->Enabled = false;
```

This process is often referred to as *command enabling* and is an important part of a professional-looking Windows program.

Font

The `Font` property is a major property and therefore needs to be included here, but there is not a lot that needs to be said about it. The `Font` property is an instance of the `TFont` class, and as such has its own properties. You can set the `Font` properties by double-clicking on the font name in the Object Inspector (which will expand the Font node and show the `Font` properties) or by invoking the Font dialog box. Figure 15.2 shows the Object Inspector with the `Font` property node expanded to reveal the `TFont` properties.

FIGURE 15.2

The Object Inspector showing the expanded Font *property.*

The `Color` property sets the color of the font, and the `Name` property allows you to choose the typeface for the font.

The `Height` and `Size` properties of `TFont` deserve special mention. The `Height` property is used to specify the height of the font in pixels, whereas the `Size` property is used to specify the height of the font in points. When you change one of these properties, the other changes automatically. The `Height` is often specified as a negative number. Refer to the online help for `TFont` for an explanation of why this is the case.

15

Finally, the Style property of TFont can be used to toggle bold, italic, underline, or strikethrough. These styles are not mutually exclusive, so you can mix styles in any way you choose.

> Although you can use the Object Inspector to change font properties, the Font dialog box (invoked when you click the ellipsis button next to the Font property) has the added benefit of showing you a sample of what the font looks like as you choose different font options. To simply change the font's Style property or Size property, use the Object Inspector. But if you are looking for just the right font, the Font dialog box is a better choice.

Hint

The Hint property is used to set hint text for a component. The hint text has two parts. The first part is sometimes called the *short hint*. This is the hint text that is displayed when the user places the cursor over the component and pauses. The pop-up window that displays the hint text is called a *ToolTip*.

The second part of the hint text is sometimes called the *long hint*. The long hint is the optional hint text that shows in the status bar when the user moves the mouse cursor over the component. The short and long hint texts are separated by a pipe (¦). For example, to specify both the short hint text and the long hint text for a File Open speed button, you would enter the following for the Hint property:

```
Open¦Open a file for editing
```

In order for short hints to show, you must have the Application object's ShowHint property set to True (the default) as well as the component's ShowHint property. After that is done, displaying the long hint in a status bar is as simple as setting the status bar's AutoHint property to True.

You can specify the short hint text, the long hint text, or both. You can use the pipe to tell C++Builder which hint text you are supplying. If you don't use the pipe, both the short hint and the long hint will use the same text.

ParentColor, ParentCtl3D, ParentFont, and ParentShowHint

The ParentColor, ParentCtl3D, ParentFont, and ParentShowHint properties all work the same way, so by understanding one, you'll understand them all.

When these properties are set to True, the component takes its Color, Ctl3D, Font, or ShowHint settings from its parent. For example, for most components the ParentFont property is set to True by default. This means that the component will inherit the font that its parent is currently using. To illustrate, do this exercise:

1. Create a blank form. Set the Font property's Size property to 16.

2. Place a Label component on the form. Notice that the label automatically uses the 16-point font.

3. Place a Button component on the form. It also uses the 16-point font.

Other Common Properties

Table 15.1 lists other common properties that are frequently used. These properties don't require as much explanation, so they are listed here for your reference. Not all components have each of the properties listed.

TABLE 15.1 ADDITIONAL COMPONENT PROPERTIES

Property	Description
BorderStyle	Can be bsSingle or bsNone. Use bsNone when you want the component to blend in with the background.
BoundsRect	The rectangle of the entire component (not limited to only the client area).
Caption	Sets the component's caption. Many components don't have captions, so for those components the Caption property is not exposed.
ClientHeight	Contains the height of the client area of the component.
ClientRect	Contains the rectangle for the client area of the component.
ClientWidth	Contains the width of the client area of the component.
Constraints	Sets the size constraints for the component (maximum width and height, minimum width and height). More important for forms than for other components.
Ctl3D	Indicates whether the control should be drawn with a 3D border. If BorderStyle is set to bsNone, this property has no effect.
Height	Sets the component's height.
HelpContext	The HelpContext property is used to associate an index number in a help file with a particular component.
Left	Sets the x-coordinate of the component.
Parent	A pointer to the parent of the component.
PopupMenu	Specifies the pop-up menu that will be displayed when the user right-clicks the component.

Property	Description
TabOrder	For windowed components. Sets this component's position in the tab order.
TabStop	For windowed components. Indicates that this component can be tabbed into. Setting this property to False removes the component from the tab order.
Top	Sets the y-coordinate of the component.
Visible	When read, indicates whether the component is currently visible. When written to, Visible either hides or shows the component.
Width	Sets the width of the component.

Primary Methods of Components

There are more than 20 methods that most components have in common. Windowed components have more than 40 common methods from which to choose. Interestingly, not many of these are widely used. Much of the functionality of components is accomplished via properties. For example, to hide a component, you can call the Hide() method or you can set the Visible property to False. In addition, components typically have methods specific to their purpose, and it will likely be those methods that you use most when dealing with a particular component.

There are a few methods worthy of note, however, so I'll list them here (see Table 15.2). Note that some of these methods are not available to all controls. These are not the most often used methods common to every component, but rather the most commonly used methods of components in general. Also, this list concentrates on components representing controls (components placed on forms) rather than components as forms. Methods particular to forms were discussed in Hour 11, "C++Builder Forms."

TABLE 15.2 COMMON METHODS OF COMPONENTS

Method	Description
Broadcast	Used to send a message to all windowed child components.
ClientToScreen	Converts client window coordinates into screen coordinates.
ContainsControl	Returns True if the specified component is a child of the component or form.
HandleAllocated	Returns True if the Handle property for the component has been created. Simply reading the Handle property automatically creates a handle if it hasn't already been created, so HandleAllocated() can be used to check for the existence of the handle without creating it.

continues

TABLE 15.2 CONTINUED

Method	Description
Hide	Hides the component. The component is still available to be shown again later.
Invalidate	Requests that the component be redrawn. The component will be redrawn at Windows's earliest convenience.
Perform	Sends a message directly to a component rather than going through the Windows messaging system.
Refresh	Requests that a component be redrawn immediately and erases the component prior to repainting.
Repaint	Requests that a component be redrawn immediately. The component's background is not erased prior to repainting.
SetBounds	Enables you to set the Top, Left, Width, and Height properties all at one time. This saves time having to set them individually.
SetFocus	Sets the focus to a component and makes it the active component. Applies only to windowed components.
Update	Forces an immediate repaint of the control. Typically, you should use Refresh() or Repaint() to repaint components.

Now look at some of the events to which a component is most likely to respond.

Common Events

As with properties and methods, there are some events that will be responded to most often. Components cover a wide variety of possible Windows controls, so each component has individual needs. Events specific to forms are not covered here because I covered that information in Hour 11. The most commonly used events are listed in Table 15.3.

TABLE 15.3 COMMONLY HANDLED COMPONENT EVENTS

Event	Description
OnChange	This event is triggered when a control changes in one way or another. Exact implementation depends on the component.
OnClick	Sent when the component is clicked with either mouse button.
OnDblClick	This event occurs when the user double-clicks the component.
OnEnter	This event occurs when a windowed component receives focus (is activated).

15

Event	Description
OnExit	This event occurs when a windowed component loses focus as the result of the user switching to a different control. It does not occur, however, when the user switches forms or switches to another application.
OnKeyDown	This event is triggered when the user presses a key while the control has focus. Keys include all alphanumeric keys as well as keys such as the arrow keys, Home, End, Ctrl, and so on.
OnKeyPress	This event is also triggered when the user presses a key, but only when alphanumeric keys or the Tab, backspace, Enter, or Esc keys are pressed.
OnKeyUp	This event occurs whenever a key is released.
OnMouseDown	This event is triggered when the mouse button is pressed while over the component. The parameters passed to the event handler give you information on which mouse button was clicked, special keys that were pressed (Alt, Shift, Ctrl), and the x,y coordinate of the mouse pointer when the event occurred.
OnMouseMove	This event occurs any time the mouse is moved over the control.
OnMouseUp	This event is triggered when the mouse button is released while over a control. The mouse button must first have been clicked while on the control.
OnPaint	This event is sent any time a component needs repainting. You can respond to this event to do any custom painting a component requires.

DEALING WITH MOUSE EVENTS

Mouse events have a couple of peculiarities that you should be aware of. If you are responding just to a mouse click on a component, you will want to keep it simple and only respond to the OnClick event. If you must use OnMouseDown and OnMouseUp, you should be aware that the OnClick event will be sent as well as the OnMouseDown and OnMouseUp events. For example, a single click will result in these events occurring (and in this order):

OnMouseDown
OnClick
OnMouseUp

Similarly, when the user double-clicks with the mouse, it could result in the application getting more events than you might think. When a component is double-clicked, the following events occur:

OnMouseDown
OnClick
OnDblClick
OnMouseUp

The point I am trying to make is that you need to take care when responding to both double-click and single-click events for a component. Be aware that you will get four events for a double-click event.

Multiple events will occur when a key is pressed, too. A keypress in an edit control, for instance, will result in OnKeyDown, OnKeyPress, OnChange, and OnKeyUp events occurring.

The CD accompanying the book contains a program called EventTst, which illustrates the fact that multiple events occur on mouse clicks and keypresses. Run this program and you will see how multiple events can be triggered based on certain user actions.

In the next hour you'll look at some of the VCL components in more detail. First, however, I want to introduce you to a class that is used by certain VCL components.

TStrings

The TStrings class is a VCL class that manages lists of strings. Several VCL components use instances of TStrings to manage their data (usually text). For example, you used TStrings when you built the ScratchPad application in the previous two hours. "I don't recall using a TStrings class," you say. Well, you did, but you just weren't aware of it. Remember when you saved and loaded files? You used something like this:

```
Memo->Lines->SaveToFile(SaveDialog->FileName);
```

The Lines property of TMemo is an instance of the TStrings class. The SaveToFile() method of TStrings takes the strings and saves them to a file on disk. You can do the same thing to load a list box from a file on disk or save the contents of a list box to disk. In the case of the TListBox class, the property that holds the list box items is called Items. For example, do this exercise:

1. Create a new application and place a ListBox component on the form. Size the list box as desired.

2. Change the Name property of the list box to ListBox.

3. Double-click the background of the form (not on the list box). The Code Editor displays the FormCreate() function.

4. Type the following code in the FormCreate() function:
   ```
   char winDir[256], fileName[256];
   GetWindowsDirectory(winDir, sizeof(winDir));
   wsprintf(fileName, "%s\\win.ini", winDir);
   ListBox->Items->LoadFromFile(fileName);
   ```

5. Click the Run button to compile and run the program.

When the program runs, the list box will contain the contents of your WIN.INI file. Using this method, it's easy to load a list box from any ASCII text data file. The ComboBox component also has an Items property, and it works in exactly the same way.

You can add, delete, insert, and move items in a list box, combo box, or memo by calling the Add(), Append(), Delete(), Insert(), and Move() methods of the TStrings class.

How Add() performs depends on the value of the Sorted property. If the Sorted property is set to True, Add() inserts the string where it needs to be in the list of items. If Sorted is False, the new string is added at the end of the list.

A component can be cleared of its contents by calling the Clear() method. An individual string can be accessed by using the Strings property of TStrings and the array subscript operator. For example, to retrieve the first string in a list of strings, you would use

```
Edit->Text = ListBox->Items->Strings[0];
```

There might be times when you need to manage a list of strings unrelated to a component. The TStringList class is provided for exactly that purpose. This class works just like TStrings but can be used outside components.

In reality, TStrings is what is called an *abstract base class*. An abstract base class is never used directly, but only serves as a base class from which to derive other classes. The Lines property of the Memo component is actually an instance of the TMemoStrings class rather than an instance of the TStrings class as I said in this section. This can be confusing because the Lines property *is* declared as a TStrings pointer but is actually an instance of TMemoStrings. Translating this into C++ might look something like this:

```
TStrings* Lines;
Lines = new TMemoStrings;
```

This is why the Lines property appears to be an instance of TStrings but is really not. I didn't mean to lead you astray, but I thought it was best to make this distinction after the discussion on TStrings rather than confuse you with this information during that discussion.

Summary

Understanding the common properties, methods, and events that most components have in common will help you in all your C++Builder applications. In this hour you learned about those elements VCL components have in common. You also learned about the TStrings and TStringList classes. The TStrings component (or a class derived from TStrings) is used in many VCL components. An understanding of TStrings is vital to using those components.

Workshop

The Workshop contains quiz questions to help you solidify your understanding of the material covered and exercises to provide you with experience in using what you have learned.

Q&A

Q **If I change the Name property of a component using the Object Inspector, C++Builder will automatically change all references to that component in my code, right?**

A Yes and no. C++Builder will change all references to that component name in C++Builder-generated code, but it will not change any user-written code.

Q **I want to use the features of the TStrings class to keep a list of strings my program needs in order to operate. The compiler won't let me use a TStrings object. What do I do?**

A Use a TStringList object instead. The TStringList class is provided for this purpose.

Quiz

1. Can you change the Name property of a component at runtime?
2. What property is used to enable and disable controls?
3. What is the difference between the long hint and the short hint?
4. Name two components that use TStrings to store their data.

Answers

1. Yes, but it is not generally a good idea. The Name property is used by VCL internally and should not be changed.
2. The Enabled property is used to enable and disable controls.

15

3. The long hint is used for the status bar text and the short hint is used for the ToolTip text.

4. Components that use instances of TStrings include the ListBox, ComboBox, RadioGroup, and RichEdit components.

Exercises

1. Write an application that contains two edit components and a button. Write code so that when the button is clicked the edit controls are disabled.

2. Using the TStringList class, write a program that creates a text file. The text file can contain any text you choose.

HOUR 16

Standard Windows Control Components

Back in the Jurassic age, there was something called Windows 3.0. Windows 3.0 gave us things like edit controls (single line and multiline), list boxes, combo boxes, buttons, check boxes, radio buttons, and static controls. These controls must have been fairly well designed because they are very prevalent in Windows programs today—even considering all the new Win32 controls.

I'm not going to go over every Windows control and its corresponding Visual Component Library (VCL) component. There are a few things, though, you should know regarding the standard components that I will point out.

Edit Controls

C++Builder comes with four edit-control components. The Edit, Memo, and MaskEdit components are based on the standard Windows edit control. The RichEdit component is based on the Win32 rich edit control, which is not one of the standard Windows controls. Still, I will discuss RichEdit here because it has many things in common with the other edit controls.

The `Edit` component encapsulates the basic single-line edit control. This component has no `Align` or `Alignment` property. It has no `Alignment` property because the text in a single-line edit control can only be left-justified. The `Edit` component has no `Align` property because it cannot (or more accurately, should not) be expanded to fill the client area of a window. (A single-line edit control that fills the entire client area of a window might give the user the impression that she could type multiple lines of text.)

> If you need text in an edit component to be right-justified or centered, use a `Memo` component but make its height that of a standard `Edit` component. Then set the `Alignment` property as needed.

The `MaskEdit` component is an `Edit` component with an input filter, or mask, attached. The `MaskEdit` does not represent a Windows control per se, but rather is just a VCL extension of a standard edit control. A mask is used to force input to a specific range of numbers or characters. In addition, the mask can contain special characters that are placed in the edit control by default. For example, a date is commonly formatted as follows:

12/16/98

An edit mask for a date can already have the slashes in place so the user only has to enter the numbers. The edit mask would specify that only numbers can be entered to avoid the possibility of the user entering a nonnumeric character.

> The `DateTimePicker` component (found on the Win32 tab) enables you to pick a date or a time from a specialized edit component. When the `Kind` property is set to `dtkDate`, the component displays a drop-down calendar from which the user can choose a date. When `Kind` property is set to `dtkTime`, the `DateTimePicker` displays a multi-field edit control that enables the user to set the hours, minutes, seconds, and AM or PM. The `DateTimePicker` is preferred over the `MaskEdit` for date and time entry.

The `EditMask` property controls the mask used. When you click the ellipsis button in the Value column for the `EditMask` property, the Input Mask Editor is displayed. This dialog box enables you to choose from one of the predefined masks or to create your own. You can choose prebuilt masks from several countries. Figure 16.1 shows the Input Mask Editor displaying the United Kingdom set of predefined input masks.

FIGURE 16.1

The Input Mask Editor dialog box.

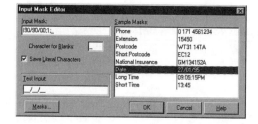

For more information on building your own masks, see the C++Builder online help.

The Memo component encapsulates a multiline edit control. The Lines property is the most significant property in a Memo component. As I mentioned in Hour 15 in the discussion on TStrings, the Lines property enables you to save the contents of the Memo component to disk or load the Memo with text from a file, as well as otherwise manipulate the individual lines in the Memo. The ScrollBars property is unique to the Memo component. This property enables you to specify whether your component has a horizontal scrollbar, a vertical scrollbar, or both. You used the ScrollBars property in Hour 13 when you wrote the ScratchPad application. The Memo component is a very versatile component that you will probably find yourself using frequently.

The RichEdit component is the biggest and the best of all the edit components. It is based on the Win32 rich edit control. The RichEdit component enables you to change fonts, use indentation, set text to bold, italic, or underlined, and much more. Basically, the RichEdit component is a mini word processor in one neat package. RichEdit has surprisingly few design-time properties over what the Memo component has. Key runtime properties include SelAttributes and Paragraph. The RichEdit component is fairly complex, but still easy to use considering its complexities. See the C++Builder online help for full details on the RichEdit component.

Table 16.1 lists the published properties specific to components based on edit controls. Table 16.2 lists the public (runtime) properties of the VCL edit controls.

TABLE 16.1 PUBLISHED PROPERTIES FOR EDIT CONTROLS

Property	Applies To	Default	Description
AutoSelect	Edit, MaskEdit	True	When set to True, text in the edit control is automatically selected when the user tabs to the control.
AutoSize	Edit, MaskEdit	True	When set to True, the edit control automatically resizes itself when the font of the edit control changes. Otherwise, the edit control does not change size when the font changes.

continues

TABLE 16.1 CONTINUED

Property	Applies To	Default	Description
CharCase	Edit, MaskEdit	ecNormal	Determines whether the edit control displays uppercase (ecUpperCase), lowercase (ecLowerCase), or mixed text (ecNormal).
HideScrollBars	RichEdit	False	When set to True, the scrollbars are shown when needed but hidden otherwise. When set to False, the scrollbars are shown as determined by the value of the ScrollBars property.
HideSelection	Edit, Memo, RichEdit	False	When set to True, any text selected will not show as selected when the user tabs to another control.
Lines	Memo, RichEdit	none	The text contained in the component. Lines is an instance of the TStrings class.
MaxLength	All	0	Specifies the maximum number of characters that the component will hold. When set to 0, the amount of text that can be input is unlimited (limited only by system considerations). When set to any nonzero value, it limits the number of characters to that value.
OEMConvert	Edit, Memo	False	Set this property to True when the text input consists of filenames.
PasswordChar	Edit, MaskEdit	#0	When this property is set to a value other than ASCII #0, any text entered will be echoed with the character provided. The actual text in the edit control is unaffected. Most password edits use the asterisk (*) as the password character.
PlainText	RichEdit	False	When set to True, RTF (rich text format) files are shown as plain text without character and paragraph formatting. When set to False, RTF files are displayed with full formatting.
ReadOnly	All	False	When set to True, the component displays its text, but new text cannot be entered. The user can, however, highlight text and copy it to the Clipboard.

Property	Applies To	Default	Description
ScrollBars	Memo, RichEdit	ssNone	Determines which scrollbars to display. Choices are ssNone, ssBoth, ssHorizontal, and ssVertical.
Text	Edit, MaskEdit	none	Contains the text in the component.
WantReturns	Memo, RichEdit	True	When set to True, the component keeps the return character and a new line is inserted in the edit control when the user presses Enter. When set to False, return characters go to the form and are not placed in the edit control. If you have a form with a default button and WantReturns set to False, pressing Enter causes the form to close.
WantTabs	Memo, RichEdit	False	When set to True, a tab character is placed in the edit control when the user presses the Tab key. When set to False, tab characters go to the form, which would enable tabbing out of the edit control.
WordWrap	Memo, RichEdit	True	When set to True, text entered wraps to a new line when the right edge of the edit control is reached. When set to False, the edit control automatically scrolls as new text is entered.

TABLE 16.2 PUBLIC PROPERTIES FOR EDIT CONTROLS

Property	Applies To	Description
Modified	All	Indicates whether the contents of the edit control have changed since the last time the Modified property was set. After saving the contents of a Memo or RichEdit component to a file, you should set Modified to False.
SelLength	All	Contains the length of the text currently selected in the edit control.
SelStart	All	Contains the starting point of the selected text in the edit control. The first character in the edit control is 0.
SelText	All	Contains the currently selected text in an edit control.

16

Edit controls have many common methods; they are too numerous to list here. The `CutToClipboard()`, `CopyToClipboard()`, `PasteFromClipboard()`, and `Clear()` methods deal with Clipboard operations and text manipulation. The `GetSelTextBuff()` and `GetTextBuff()` methods retrieve the selected text in the component and the entire text in the component, respectively. See the C++Builder online help topics `TEdit`, `TMaskEdit`, `TMemo`, and `TRichEdit` for a complete list of methods associated with each edit component.

The edit component events that you are most likely to be interested in are dependent on the type of edit control you are using. In general, though, the `OnEnter`, `OnExit`, `OnChange`, `OnKeyDown` (or `OnKeyPress`), and `OnKeyUp` events are the most widely used.

The `ListBox` and `ComboBox` Components

The `ListBox` and `ComboBox` components are also widely used. The `ListBox` component represents a standard Windows list box, which simply presents a list of choices. If the list box contains more items than can be shown at one time, scrollbars appear to enable access to the rest of the items in the list box.

NEW TERM   Some list boxes are *owner-drawn* list boxes. In an owner-drawn list box, the programmer takes the responsibility for drawing the items in the list box.

Combo boxes are specialized list boxes. Actually, a combo box is a combination of a list box and an edit control. The user can choose from the list or type in a value in the edit portion. When the user chooses an item from the list, that item is placed in the edit control. There are three different types of combo box. The combo box type is determined by the `Style` property. Table 16.3 lists the types of combo boxes and a description of each.

TABLE 16.3   TYPES OF COMBO BOXES

Type	Description
Simple	The simple style of the combo box is nothing more than an edit control placed on top of a list box. The user can choose from the list or type text in the edit portion.
Drop-down	Similar to the simple style, except the list box portion is not initially displayed. A drop-down button is provided so that the user can view the list and choose an item. The user can also type text in the edit portion.
Drop-down list	This is the most restrictive type of combo box. As with the drop-down style, the list is not initially exposed. The user can click the drop-down button to expose the list and choose an item from the list, but cannot enter text in the edit portion. Use this style when you want the user to select only from a predetermined set of choices.

The CD-ROM accompanying the book contains a program called ComboBox Test that illustrates the different types of combo boxes.

Table 16.4 lists the published properties common to list boxes and combo boxes. Table 16.5 lists the public (runtime) properties.

TABLE 16.4 PUBLISHED PROPERTIES FOR LIST BOXES AND COMBO BOXES

Property	Applies To	Default	Description
Columns	ListBox	0	Contains the number of columns in the list box. You can create multiple columns by making this property greater than 1.
ExtendedSelection	ListBox	True	Determines whether extended selection is allowed. Extended selection enables the user to select items using Shift+click and Ctrl+click. Has no effect if MultiSelect is set to False.
IntegralHeight	ListBox	False	When True, the list box height will be resized to be sure that no partial lines are displayed. When False, the list box might show partial lines.
ItemHeight	Both	13	For use with owner-drawn list boxes and combo boxes. Sets the height of the items in the control.
Items	Both	none	A TStrings instance that contains the list of items in the list box. (See the section on TStrings in Hour 15 for a description of available properties and methods.)
MaxLength	ComboBox	0	The maximum number of characters the user can type in the edit portion of the combo box. Same as MaxLength in edit controls.
MultiSelect	ListBox	False	When True, the list box enables multiple items to be selected.
Sorted	Both	False	When set to True, the list box items are sorted in ascending order. When set to False, the items are not sorted at all.
Style	ComboBox	csDropDown	The style of the combo box. Choices are csSimple, csDropDown, csDropDownList, lbOwnerDrawFixed, and csOwnerDrawVariable. (See Table 16.3 for a description of the three basic styles.)

continues

16

TABLE 16.4 CONTINUED

Property	Applies To	Default	Description
	ListBox	lbStandard	Style choices for list boxes are lbStandard, lbOwnerDrawFixed, and csOwnerDrawVariable.
TabWidth	ListBox	0	List boxes can use tabs. This property sets the tab width, in pixels.
Text	ComboBox	none	Contains the text in the edit portion of the combo box.

TABLE 16.5 PUBLIC PROPERTIES FOR LIST BOXES AND COMBO BOXES

Property	Applies To	Description
ItemIndex	ListBox	Contains the index of the currently selected item, with 0 being the first item in the list. Returns –1 if no item is selected. When written to, selects the specified index.
SelCount	ListBox	Contains the number of items selected in a multiple-selection list box.
Selected	ListBox	Returns True if the specified item is selected or False if it is not.
SelLength	ComboBox	Contains the length of the text currently selected in the edit control part of the combo box.
SelStart	ComboBox	Contains the starting point of the selected text in the edit control. The first character in the edit control is 0.
SelText	ComboBox	Contains the currently selected text in the edit control.
TopIndex	ListBox	Returns the list box item that is at the top of the list box. Can be used to set the top item to a certain list box item.

There are very few ListBox and ComboBox methods. The Clear() method will clear the control of all data. The ItemAtPos() method will return the index number of the item at the specified x and y coordinates. The SelectAll() method will select the text in the edit control portion of a combo box.

Easily the most-used event when dealing with combo boxes and list boxes is the OnClick event. Use this event to determine when a selection has been made in the list box.

Clicking the edit portion of a combo box or the drop-down button does not result in an OnClick event being sent. Only when the list box portion of a combo box is clicked will the OnClick event occur.

The OnChange event can be used to detect changes to the edit portion of a combo box just as it is used with edit controls. The OnDropDown event is used to detect when the drop-down button on a combo box has been clicked. The OnMeasureItem and OnDrawItem events are used with owner-drawn list boxes and owner-drawn combo boxes.

Using Button Controls

VCL contains several types of buttons that you can use in your applications. Although not all of them are based on the standard Windows button control, I will still address all the button types here. Before we look at the specific button components, though, let's cover some of the basics.

16

> When setting a button's Caption property, use the ampersand (&) just as you would when setting the Caption property of menu items. The character after the ampersand will be underlined and will be the accelerator for the button.

The button components only have about four properties of note.

ModalResult

The ModalResult property is used to provide built-in form closing for forms displayed with ShowModal(). By default, ModalResult is set to mrNone (which is 0). Use this value for buttons that are used as regular buttons on the form, and that don't close the form when pressed.

If you use any nonzero value for ModalResult, pressing the button will close the form and return the ModalResult value. For example, if you place a button on a form and set the ModalResult property to mrOk, pressing the button will close the form, and the return value from ShowModal() will be mrOk (1). Given that, then, you can do something like the following:

```
int result = MyForm->ShowModal();
if (result == mrOK) DoSomething();
if (result == mrCancel) return;
```

See the TModalResult topic in the C++Builder online help for a complete list of modal result constants.

You don't have to use one of the predefined ModalResult constants for your buttons. You can use any value you like. Let's say, for example, you had a custom dialog box that could be closed by using a variety of buttons. You could assign a different ModalResult value to each button (100, 150, and 200, for example), and you would then know which button closed the dialog box. Any nonzero number is valid, up to the maximum value of an int. The return value from the ShowModal() function will be the value of the ModalResult property.

The CD contains a program called ButtnTst that demonstrates the use of ModalResult. The program enables you to execute a form containing several buttons. When you click a button the ModalResult will be reported back on the main form.

Default

The Default property is another key property of buttons. Windows has a standard mechanism for dealing with dialog boxes. One of the features of this mechanism is as follows:

If a control other than a button has keyboard focus and the user presses the Enter key on the keyboard, the dialog box behaves as if the user had clicked the *default button*.

The default button is the button that has the BS_DEFPUSHBUTTON style set (usually the OK button). This feature has been the bane of programmers and the curse of data-entry personnel for years. The Default property is used to set a button as the default button for a form. The default value for this property is false. To make a button the default button, set its Default property to true. If you don't specifically set any button's Default property to true, the form will not close when the user presses the Enter key.

Cancel

The Cancel property works with the Esc key in much the same way as the Default property works with the Enter key. When the user presses the Esc key to close a form, the return value from ShowModal() will be the ModalResult value of the button whose Cancel property is set to True. If no button has its Cancel property set to True, mrCancel will be returned if the user uses the Esc key to close the form (mrCancel is equal to 2).

Closing a form by clicking the system close box or by pressing Alt+F4 results in mrCancel being returned from ShowModal(), as you would expect. Pressing the Esc key, however, results in a return value of the ModalResult property being set to whatever button has the Cancel property set to True. The OnClick handler for the Cancel button is called before the form closes. No OnClick handler is called if the user uses the system close box or Alt+F4 to close the form. Be sure to anticipate the different ways users might use (or abuse) your forms.

You can have more than one button with a `Default` property set to `True`. Likewise, you can have more than one button with the `Cancel` property set to `True`. However, when the user presses Enter on the keyboard, the first button in the tab order that has its `Default` property set to `True` will be invoked. Similarly, when the user presses the Esc key to close the form, the return value from `ShowModal()` will be the `ModalResult` value of the first button in the tab order that has its `Cancel` property set to `True`.

Enabled

In Hour 15 I discussed the `Enabled` property when I discussed components in general. This property is used a lot with buttons to enable or disable the button depending on the current state of the program or of a particular form. When a button is disabled (its `Enabled` property is set to `False`), its text is grayed out and the button does not function. In the case of buttons with bitmaps on them (`BitBtn` and `SpeedButton`), the bitmap will also be grayed out automatically.

Button components have only one method of interest: The `Click()` method, which simulates a mouse click. When you call `Click()` for a button, the `OnClick` event of the button is executed just as if the user had clicked the button. As for events, typically only the `OnClick` event is used.

Now let's take a look at the different button components C++Builder provides.

The Button Component

The standard `Button` component is sort of like actor Danny DeVito—he ain't pretty, but he sure gets a lot of work. There really isn't anything to add concerning the standard `Button` component. It has a default `Height` property value of 25 pixels and a default `Width` property value of 75. Typically you will place a button on a form and respond to its `OnClick` event, and that's about it.

The BitBtn Component

The `BitBtn` component is a perfect example of how a component can be extended to provide additional functionality. In this case the standard `Button` component is extended to enable a bitmap to be displayed on the face of the button.

The `BitBtn` component has several properties in addition to what the `Button` component provides. All these properties work together to manage the bitmap on the button and the layout between the bitmap and the button's text. They are explained in the following sections.

Glyph

The Glyph property represents the bitmap on the button. The value of the Glyph property is a picture, or glyph.

NEW TERM A *glyph* is a picture that is usually in the form of a Windows bitmap file (.BMP).

The glyph itself consists of one or more bitmaps that represent the four possible states a button can be in: up, down, disabled, and stay down. If you are creating your own buttons, you can probably get by with supplying just one glyph, which the BitBtn component will then modify to represent the other three possible states. The bitmap will move down and to the right when the button is clicked and will be grayed out when disabled. The glyph in the stay-down state will be the same as in the up state, although the button face will change to give a pressed look.

> The BitBtn component automatically applies transparency to the button's glyph. Transparency means that part of the bitmap will be transparent and anything beneath the bitmap will show through. This allows you to design bitmaps that blend with the button they are on, regardless of the color of the button.
>
> The pixel in the lower-left corner of the bitmap is the color that will be used for the transparent color. Any pixels in the bitmap having that color will be transparent when the glyph is displayed on the button. You must keep this in mind when designing your bitmaps. If you are not using transparency, you will need the pixel in the lower-left corner to be a color not present anywhere else on the bitmap.

To set the glyph for a BitBtn, double-click the Value column in the Object Inspector next to the Glyph property. The Picture Editor will be displayed, and you can choose the bitmap that will be used for the glyph.

Kind

The Kind property is a nice feature of the BitBtn component that enables you to choose from several predefined kinds of buttons. The default value for the Kind property is bkCustom, which means that you will supply the glyph and set any other properties for the button. Choosing any of the other predefined kinds will produce these five results:

1. The Glyph property is automatically set for the kind of button chosen.
2. The Cancel or Default properties are modified according to the kind of button chosen.

3. The `Caption` property is modified for the type of button chosen.

4. The `ModalResult` property is set according to the kind of button chosen.

5. The button on the form is updated to reflect all these settings.

For example, if you set the value of `Kind` to `bkOK`, the button will become an OK button. The glyph is set to a green check mark, the `Cancel` property is set to `False`, the `Default` property is set to `True`, the `ModalResult` property is set to `mrOk`, the `Caption` property is set to `OK`, and the results show up on the form. You can always override any of the properties modified by changing the `Kind` property, but it is not usually necessary to do so. The CD-ROM that comes with this book contains a program called `BtnTest` that illustrates the use of the `BitBtn` component.

The `SpeedButton` Component

The `SpeedButton` component is a non-windowed component. It is different from the `Button` and `BitBtn` components in that a speed button cannot receive input focus, nor can you tab to it. On the other hand, the `SpeedButton` component has several things in common with the `BitBtn` component. The way in which the `Glyph` property is handled by the `SpeedButton` component is exactly the same as with the `BitBtn` component, so I'm not going to go over that ground again. There are a couple of major differences, though, so let's look at those.

By default, speed buttons are square and are 25×25 pixels. Your speed buttons can be any size you like and can contain text, although speed buttons don't usually contain text. There are some properties specific to speed buttons that you should be aware of, which I've broken down in the following sections.

> The C++Builder 1.0 method of creating toolbars involved using a `Panel` component on which various components (`SpeedButtons`, primarily) were placed. C++Builder 4 has the `ToolBar` component, which is the preferred method of creating a toolbar. The `ToolBar` component has some added benefits, but is slightly more complicated to use. You used the ToolBar component in Hour 12, "Writing an MDI Application," when you created the Picture Viewer program.

`GroupIndex`

Speed buttons can be grouped to make them behave like radio buttons (radio buttons are discussed later in the hour in the section "Radio Buttons and Check Boxes"). When one

16

button in the group is pressed, it stays down, and the button that was previously pressed pops up again.

To group speed buttons, simply assign the same value to the GroupIndex property for all buttons in a group. (The default value of 0 indicates that the button is not part of any group.) To illustrate, do the following exercise:

1. Create a blank form and place five speed buttons on the form. (I won't bother adding glyphs to the buttons in this simple exercise, but you certainly can if you want.)

2. Select all the buttons and change the value of the GroupIndex property to 1. The GroupIndex for all buttons will be changed to 1.

3. Optional: Change the Down property of one of the buttons to true.

4. Click the Run button to compile and run the program.

When you run the program, click several of the buttons. You will notice that only one button can be in the down state at one time. As you can see when you assign a nonzero value to GroupIndex, the speed buttons change their behavior. A speed button with a GroupIndex of 0 pops back up when you click it, whereas a speed button that is part of a group stays down when clicked.

AllowAllUp

By default, one button in the group must be down at all times. You can change that behavior by setting the AllowAllUp property to true. Doing this for one button automatically changes the AllowAllUp property for all other buttons in the group to True as well. Now you can have any one button in the group selected or no buttons at all.

> Sometimes you want a speed button to act as a toggle button. A toggle button is used to turn an option on or off and is not part of a button group. To make an individual speed button a toggle button, assign a nonzero value to its GroupIndex property and set its AllowAllUp property to True. Be sure to set the GroupIndex property to a value not used by any other components on the form. When the user clicks the button, it stays down. When the button is clicked again, it pops back up.

Down

The Down property, when read, returns True if the button is currently down and False if it is not. When written to, the Down property can be used to toggle a button as pressed or not pressed. Writing to the Down property has no effect unless the speed button is part of a group.

Radio Buttons and Check Boxes

Although radio buttons and check boxes are specialized buttons, they are, in the end, still buttons. I'm not going to spend a lot of time discussing these two components because implementing them is straightforward. Both the `RadioButton` and `CheckBox` components have a property called `Checked` that can be used to set the check state and can be read to retrieve the current check state.

The radio button is usually used in a group of buttons. A radio button typically signifies a group of options, only one of which can be selected at one time (like a group of speed buttons, which you just learned about). Although you can use a radio button by itself, it is not recommended because it is confusing to your users. When tempted to use a radio button by itself, use a check box instead—that's what a check box is for, after all.

16

Any buttons placed on a form will automatically be considered part of the same group. If you have more than one group of radio buttons, and those groups need to operate independent of one another, you need to use a `RadioGroup` component. This component enables you to quickly set up a group of radio buttons with a 3D frame around the buttons and a caption as well. To illustrate this concept, do the following exercise:

1. Create a blank form or use the form you created in the previous exercise. Place a `RadioGroup` component on the form.

2. Locate the `Items` property and double-click the Value column.

3. The String list editor is displayed. Type the following lines in the String list editor:
   ```
   Redtailed Hawk
   Peregrine Falcon
   Gyrfalcon
   Northern Goshawk
   ```

4. Click OK to close the String list editor. The group box is populated with radio buttons containing the text you typed.

5. Change the `Caption` property of the radio group box to
   ```
   Apprentice Falconers Can Legally Possess:
   ```

6. Click Run to compile and run the program.

When you click one of the radio buttons, the previously selected button pops up as expected. Using the `RadioGroup` component, you can put more than one group of radio buttons on a form. Like the list box and combo box components discussed earlier, the `RadioGroup` component has an `ItemIndex` property that you can read at runtime to determine which item in the group is selected. Oh, by the way—if you live in the United States, the answer to the quiz is Redtailed Hawk (American Kestrel would also have been an acceptable answer, but it was not presented in the list).

You can also use a GroupBox component to hold radio buttons. The GroupBox component is less convenient to use than the RadioGroup component, but it has more flexibility. You can place any type of control in a group box. After placed in the group box, the controls and the group box itself can be moved as a unit at design time.

The CheckBox component is used to enable users to turn an option on or off or to indicate to a user that an option is currently on or off. A check box can have up to three states, depending on its style: on, off, or grayed. If the check box's AllowGrayed property is False, it can only be checked or unchecked. When the AllowGrayed property is True, the check box can be any one of the three states. The grayed, or indeterminate, state is handled [programmatically]. In other words, it's up to you to decide what the grayed state means for your application. If the AllowGrayed property is False (the default), you can use the Checked property to determine if the check box is checked or unchecked. If the AllowGrayed property is True, you must use the State property to determine (or set) the check box state. State will return either cbChecked, cbUnchecked, or cbGrayed.

The Label Component

The Label component is used to display text on a form. It is a non-windowed control. Sometimes the label text is determined at design time and never changed. In other cases, the label is dynamic and is changed at runtime as the program dictates. Use the label's Caption property to set the label text at runtime. The Label component has no specialized methods or events beyond what is available with other components. Table 16.6 lists the properties specific to the Label component.

TABLE 16.6 PROPERTIES FOR THE Label COMPONENT

Property	Description
AutoSize	When set to True, the label sizes itself according to the text contained in the Caption property. When set to False, text is clipped at the right edge of the label.
FocusControl	A label is a non-windowed component, so it cannot receive input focus and it cannot be tabbed to. Sometimes, however, a label serves as the text for a control such as an edit control. In those cases you could assign an accelerator key to the label (using the ampersand) and then change the FocusControl property to the name of the control you want to receive focus when the label's accelerator key is pressed.

Property	Description
ShowAccelChar	Set this property to True if you want an actual ampersand to show up in the label rather than the ampersand serving as the accelerator key.
Transparent	When this property is set to True, the Color property is ignored and anything beneath the label shows through. This is useful for placing labels on bitmap backgrounds, for instance.
WordWrap	When set to True, text in the label wraps around to a new line when it reaches the right edge of the label.

16

The ScrollBar Component

The ScrollBar component represents a standalone scrollbar. It's standalone in the sense that it is not connected to an edit control, list box, form, or anything else. I have not found that the scrollbar is a control I use very frequently. Certain types of applications use scrollbars heavily, of course, but for day-in, day-out applications its use is fairly uncommon. The scrollbar's performance is set by setting the Min, Max, LargeChange, and SmallChange properties. The scrollbar's position can be set or obtained via the Position property. The Kind property enables you to specify a horizontal or vertical scrollbar. See the Scroller example on the book's CD for an example.

The Panel Component

The Panel component is sort of a workhorse in C++Builder. There is almost no limit to how you can use panels. Panels can be used to hold toolbar buttons, to display text labels such as a title for a form, display graphics, and to hold regular buttons as well. One of the advantages of a panel is that components placed on the panel become children of the panel. As such, they go with the panel wherever the panel goes. This can be a great aid at runtime and at design time.

Much of the power of the Panel component lies in its Align property. For instance, let's say you want a title to be displayed on the top of a form. Let's further assume that you want it centered no matter how the user sizes the window. By setting the Align property to alTop and the Alignment property to taCenter, your title will always be centered. It's a simple as that.

A panel can have many different appearances. The panel's appearance can be altered by changing the BevelInner, BevelOuter, BorderStyle, and BorderWidth properties. The Panel component is so versatile that it will take you a while to discover all its possible uses. See the Panel example on the book's CD to get an idea how the different border and bevel styles can be used in combination.

Summary

Unfortunately, there isn't sufficient space in this book to go over all the components C++Builder provides. You saw the Image, ToolBar, and ImageList components in Hour 12, when you created the Picture Viewer program. You also got a brief glimpse at the Shape component in Hour 13 as part of an exercise on aligning components. These represent just a sampling of the components that are waiting for you. You need to test drive each one of them to determine their usefulness for you. It is important to understand the basic controls available in Windows and the C++Builder components that represent those controls.

Workshop

The Workshop contains quiz questions to help you solidify your understanding of the material covered and exercises to provide you with experience in using what you have learned.

Q&A

Q I need an edit control in which my users can enter date values. Can I do that with C++Builder?

A Yes. Just use a MaskEdit component and set the EditMask property to display a date mask.

Q I need a single-line edit control to be right-justified, but there is no Alignment property for the Edit component. Can I right-align text in a single-line edit?

A No. What you can do, though, is use a Memo component and make it appear to be a regular Edit component. Be sure to set the Memo component's WantReturn property to false, its Height to the height of a standard edit component (21 pixels), and its Alignment property to taRightJustify. The component will give all appearances of being a single-line edit control that is right-justified.

Quiz

1. Name the three primary VCL edit components.

2. Is the CheckBox component a button?

3. Does the Label component have a window handle?

4. What component is often used as a container for other components?

Answers

1. The primary VCL edit components are the Edit, Memo, and RichEdit components. The MaskEdit is also an edit component.

2. Yes. While the CheckBox component does not look like a traditional button it is a button as far as Windows is concerned.

3. No. The Label is a non-windowed control.

4. The Panel component is used as a container component. Several other components qualify, too, such as the GroupBox and ScrollBox components.

16

Exercises

1. Create a program that contains two edit components. When the user types information in the first control, make it appear in the second edit control as it is entered.

2. Create a program with a list box. Write code to load the list box from a text file prior to the application being visible.

3. Add a button to the program in Exercise 2. Write code so that when the button is clicked, any text in the edit control is added as a new item in the list box.

HOUR **17**

Common Dialogs and the Object Repository

In this hour I continue the discussion of Visual Component Library (VCL) components by explaining the common dialog components. After that I explain the Object Repository, which is where C++Builder stores any pre-built forms, applications, or other objects for you to reuse.

The Common Dialog Boxes

Windows provides a set of common dialog boxes that any Windows program can use, including

- File Open
- File Save
- File Open Picture
- File Save Picture
- Font

- Color
- Print
- Printer Setup
- Find
- Replace

The common dialog boxes are found on the Dialogs tab of the Component palette. These components are considered nonvisual because they don't have a visual design-time interface. The following sections discuss the most commonly used common dialog boxes.

The Execute Method

One thing that all the common dialog boxes have in common is the `Execute()` method, which is used to create and display the dialog box. The dialog box is displayed modally except for the Find and Replace dialog boxes, which are displayed modelessly. `Execute()` returns `True` if the user clicked OK, double-clicked a filename (in the case of the file dialogs), or pressed Enter on the keyboard. `Execute()` returns `False` if the user clicked the Cancel button, pressed the Esc key, or closed the dialog box with the system close box. A common dialog box is often implemented like this:

```
if (OpenDialog->Execute()) {
  // user pressed OK so use the filename
  Memo->Lines->LoadFromFile(OpenDialog->FileName);
}
return;
```

You have seen code like this several times up to this point in the book. It displays the File Open dialog box and gets a filename from the user. If the user clicked OK, the code inside the `if` block is executed and the file is loaded in to a `Memo` component. If OK was not clicked, the code inside the `if` block is ignored and no action takes place.

The File Open and File Save Dialog Boxes

The File Open and File Save dialog boxes have several properties in common. File Open is used when you want to allow the user to open a file in your application (see Figure 17.1). It is encapsulated in the `OpenDialog` component. The File Save dialog box is used when getting a filename from the user in order to save a file. It is also used as the Save As dialog box. The File Save dialog box is encapsulated by the `SaveDialog` component.

Figure 17.1

A typical File Open dialog box.

The file dialog boxes are fairly easy to use in their most basic form. They do have a few features, however, that need to be explained in order for you to get the full benefit of using them. The following sections examine the properties that are specific to the file dialog boxes.

> The OpenDialog and SaveDialog components merely retrieve a filename from the user. It is up to the programmer to write code that actually does something with the filename.

The DefaultExt Property

NEW TERM   Use the DefaultExt property to set the default extension that the dialog box will use. The *default extension* is the extension that will automatically be appended to the filename if the user does not supply an extension.

The FileName Property

The FileName property is the most obvious file dialog box property: It holds the text of the file that the user chooses. Set this property before calling the dialog box if you want a filename to show in the edit portion of the file dialog box when it is initially displayed. After the user clicks OK to close the dialog box, this property contains the full path and filename of the file chosen.

The Files Property

Files, a read-only property, is a TStrings instance that contains the list of files selected when multiple file selection is enabled.

The Filter Property

The Filter property contains a list of the file types from which the user can choose. The list of file types is displayed in the Files of Type: combo box in the file dialog box.

You can set `Filter` to reflect types of files specific to your application. For instance, a simple text-editing program could have the filter set to show files of type .TXT, .INI, and .LOG, to name just a few. The filter can easily be set at design time through the Filter Editor dialog box. To invoke the Filter Editor, double-click the Value column next to the `Filter` property in the Object Inspector. Figure 17.2 shows the Filter Editor for a File Open dialog box.

FIGURE 17.2

The Filter Editor dialog box.

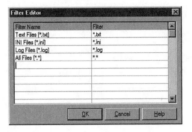

The Filter Name column contains a textual description of the file type. The Filter column is the actual file mask that is used to display files of that type.

Although you can enter the filter string directly in the Value column of the Object Inspector, it is easiest to use the Filter Editor. If you are only using a single filter, you can type it directly into the Value column for the `Filter` property. Separate the description and filter with a pipe. For example, to have a single filter for all file types, you would enter the following:

```
All Files (*.*)|*.*
```

The `FilterIndex` Property

The `FilterIndex` property is used to set the filter that is used when the dialog box is initially displayed. The index is not 0-based as you might expect, however. The first filter in the list is 1, the second is 2, and so on. For example, refer back to Figure 17.2. If you wanted the All Files filter to be the one initially displayed, you would set the `FilterIndex` property to 4.

The `InitialDir` Property

The `InitialDir` property is used to specify the directory that is used as the initial directory when the file dialog box is displayed. If no value is supplied for the `InitialDir` property, the current directory is used (as determined by Windows).

The `Options` Property

The `Options` property controls the way the file dialog box is used. The list of options is too long to list here, but common items include whether you allow new files or directories to be created, whether the Help button is shown on the dialog box, whether long filenames are allowed, whether multiple file selection is allowed, and others. See the C++Builder online help for the `OpenDialog` and `SaveDialog` components for complete information.

The `Title` Property

The `Title` property is used to set or read the title of the file dialog box. If no title is specified, the common dialog box defaults of Open for the `OpenDialog` component and Save for the `SaveDialog` component will be used.

> A Save As dialog box is nothing more than a `SaveDialog` component with the `Title` property set to `Save As`.

17

The File Open Picture and File Save Picture Dialog Boxes

These two dialog boxes are nothing more than the regular File Open and File Save dialog boxes with an extra feature—they display a preview window that enables you to see the image that is currently selected. These dialog boxes also have the `Filter` property preset to the common Windows image formats. Otherwise they behave just like the File Open and File Save dialog boxes.

The Color Dialog Box

The Color dialog box enables the user to choose a color. When the OK button is clicked, the `Color` property contains the color information. (Refer to Figure 15.1 in Hour 15, "Working with the Visual Component Library (VCL)," to see the Color dialog box.) The Color dialog box, like the file dialog boxes, has no events to respond to.

The Font Dialog Box

The Font dialog box enables the user to choose a font from the list of fonts available on his system. Through the `Device` property, you can choose whether you want screen fonts, printer fonts, or both types of fonts to be displayed. You can limit the maximum and minimum font sizes that the user can select by modifying the `MaxFontSize` and `MinFontSize` properties. As with the file dialog boxes, the `Options` property contains a wide variety of options you can use to control how the Font dialog box functions.

If the user clicks OK, the Font property will contain all the information you need to implement the new font. Figure 17.3 shows the Font dialog box in the default configuration.

FIGURE 17.3

The Font dialog box.

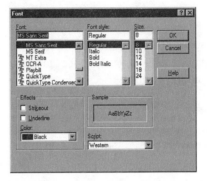

The Font dialog box has a single event, OnApply, that occurs when the user clicks the Apply button on the Font dialog box. The Apply button will not be present on the Font dialog box unless you have first created a valid (not empty) event handler for the OnApply event.

The Find and Replace Dialog Boxes

The Find and Replace dialog boxes provide users the capability to enter text to search for and text to replace, and a variety of search and replace options. The Find dialog box is encapsulated in the VCL component FindDialog, and the Replace dialog box is represented by the ReplaceDialog component. The Replace dialog box, which contains everything found on the Find dialog box plus the extra replace features, is shown in Figure 17.4.

FIGURE 17.4

The Replace dialog box.

Major properties of the FindDialog and ReplaceDialog components include FindText (the text to find), ReplaceText (the text with which to replace the found text), and Options. Obviously, the FindDialog does not have a ReplaceText property. The Options property contains a wide variety of information about the various options that the user had set at the time the Find Next, Replace, or Replace All button was clicked.

The Execute() method for the FindDialog and ReplaceDialog components is a little different than it is with the other common Dialog components. First of all, the Find and Replace dialog boxes are modeless dialog boxes. As soon as the dialog box is displayed, the Execute() method returns. Because the dialog box is modeless, the return value from Execute() is meaningless (it's always True). Instead, the Find and Replace dialog boxes use the OnFind and OnReplace events along with the Options property to determine what is happening with the dialog box. The OnFind event occurs when the Find Next button is clicked. The ReplaceDialog has an OnFind event, but it also has an OnReplace event that is fired when the Replace or Replace All button is clicked. Use these events to determine when the user has requested a find or replace action. Your programs should read the Options property to determine how the user intended the find or replace operation to be carried out.

Introduction to the Object Repository

The Object Repository dialog box is the means by which you can select predefined objects to use in your applications.

> The Object Repository itself is actually a text file (BCB.DRO in the BIN directory, if you want to take a look), which contains the information that the Object Repository dialog box displays. For the sake of simplicity, I will refer to the Object Repository dialog box and the repository file collectively as simply the Object Repository.

The Object Repository enables you to do the following:

- Choose a predefined application, form, or dialog box to implement in your application.
- Add your own forms, dialog boxes, and applications to the Object Repository.
- Add other objects to your application such as ASCII text files and additional source code units.
- Create new components.
- Create new packages.

That's just a sampling of what the Object Repository provides. There are other objects you can create in addition to those listed here.

Object Repository Pages and Options

The Object Repository is displayed automatically whenever you choose File, New from the main menu. Figure 17.5 shows the Object Repository window as it initially appears if you choose File, New with the PictView project open.

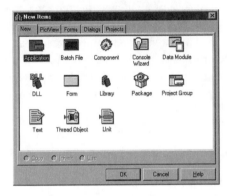

Strange as it might seem, the Object Repository dialog box is titled New Items, and the Object Repository configuration dialog box is titled Object Repository. To say that this is confusing is a bit of an understatement.

The Object Repository has several pages, each of which contains different objects that you can incorporate into your applications. As you can see from Figure 17.5, the New tab is what is initially selected when the Object Repository is displayed. Table 17.1 lists the Repository pages and a description of the items you will find on each page.

TABLE 17.1 THE OBJECT REPOSITORY PAGES

Page/Tab	Description
New	Enables you to create a new application, console app, form, or source code unit for use in your application. Also enables you to create advanced objects such as packages, DLLs, and components.
Forms	Enables you to create standard forms from prebuilt forms such as an About box, a dual list box, or a tabbed dialog box.
Dialogs	Presents choices of several different basic dialog box types from which you can choose.
Projects	Displays full projects that you can choose from to initially set up an application.

If you invoke the Object Repository when you already have a project open, you will see an additional tab in the Object Repository. The tab will have the name of your project on it. Clicking this tab displays a page that contains all the objects currently in the project. This enables you to quickly reuse a form or other object by simply selecting it from the Object Repository.

The Copy, Inherit, and Use Buttons

Across the bottom of each page on the Object Repository, you see three radio buttons. These buttons, labeled Copy, Inherit, and Use, determine how the selected object is implemented. Depending on the object selected, some of the radio buttons (or all) might be disabled. For example, all three radio buttons are always grayed out when the New page is displayed. This is because Copy is the only option available for objects on this page, so C++Builder grays out all choices and applies the Copy option automatically.

Copy

When you choose the Copy radio button, C++Builder creates a copy of the selected object and places it in your application. At this point you are free to modify the object in any way you choose. The original object in the Repository is not altered when you make changes to the new object in your application.

To illustrate, let's say you had an often used form (a form in the traditional sense, not in the C++Builder sense) printed on paper—a work schedule, for instance. Let's say that you wanted to fill in that form with scheduling information. You wouldn't modify the original form because it would then be unusable for future reuse. Instead, you would put the original form in the copy machine, make a copy, and then return the original to some location for safekeeping. You would then fill out the copy of the form as needed. Making a copy of an object in the Repository works in exactly the same way. You are free to modify the copy in any way you choose while the original remains safely tucked away. Making a copy is the safest method of object usage.

Inherit

The Inherit method of usage is similar to Copy, but with one important distinction: The new object is still tied to the base object. If you modify the base object, the newly created object is updated to reflect the changes made to the base object. The inverse is not true, however. You can modify the new object without it having any effect on the base object.

To illustrate this type of object usage, consider the following scenario: Frequently, information managers will create a spreadsheet in a spreadsheet program and use the contents of that spreadsheet in a word-processing program to present a report. They will usually opt to link the data to the spreadsheet when pasting from the clipboard or importing the spreadsheet into the word processor. That way, when changes are made to the spreadsheet, the word-processing document is automatically updated to reflect the new data. In the same way, changes made to a base form will automatically be reflected in all forms inherited from the base form. Use the Inherit option when you want to have several forms based on a common form that might change at some point. Any changes in the base form will be reflected in all inherited forms.

Use

The Use option is not common. When you Use an object, you are opening that object directly for editing. Use this option when you have saved an object in the Repository and you want to make permanent changes to that object. In the section about the Inherit option, I said that changes made to a base form would be reflected in all inherited forms. If you wanted to make changes to a base form, you would open it in the Object Repository with the Use option.

Using the Object Repository

Exactly what takes place when you select an object from the Object Repository depends on several factors. The factors include the type of object selected, whether a project is currently open, and the usage type you have selected (Copy, Inherit, or Use). If you have an application open and you choose to create a new application from the Object Repository, you will be prompted to save the current project (if necessary) before the new project is displayed.

> Choosing File, New Application from the main menu is a shortcut for starting a new application. It is equivalent to choosing New from the main menu and then choosing the Application object from the Object Repository. Similarly, the New Form, New Data Module, and New Unit items on the main menu are shortcuts for their equivalents in the Object Repository.

Creating a new form from the Object Repository is treated differently based on whether a project is open at the time. If a project is open, the new form is added to the application as a form/unit pair. If no project is open, a new form and unit are created as a standalone form. A form created outside of a project must be added to a project before it can be used at runtime. Use this option when creating a new base form to add to the Object Repository.

If you choose to create a new unit or text file, the new file is simply created in the Code Editor (and, in the case of a new unit, added to the current project). You might create a new text file for several reasons. For example, let's say you wanted to implement a configuration file (an .INI file) in your application. You could create a new text file in the Object Repository to initially create the configuration file. Create a new unit any time you want to start a new source file for your application that is not associated with a form (a specialized header file, for instance).

Choosing a new DLL or Console Wizard results in a new project being created with the project set up for a DLL or console application target.

Creating New Objects from the Object Repository

Certainly the most basic use of the Object Repository is creating a new object using an object from the Repository. To illustrate, let's create a simple application with a main form, an About dialog box, and a second form. Follow these steps:

17

1. Ensure that no other application is open. Choose File, New from the main menu. The Object Repository is displayed.

2. Click the Application icon and click OK to create a new application. A new application is created, and a blank form is displayed.

3. Place two buttons on the form. Change the Caption property of one of the buttons to About... and the Caption property of the other button to Display Form2. Change the Name properties if desired.

4. Choose File, New from the main menu. The Object Repository is displayed again.

5. Click the Forms tab in the Object Repository.

6. Choose the About box object. Ensure that the Copy radio button is selected, and click OK to create a new About box form.

The About box is displayed and added to your project. Now that you have created the About box you can customize it as you choose. For example you can enter your own company information, copyright notice, change the icon, size, position, and so on. Let's do one more:

1. Select File, New from the main menu again. The Object Repository is displayed for the third time.

2. Click the Forms tab and choose the Dual list box object. Click OK to close the Object Repository. A dual list box form is displayed. (I had you choose this one just so you could see it.)

3. Write event handlers for the two buttons that display the About box and the second form as required.

4. Compile, run, and test the program.

No, this program doesn't do anything, but it does illustrate how you can use the Object Repository to quickly prototype an application. As time goes on, you will add your own custom objects to the Object Repository and then you can really be effective! Let's look at that next.

Adding Objects to the Object Repository

The Object Repository wouldn't be nearly as effective a tool if you couldn't add your own objects to it. But you can add your own objects and you should. Adding often used objects to the Object Repository makes you a more efficient and, therefore, a more valuable programmer. There is no point in re-inventing the wheel over and over again. After you have an application, form, or other object created, save it to the Repository so that you can reuse it whenever you want. Of course, you don't want to save every form you ever created in the Object Repository, just the ones you will reuse most often.

You can set out to create an object with the express purpose of adding it to the Repository, or you can add an object to the Repository during the normal course of application development. (The term *object* is pretty broad, so I'll have to use a specific example in order for this to make sense.) Let's say that you create an About box form while creating an application. Suddenly it dawns on you that you'd like to save this About box to use in all your programs. After all, it has your company name, logo, and all the copyright information all laid out just the way you like it, so it'd be a shame to have to re-create the same About box for every application you write. No problem—just add it to the Repository.

To add a form to the Object Repository, first save the form (if you don't save the form, you will be prompted to save it before continuing). Next, right-click anywhere on the form and choose Add To Repository from the context menu. When you do, the Add To Repository dialog box is displayed as shown in Figure 17.6.

FIGURE 17.6

The Add To Repository dialog box.

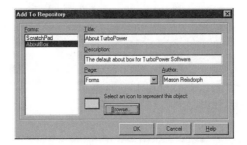

The Forms list box on the left side of this dialog box lists the current forms as well as any other objects in the application. First, select the form that you want to add to the Object Repository.

> The active form in the Form Designer will already be selected in the Forms list box in the Add To Repository dialog box.

Now enter the object's title. This is the title that will appear below the icon in the Object Repository. The Description field is used to give further information about the object. This description is displayed when the Object Repository view is set to display all object details. The Author field is where you type your name as the author of the object. You can enter your personal name, a company name, or any other identifying name.

The Page field is used to select the Object Repository page where the new object will be placed. You can choose from one of the existing pages or simply type in the name of a new page in the Page field. If a page with the name you type doesn't exist, C++Builder creates a new page with that name. Near the bottom of the dialog box is a button labeled Browse that you can use to select the icon used to represent the object.

17

> You can choose icons from the `Program Files\Common Files\Borland Shared Files\Images\Icons` directory or the `CBuilder4\ObjRepos` directory. The icons in the `CBuilder\ObjRepos` directory are the icons used by C++Builder for the items it places in the Object Repository.

After you've filled in all the fields and selected an icon, you can click OK to add the object to the Repository. The object is added to the Object Repository on the page you specified. You can now reuse that object any time you want. As you can see, adding an object to the Object Repository is nearly as easy as using an object.

> When you add an object to the Object Repository, C++Builder makes an entry in the object repository file that describes the object. This information includes the pathname where the form and source file for the object are located. If you move or delete an object's form or source file, you will not be able to use the object from the Object Repository.

Adding Projects to the Object Repository

Adding projects to the Object Repository is not much different from adding individual forms. To add a project to the Object Repository, choose Project, Add to Repository from the main menu. The Add to Repository dialog box is displayed just like it is when adding objects to the Repository, except the Forms list box is not displayed. Fill in any required information (Title, Description, Author, and so on) and click OK, and the project is added to the Repository.

When you are familiar with C++Builder, you should create an application shell that has the features you use most often in your applications. Each time you start a new standard application, make a copy of the shell from the Object Repository. This way you can have your menus, toolbar, About box, and other standard dialog boxes all set up and ready to go in a matter of seconds. After the new application has been created, it can then be modified as with any project. You can add new forms, delete any unwanted forms, and so on.

Object Repository Housekeeping

You can manage the pages and objects in the Object Repository by using the Object Repository configuration dialog box.

To view the Object Repository configuration dialog box, choose Tools, Repository from the main menu or, if you have the Object Repository open, choose Properties from the Object Repository context menu. The configuration dialog box is displayed as shown in Figure 17.7.

FIGURE 17.7

The Object Repository configuration dialog box.

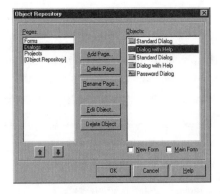

This dialog box enables you to delete objects and pages from the Object Repository, move objects from one page to another, change the order of pages in the Object Repository, and more. The list of pages in the Object Repository is displayed in the list box labeled Pages on the left side of the dialog box. When you select one of the pages in the Pages list, the list box on the right (labeled Objects) displays the objects contained on that page.

> The Pages list box has two important items of note. First, notice that the New page, which is always the first page displayed when the Object Repository is invoked, is not listed here. The New page is fixed and cannot be altered. Also notice that there is an item labeled [Object Repository]. This item is actually a list of all items on all pages of the Repository.

17

Managing Objects

Before you can edit, delete, or move an object you must first select it. To select an object, click the object in the Objects list box. After you have selected an object, you can edit it by clicking the Edit Object button. Editing an object enables you to change the object's name, description, and author, as well as the page on which the object is displayed.

> To quickly edit an object, double-click the object in the Objects list box.

You can delete an object by selecting it and then clicking the Delete Object button. You are prompted for confirmation before the object is removed from the page and from the Repository.

> When an object is deleted from the Object Repository, it is removed from the object repository file and no longer shows up on any page in the Object Repository. However, the actual form file and source file that describe the object are not deleted from your hard drive.

Objects can be moved from one page to another by simply dragging the object from the Objects list box to the Pages list box. Drop the object on the page on which you want the object to be located, and the object is moved.

Managing Pages

The previous section deals with editing, deleting, and moving individual objects. You can also add, delete, or rename Object Repository pages through the Object Repository configuration dialog box.

Before you can delete a page, you must first delete all the objects on the page. After a page is empty, you can remove the page by clicking on the page name in the Pages list box and then clicking the Delete Page button. After checking to be sure the page is empty, C++Builder deletes the page from the Object Repository.

A new page can be by clicking the Add Page button. A dialog box pops up, asking for the name of the new page. Just supply a new page name, and when you click OK, the new page appears in the Pages list box. Renaming a page works essentially the same way. When you select a page and click the Rename Page button, a dialog box appears, prompting you for the new page name.

The order in which the pages appear in the Object Repository can be changed. To change a page's position in the page order, click the page to highlight it and then click the up or down arrow button underneath the Pages list box to move the page up or down in the list. You can also drag a page to its new location if you want.

Setting Default Forms and Projects

The Object Repository configuration dialog box enables you to set three default objects:

- The default form that is used when you choose File, New Form from the main menu.
- The default form that is used as the main form when you choose File, New Application from the main menu.
- The default project that is used when you choose File, New Application from the main menu.

Notice that, depending on the object you have selected, one or two check boxes appear beneath the Objects list box. If you have selected a form, the New Form and Main Form check boxes appear. If you have selected a project, the New Project check box appears.

Making a form or project the default is easy. Let's say you created a main form that you want to be the default main form when a new application is created. Select the form from the Objects list box and click the Main Form check box at the bottom of the screen.

When you click OK, that form will now be the default. Similarly, if you have a project that you want to be the default project, first locate it in the Object Repository configuration dialog box, click on it, and then check the New Project check box. From that point on, when you choose File, New Application from the main menu, the project you set as the default will appear.

> If you aren't careful, you might accidentally select a form as the default form for a new application without intending to. If this happens, be sure you look at each form in the Object Repository configuration dialog box. One form will have the Main Form check box checked. Clear the check box and all will be back to normal. This also applies to the default project. Examine the Projects page for any items that have the New Project check box checked.

17

Summary

The VCL common dialog components offer a way of easily displaying Windows' common dialogs. You will likely use the OpenFile and SaveFile dialogs a lot in your C++Builder applications. You also learned about the Object Repository in this hour. The Object Repository is a great tool for reusing previously created forms, dialog boxes, projects, and other objects.

Workshop

The Workshop contains quiz questions to help you solidify your understanding of the material covered and exercises to provide you with experience in using what you have learned.

Q&A

Q The OpenDialog component is obviously a visible component. Why is it called a nonvisual component?

A Because it is not visible at design time. It is visible only at runtime when you invoke it with the Execute() method.

Q **Is there a limit to the number of objects that can be stored in the Object Repository?**

A Technically, you can store as many objects as you like. Remember, though, that the purpose of the Object Repository is to help you quickly locate and reuse your forms, dialog boxes, and other objects. If you put too many seldom-used objects in the Object Repository, you will start to lose efficiency because it takes longer to find the specific object you are looking for. It also takes longer for the Object Repository to load and display all those objects.

Quiz

1. At what time do you use the Inherit option when selecting an object in the Object Repository?

2. What happens to inherited forms when you change the base form?

3. What is the return value from the `Execute()` method for an `OpenDialog` component if the user clicks OK to close the dialog box?

4. How do you make the `SaveDialog` component into a Save As dialog box?

Answers

1. When you want all the features of the base object and you want the inherited object to change if the base object ever changes.

2. All the inherited forms change to reflect the change made to the base form.

3. If the user closes a common dialog by clicking the OK button, the return value from `Execute()` is `true`.

4. Just change its `Title` property to `Save As`.

Exercises

1. Add filters to the `ScratchPad` program's `OpenFile` and `SaveFile` dialogs. The filter list should include "Text file" and "Any file" filters at a minimum.

2. Create a new form. Add several components of your choosing to the form. Save the form to the Forms page of the Object Repository with the name `BaseForm`. Now start a new application. Choose File, New to view the Object Repository. Switch to the Forms page. Click the Copy radio button. Choose the `BaseForm` object you created in Exercise 1 and add it to the application.

Hour **18**

Adding Functions, Data Members, and Resources

In this hour you learn about adding your own functions and data members to your projects. As you have learned, C++Builder adds code to your projects each time you add a new component or event handler. Sooner or later, though, you will have to add your own functions and data members to the code that C++Builder provides you with. I'll also introduce you to component templates. Component templates can speed application development. Later in the hour I'll show you how to add resources such as string tables, wave files, and bitmaps to your projects.

Adding Functions and Data Members to Code

As you know by now, C++Builder is a great tool for quickly creating the user interface (UI) portion of a Windows application. It creates event handlers for you so that you can begin entering code to drive your application.

It won't be long, however, before you find the need to start adding more complicated code to your applications. Part of that means adding your own data members and functions to the code that C++Builder generates. For example, a simple application might contain two dozen event handlers of various types. C++Builder creates all these event handlers for you; you simply fill in the blanks with working code. To make the application a viable, working application, however, you might have to write another two dozen functions of your own.

Adding your own functions and data members to code generated by C++Builder is not a difficult task, but you need to know the rules or you can get into trouble.

Managing Class Declarations

As you know, when you create a new form in the Form Designer, C++Builder creates three files for you: the form file, the source code unit, and the unit's header. When C++Builder creates the class declaration in the header, it essentially creates two sections. The first section is the part of the class declaration that C++Builder manages. The second section is the part that you manage. To illustrate, let's do a quick example.

First, create a new application. Next drop a button, a label, and an edit component on a blank form. Double-click the button to create an OnClick event handler for the button. Now switch to the Code Editor and bring up the main unit's header. Listing 18.1 shows the main form's class declaration as it appears at this point.

LISTING 18.1 THE MAIN FORM'S CLASS DECLARATION

```
 1: class TForm1 : public TForm
 2: {
 3: __published:  // IDE-managed Components
 4:     TEdit *Edit1;
 5:     TLabel *Label1;
 6:     TButton *Button1;
 7:     void __fastcall Button1Click(TObject *Sender);
 8: private:    // User declarations
 9: public:     // User declarations
10:     __fastcall TForm1(TComponent* Owner);
11: };
```

ANALYSIS Look at line 3 in the code. Notice the __published keyword and the comment that says IDE-managed Components. The section between the __published keyword and the private keyword (on line 8 in this case) should be considered off-limits. Leave the __published section to C++Builder to manage.

Placing any code between the __published keyword and the private key-word can cause problems with your program. In some cases, you might just get compiler or linker errors. In other cases, your program might be beyond repair (unusual, but possible). Get in the habit of avoiding the __published section like the plague.

If you're an astute student, you might be scratching your head right now. In the first few hours we covered the basics of the C++ language. You learned about private, protected, and public class access, but not a word about the __published keyword. The reason is simple: __published is not a C++ key-word. The __published keyword is a Borland extension to C++ and doesn't exist in ANSI standard C++. This keyword was added to allow the C++ lan-guage to take advantage of the power of components.

Notice that lines 8 and 9 in Listing 18.1 have comments that say User declarations. You can safely place any of your own class data members or class member function dec-larations in either the private or the public section of the class declaration. You could add a protected section and place data members or functions there too, of course.

Adding a Function to Your Code

To illustrate adding a function to an application, let's do a quick exercise. In this exercise you will create a button component via code rather than using the Form Designer. First create a new application and add a label component to the form. Next, you need to add a data member and a method to the form's class declaration. Follow these steps:

1. Bring up the Code Editor and switch to the main form's header.

2. Add the following declarations to the private section of the form's class declaration:

   ```
   void __fastcall MyOnClick(TObject* Sender);
   ```

   The entire class declaration now looks like this:

   ```
   class TForm1 : public TForm
   {
   __published:      // IDE-managed Components
     TLabel *Label1;
   private:     // User declarations
     void __fastcall MyOnClick(TObject* Sender);
   public:          // User declarations
     __fastcall TForm1(TComponent* Owner);
   };
   ```

What you have done here is add a method called MyOnClick(). This method will be used as the OnClick event handler for the button you will dynamically create in a moment. Continuing on:

3. Switch back to the main form's source unit. Add the following code to the end of the unit:

```
void __fastcall TForm1::MyOnClick(TObject* Sender)
{
  Label1->Caption = "It works!";
}
```

This is the implementation of the MyOnClick() method that you declared in step 2.

Now you need to dynamically create a button at runtime and assign the MyOnClick() method to that button's OnClick event.

4. Generate an event handler for the form's OnCreate event. Enter code so that the OnCreate event handler looks like this:

```
void __fastcall TForm1::FormCreate(TObject *Sender)
{
  TButton* button = new TButton(this);
  button->Top = 50;
  button->Left = 20;
  button->Caption = "Test";
  button->OnClick = MyOnClick;
  button->Parent = this;
}
```

Methods that will be used as event handlers need to be declared with the __fastcall modifier. Functions you create for general purpose use don't need the __fastcall modifier.

This code creates a new button component dynamically. Notice that you pass this in the button's constructor to assign the form as the button's owner (the this pointer refers to the main form in this case). Next you set the button's Top and Left properties to position the button. You also set the caption of the button. Consider this line:

```
button->OnClick = MyOnClick;
```

This line of code assigns the MyOnClick() method you created earlier to the button's OnClick event. When the button is clicked, the MyOnClick() method is called.

The last line of code assigns the form to the Parent property of the button. It is vital that you assign the form as the parent of any component you create at runtime. If you do not assign the Parent property of the dynamically created component, it will not show on the form.

Notice that you don't delete the button pointer in the OnCreate event handler. This is another case where the VCL will take care of deleting the component when the form is destroyed. You can create the button object and hand it off to VCL to manage from there.

Run the program. When the application appears you will see the button on the form. Click the button and the label's text changes as a result of the MyOnClick() function being called.

Adding a Class Data Member

Adding a class data member to a class generated in C++Builder works in exactly the same way. All you have to do is to ensure that you add the data member to the private or public section of the class declaration as you did earlier when adding a class member function.

Deleting C++Builder-Generated Code

There might be times when you'll need to delete code that C++Builder generated in your application. For instance, you might have a button on a form that, because of design changes, is no longer needed. To delete the button, of course, all you have to do is select the button in the Form Designer and press the Delete button on the keyboard. No more button. C++Builder deletes the button, but the OnClick handler associated with that button is still in the code. C++Builder knows that the button associated with that OnClick handler is gone, but it still doesn't delete the event handler because it is possible that other components are using the same event handler. It's up to you to delete the event handler if you want it removed from your code.

The fastest and easiest way to remove an event handler from your code is to delete all the code inside the event handler and save the project. C++Builder removes any empty event handlers it finds.

The actual deletion of the event handler is a trivial task:

- Delete the function definition from the source unit.
- Delete the function declaration from the header.

> This is the exception to the rule that you should never modify the
> __published section of your forms' class declaration.

Before you delete the event handler, you need to make sure that no other components are using that handler. Unfortunately, there is no simple way of determining whether another component is using a particular event handler. You need to be aware of how the components in your application interact.

> Some might say that if you are unsure about an event handler being used
> by other components, just leave it in the code. That's a bad solution, in my
> opinion. You need to take the responsibility for knowing what is in your
> code and getting rid of any unused functions. Although unused code
> doesn't hurt anything, it leads to a larger .EXE file. In some cases, unused
> code can lead to performance degradation. Be diligent in paring your pro-
> grams of unused or inefficient code.

Using Component Templates

Component templates enable you to create, save, and reuse groups of components. In fact, a component template doesn't have to be a group of components at all—it can be a single component. A quick example would probably help you see how useful component templates can be. First a quick lesson on the Windows edit control.

The standard Windows single-line edit control, like all Windows controls, has certain predefined behaviors. One of those behaviors deals with the way the Enter key is handled. If the user presses the Enter key when in an edit control, Windows looks for a default button on the window. If a default button is found, Windows essentially clicks the button. What does this mean to you? Let's say you have several edit controls on a form and a default button such as an OK button (or any button with the Default property set to True). When you press the Enter key when an edit control has focus, the form closes. If there is no default button on the form, Windows just beeps. Although this is standard

Windows behavior, many users find it annoying and confusing. What many users prefer, particularly when working with a form that has several edit fields, is that the Enter key moves focus to the next control rather than closing the form.

The solution to this problem is really pretty simple. All you have to do is provide an event handler for the form's OnKeyPress event and add code so that it looks like this:

```
void __fastcall TForm1::Edit1KeyPress(TObject *Sender, char &Key)
{
  if (Key == VK_RETURN) {
    Key = 0;
    PostMessage(Handle, WM_NEXTDLGCTL, 0, 0);
  }
}
```

This code first checks to see whether the key pressed was the Enter key (VK_RETURN). If so, it sets the value of Key to 0. This eliminates the beep that Windows emits when the Enter key is pressed in an Edit control. The next line posts a WM_NEXTDLGCTL message. This message sets focus to the next control in the tab order. That's all there is to it.

After you have written the code for your new Edit component, you can save it as a component template. When you do, all the code is saved as well. Any code templates you create go into the Templates page of the Component palette. Let's create a component template so you can see how it works. Perform these steps:

1. Place an Edit component on a blank form. Change its Name property to EnterAsTab and clear its Text property.

2. Switch to the Events page in the Object Inspector and create an event handler for the OnKeyPress event. Enter this code in the event handler:
   ```
   if (Key == VK_RETURN) {
     Key = 0;
     PostMessage(Handle, WM_NEXTDLGCTL, 0, 0);
   }
   ```

3. Be sure the Edit component is selected and choose Component, Create Component Template from the main menu. The Component Template Information dialog box is displayed.

4. Type TEnterAsTab in the Component name field. The Component Template Information dialog box should now look like the one in Figure 18.1.

5. Click OK to save the component template.

18

FIGURE **18.1**

*The Component
Template Information
dialog box.*

Now your Component palette will have a tab called Templates. Switch to the Templates
tab (you might have to scroll the Component palette tabs to find it), select your new
component, and place it on the form. You will see that the code for the OnKeyPress event
handler was included when the component was placed on the form.

If you had several of these components on a form, the code for the
OnKeyPress event handler would be repeated for every EnterAsTab compo-
nent on the form. Rather than duplicating code you could just place one
EnterAsTab component on the form. Any other components could be stan-
dard Edit components that have their OnKeyPress events hooked up to the
OnKeyPress event handler for the EnterAsTab component.

One of the biggest advantages of component templates is that the code written for each
component's event handlers is saved along with the component. Component templates
enable you to have a collection of customized components at your disposal: common dialog boxes with predefined filters and titles, toolbars with buttons and glyphs already
included, list boxes or combo boxes that automatically load items from a file, or any of a
number of other possibilities.

Although the concept of a component template works for a single component, it makes
even more sense when dealing with multiple components. If you have a group of components that you place on your forms over and over again, you can create a component template from those components. After you have created a component template, reusing a
group of components is only a click away.

There are certainly some similarities between component templates and saving forms in the Object Repository. Use component templates for groups of
components that you typically use as part of a larger form. Use the Object
Repository to save entire forms that you want to reuse.

Using Resource Files

 Every Windows program uses resources. *Resources* are those elements of a program that support the program but are not executable code.

A typical Windows program's resources include

- Accelerators
- Bitmaps
- Cursors
- Dialog boxes
- Icons
- Menus
- Data tables
- String tables
- Version information
- User-defined specialty resources (sound files and AVI files, for example)

18

> Version information can be easily added to your C++Builder projects through the Version Info tab of the Project Options dialog box. The Project Options dialog box is discussed in detail in Hour 19, "Managing Projects with C++Builder."

Resources are generally contained in a *resource script file* (a text file with an .RC extension), which is compiled by a resource compiler and then bound to the application's .EXE file during the link phase.

Resources are usually thought of as being bound to the executable file. Some resources, such as bitmaps, string tables, and wave files, can be placed in external files (.BMP, .TXT, and .WAV), or they can be bound to the .EXE and contained within the application file. You can opt to do it either way. Placing resources in the .EXE file has two main advantages:

- The resources can be accessed more quickly because it takes less time to locate a resource in the executable file than it does to load it from a disk file.
- The program file and resources can be contained in a single unit (the .EXE file) without the need for a lot of supporting files.

The downside to this approach is that your .EXE will be slightly larger. The program file won't be any larger than the combined external resource files plus the executable, but the extra size could result in slightly longer load times for the program.

Your exact needs will determine whether you decide to keep your resources in external files or have your resources bound to the .EXE. The important thing to remember is that you can do it either way (or even both ways in the same program).

A traditional Windows program will almost always contain at least one dialog box and an icon. A C++Builder application, however, is a little different. First of all, there are no true dialog boxes in a C++Builder application, so there are no dialog box resources per se (C++Builder forms are stored as resources, but they are RCDATA resources and not dialog box resources). A C++Builder application does have a traditional icon resource, though. C++Builder takes care of creating the resource file for the icon for you when you create the application. Similarly, when you choose bitmaps for speed buttons, Image components, or BitBtn components, C++Builder includes the bitmap file you chose as part of the form's resource. The form and all its resources are then bound to the program file when the application is built. It's all more or less handled for you automatically.

There are times, however, when you will want to implement resources aside from the normal C++Builder processes. For instance, if you want to do animation, you must have a series of bitmaps that can be loaded as resources for the fastest possible execution speed. In this kind of situation, you are going to need to know how to bind the resources to your C++Builder program file.

The act of binding the resource file to the executable is trivial, actually. It's much more difficult to actually create the resources. Creating basic resources such as bitmaps, icons, and cursors is not difficult with a good resource editor, but creating professional quality 3D bitmaps and icons is an art in itself. How many times have you seen a fairly decent program with really awful bitmap buttons? I've seen plenty. (Sorry, I'm getting off track here.) You can create bitmaps, icons, and cursors with the C++Builder Image Editor. If you are going to create string resources, user data resources, wave file resources, or other specialty resources, you will probably need a third-party resource editor.

C++Builder Professional and Enterprise versions come with Resource Workshop, which can be used to create resource script files. After creating the resources, you will have an .RC file that you can add to your C++Builder project directly, or compile into a .RES file using the Borland Resource Compiler (BRCC32.EXE). The Borland Resource Compiler comes with all versions of C++Builder. Technically, you could create the .RC file with any text editor and compile it with the Resource Compiler, but in reality it is much easier to use a resource editor.

You can add either a .RES file or an .RC file to your project via the Project Manager. To add a resource file to a project, you first choose View, Project Manager from the main menu to display the Project Manager. If there is more than one project in the project group, double-click the project name of the project to which you want to add the resource file. Now click the Add File To Project button on the C++Builder toolbar or right-click the project name and choose Add from the Project Manager context menu. When the File Open dialog box appears, select the resource file you want to add to the project and click Open. The resource file shows up in the Project Manager with the rest of the application's files. I'll discuss the Project Manager in more detail in the next hour.

Listings 18.2 and 18.3 contain the header and main form unit for a program called Jumping Jack. This program shows a simple animation with sound effects. The main form contains just two buttons, an `Image` component and a `Label` component. The Jumping Jack program illustrates several aspects of using resources in a C++Builder application. Specifically, it shows how to load a bitmap stored as a resource, how to load and display a string resource, and how to play wave audio contained as a resource. Listing 18.4 is a partial listing of the resource file that is used by the Jumping Jack program. Examine the listings, and then I'll discuss what the program does.

LISTING 18.2 JJMAIN.H, THE JUMPING JACK APPLICATION HEADER

```
 1: //-------------------------------
 2: #ifndef JJMainH
 3: #define JJMainH
 4: //-------------------------------
 5: #include <Classes.hpp>
 6: #include <Controls.hpp>
 7: #include <StdCtrls.hpp>
 8: #include <Forms.hpp>
 9: #include <ExtCtrls.hpp>
10: //-------------------------------
11: class TMainForm : public TForm
12: {
13: __published:    // IDE-managed Components
14:     TButton *Start;
15:     TButton *Stop;
16:     TImage *Image;
17:     TLabel *Label;
18:     void __fastcall FormCreate(TObject *Sender);
19:
20:     void __fastcall StartClick(TObject *Sender);
21:     void __fastcall StopClick(TObject *Sender);
22: private:        // User declarations
23:     bool done;
24:     void DrawImage(String& name);
```

continues

18

LISTING **18.2**   CONTINUED

```
25: public:          // User declarations
26:     virtual __fastcall TMainForm(TComponent* Owner);
27: };
28: //------------------------------
29: extern PACKAGE TMainForm *MainForm;
30: //------------------------------
31: #endif
```

LISTING **18.3**   JJMAIN.CPP, THE JUMPING JACK APPLICATION MAIN PROGRAM

```
 1: //-----------------------------------------------------------
 2: #include <vcl\vcl.h>
 3: //
 4: // have to add this include for the PlaySound() function
 5: //
 6: #include <mmsystem.hpp>
 7: #pragma hdrstop
 8:
 9: #include "JJMain.h"
10: #pragma package(smart_init)
11: #pragma resource "*.dfm"
12: //
13: // defines for the string resources
14: //
15: #define IDS_UP    101
16: #define IDS_DOWN  102
17:
18: TMainForm *MainForm;
19: //-----------------------------------------------------------
20: __fastcall TMainForm::TMainForm(TComponent* Owner)
21:     : TForm(Owner),
22:     done(false)
23: {
24: }
25: //-----------------------------------------------------------
26: void __fastcall TMainForm::FormCreate(TObject *Sender)
27: {
28:     //
29:     // load and display the first bitmap
30:     //
31:     Image->Picture->Bitmap->
32:        LoadFromResourceName((int)HInstance, "ID_BITMAP1");
33: }
34: //-----------------------------------------------------------
35: void __fastcall TMainForm::StartClick(TObject *Sender)
36: {
```

```
37:   //
38:   // When the Start button is clicked the animation
39:   // loop starts. The bitmap resources are named
40:   // ID_BITMAP1 through ID_BITMAP5 so we'll start with
41:   // a string called "ID_BITMAP" and append the last
42:   // digit when needed.
43:   //
44:   String s = "ID_BITMAP";
45:   //
46:   // a buffer for the string resources
47:   //
48:   char buff[10];
49:   //
50:   // a flag to let us know when we're done
51:   //
52:   done = false;
53:   //
54:   // start the loop and keep looping until the 'Stop'
55:   // button is pressed
56:   //
57:   while (!done) {
58:     //
59:     // loop through the five bitmaps starting with
60:     // 1 and ending with 5
61:     //
62:     for (int i=1;i<6;i++) {
63:       //
64:       // append the value of 'i' to the end of the string
65:       // to build a string containing the resource name
66:       //
67:       String resName = s + String(i);
68:       //
69:       // call a class member function to display the bitmap
70:       //
71:       DrawImage(resName);
72:     }
73:     //
74:     // load the "Up" string resource using the WinAPI
75:     // function LoadString(), display the string,
76:     // and tell Windows to repaint the Label
77:     //
78:     LoadString(HInstance, IDS_UP, buff, sizeof(buff));
79:     Label->Caption = buff;
80:     Label->Refresh();
81:     //
82:     // play the 'up' sound using the WinAPI function
83:     // PlaySound(), play it asynchronously
84:     //
85:     PlaySound("ID_WAVEUP",
```

continues

LISTING 18.3   CONTINUED

```
 86:        HInstance, SND_ASYNC | SND_RESOURCE);
 87:      //
 88:      // pause for a moment at the top of the jump
 89:      //
 90:      Sleep(200);
 91:      //
 92:      // repeat all of the above except in reverse
 93:      //
 94:      for (int i=5;i>0;i--) {
 95:        String resName = s + String(i);
 96:        DrawImage(resName);
 97:      }
 98:      PlaySound("ID_WAVEDOWN",
 99:        HInstance, SND_ASYNC | SND_RESOURCE);
100:      LoadString(HInstance, IDS_DOWN, buff, sizeof(buff));
101:      Label->Caption = buff;
102:      Label->Refresh();
103:      Sleep(200);
104:    }
105: }
106: //-------------------------------------------------------------
107: void __fastcall TMainForm::StopClick(TObject *Sender)
108: {
109:    //
110:    // Stop button pressed, so tell the loop to stop executing
111:    //
112:    done = true;
113: }
114: //-------------------------------------------------------------
115: //
116: // a class member function to display the bitmap
117: //
118: void
119: TMainForm::DrawImage(String& name)
120: {
121:    //
122:    // load the bitmap from a resource
123:    // using the name passed to us
124:    //
125:    Image->Picture->Bitmap->
126:      LoadFromResourceName((int)HInstance, name);
127:    //
128:    // must pump the message loop so that Windows gets
129:    // a chance to display the bitmap
130:    //
131:    Application->ProcessMessages();
132:    //
```

```
133:    // take a short nap so the animation doesn't go too fast
134:    //
135:    Sleep(20);
136: }
```

LISTING 18.4 JJRES.RC, THE JUMPING JACK APPLICATION RESOURCE SCRIPT

```
 1: #define IDS_UP      101
 2: #define IDS_DOWN    102
 3:
 4: STRINGTABLE
 5: {
 6:   IDS_UP, "Up"
 7:   IDS_DOWN, "Down"
 8: }
 9:
10: ID_WAVEUP    WAVE "up.wav"
11: ID_WAVEDOWN WAVE "down.wav"
12:
13: ID_BITMAP1 BITMAP LOADONCALL MOVEABLE DISCARDABLE IMPURE
14: {
15:   '42 4D 76 02 00 00 00 00 00 00 76 00 00 00 28 00'
16:   '00 00 20 00 00 00 20 00 00 00 01 00 04 00 00 00'
17: //
18: //   remainder of bitmap data to follow
```

ANALYSIS Notice lines 23 and 24 in the header for the main form class in Listing 18.2.
Line 23 declares a `bool` data member that is used to determine when to stop the animation. The class member function declared on line 24 is used to display the bitmap in the `Image` component.

In Listing 18.3, notice that two Windows API functions are used to load the string and wave file resources. On line 78, the `LoadString()` function loads a string resource into a text buffer based on the numerical identifier of the string (lines 1–8 of Listing 18.4 show how the string resources are created). The string is then assigned to the `Caption` property of the label component on the form. On line 83, the `PlaySound()` function is used to play a wave file contained as a resource. The `SND_ASYNC` flag used with the `PlaySound()` function tells Windows to play the sound and immediately return control to the program. This enables the animation to continue while the sound is being played. The `SND_RESOURCE` flag tells Windows that the sound is contained as a resource and not as a file on disk. Both the `LoadString()` and `PlaySound()` functions use the `HInstance` global variable to tell Windows to look in the executable file for the resources.

18

Lines 1–8 of Listing 18.4 illustrate how a string table looks in a resource script file. Creating string tables is very easy with any text editor. On lines 10 and 11, a WAVE resource is created for each of the two wave files, which were previously recorded and reside in the project's directory. When the resource compiler sees the WAVE declaration, it reads the individual sound files and compiles them into the binary resource file.

> As you can see from Listing 18.4, you can create some types of resources easily with a text editor. If you have bitmaps or wave audio stored as external files, you can include them in an .RC file as illustrated in Listing 18.4. Simply add the .RC file to your project and C++Builder compiles the resources and binds them to the executable file.

Listing 18.4 is a partial listing. Bitmaps created with a traditional resource editor are often contained in the resource file as numerical data. The resource descriptions for bitmaps can get very long. The rest of the bitmap resource descriptions for the Jumping Jack bitmaps require about 200 lines of resource code, so I decided not to list them all. The full project is on the book's CD if you want to look at the resource script file in its entirety. Figure 18.2 shows Jumping Jack in mid-stride.

FIGURE 18.2

The Jumping Jack program in action.

Creating additional resources for your programs is not rocket science, but it is not exactly trivial, either. It takes some time to realize how it all fits together. You might never need to add additional resources to your applications. If you do, though, it's good to have an idea where to begin. If this section left you a little dazed and confused, don't worry. Over time, it all starts to make sense.

Bitmaps, icons, and cursors found in other programs are usually copyrighted material. Don't use resources from any copyrighted program without permission. Further, assume all images are copyrighted unless they are specifically said to be freeware. You are free to use the bitmaps, icons, and cursors that are provided with C++Builder (in the `Common Files\Borland Shared Files\Images` directory) in your applications without permission from Inprise.

Summary

In this hour you learned about adding data members and functions to your code. Although C++Builder does a great deal of work for you, there will certainly be times when you will need to add your own functions to your application. You also learned about Windows resources and resource script files. Resources allow you to place bitmaps, string tables, icons, and wave files in your application. Those resources can then be accessed using the VCL or using the Windows API.

Workshop

18

The Workshop contains quiz questions to help you solidify your understanding of the material covered and exercises to provide you with experience in using what you have learned.

Q&A

Q I added a function to my main form class. Now I can't compile. What's the problem?

A You probably added the function declaration to the `__published` section of the class declaration accidentally. Be sure that the declaration for your function is in either the `public` or the `private` section of the class declaration (or the `protected` section if you have one).

Q I have a lot of bitmaps and sound files that go with my application. Can I put all those resources in a file other than the program's executable file?

A Yes. You can have resources stored in a dynamic link library (DLL).

Quiz

1. Should you place functions you create in the __published section of the form's class declaration?

2. What calling convention must be applied to any functions that are to be used as event handlers?

3. Name three types of resources used in Windows applications.

4. Can you create a resource script file containing a string table with a text editor?

Answers

1. No. You should never place functions you create in the __published section. Always place the function declaration in the private, protected, or public sections.

2. Any functions that are to be used as event handlers must include the __fastcall calling convention.

3. Resources used in Windows applications include accelerators, bitmaps, strings, menus, icons, and version information.

4. Yes. A string table is just a resource description placed in a file with an .RC extension. You can use any text editor to create the string table.

Exercise

1. Create a string table resource with a text editor and compile it with the resource compiler (BRCC32.EXE). (**Extra Credit:** Write a program to load the strings and display them on a form.)

HOUR **19**

Managing Projects with C++Builder

Projects are a fact of life with C++Builder. You cannot create a program without a project. The project makes sure that everything works together to create a working application. In this hour I will talk about

- The Project Manager
- Project groups
- The Project Options dialog box

Project Groups

In Hour 10 I said that a project is a collection of files that work together to create a standalone executable file or DLL. That's the definition of a project as far as the C++Builder IDE is concerned. In the real world you might have a different kind of project; a job that you have to complete. A large project might include one or more executable files and several DLLs. Because some projects consist of more than a single executable program, C++Builder enables you to group several C++Builder projects together and deal with them as a single unit. This unit is called a *project group*.

Why use project groups? Project groups give you the following:

- Better control over a complete software project.
- The ability to work on a DLL and a test EXE for the DLL at the same time.
- The ability to build (compile and link) a group of projects all at one time.
- The ability to have several projects open at one time and to easily switch between open projects.
- A way to organize related projects.

A project that creates a single executable file doesn't need a project group. A single project can hardly be considered a group, right? In the case of a single project the concept of a project group is out of place. But imagine for a moment a program that includes an EXE and a single supporting DLL. Both the DLL and the EXE go together. Usually, if you are working on the DLL, you will want the EXE present so you can immediately test any changes you make to the DLL. In this scenario a project group makes perfect sense because EXE and DLL go everywhere together. You can create a project group that contains these two individual projects and save it. When you want to work on the application, you can open the project group rather than an individual project. When you open the project group, both the EXE project and the DLL project will be displayed. You can work on either the DLL or the EXE in the Code Editor and switch back and forth between them any time you want. Figure 19.1 shows the Project Manager window with this type of project group open.

FIGURE 19.1

The Project Manager window showing a simple project group.

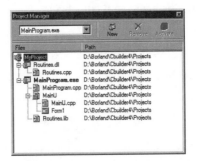

Another reason to have a project group is so that you can group related projects. That probably sounds like it doesn't make much sense, so let me explain. Here at TurboPower Software we have a product called Async Professional, which is a collection of serial communications components. These components include three main categories: basic serial communications, faxing, and TAPI. We include dozens of sample programs with Async Professional covering each of these three categories. Given that scenario, we could create a project group for all our faxing examples, one for all our TAPI examples, and one for all our basic serial communications examples. Our users could then open the TAPI Examples project group and have all the TAPI examples in one neat package. The entire project group could be built at one time, thereby saving the time and aggravation of opening and building each project individually. In this case the projects don't work together like a DLL and EXE do, but the projects are related so the concept of a project group makes just as much sense.

In any project group there is always an active project. The active project is displayed in the Project Manager in bold type. In Figure 19.1 the active project is the project called MainProgram. The active project is the project that will be built when you choose Make or Build from the Project menu on the C++Builder main menu. These menu items are modified each time a project is made the active project. For example, if the active project is called Project1, the menu items will be called Make Project1 and Build Project1. If a project called PictView is made the active project, these two menu items will be called Make PictView and Build PictView.

The active project also has significance when a new form or a new unit is added using the Project Manager. When you create a new form using the Project Manager, the new form will be added to the active project regardless of which node in the Project Manager is currently selected. The active project is also the project to which new forms or units will be added if you add new elements via the C++Builder main menu or the C++Builder toolbar.

You can make a project the active project in one of several ways. One way is to select any item in the project node you want to make the active project and click the Activate button on the top of the Project Manager. Another way is to simply double-click the project node itself. Finally, you can choose Activate from the project node context menu to activate a particular project.

The Project Manager Window

The Project Manager is the central controller for all your projects and your program groups. It enables you to add files to a project, delete files from a project, view a unit or form, add projects to the project group, change the order of projects, and more. To display the Project Manager, choose View, Project Manager from the main menu, or press Ctrl+Alt+F11.

19

The Project Manager window contains a tree view control that displays up to four levels. Those levels are

- The project group
- The projects within the project group
- Forms and other files within the project
- Individual form files and units under the form node

Naturally, the individual nodes can be collapsed or expanded as with any tree view control. The Project Manager nodes have icons that indicate whether the node contains a project, an individual file, a form, or a form/unit pair. Refer to Figure 19.1 to see the different icons and levels that the Project Manager displays.

The Project Manager Context Menus

Most of the Project Manager's work is done through its context menus. There are three separate context menus for the Project Manager. The first is the Project Group context menu you see when you right-click the project group node at the top of the Project Manager tree. The second is the Project Node context menu. This menu appears when you right-click on a project. The third is the Unit Node context menu you see when you right-click on an individual unit within a project. Table 19.1 lists the Project Manager context menu items that appear on the Project Group context menu.

TABLE 19.1 THE PROJECT GROUP CONTEXT MENU ITEMS

Menu Item	Description
Add New Project	Opens the Object Repository so you can choose a new target. Targets include applications, DLLs, forms, or any other object available from the Object Repository.
Add Existing Project	Opens a target file from disk and adds it to the project group or the active project.
Save Project Group	Saves the project group. Project groups have a .BPG extension.
Save Project Group As	Saves the project group with a new name.
View Project Group Source	Displays the project group source. The project group source is a special makefile that contains references to all projects within the project group.

In addition to the items listed in Table 19.1, the Project Manager menus include items called Toolbar, Status Bar, and Dockable. These menu items are self explanatory, so I didn't list them in Table 19.1.

The behavior of the Add New Project and Add Existing Project menu items depends on the type of target that you are creating or opening. For example, if the new target is an application or DLL, that application or DLL is added to the project group as a new project node. If you are creating a form, the new form is added to the active project.

The project context menu is the second menu displayed when you right-click a project node in the Project Manager. Table 19.2 lists the context menu items specific to the project node context menu. Remember, this context menu also includes the items listed in Table 19.1.

TABLE 19.2 ADDITIONAL PROJECT CONTEXT MENU ITEMS

Menu Item	Description
Add	Opens the Add to project dialog box so you can add a file to the project. The same as choosing Project, Add to Project from the main menu or from the C++Builder toolbar.
Remove File	Opens the Remove From Project dialog box so you can remove a file from the project. The same as choosing Project, Remove from Project from the main menu or from the C++Builder toolbar.
Save	Saves the project. The same as choosing File, Save Project As from the C++Builder main menu.
Options	Displays the Project Options dialog box for this project. The same as choosing Project, Options from the C++Builder main menu.
Activate	Makes this project the active project.
Make	Makes this project. The difference between make and build is discussed in Hour 10, "Exploring the C++Builder IDE."
Build	Builds this project.
View Source	Displays the project source file. The same as choosing Project, View Source from the C++Builder main menu.
View Makefile	Displays the project's makefile. The same as choosing Project, View Makefile from the C++Builder main menu.
Close	Closes this project and all its files. If the project is part of a saved project group, the project node icon is displayed as grayed out. The project is still part of the group but is not open in the IDE. If the project is part of the default project group, the project is closed and removed from the default group.
Remove Project	Removes this project from the project group. The project is not deleted from your hard drive, just removed from the project group.
Build Sooner	Moves the project up in the project tree. Projects are built from the top of the Project Manager down.
Build Later	Moves the project down in the project tree.

19

In addition to these two menus, a third menu is displayed when you right-click a node other than the project group node or a project node. This menu contains items called Open, Save, Save As, and Compile. The Open menu item displays the selected node in either the Code Editor or the Form Designer depending on the type of the selected node. This does not apply to binary files such as .RES files or .LIB files. The Compile menu item will compile the node, if applicable.

The Project Manager Toolbar and Keyboard Commands

In addition to the Project Manager context menus, the Project Manager has a toolbar to make working with it easier. The Project Manager toolbar contains three buttons. The New button displays the Object Repository, so you can create a new object whether that be an application, a DLL, a form, a unit, or any other object available from the Object Repository. This is essentially the same as clicking the Add New Project menu item from any of the Project Manager's context menus. The Remove button removes the selected project from the project group. Use this button only to remove an entire project, and not to remove a particular form or file from a project. The Activate button makes the selected target the active project.

Keyboard commands include the Delete key and the Insert key. When you press Delete, the Remove From Project dialog box is displayed just as it is if you choose Remove File from the project context menu. The Remove From Project dialog box presents a list of all forms and units in the active project regardless of which node was selected when you pressed Delete. The Insert key behaves exactly the same as choosing Add from the project context menu.

> The Project Manager toolbar buttons can be either large or small. By default, the Project Manager toolbar buttons are large. You can change the toolbar button size by dragging the bottom of the toolbar either up (to show the small buttons) or down (to show the large buttons).

Creating and Using Project Groups

Project groups are a great benefit for complex projects, but using a project group is not mandatory. You don't have to use project groups with every project. The Project Manager has a default project group called `ProjectGroup1` that is used if you don't specifically open or create a project group. Try this:

1. Choose File, Close All to close any open projects or project groups.

2. Choose File, New Application to create a new application.

3. Choose View, Project Manager to display the Project Manager. The Project Manager is displayed as shown in Figure 19.2.

FIGURE 19.2

The Project Manager showing the default project group.

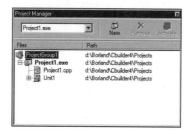

The project group called `ProjectGroup1` is a temporary project group. When you choose Save All from the File menu, you are prompted to save the project but not the project group. If you want to save the project group, you must explicitly save it using the Save Project Group or Save Project Group As menu item from one of the Project Manager context menus.

Adding Units

When you add files to your projects, you use the Add to Project dialog box. The Add to Project dialog box has file filters for the following types of files:

- C++Builder unit (.cpp)
- Pascal unit (.pas)
- C source file (.c)
- Resource script file (.rc)
- Assembler file (.asm)
- Module definition file (.def)
- Compiled resource files (.res)
- Object file (.obj)
- Library file (.lib)
- Type Library (.tlb)
- IDL File (.idl)

19

If you add files of any of these types, C++Builder will know what to do with them. For example, if you add a C source file (.c), C++Builder compiles it as C rather than C++ (the differences are subtle, and most people don't care about the differences, but it matters to some programmers). If you add a Pascal file (.pas), the Pascal compiler compiles the source file before passing it to the linker. If you add a binary object file (.obj), C++Builder passes it to the linker at link time.

You can add some file types to your project other than those listed here. For example, you might want to add a text file to your project that describes what the project does and how it is expected to be used.

Removing Units

You use the Remove option to remove files from the project. Files removed from the project are not deleted from your hard drive, but are just removed from the project compile/link process.

> Be careful when removing units from your projects. You must be careful to not remove units that are referenced by other units in the project. If you remove units that are required by your project, a compiler or linker error will result. Before removing a unit, be sure it is used nowhere else in your project.

The Remove From Project dialog box enables multiple selection, so you can remove several units from a project at one time if you want.

Viewing Units or Forms

To view a unit, form, or other file just double-click the node representing the form or unit you want to view. You can also choose Open from the Project Manager context menu. The form or unit is displayed in the Form Designer or Code Editor, depending on the type of node you are viewing.

Building Projects or Project Groups

To make a particular project, you can do one of the following:

- Right-click the project node in the Project Manager and choose Make from the context menu.

- Choose Project, Make Project from the C++Builder main menu. The name of this menu item changes based on the name of the active project.
- Press Ctrl+F9 on the keyboard to make the active project.

To build a project choose Project, Build Project from the main menu or right-click a project node in the Project Manager and choose Build from the context menu.

To build an entire project group, choose Project, Build All Projects from the C++Builder main menu. All projects in the project group are built starting with the first project in the group (the project at the top of the Project Manager tree) and proceeding down through the last project in the group.

Understanding Project Options

Project options are another of those things that are easy to ignore. For one thing, the defaults are usually good enough when you are just starting out. After all, who has time to worry about all those compiler/linker options when you are just struggling to learn a new programming environment? At some point, though, you will start to become more interested in what all those options do, and it's good to have some reference when the time comes.

This section looks at the Project Options dialog box. You can invoke this dialog box by choosing Project, Options from the main menu. The Project Options dialog box is a tabbed dialog box with several pages:

- Forms
- Application
- Compiler
- Advanced Compiler
- C++
- Pascal
- Linker
- Directories/Conditionals
- Version Info
- Packages

19

I won't discuss every page of the Project Options dialog box, but take a look at the most important pages so that you can better understand what each of these pages do. I'll start you out easy by discussing the Forms and Application pages. After that we'll move on to the more complicated pages.

At the bottom of each page of the Project Options dialog box is a check box labeled Default. If you want the current settings to become the default settings for all new projects created, check the Default box. When you click OK, the current settings become the new default settings.

The Forms Page

The Forms page of the Project Options dialog box is where you control how your application handles its forms. Figure 19.3 shows the Forms page of the Project Options dialog box for the ScratchPad program.

FIGURE 19.3

The Forms page of the Project Options dialog box.

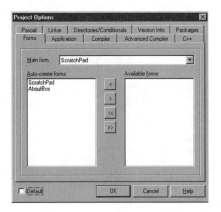

At the top of the Forms page is the Main form combo box. This is where you tell C++Builder which form to display when the application starts. By default, the first form you create will be the main form. If you change your project around in such a way that a different form becomes the main form, you must change this setting so that the new form becomes the application's main form.

In the middle of the dialog box are two list boxes. The list box on the left is labeled Auto-create forms; the one on the right is labeled Available forms. Before I talk about how to use these two list boxes, take a moment to learn about auto-creation of forms.

Each time you create a form, C++Builder places that form in the auto-create list for the application. *Auto-creation* means that C++Builder constructs the form during the application startup process. Forms that are auto-created will display more quickly than forms that are not auto-created. The disadvantage to auto-creation of forms is that your application will use more memory than it would if your forms were not auto-created. Another disadvantage, although probably insignificant, is that your application will take slightly longer to load if you are auto-creating a lot of forms.

The nice thing about auto-creation is that displaying an auto-created form is easy. All you must do is call that form's `Show()` or `ShowModal()` function:

```
AboutBox->ShowModal();
```

If you do not have your forms auto-created by C++Builder, you must take the responsibility of creating the form before you use it:

```
TAboutBox* aboutBox = new TAboutBox(this);
aboutBox->ShowModal();
delete aboutBox;
```

This example does not use the C++Builder–generated pointer to the About box. It creates a local pointer, displays the form, and then deletes the pointer as soon as the form is no longer needed. This is how I always create my forms. I prefer to allocate memory only when needed and free it immediately after I am done with it.

Each time you create a form in the Form Designer, C++Builder creates a pointer to the form. If you allow C++Builder to auto-create a form, you don't have to worry about the pointer being valid. If you choose not to have a form auto-created, the pointer to the form is NULL until you explicitly create the form and initialize the pointer. If you forget and use the pointer before it is initialized, Windows generates an access-violation error.

Okay, now turn your attention back to the Project Options dialog box. The Auto-create forms list box contains a list of the forms that will be auto-created. If you do not want a form to be auto-created, drag the form from the Auto-create forms list box to the Available forms list box. To move several forms at one time, simply select the forms you want to move (both list boxes support multiple selection) and drag and drop them all at once. It's that easy.

You can use the buttons between the two list boxes to move forms from one list box to the other, but it's usually easier to use drag and drop.

The Application Page

The Application page of the Project Options dialog box is very simple. (See Figure 19.4.)

19

FIGURE 19.4

The Application page of the Project Options dialog box.

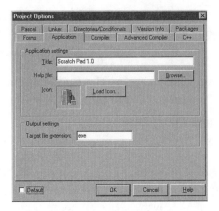

The Title field on this page is used to set the title of the application. The title is the text that appears on the Windows taskbar when your application is minimized.

The application's title and the caption of the main form are two separate items. If you want your program's name to show up when you minimize your program, you must be sure that you set the title for the application in the Project Options dialog box. If you do not provide an application title, the name of the project file will be used by default.

The Help file field of the Application page is used to set the help file that your application will use. This is the help file that the program will load when you press F1 while your application is running. You can use the Browse button to locate the help file if you can't remember the name or location of the help file. If you do not supply a help file, pressing F1 in your application will have no effect.

The Icon option enables you to choose an icon for your application. This is the icon that will be displayed in the Windows taskbar when your application runs and when it is minimized. In addition, this icon will be displayed on your main form's title bar unless you have explicitly set an icon for the main form. To choose an icon, click the Load Icon button and locate the icon file (.ico) using the Application Icon dialog box.

You use the Target file extension to specify the filename extension of the project when the project is built. For example, if you were creating a screen saver, you would change this field to scr so that your screen saver would be created with an extension of .scr rather than .exe. This field is automatically set to .exe for executable projects (console applications and GUI applications) and to .dll for DLLs, and normally you won't have to change it.

The Compiler Page

The Compiler page of the Project Options dialog box is where you set the options that the compiler uses to build your project. Figure 19.5 shows this page of the Project Options dialog box.

FIGURE 19.5

The Compiler page of the Project Options dialog box.

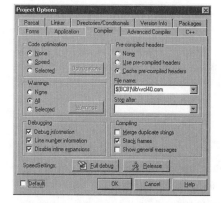

At the bottom of this page is a section called SpeedSettings that contains two buttons. The Full debug button sets the default compiler options for a typical debug session. These are the settings you will be most likely to use while debugging your application. The Release button sets the compiler options for a typical release build. Use the Release settings after you have debugged your application and are ready to ship the final product. Be sure that you do a Build of your project after changing compiler settings.

> The Full debug and Release buttons set the compiler settings to the suggested settings for debugging or final release, respectively. You can always change individual options after choosing one of these speed buttons.

The rest of the Compiler page is broken down into five sections. I won't discuss all the sections but will cover a couple of the more critical ones.

Code Optimization

The compiler can be configured to perform optimizations on your code. When optimizations are turned off (the None radio button is selected), the compiler makes no attempts to optimize code in any way.

19

If you choose the Speed option, the compiler generates the fastest code possible without regard to code size. When optimizations are set to Selected, the specific optimizations you select are implemented. Click the Optimizations button to see a list of available optimization methods from which you can choose. In most cases you should leave this option on the default setting, chosen when you press either the Full debug or Release speed buttons.

> The results of changing optimization settings can vary widely. Each application is different. Sometimes optimizing for speed has a major impact on the final executable file size and speed; other times the difference is negligible.

Debugging

When the Debug information option is enabled, C++Builder generates debug information for the project. The debug information is stored in a separate file in the project's directory. The filename of the file containing the debug information has a .TDS extension. For example, if you had a program with a project name of MyApp, C++Builder would generate a symbol file called MyApp.tds. This file is read by the debugger during debug sessions. If you do not generate debug information, you will not be able to stop on breakpoints and inspect variables during debugging. Put another way, you can't debug your program unless you tell C++Builder to generate debug information. I discuss debugging in Hour 23, "Using the Debugger."

Pre-Compiled Headers

The settings in this section of the C++ page enable you to control how pre-compiled headers will be used in your application. A *pre-compiled header* is essentially an image of the project's symbol table stored on disk. (I realize you probably don't know what a symbol table is at this point, but I can assure you that it's not something you'll ever need to think about.) The first time you build your program, C++Builder creates the pre-compiled header. On subsequent makes, C++Builder can load the pre-compiled header from disk, which is much faster than compiling the headers for each build. In addition, you can opt to cache the pre-compiled header in memory. This increases compile speed even more because the pre-compiled header can be held in memory rather than be loaded from disk when needed. You can set the Pre-compiled headers option to None, Use pre-compiled headers, or Cache pre-compiled headers depending on your needs and the hardware available on your system. Generally, you will use pre-compiled headers in one way or another. Turning off pre-compiled headers almost always results in much slower build times.

The option to cache pre-compiled headers will dramatically speed up compile and build times *if* you have enough system RAM. If you do not have enough system RAM, caching pre-compiled headers can actually slow down your builds. Do your own tests to determine whether caching pre-compiled headers is faster or slower on your system. In general, though, I would recommend turning caching off if you have less than 32MB of system RAM.

The C++ and Advanced Compiler Pages

These two pages are used to set advanced compiler options. Because these are advanced options that you might never use, I won't discuss them here. Instead I'll refer you to the C++Builder online help. A related page, the Pascal page, contains compiler options specific to C++Builder's built-in Pascal compiler.

The Linker Page

The Linker page of the Project Options dialog box is where you set options that specify how you want the linker to function. Until you become very familiar with C++Builder, you can leave this page alone and accept the default settings. Figure 19.6 shows the Linker page of the Project Options dialog box. As with the other pages, I'll explain only the linker options you're most likely to use.

FIGURE 19.6

The Linker page of the Project Options dialog box.

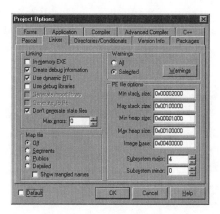

19

The Linking section has several linker options that I will go over briefly. The In-memory EXE option tells C++Builder to create the project's executable file in memory rather than on disk. This speeds build times because the executable file is never written to disk. This option is available only when running under Windows NT. (If you are using Windows 95 or 98, this option is grayed out.) Use this option only if you have plenty of system RAM. Exactly how much RAM is enough depends on your system. Experiment to see whether using this option enhances your build times. This option is used only during development. Eventually you will have to turn the In-memory EXE option off in order to get an executable file on disk that you can ship.

The Create debug information option goes with the Debug information on the Compiler page. This item must be checked in order for you to debug your application in the IDE. This option is set for you automatically when you choose either the Full debug or Release speed settings on the Compiler page.

The Use dynamic RTL option determines whether the runtime library code is linked into your application or extracted from the RTL DLL. If you are using runtime packages with your application, you will probably want to use the dynamic RTL as well. If you choose this option, you must ship the runtime library DLL (CP3245MT.DLL) with your application.

The Generate import library option pertains only to DLLs. When this option is on (the default for DLL projects) an import library file will automatically be created for the DLL. This is a great feature when creating DLLs because you don't have to manually create the LIB file yourself using the IMPLIB utility.

The Directories/Conditionals Page

The Directories/Conditionals page of the Project Options dialog box is where you set the directories that your project uses to find library files and headers. Figure 19.7 shows the Directories/Conditionals page. The fields on this page are described in the following sections.

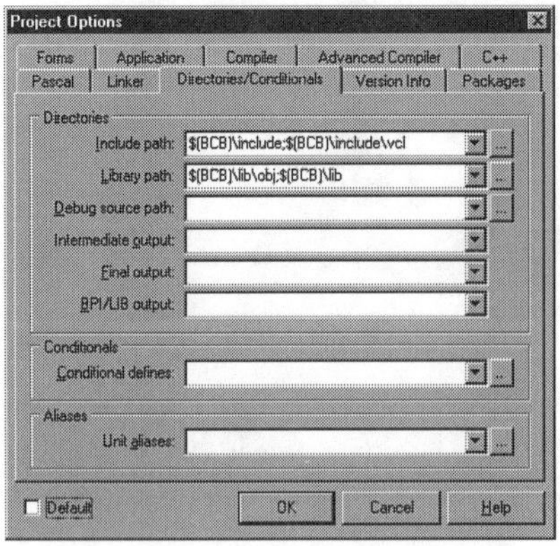

FIGURE 19.7

The Directories/ Conditionals page of the Project Options dialog box.

Include Path

The Include Path setting is the path where C++Builder looks for the headers it needs to build your application (the .h and .hpp files). By default, this field is set to point to the various C++Builder directories where the system headers are found. You should leave this field set to the default directories unless you have a third-party library that resides in a separate directory. If you must add directories to the Include path, you can add them to the end of the existing directories. Separate each directory with a semicolon, and be sure to include the full path.

Notice that the Include and Library path fields have something like the following:

`$(BCB)\include;$(BCB)\include\vcl`

The `$(BCB)` symbol is an IDE-defined macro that contains the location of the C++Builder root directory.

Library Path

The Library Path field contains the paths where the C++Builder library files (.lib) can be found. As with the Include Path field, you can add directories by separating each with a semicolon.

Do not remove the list of default directories in either the Include Path or Library Path fields. If you must modify these fields, add directories to the end of the directories listed, but do not delete any of the default directories. If you remove the default directories, your application will not compile.

19

Debug Source Path

The Debug Source Path field is used to specify the path to any source modules that you want to debug, but which aren't in the current project's directory. For example, if you wanted to step into a DLL while debugging, you would have to enter the path to the DLL's source code in this field.

Output Directories

The final three fields in the Directories section control where C++Builder creates the intermediate files it generates when it builds a project and where it places the final output file (EXE, DLL, or BPL). Intermediate files (.OBJ and .RES files, for example) are placed in the Intermediate output directory. The final output file is placed in the Final output directory. The BPI/LIB output directory is where C++Builder places the .BPI and .LIB files when building a component package. If these directories are blank, the .BPI and .LIB files will be placed in the \CBuilder4\Projects\Lib directory by default.

Conditional Defines

You use the Conditional Defines field to specify any defines that you want to add at the project level. For example, to add support for the TRACE and WARN diagnostic macros you would add this text to the Conditional defines field:

```
__TRACE;__WARN
```

Note that each defined symbol is separated by a semicolon. Sometimes C++Builder will add symbols to this field as well.

The Version Info Page

The Version Info page enables you to set the version info for your applications. Version information is stored in your program's executable file, DLL, or package file (depending on the project type). It is used by installation programs to determine whether a file being installed is older or newer than the file it is replacing. Version Info has other uses as well. You can view the version information for a file from Windows Explorer. Just right-click the file and choose Properties from the Explorer context menu. When the Properties dialog box comes up, click the Version tab to view the Version information for the file.

Figure 19.8 shows the Version Info page of the Project Options dialog box. At the top of the page is a check box labeled Include Version Information In Project. When this check box is checked, version information will be included in the project's executable file. When this check box is not checked, version information is not included in the project, and the rest of the page is disabled.

The remaining fields on the Version Info page are used to specify the various pieces of version information. The Major Version, Minor Version, Release, and Build fields work together to form the file version number. The version number of the file in Figure 19.8 is version 2.02, build 11. If you check the Auto-Increment Build Number option, the build number will automatically increment by one each time you perform a make or a build.

FIGURE 19.8

The Version Info page of the Project Options dialog box.

The Module Attributes section can be used to specify any special attributes you want specified for the file. The Language section enables you to select a locale identifier for the file. For more information on the possible values for the Locale ID field see the Windows API online help under the topic "Language Identifiers and Locales."

The table at the bottom of the Version Info page can be used to set a variety of information. This information includes your company name, the file description, the internal name of the file, the legal copyright or trademark information, the product name, product version, and any comments you want to add. You can provide information for any of these fields or none at all (the FileVersion field is set based on the fields in the Module version number section). Adding version information to a project has never been so easy!

The Packages Page

The Packages page is where you determine the packages that your application uses, or whether to use runtime packages at all. I discuss the Packages page in Hour 21, "Deploying Applications Using Packages," so I won't go into further detail here.

Summary

This chapter presents information that often gets overlooked in most users' zeal to immediately begin programming in C++Builder. I hope you picked up some tips that you can use as you work with C++Builder projects. Don't worry about understanding all the project options. In general you shouldn't have to bother with the default project options.

19

Workshop

The Workshop contains quiz questions to help you solidify your understanding of the material covered and exercises to provide you with experience in using what you have learned.

Q&A

Q Must I use a project group even if I have just one project?

A No. You don't need a project group for a single project. You can use the default project group instead.

Q All those project compiler and linker options confuse me. Do I need to know about each of those options to write programs with C++Builder?

A No. The default project options work well for almost all C++Builder applications. At some point you might get further into the mysteries of the compiler and linker, and at that time you can learn more about the project options. Until then, don't worry about it.

Quiz

1. If you remove a file from your project via the Project Manager, does the file get removed from your hard drive?

2. How do you set the main form for an application?

3. What is the significance of generating debug information for your application?

4. How do you add version information to your projects?

Answers

1. No. It is only removed from the project.

2. On the Forms page of the Project Options dialog. Move the form you want to be the main form to the top of the Auto-create forms list box.

3. When debug info is generated, you can step through your code during debugging sessions.

4. Fill in the version information for your project on the Version Info page of the Project Options dialog.

Exercises

1. Create a new application. Save the project and the project group. Now add a new project to the project group.

2. Open the ScratchPad program. Open the Project Options dialog. On the Compiler page, turn off the Debug information option. Build the application. Place a breakpoint on any line and run the program. What happens?

19

Hour **20**

Using the Code Editor

There is no question that C++Builder is highly visual in nature—that's one of the great things about programming with it. Still, any program of any significance will have a great deal of code that must be written by hand. After you get the user interface (UI) part of your application written with C++Builder's impressive visual tools, you'll likely spend a long stretch with the C++Builder Code Editor. The Code Editor has some features you'll learn to appreciate when you discover them.

In this hour you will learn about

- Basic editor operations
- Specialized editor features
- The Code Editor context menu
- Changing the editor options

The C++Builder Code Editor enables you to choose from four keyboard-mapping configurations: Default, IDE Classic, BRIEF, Epsilon, and Visual Studio. This hour assumes Default keyboard mapping. If you are using one of the other keyboard mapping configurations, you can ignore any references to specific keystrokes.

Basic Editor Operations

I'm going to assume that you know enough to be able to enter and delete text, highlight text with the mouse, cut, copy, paste, and so on. I won't spend any time going over things at that level.

If you have spent a lot of time writing code, you might be a heavy keyboard user. If that is the case, you will likely use the keyboard shortcuts for simple things like cut, copy, and paste. If you are not as experienced with the keyboard (or you just prefer using the mouse), you might want to customize your C++Builder toolbar to add speed buttons for operations like cut, copy, and paste. Whichever method you choose, you will probably get lots of practice—if you are anything like me, you will do a lot of cut, copy, and paste while writing your programs.

When it comes right down to it, the C++Builder Code Editor is a typical code editor. It features syntax highlighting, which makes identifying keywords, strings, numeric constants, and comments at a glance easy. You'll look at setting the editor preferences a little later.

The Code Editor is a tabbed window. You can open as many editor windows as you like; each one is represented by a tab along the top of the editor window. The tab displays the name of the file. To switch to a source file, simply click the tab corresponding to the file you want to view. If more tabs exist than can be displayed at one time, scroll buttons appear so that you can scroll among the tabs.

You might have noticed the two grayed out buttons on the top-right of the Code Editor window. These buttons are used for the code browser that ships with the Professional and Enterprise editions of C++Builder. They are not active in the Standard version.

The status bar at the bottom of the Code Editor gives status information (obviously). The current line number and the cursor position on the line are reported in the left panel of the status bar. If the file has changed since it was last saved, the status bar says Modified in the center panel of the status bar. The right panel of the status bar shows the current mode, either Insert or Overwrite. If the file has been set to read-only, this panel says Read Only.

The editor window has a gray strip in the left margin that is called the *gutter*. The gutter is used to display icons at different stages of the development process. For example, when you set a debugger breakpoint (discussed in Hour 23, "Using the Debugger"), a red dot is placed in the gutter. When you set a bookmark (discussed in the section "Using Bookmarks"), an icon representing the bookmark is placed in the gutter.

If you accidentally click on the gutter when trying to select text or place the cursor, you will find that a breakpoint is set on that line. Click the gutter again to clear the breakpoint.

Opening and Saving Files

Nothing is very mysterious about opening and saving files in the Code Editor. It should be pointed out, though, that there is a difference between opening a project and opening a source file. When you choose File, Open Project from the main menu, you are prompted for the name of a project file to open. When you choose File, Open from the main menu, you can open any text file (.cpp, .rc, .h, .hpp, .pas, .txt, and so on). Both the Open and Open Project menu items have corresponding toolbar buttons.

If you open a source file (.cpp) that is the source code unit for a form, C++Builder opens the source file in the Code Editor and also opens the form in the Form Designer.

You can open multiple files at one time. To open multiple files, choose the files you want to open in the Open dialog box and click OK. Each file selected is loaded, and a tab for each file is placed at the top of the editor window.

20

You can also use drag and drop to open files. For example, you can choose a file (or a group of files) in Explorer, drag it onto the Code Editor, and drop it. The file will be opened in the Code Editor.

To save a file, choose File, Save or File, Save As from the main menu or type Ctrl+S on the keyboard. If the file has not been previously saved, the Save As dialog box appears, and you can enter a filename at that time.

Highlighting Text

Although text highlighting is basic text-editor stuff, I thought it wouldn't hurt to remind you of a few basic highlighting techniques you can use in the C++Builder Code Editor.

To highlight a short block of text, you can use the mouse to drag across any text you want to highlight. After you've selected the text you can cut, copy, or paste as needed. To highlight longer blocks of code, you can use the Click+Shift+Click method. First, click at the beginning of the block you want to highlight. Next, hold the Shift key on the keyboard and then click again at the end of the block. All text between the starting point and the ending point is highlighted.

Another useful feature is the capability to quickly select an individual word. To select a keyword, function name, or variable, just double-click on the word. Now you can perform any editing operations you want with the highlighted word.

To select a single line of code with the mouse, click at the beginning of the line and drag straight down to the beginning of the next line. To highlight a single line of code with the keyboard, first press the Home key to move to the beginning of the line and then use Shift+down-arrow key to highlight the line.

Dozens of keyboard combinations can be used to highlight text and do other editing chores. For a complete list of all the keyboard shortcuts available, consult the C++Builder online help.

As you program you often add, delete, or move blocks of text. Sometimes you will need to indent an entire block of code. At other times you will need to un-indent (outdent?) an entire block of code. To indent a block of code, highlight the lines that you want to indent and then press Ctrl+Shift+I on the keyboard. The entire block will be indented. To un-indent a block of code, press Ctrl+Shift+U on the keyboard.

The Code Editor also supports drag-and-drop editing. To move a section of code first highlight it. Next, place the mouse cursor over the highlighted text and drag. Drag until the cursor reaches the location where you want the code to be placed. Release the mouse button, and the code will be moved to the new location. To copy text rather than move it, repeat the preceding steps, but hold down the Ctrl key before you drop the text.

Undo

The Code Editor has a virtually limitless number of undo levels (32,767 by default). Normally, you can only undo commands up to the last time you saved a file. By changing the editor options, you will be able to undo past commands even after saving the file. I'll talk about editor options and preferences later in the chapter in the section titled "Changing the Editor Options."

In general, it pays to remember this simple maxim: "Undo is your friend."

Find and Replace

Find and Replace are used fairly heavily in programming. You might use Find to find a specific piece of code or a specific variable in your code. You might use Replace to change a variable's name or to change the name of a function. The possibilities are endless.

The C++Builder Find Text and Replace Text dialog boxes implement more or less standard find-and-replace operations. To bring up the Find Text dialog box, choose Search, Find from the main menu or press Ctrl+F. Enter text in the Text to find field and click OK or press Enter. If the text is found, it is highlighted.

Text highlighted by the Find Text dialog box is not the same as text highlighted with the mouse. You will notice that searched text is highlighted in black, whereas text selected with the mouse is highlighted in blue (assuming you haven't changed the editor defaults or the Windows' default color scheme). Text highlighted after a search operation is not selected for editing, but is just marked so you can see it better.

20

To invoke the Replace Text dialog box, choose Search, Replace from the menu or press Ctrl+R. Figure 20.1 shows the C++Builder Replace Text dialog box. With a few obvious exceptions, the Find Text dialog box contains the same options.

FIGURE 20.1

*The Replace Text
dialog box.*

For the most part, the options on the Find Text and Replace Text dialog boxes do exactly what they indicate. If you choose the Case Sensitive option, you must type the search text exactly as it appears in the source file.

Use the Whole Words Only option when you want to be sure that text for which you are searching is not part of a longer word or variable name. For example, suppose you were converting a Delphi application to C++Builder. In that case you might search for all occurrences of the word end and replace them with a closing brace, }. In this case you would want to search for whole words only because the e-n-d sequence of characters is commonly used within words. Failing to use this option would cause this code:

```
DataSet->Append();
```

to be modified like this:

```
DataSet->App}();
```

The Regular Expressions option requires explanation as well. When this option is on, you can use special and wildcard characters when doing searches. The special characters enable you to find things such as the beginning of a line or the end of a line in your search strings. Wildcard characters work much like they do in directory operations. For a complete description of regular expressions see the C++Builder online help under the topic Regular Expressions.

When replacing text, it is safest to leave the Prompt On Replace option on. When you do a Replace All operation with this option on, the editor highlights each found word and prompts you whether to replace it. It is easy to miscalculate the results of a Replace All operation, so always use Replace All with care. Even then, it still pays to remember that maxim: "Undo is your friend."

The rest of the Find and Replace options are self-explanatory and therefore don't need additional mention.

Find in Files

Find in Files is a great tool for searching for text in multiple files. This tool replaces the venerable old GREP utility. I frequently use Find in Files to search the VCL source code for particular functions, variables, or classes. This tool is useful and convenient, and you should learn how to use it. To display the Find in Files dialog box you can choose Search, Find in Files from the main menu. Perhaps an easier way is to type Ctrl+F on the keyboard to bring up the Find Text dialog box and then click the Find in Files tab. Figure 20.2 shows the Find Text dialog box with the Find in Files page displayed.

FIGURE 20.2

The Find in Files tab of the Find Text dialog box.

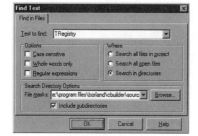

Find in Files uses some of the same search options as the regular Find operation (Case Sensitive, Whole Word Only, and Regular Expressions). In addition, you have the option to search all files in the project, all open files, or files in a particular directory, including subdirectories. When you start Find in Files, a small window with a title of Searching appears in the lower-right portion of your screen. This window shows the status of the Find in Files operation. It shows you the current file being searched and the number of matches up to this point. To cancel the search just close the Searching window.

Any matches are reported in the Code Editor's message window. The message window shows the filename of the file in which the text was found, the line number where the text was found, and the line containing the search text with the search text displayed in bold. To view the file that contains a match, just double-click a line in the message window. C++Builder opens the appropriate file and displays the exact line containing the text for which you are searching. Figure 20.3 shows C++Builder searching a set of files.

When specifying the file mask, all the usual wildcard characters apply. For example, if you wanted to search all VCL headers, you would enter the following in the File masks field:

```
c:\Program Files\Borland\CBuilder4\Include\VCL\*.hpp
```

20

FIGURE 20.3

C++Builder searching for text.

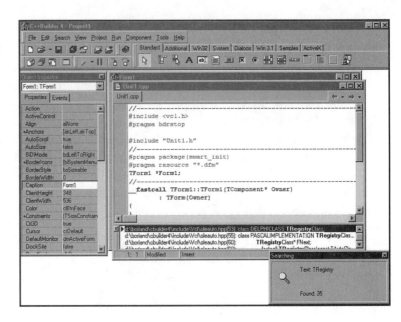

Find in Files is an indispensable tool. I find myself using it all the time. Learning to use Find in Files will save you a lot of time.

Getting Help

One of the most useful features of the Code Editor is its integration with the C++Builder help system. Just place the editor cursor over a C++ keyword, a VCL property or method, or any other C++Builder–specific text and press F1. If a help topic for the text under the cursor exists in the C++Builder help files, Windows Help runs with the appropriate page showing. If no help topic exists for the selected text, an error message is displayed. This feature is extremely useful when you can't remember how to use a particular aspect of C++Builder, C++, or VCL. Help, as they say, is just a keystroke away.

Specialized Editor Features

The C++Builder Code Editor has a few features that are extremely useful when you are writing a lot of code. They are explained in the following sections.

Code Templates

Code templates are another nice feature of the C++Builder Code Editor. Code templates enable you to insert any predefined code (or any text, for that matter) in your source units. To use Code templates, just type Ctrl+J on the keyboard while editing in the Code Editor. When you do, a list box pops up giving you a list of templates from which to choose. Choose a template from the list, press Enter, and the text corresponding to that code template is inserted into your source code. Figure 20.4 shows the code template list box as it appears when you type Ctrl+J.

FIGURE 20.4

The C++Builder code template list box.

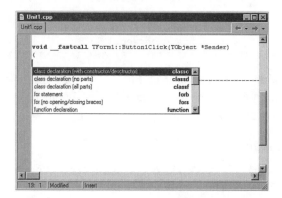

You can add new templates or edit existing templates via the Code Insight page of the Environment Options dialog box. Or if you prefer, you can open the code template file with any text editor (such as the C++Builder Code Editor) and edit the code templates there. The code template file is called BCB.DCI and is located in the CBuilder4\Bin directory.

Feel free to modify the code templates in any way you see fit. For example, I have modified my code template representing the for statement to look like this:

```
for (int i=0;i<|;i++) {

}
```

Notice the pipe character (|) in the code snippet. The pipe in a code template entry is a placeholder that determines where the cursor will be placed after the text is inserted into your source code.

20

If you make a lot of modifications to the code template file, be sure to keep a backup of the file in a safe location. You will need a backup because the C++Builder installation program might overwrite your modified BCB.DCI file when you update or reinstall C++Builder.

You can use code templates for more than just code. Here at TurboPower Software our source files always have a header at the top of the unit. It looks something like this:

```
{*********************************************************}
{*                  Filename and version                 *}
{*        Copyright (c) TurboPower Software 1999          *}
{*                 All rights reserved.                   *}
{*********************************************************}
```

Because most of this text stays constant, I have a template that quickly inserts the header in any new source units I create. Use code templates for any text that you use frequently in your day-to-day programming.

Using Bookmarks

You can set bookmarks in your code to temporarily mark your place in a source file. For example, you often must temporarily leave a block of code on which you are working to review previously written code or to copy code from another location. By dropping a bookmark at that point in your code before running off to do your other work, you can return to that section of code with a simple keystroke. You can have up to 10 bookmarks set at any one time.

To set a bookmark at a particular location, press Ctrl+Shift and the number of the bookmark to set. For example, to set bookmark 0 (the first bookmark), place the editor cursor at the location you want to mark and then press Ctrl+Shift+0 (Ctrl+K+0 works as well). When you set a bookmark, an icon is placed in the Code Editor gutter to indicate that a bookmark exists on that line. The icon shows the number of the bookmark. Figure 20.5 shows the Code Editor with a bookmark dropped on a line.

To return to the bookmark, press Ctrl plus the number of the bookmark to which you want to return. Using the same example, you would type Ctrl+0 to go back to the bookmark. To clear a bookmark, place the editor cursor anywhere on the line containing the bookmark and again press Ctrl+Shift+0.

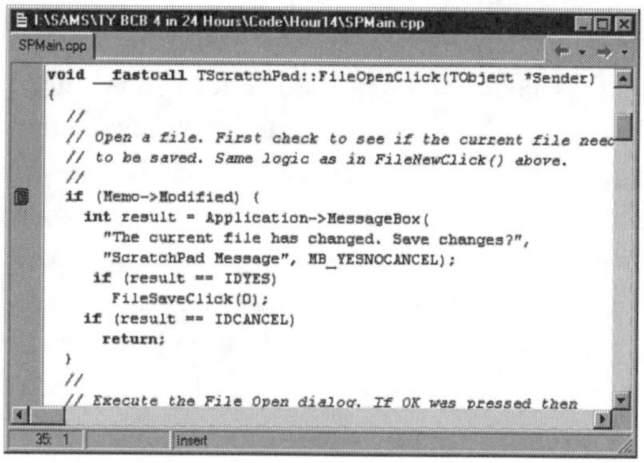

FIGURE 20.5

The Code Editor with a bookmark set.

```
F:\SAMS\TY BCB 4 in 24 Hours\Code\Hour14\SPMain.cpp
SPMain.cpp
void __fastcall TScratchPad::FileOpenClick(TObject *Sender)
{
  //
  // Open a file. First check to see if the current file need
  // to be saved. Same logic as in FileNewClick() above.
  //
  if (Memo->Modified) {
    int result = Application->MessageBox(
      "The current file has changed. Save changes?",
      "ScratchPad Message", MB_YESNOCANCEL);
    if (result == IDYES)
      FileSaveClick(0);
    if (result == IDCANCEL)
      return;
  }
  //
  // Execute the File Open dialog. If OK was pressed then
```

Bookmarks can be set for each file you have open in the Code Editor. For example, you can have bookmark #0 set in one source file and another bookmark #0 set in another source file. This means that bookmarks cannot be found across source files. If you set bookmark #0 in Unit1.cpp, you cannot press Ctrl+0 from Unit2.cpp and expect to be taken to the bookmark in Unit1.cpp.

To illustrate the use of bookmarks, do the following:

1. Open any source file in the Code Editor.

2. Scroll almost to the bottom of the file and click on a line of code.

3. Press Ctrl+Shift+0 to set a bookmark. The bookmark icon shows in the Code Editor gutter.

4. Press Ctrl+Home to move to the top of the source file.

5. Now press Ctrl+0 to jump back to the bookmark. The Code Editor changes to show the line of code where the bookmark was set, and the cursor is placed exactly where it was when you set the bookmark.

6. Type Ctrl+Shift+0 again to clear the bookmark. The bookmark is cleared, and the bookmark icon disappears from the Code Editor gutter.

Bookmarks are temporary. When you close the source file and reopen it, the bookmark is not preserved.

20

Finding Matching Braces and Parentheses

As you have seen, C++ code can often become fairly convoluted when you start nesting if statements, if/else pairs, and so on. To tell the truth, getting lost is easy. The Code Editor has a feature to help you find a brace that matches the brace the cursor is currently on. To find a matching brace, first place the cursor before a brace (it doesn't matter whether it's the opening or closing brace). Now press Alt+[on the keyboard. The cursor jumps to the brace that matches the brace on which you started. Press Alt+[again, and the cursor jumps back to where you started. Getting lost in the maze of braces in a long series of if statements is still a possibility, but at least now you know how to find your way out again. This feature also works with parentheses.

The Code Editor Context Menu

Like most of the different windows you encounter in C++Builder, the Code Editor has its own context menu. The Code Editor context menu can essentially be broken down into two parts: editor items and debugger items. I will leave the debugger items of the context menu for Hour 23 when I discuss debugging, but I'll go over the editor items on the context menu now. Table 20.1 contains a list of the context menu items that pertain to the editor, along with a description of each.

TABLE 20.1 THE CODE EDITOR CONTEXT MENU ITEMS

Menu Item	Description
Open Source/Header File	If the header file corresponding to the current source file is not opened in the Code Editor, choosing this menu item opens the header file, creates a new tab for it, and changes focus to that window. Choosing this option when both the .cpp and .h files are open switches focus back and forth between the two files.
Close Page	Closes the active page in the edit window. If the file on the page has been modified since it was last saved, you will be prompted to save the file.
Open File at Cursor	Opens the file under the cursor. This option has an effect only when the text under the cursor represents a source code file. For example, if you had a header included with #include "myclass.h", you could place the cursor over the filename and choose this menu item to open the file. The file will be placed in a new editor window, and focus will be set to the window.
New Edit Window	Opens a new copy of the Code Editor. This is convenient if you want to compare two source files side by side.

Menu Item	Description
Topic Search	Displays the help topic for the item under the cursor (if it can be found). Same as pressing F1 on the keyboard.
Toggle Bookmarks	Allows you to set a bookmark on the current line in the Code Editor.
Goto Bookmarks	Allows you to go to a bookmark previously set.
View As Form	If the active file in the Code Editor is displaying a form's contents as text, choosing this option will again display the form in the Form Designer.
Read Only	Toggles the currently active file between read-only and read/write mode. When set to read-only, the file cannot be modified, although text can be selected and copied to the clipboard. The status bar displays Read only to indicate the file is read-only. When the file is closed and reopened, it is again in read/write mode.
Message View	Displays or hides the C++Builder message window. The message window automatically appears when there are compiler or linker errors or warnings, but can be specifically shown or hidden with this command.
Properties	Displays the Environment Options dialog box so that the editor options can be set.

Depending on the current state of the Code Editor and the particular type of file open, some of the items in Table 20.1 can be disabled at any given time.

Changing the Editor Options

The editor options occupy four pages of the Environment Options dialog box. To view this dialog box, choose Tools, Environment Options from the main menu.

20

> You can also choose Properties from the Code Editor context menu to view the editor options. The difference with this method is that only the four pages pertaining to the editor options are displayed in the Environment Options dialog box.

The four pages of the Environment Options that are specific to the Code Editor are the Editor, Display, Colors, and Code Insight pages. We'll examine the first three of these pages next. I'll discuss the Code Insight page in Hour 24, "New Features in C++Builder 4."

The Editor Page

The Editor page of the Environment Options dialog box enables you to control how the editor works for you. As you can see from Figure 20.6, a lot of options are available on this page.

FIGURE 20.6

The Editor page of the Environment Options dialog box.

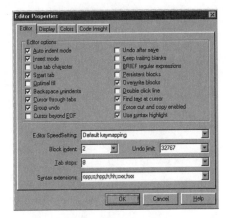

In the bottom section of the page is a combo box labeled Editor SpeedSetting. You can choose Default keymapping, IDE Classic, BRIEF emulation, Epsilon emulation, or Visual Studio emulation from the combo box. If you change the setting in this combo box, the Editor Options will change to reflect the defaults for the type you chose.

If you are new to programming or if you have been using other Borland compilers using the Default keymapping, you don't have to worry about what you are missing. If you are accustomed to years of using a particular type of editor, you will be glad to know that you can still use the keyboard shortcuts and editor options you know and love simply by changing the Editor SpeedSetting on this page and on the Display page.

Toward the bottom of the screen you will see the Block Indent and Tab Stops fields. You can use these two fields to change the amount by which code is indented when you block indent or when you tab to the next tab stop. Block indenting is discussed in the section "Highlighting Text."

Real programmers use tab stops of either two or three characters. (I use two-character tabs.)

The Undo limit of 32,767 is probably sufficient for most needs (I hope!), so I doubt you'll feel the need to modify that setting. The Syntax Extensions field enables you to select the types of files for which syntax highlighting will be applied. For example, you probably don't want syntax highlighting applied to regular text files (.txt) that you open in the Code Editor, so that file type is not listed by default.

In the top section of the Editor page, you will find a whole gaggle of editor options from which to choose. Because so many options are available, and because determining exactly which of the available options are the most important is difficult, I'll refer you to the C++Builder online help. Simply press F1 while on this page or click the Help button, and you will have explanations of each of the editor options you see on this page. As with some of the project options I discussed in Hour 19, you can probably feel comfortable in accepting the C++Builder defaults.

The Display Page

The Display page of the Environment Options dialog box has additional options from which you can choose. These options pertain to the actual display of the text in the Code Editor window. (See Figure 20.7.)

FIGURE 20.7

The Display page of the Environment Options dialog box.

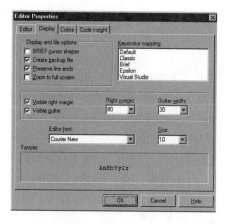

20

In the Display And File Options section, you will find the BRIEF Cursor Shapes option. Turn on this option if you want the horizontal cursor in the editor window rather than the vertical cursor. Check the Create Backup File option if you want C++Builder to create a backup file every time you save your file or your project. Backup file extensions begin with a tilde (~). For example, the backup file for a source file called MyApp.cpp would be MyApp.~cp.

I usually tire of the backup files cluttering up my project directories and turn off file backups. I would recommend, however, that you leave backups on until you have a degree of experience with C++Builder.

The Zoom To Full Screen option controls how the Code Editor acts when maximized. If this option is on, the Code Editor fills the entire screen when maximized. When this option is off (the default), the top of the Code Editor window stops at the bottom of the C++Builder main window when maximized. In other words, the C++Builder main window is always visible when the Code Editor is maximized if this option is off.

You can also choose whether your editor windows have a visible right margin. The right margin is not binding—you can still type text beyond it—but it gives you a visual cue that your lines might be getting too long. This section also enables you to determine whether you want a visible gutter and how wide the gutter should be (in pixels).

You can also change the Code Editor font and point size. A combo box is provided for you to choose these options. Only fixed-space screen fonts are listed; proportional and printer fonts are not. Choose the typeface and point size that best suit your needs. A preview window is provided so that you can see how the font you have chosen will look.

The Colors Page

The Colors page of the Environment Options dialog box enables you to fully customize the Code Editor's window and syntax highlighting options. (See Figure 20.8.)

FIGURE 20.8

The Colors page in the Environment Options dialog box.

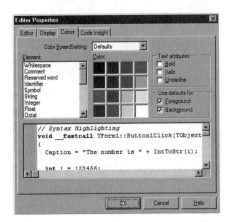

At the top of the page is the Color SpeedSetting combo box. This combo box gives you four predefined color schemes from which to choose. You can choose one of these color schemes or use one of them as a base for creating your own color scheme.

The Colors page is very easy to use. At the bottom of the page is a text window that contains sample code. If you click one of the key elements of the code, that element is selected in the Elements list box, and its current settings are displayed on the Color grid. To change the foreground, background, and text attributes for that element, simply choose the settings you like. For example, keywords are displayed in bold text with a black foreground and a white background (assuming the default color scheme). To change the keywords to green, bold text, click the void keyword in the sample code window and then change the foreground color to green. The text colors in the sample window change to reflect the new color you have chosen. Continue changing colors until you have the sample window just the way you want it. When you click OK, the Code Editor changes to the new colors you have chosen.

Summary

In this hour you learned about the C++Builder Code Editor. You'll spend a lot of time with the Code Editor as you begin writing applications in C++Builder. Knowing how to use the Code Editor to its fullest will make you a more efficient programmer. You learned about basic editor features such as opening and saving files, entering code, and finding and replacing text. You also learned about specialized editor techniques such as code templates and bookmarks. You ended this hour learning about the editor options and how to use them to customize the editor to your liking.

Workshop

The Workshop contains quiz questions to help you solidify your understanding of the material covered and exercises to provide you with experience in using what you have learned.

20

Q&A

Q Can I open several source files at one time in the Code Editor?

A Yes. You can also select multiple files in Windows Explorer and drop them onto the Code Editor.

Q I find that 32,767 undo levels is not enough for my needs. What do you suggest?

A Don't quit your day job.

Quiz

1. What is the Find in Files option used for?
2. What is the keyboard shortcut for saving a file in the Code Editor?
3. How do you set a bookmark in an editor window?
4. What keystroke do you use to find a matching brace in the Code Editor?

Answers

1. Find in Files is used to find text in files.
2. The keyboard shortcut for saving a source file is Ctrl+S (assuming the Default keymapping).
3. Set a bookmark with Ctrl+K+0 through Ctrl+K+9 (or Ctrl+Shift+0 through Ctrl+Shift+9).
4. Use Alt+[or Alt+] to find a matching brace.

Exercises

1. Open any source file in the Code Editor. Set four bookmarks at random locations in the source file. Jump from bookmark to bookmark and observe the effects in the Code Editor. When you are finished, clear all the bookmarks.
2. Open the ScratchPad project (or any other project) and switch to the Code Editor. View the project's main form source file. Choose Search, Find from the main menu. Type `Click` in the Text To Find box and click OK to find the first occurrence of the word Click.
3. Press F3 several times to repeat the search until the entire file has been searched.

Hour 21

Deploying Applications Using Packages

After your application is written, you can deploy it in one of two ways. (*Deploying* means the act of distributing your application to your users.) You might be distributing your application to the general public or possibly to users within your company. Either way, you need to know what options are available to you. Essentially you have two choices: static linking or dynamic linking using packages. In this hour, I'll discuss those options so that you can make an informed choice on how to deploy your application. I'll start with a discussion of packages, and then I'll discuss deployment options.

In this hour, you will learn about

- Defining a package
- Static linking versus dynamic linking
- Static linking your applications
- Linking your applications dynamically

Defining a Package

Before I discuss the options available to you, it would be a good idea to define what a package is. When you take off the wrappings, a package is, essentially, just a dynamic link library (DLL) with an extension of .BPL rather than the traditional .DLL extension. (BPL stands for Borland Package Library, in case you were wondering.)

There are two types of packages in C++Builder—runtime packages and design packages. I'll go over each of these two types next, so you can get an understanding of how packages work. Because a package is just a form of DLL, I'll use the term package and DLL interchangeably.

Runtime Packages

A runtime package contains code your application needs to run. Although C++Builder provides many different packages, the primary package is called VCL40.BPL. This package contains all the base Visual Component Library (VCL) code in one DLL. If you choose to use packages in your application, your application will load the VCL40.BPL package and call routines from that package as needed. If your application uses additional VCL controls, it will also load VCLX40.BPL and call routines from that package as needed. There are other C++Builder packages in addition to the two mentioned here.

In addition to the VCL packages, your application might require other packages. This is the case if you are using any third-party components or any components that you write yourself. For components that you write, you will naturally know the package name. For third-party components, you will have to check the documentation that comes with those components to find out which packages your application requires in order to run. Before going into detail on this, I will talk about design packages.

Design Packages

To explain design packages, it might be a good idea to first give you a short tutorial on component design. Most components created for C++Builder include a runtime package and a design package. The runtime package contains all the code needed for a component to operate. The design package contains the code needed for the component to operate on a form at design time. For example, a design package often includes component and property editors. Component and property editors contain code (and usually forms) that don't need to be in the executable at all; they are only used at design time.

The design package has a Requires list that tells C++Builder which packages it requires to operate. The design package almost always requires code from the runtime package and probably code from one or more VCL packages as well. It's important to understand that one package (both runtime and design) can contain the code for several components. It's not necessary to have a separate package for each component.

Because design packages contain just the code needed to display components at design time, they are usually much smaller than their runtime counterparts. Design packages are only used by C++Builder at design time—they are not needed for your application to operate.

 A package can be written as both a design and a runtime package. This is done when the components in the package do not contain component and property editors. Most professional component packages, however, contain both design and runtime packages.

Static Linking Versus Dynamic Linking

Now that you know a little about packages, I can talk about static linking versus dynamic linking.

Static Linking

When an application uses static linking of the Visual Component Library (VCL) and C/C++ runtime library (RTL), it doesn't use packages at all. Any code your application requires to run is linked directly into your application's executable file. Your application is a standalone program and doesn't require any supporting packages or DLLs.

Static linking has two primary advantages over dynamic linking. The first is that you don't have to worry about shipping any additional files with your application. Your application contains all the code it needs to run and no extra libraries are required. The second advantage is that a statically linked application is generally smaller in total size than an application that requires packages. I'll talk about this more in just a bit when I talk about the advantages and disadvantages of dynamic linking.

Static linking has one major drawback, but it only shows up in applications that use many supporting DLLs. The drawback is that the VCL and RTL code is duplicated in every module (the main application itself) and in every DLL. This means that code is duplicated unnecessarily. For example, let's say that every module requires a minimum of 200KB of VCL base code and RTL code. Now let's say that you have a main application and 10 supporting DLLs; this means that 2200KB of code is used (11 modules × 200KB each) when only 200KB is actually required. The application and DLLs are all statically linked and can't share the VCL and RTL code amongst themselves.

21

Dynamic Linking

Dynamic linking refers to a scenario where an application dynamically loads its library code at runtime. In the case of a C++Builder application, this means that any required packages and the runtime library DLL are loaded at runtime. Required packages will certainly include one or more VCL packages and might include third-party packages as well. The default for new C++Builder projects is to use dynamic linking.

 The loading of packages by your application is automatic. You don't have to write code to load the packages or the runtime library DLL. C++Builder takes care of that for you. Choosing dynamic linking over static linking doesn't require any changes to your code. It does require changes to the way you deploy your application, which I will tell you about shortly.

Dynamic linking has one primary advantage over static linking: Several modules can share code from a central location (the packages and RTL DLL). Remember earlier when I gave an example of an application and 10 supporting DLLs? Using dynamic linking, the application and all DLLs can share code from the VCL package and the RTL DLL. Each module will be at least 200KB smaller because all the base code is contained in the runtime DLLs. This is an advantage when your overall product contains several applications or many DLLs.

Dynamic linking comes with a couple of problems. The first problem is that the packages and DLLs that you need to ship with your application can be quite large. The primary VCL package, VCL40.BPL, is 1.8MB alone. The runtime library DLL, CP3245MT.DLL, is another .9MB or so. This means that your application will require at least 2.7MB of DLLs to run.

A second problem with dynamic linking is more subtle and more troublesome. The problem could be summed up in one word: versioning. To explain the problem, I will give you a possible scenario. Let's say you create an application using C++Builder 4.02 (assuming a couple of revisions to C++Builder) and that you use dynamic linking, requiring you to ship the VCL packages and RTL DLL. Your customer installs your application on his machine and everything works fine. Meanwhile, I build an application using C++Builder 4.0 (I'm too cheap to pay the shipping for the upgrade) and I also use dynamic linking. Your customer buys my application and installs it. My installation program is homemade and doesn't play by the rules, so I overwrite the packages and DLLs that your application installed. Suddenly your application quits working because my packages and RTL DLL are older than yours and the two are not compatible. Do you see the problem?

In reality, commercial software companies like Inprise prevent this problem by naming their packages and DLLs by different names for each release of a product and by embedding version information in the packages and DLLs. (A good installation program checks the version number and only installs a package if it is newer than any existing packages on the user's system.) But packages from Inprise aren't the real problem. The real problem comes when using components from companies that are less careful about how they do business. If you buy a component package from Billy Bob's Software Company, you are trusting that Billy Bob knows what he is doing when it comes to creating packages. That might or might not be a good assumption. Let's face it, with the boom of the Internet, components are available from a wide variety of sources. You don't know what you are getting in a lot of cases, so be careful when purchasing inexpensive or freeware components.

I can hear you thinking, "So should I use static linking or dynamic linking?" The answer to that question depends on the type of applications you write. In general, if you are writing a single small- or medium-sized application, you should use static linking. If you are writing very large applications, or applications with a large number of DLLs, you should probably use dynamic linking.

A simple case study might help put this in perspective. In Hours 13 and 14 you created the Scratch Pad program. That program compiles to around 415KB (give or take a few KB) when static linking is used. If you link Scratch Pad using packages and the dynamic version of the RTL, you can get the EXE size down to around 41KB, but you have to ship 2.7MB of DLLs. As you can see, dynamic linking is not a good choice in this case.

Static Linking Your Applications

If you choose to use static linking, you only need to change a couple of settings in the project options. Here's what you need to do:

1. Choose Project, Options from the main menu to bring up the Project Options dialog box.
2. Click the Linker tab and uncheck the Use Dynamic RTL option.
3. Click the Packages tab and uncheck the Build With Runtime Packages option near the bottom of the page (see Figure 21.1).
4. Click OK to close the Project Options dialog box.
5. Rebuild the project.

That's all there is to it. Remember, using static linking doesn't require any changes to your code.

21

FIGURE 21.1

*The Packages page of
the Project Options
dialog.*

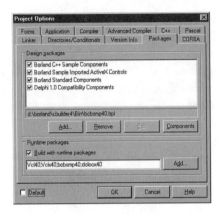

Linking Your Applications Dynamically

Deploying an application that uses dynamic linking requires you to know which packages and DLLs your application uses. If you accept the default project option of dynamic
linking, you can be assured that you need VCL40.BPL and CP3245MT.DLL at a minimum.
You might need other VCL packages as well, depending on the components your application uses. To find out for sure you will have to run a utility such as TDUMP.EXE and
examine the imports that your EXE references. TDUMP can be found in your
\Cbuilder4\bin directory. To run TDUMP just open a command-prompt box and switch to
the directory where your application resides. Then type the following at the command
line (because TDUMP is on your path, you don't have to type the path to your bin directory):

```
tdump myproject.exe
```

Get ready on the Pause button because TDUMP starts displaying information right away.
Somewhere along the line you will see some lines like this:

```
Imports from VCL40.bpl
    __fastcall Sysconst::initialization()
    __fastcall Sysconst::Finalization()
```

This might be repeated several times. You will have to watch for any files with a .BPL
extension and make note of their filenames. When you are done, you will have a list of
packages that you will have to ship with your application. Don't forget CP3245MT.DLL if
you are using the dynamic RTL.

The output from TDUMP can be redirected to a text file for easier viewing. Sending the output to a text file eliminates the scenario where you sit with your finger poised above the Pause button while the TDUMP output scrolls by at light speed. To redirect the output to a text file, do this:

```
tdump myproject.exe > dump.txt
```

Now you can open DUMP.TXT in the C++Builder Code Editor and view the contents.

You can save yourself a lot of time and trouble by getting a good installation program. I like Wise Install from Wise Solutions (http://www.wiseinstall.com). Install Shield Express comes with C++Builder Professional and Enterprise versions, so if you end up buying one of those versions, you might have everything you need. You can find out more about the full version of Install Shield at www.installshield.com. The better installation programs will figure out which packages your application requires and automatically include them in the installation. I don't recommend writing your own installation program under any circumstances. There are just too many things that you can fail to take into account when writing an installation program.

Most of the time you probably won't use runtime packages in your applications. On the other hand, sometimes packages are just what you need.

Summary

Packages are used both by the C++Builder IDE and by applications built with C++Builder. Choosing static linking over dynamic linking alleviates the need for shipping packages with your applications. For small- to medium-sized applications, static linking is preferred. For large applications or applications with a large number of supporting DLLs, dynamic linking is preferred.

Workshop

The Workshop contains quiz questions to help you solidify your understanding of the material covered and exercises to provide you with experience in using what you have learned.

21

Q&A

Q I don't like the default project options that require dynamic linking. Can I change that?

A Yes. First close all projects. Next open the Project Options dialog. Clear the Use Dynamic RTL option on the Linker page and the Build With Runtime Packages option on the Packages page. Close the Project Options dialog by clicking OK. The new settings are now the default for any new projects you create.

Q I turned off the Build with runtime packages option, but I still can't run my application on another machine. It says it needs CP3245MT.DLL. What I have done wrong?

A You forgot to clear the Use dynamic RTL option on the Linker page of the Project Options dialog.

Quiz

1. What does static linking mean?
2. What is a design package?
3. What's best for a small application, dynamic or static linking?
4. What is the name of the primary VCL runtime package?

Answers

1. Static linking means that all the code your application needs is linked into the executable file. You don't need to ship DLLs or packages for statically linked applications.
2. A design package is a package that is used by the C++Builder IDE to show components on the Component palette.
3. Static linking is best for a small application.
4. The primary VCL runtime package is VCL40.BPL.

Exercise

1. Create a simple program and build it. Run Windows Explorer and examine the size of the .EXE created by C++Builder. Now change the project options to not use runtime packages and the dynamic RTL. Rebuild the program. Check the size of the .EXE now. What is the difference in size?

Hour **22**

Printing from C++Builder Applications

Printing is an everyday necessity for most Windows users. While there are plenty of programs without printing capability, the majority of Windows applications have some form of printing support. I'll cover the basics of printing in this session.

In this hour, you will learn about

- The common printing dialog boxes
- Printing the easy way
- Printing the hard way
- Printing a bitmap

Providing printing capabilities in a DOS application used to be a real chore. A DOS program had to provide and install printer drivers for every type of printer that the program supported. This put a huge burden on software developers, especially on small companies or shareware developers. Windows changed all that. For the most part, Windows takes on the burden of dealing with different printers, printer drivers, and so on. All you have to do is send output to the printer just as you would send output to a window. I'll get to that soon.

Printing in C++Builder applications comes in several flavors. You'll probably be relieved to learn that in many cases printing is built into Visual Component Library (VCL) and comes nearly automatically. In other cases, though, you have to do some specialized printing. Before you learn how to go about that, let's look at the common dialog boxes that pertain to printing. After that I'll discuss the different ways you can print from a C++Builder application.

The Common Printing Dialog Boxes

Windows provides the Print and Print Setup common dialog boxes for use in your applications. You use the Print dialog box just before printing begins and the Print Setup dialog box to configure the printer.

The Print Dialog Box

As I've mentioned, the Print dialog box is displayed just before printing begins, usually when the user chooses File, Print from the main menu. If the user clicks OK, printing begins; if the user clicks Cancel, printing is aborted. Figure 22.1 shows the Windows Print dialog box in its most basic form.

FIGURE 22.1

The Windows Print dialog box.

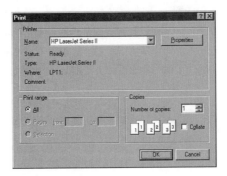

No doubt this is not the first time you have seen this particular dialog box. The combo box at the top of the dialog box enables you to choose the particular printer to which you want to print. The Properties button brings up a dialog box specific to the printer currently selected. The Properties dialog box enables you to set the orientation, resolution, and other properties specific to that printer. The Print Range section enables the user to print all pages, a page range, or any objects or text currently selected in the application. The Copies section enables the user to specify the number of copies to print, as well as whether to collate the copies.

22

The Print dialog box is encapsulated in VCL in the `PrintDialog` component. As with the other common dialog boxes, you display the Print dialog box by calling its `Execute()` method. It shouldn't disappoint you to learn that Windows accomplishes much of what the Print dialog box does. The printer selection, number of copies, and collating options are all handled by Windows, so you don't have to worry about them. Depending on your application, you might need to allow the user to print a specified range of pages or to print the current selection in the application. If you are providing that kind of support, you need to examine some of the `PrintDialog` properties before printing begins.

The `PrintDialog` component has the `Execute()` method only and no events. All the functionality of the `PrintDialog` component takes place through its properties, listed in Table 22.1.

TABLE 22.1 THE `PrintDialog` PROPERTIES

Property	Description
Collate	Specifies collated copies. If this is set to `True`, Windows prints so that the copies are collated.
Copies	Specifies the number of copies to print. You can set this property before calling the Print dialog box if one of your application's options is the number of copies to print. Windows takes care of printing the correct number of copies.
FromPage	Specifies the starting page when the option of printing a range of pages is enabled. Applications that support page-range printing should read this property to determine which pages to print.
MaxPage	Specifies the maximum page number that can be specified in the To field when printing a range of pages. The Print dialog box takes care of validating entry in the From and To fields.
MinPage	Specifies the minimum page number that can be specified in the From field when printing a range of pages.
Options	Contains a set of options that control which features of the Print dialog box are enabled. You can elect to have a Help button, to display the Print to File option, or to enable the Page Range or Print Selection options.
PrintRange	Controls which of the Print Range radio buttons is selected when the Print dialog box is initially displayed.
PrintToFile	Indicates whether the user has chosen the Print to File option. It is up to the application to write the output to a file.
ToPage	Specifies the ending page number when printing a range of pages. Applications that support page-range printing should read this property to determine which pages to print.

The application doesn't have much to do in response to the Print dialog box closing unless the Print Range and Print to File options are enabled. For example, if your application enables printing a range of pages, you need to read the FromPage and ToPage properties to determine which pages to print. Other than that, you begin printing if the user chooses OK.

The Print Setup Dialog Box

The Print Setup dialog box, shown in Figure 22.2, is used when the user wants to change printers, page size, paper source, or orientation.

FIGURE 22.2

The Print Setup dialog box.

The Print Setup dialog box isn't necessary in most applications because the user can always press the Properties button on the Print dialog box to change the setup options (refer back to Figure 22.1). On the other hand, implementing the Print Setup dialog box is so easy that you might as well include it in your applications. How easy is it? Well, the PrinterSetup component has no properties, methods, or events specific to it. As with the PrintDialog component, the Execute() method is the only method in which you are interested. To further simplify things, Windows handles everything that the Print Setup dialog box does. In fact, the Execute() function doesn't even return a value. This is because Windows handles everything for you. If the user clicks Cancel, Windows does nothing. If the user clicks OK, Windows makes the appropriate changes in preparation for printing. All you have to do is display the Print Setup dialog box and forget about it. A typical event handler for the File, Printer Setup menu item would look like this:

```
void __fastcall TScratchPad::FilePrintSetupClick(TObject *Sender)
{
  PrinterSetupDialog->Execute();
}
```

That's all there is to it. As I said, implementing the Print Setup dialog box is so simple you might as well add it to your application.

Printing the Easy Way

Printing is an application-specific task. That might not sound profound, but it's true. Depending on what kind of application you have developed, printing can be as simple as one line or it can entail hundreds of lines of code. I will first discuss the easiest forms of printing, and then I'll progress to the more difficult printing operations.

The `Print()` Method for Forms

The TForm class has a method called Print() that can be used to print the contents of a form. Only the client area of the form is printed; the form's frame and menu bar are not. Although this method works well for a simple screen dump, it is limited in its implementation. You can choose from three print options, which are controlled through the PrintScaled property. Table 22.2 lists the print scaling choices and their descriptions.

TABLE 22.2 THE PrintScaled PROPERTY OPTIONS

Option	Description
poNone	No special scaling is applied. The printed output of the form varies from printer to printer.
PoProportional	This option attempts to print the form in roughly the same size as it appears on the screen.
poPrintToFit	This increases or reduces the size of the image to fit the current printer settings.

You can set the PrintScaled property at runtime or at design time. The Print() method's use is limited to simple screen dumps and isn't likely to be used for any serious printing.

The `Print()` Method for the `RichEdit` Component

The RichEdit component is powerful, primarily because of the amount of work done by the underlying Windows rich edit control. Printing in the RichEdit component is accomplished via a call to the Print() method. This function takes a single parameter called Caption that is used by the Windows print manager when it displays the print job. Printing the contents of a RichEdit component is as simple as this:

```
RichEdit->Print("MyApp.exe - readme.txt");
```

Everything is taken care of for you. Word wrapping and pagination are automatically implemented. If you are using a multiline edit control that requires printing, the RichEdit component is the way to go.

You can use the Windows API function ShellExecute() to print a text file. ShellExecute() is used, among other things, to run a program based on a filename extension. For example, by default Windows registers the .txt extension as belonging to Windows Notepad. If you double-click on a file with a .txt extension in Explorer, Windows looks up the .txt extension in the Registry, sees that Notepad.exe is registered to handle .txt files, and runs Notepad. The file you double-clicked will be loaded automatically.

You can use this behavior to your advantage. Take this line of code, for instance:

```
ShellExecute(Handle, "print", "readme.txt", 0, 0, SW_HIDE);
```

This code loads Notepad, prints the file called Readme.txt, and then exits Notepad. In fact, you never see the Notepad program's main window because the SW_HIDE style is specified for the Show parameter. Actually, this code invokes whatever text editor the user has associated with the .txt extension, whether it be Notepad or some other program.

Printing the Hard Way

Don't let the title of this section put you off. Printing isn't all that difficult; it just takes some time and organization. First, let's look at some things you need to know in order to implement printing in your applications. After that you will delve into the actual code.

Managing the Device Context

A *device context* (DC) is like a slate that Windows programs can draw on. A better word would be canvas. On this canvas you can draw text, lines, bitmaps, rectangles, ellipses, and so on. The type of line used when drawing on a device context depends on the current pen selected in the DC. The current fill color and fill pattern are taken from the brush that is currently selected in the DC. DCs must be carefully managed. There are a limited number of DCs available to Windows, and you have to be careful to release the DC as soon as you are finished with it. Also, if you don't properly delete the objects you select in the DC, your program will leak memory and perhaps even leave Windows itself in a precarious state. As you can imagine, working with DCs can be complicated.

The good news is that VCL shields you from having to know every detail of device contexts. VCL encapsulates Windows DCs in the TCanvas class. The Canvas property represents the canvas of each C++Builder form. Any time you need to draw directly on a form, you can do so by accessing the Canvas property. For instance, the following code draws a line diagonally on a form from the top-left corner to the bottom-right corner:

```
Canvas->MoveTo(0, 0);
Canvas->LineTo(ClientRect.Right, ClientRect.Bottom);
```

The line will be drawn with the current pen for the canvas, as determined by the canvas's `Pen` property.

The nice thing about the `Canvas` property is that you don't have to worry about all the little details that can drive you nuts when dealing with Windows DCs. VCL takes care of obtaining the DC, selecting the appropriate objects in the DC, and releasing the DC when it is no longer needed. All you have to do is draw on the canvas and let VCL worry about the rest.

So what does this have to do with printing? (Inquiring minds want to know.) Well, it's like this: Windows enables you to obtain a *printer device context* on which you can draw text, graphics, lines, and so on. In other words, you draw on a printer DC just as you draw on a screen DC. This concept represents quite a switch from the way printing was approached back in the good old days of DOS. In this case, it is Windows that comes to your rescue by enabling the use of a printer DC. VCL further aids you by encapsulating DCs in the `Canvas` property. The bottom line is that printing is easier than it's ever been.

The `TPrinter` Class and the `Printer()` Function

VCL aids in printing operations by providing the `TPrinter` class. This class encapsulates the whole of printing in Windows. `TPrinter` has a `Canvas` property that you can use to output lines, text, graphics, and other drawing objects to the printer. I don't want to make it sound too easy, but all you have to do to print in your C++Builder programs is include Printers.hpp and then do something like the following:

```
Printer()->BeginDoc();
Printer()->Canvas->TextOut(20, 20, "Hello There!");
Printer()->EndDoc();
```

The `Printer()` function enables you access to a `TPrinter` object that is set up and ready to go. All you have to do is put it to work.

Now let's take a quick look at `TPrinter`'s properties and methods. Table 22.3 lists the primary `TPrinter` properties, and Table 22.4 shows the primary `TPrinter` methods.

TABLE 22.3 `TPrinter` PROPERTIES

Property	Description
Aborted	This property is `True` if printing was started and then aborted before it was finished.
Canvas	The mechanism through which you can draw on the printer (the printer device context).
Capabilities	The current settings of a printer device driver.

continues

TABLE 22.3 CONTINUED

Property	Description
Copies	The number of copies printed.
Fonts	A list of fonts supported by the current printer.
Handle	The handle to the printer device context (HDC). Use this property when you have to call a Windows API function that requires a handle to a device context.
Orientation	The printer orientation (poPortrait or poLandsacpe). This is automatically set when the user chooses a printer or modifies the printer setup, but you can also set it via code.
PageHeight	The height of the current printer page, in pixels. This value varies from printer to printer. In addition, this property can contain a different value based on the orientation of the printer. Some printers can use more than one resolution, which also causes this value to vary.
PageNumber	The page number of the page currently printing. This property is incremented each time you call NewPage() to begin printing a new page.
PageWidth	The width of the page, in pixels. As with the PageHeight property, this value varies, depending on the printer resolution, paper orientation, and paper size.
PrinterIndex	The index value of the currently selected printer in the list of available printers. Specify -1 to select the default printer.
Printers	A list of available printers on the system.
Printing	This property is True if the printer is currently printing.
Title	The text that identifies this printing job in the print manager window.

TABLE 22.4 TPrinter() METHODS

Method	Description
Abort	Used to abort the printing before normal completion.
BeginDoc	Begins the printing process. Sets up the printer with Windows in preparation for printing.
EndDoc	Ends the printing process. Forces the current page to be printed and performs printing cleanup with Windows.
GetPrinter	Retrieves the current printer. Use the Printers property instead of this method. (The Printers property is the preferred method for accessing printers because you can use it for both retrieving and setting the current printer.)
NewPage	Used to force printing of the current page and start a new page. Increments the PageNumber property.
SetPrinter	Sets the current printer. Use the Printers property instead of this method.

The TPrinter class has no design-time interface. Everything is accomplished at runtime.

Adding Print Capability to Your Application

It's time to put your newly acquired knowledge to work. Once again we'll dust off the ScratchPad program and spruce it up a bit. After all, what good is a text editor that doesn't print?

First, you need to modify the main form slightly. You already have menu items set up for Print and Print Setup, but you need to enable them and add the Print and Printer Setup dialog boxes to the form. Here goes:

1. Double-click the `MainMenu` component to bring up the Menu Designer.
2. Choose File, Print from the ScratchPad menu in the Menu Designer. Change the `Enabled` property to `True`.
3. Do the same for the File, Print Setup menu item. Close the Menu Designer.
4. Place a `PrintDialog` component on the form. Change its `Name` property to `PrintDialog`.
5. Place a `PrinterSetupDialog` on the form and change its `Name` property to `PrinterSetupDialog`.

Okay, now that you've completed the form, it's time to go to work modifying the code. To start, you have to add a couple items to the `SPMain.h` header file by doing the following:

1. Switch to the Code Editor and open the `SPMain.h` file.
2. Add the following at the end of the other `#include`s near the top of the file:

   `#include <Printers.hpp>`
3. Add this line to the `private` section of the class declaration:

   `void PrintFooter(TRect& rect, int lineHeight);`

   This is the declaration for a function that prints the footer at the bottom of each page.

That takes care of the unit's header. Now you add code to the SPMain.cpp source code unit:

1. Switch back to the Form Designer and choose File, Print from the form's main menu. The `FilePrintClick()` function is displayed. For now, leave the function empty.

22

2. Switch back to the Form Designer and choose File, Print Setup from the main menu. Enter one line at the cursor so that the entire FilePrintSetupClick() function looks like this:

```
void __fastcall TScratchPad::FilePrintSetupClick(TObject *Sender)
{
  PrinterSetupDialog->Execute();
}
```

3. Still in the Code Editor, move to the end of the file and type the following:

```
void TScratchPad::PrintFooter(TRect& rect, int lineHeight)
{
}
```

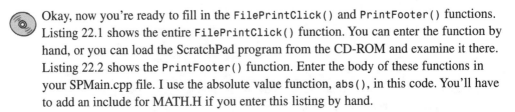 Okay, now you're ready to fill in the FilePrintClick() and PrintFooter() functions. Listing 22.1 shows the entire FilePrintClick() function. You can enter the function by hand, or you can load the ScratchPad program from the CD-ROM and examine it there. Listing 22.2 shows the PrintFooter() function. Enter the body of these functions in your SPMain.cpp file. I use the absolute value function, abs(), in this code. You'll have to add an include for MATH.H if you enter this listing by hand.

LISTING 22.1   THE FilePrintClick() FUNCTION USED IN THE SCRATCHPAD APPLICATION

```
 1: void __fastcall TScratchPad::FilePrintClick(TObject *Sender)
 2: {
 3:   //
 4:   // Display the Print dialog.
 5:   //
 6:   if (PrintDialog->Execute()) {
 7:     //
 8:     // Set the title for the printer object.
 9:     //
10:     Printer()->Title =
11:       "ScratchPad - " + OpenDialog->FileName;
12:     //
13:     // Set the printer font to the same font as the rich edit.
14:     //
15:     Printer()->Canvas->Font = Memo->Font;
16:     //
17:     // Determine the line height. Take the Size of the
18:     // font and use the MulDiv() function to calculate
19:     // the line height, taking into account the current
20:     // printer resolution. Use the abs() function to get
21:     // the absolute value because the result could be a
22:     // negative number. After that add 40% for leading.
23:     //
24:     int lineHeight = abs(
25:       MulDiv(Printer()->Canvas->Font->Size,
```

```
26:        GetDeviceCaps(Printer()->Handle, LOGPIXELSY), 72));
27:      lineHeight *= 1.4;
28:      //
29:      // Determine how many lines will fit on a page. Trim
30:      // it back by three lines to leave some bottom margin.
31:      //
32:      int linesPerPage =
33:        (Printer()->PageHeight/lineHeight) - 4;
34:      //
35:      // Start printing on line 4 rather than line 0 to leave
36:      // room for the header and to allow for some top margin.
37:      //
38:      int lineCount = 4;
39:      //
40:      // Tell Windows we're starting and print the header.
41:      //
42:      Printer()->BeginDoc();
43:      TRect rect;
44:      rect.Top = lineHeight;
45:      rect.Left = 20;
46:      rect.Right =  Printer()->PageWidth;
47:      rect.Bottom = lineHeight * 2;
48:      DrawText(Printer()->Handle,
49:        OpenDialog->FileName.c_str(), -1, (RECT*)&rect, DT_CENTER);
50:      //
51:      // Loop through all the lines and print each one.
52:      //
53:      for (int i=0;i<Memo->Lines->Count;i++) {
54:        //
55:        // When we get to the bottom of the page, reset the
56:        // line counter, eject the page, and start a new page.
57:        //
58:        if (lineCount++ == linesPerPage) {
59:          PrintFooter(rect, lineHeight);
60:          lineCount = 4;
61:          Printer()->NewPage();
62:        }
63:        //
64:        // Get the next string and print it using TextOut()
65:        //
66:        String s = Memo->Lines->Strings[i];
67:        Printer()->Canvas->TextOut
68:          (0, lineCount * lineHeight, s);
69:      }
70:      //
71:      // All done.
72:      //
73:      PrintFooter(rect, lineHeight);
74:      Printer()->EndDoc();
75:    }
76: }
```

LISTING 22.2   THE `PrintFooter()` FUNCTION USED IN THE SCRATCHPAD APPLICATION

```
 1: void TScratchPad::PrintFooter(TRect& rect, int lineHeight)
 2: {
 3:   //
 4:   // Build a string to display the page number. We'll use the
 5:   // C++ char* method rather than a String object because
 6:   // DrawText() will want a char* anyway.
 7:   //
 8:   char buff[10];
 9:   wsprintf(buff, "Page %d", Printer()->PageNumber);
10:   //
11:   // Set up the rectangle where the footer will be drawn.
12:   // Find the bottom of the page and come up a couple
13:   // lines.
14:   //
15:   rect.Top = Printer()->PageHeight - (lineHeight * 2);
16:   rect.Bottom = rect.Top + lineHeight;
17:   //
18:   // Display the text using DrawText so we can center the
19:   // text with no fuss.
20:   //
21:   DrawText(Printer()->Handle, buff, -1, (RECT*)&rect, DT_CENTER);
22:   //
23:   // Draw a line across the page just above the Page x text.
24:   //
25:   Printer()->Canvas->MoveTo(0, rect.Top - 2);
26:   Printer()->Canvas->LineTo(rect.Right, rect.Top - 2);
27: }
```

This code illustrates how you can print directly through Windows rather than rely on the built-in printing that VCL provides. Although I always opt to do something the easy way when possible, there are times when the easy way isn't flexible enough. In those times it's good to have the knowledge to do the job without trouble.

Printing a Bitmap

Printing a bitmap is simple. All you need to do is create an instance of the TBitmap class, load a bitmap into the bitmap object, and send it to the printer, using the Draw() method of TCanvas. Here's the entire code:

```
Graphics::TBitmap* bitmap = new Graphics::TBitmap;
bitmap->LoadFromFile("c:\\winnt\\winnt.bmp");
Printer()->BeginDoc();
Printer()->Canvas->Draw(20, 20, bitmap);
Printer()->EndDoc();
delete bitmap;
```

22

When you print a bitmap, be aware that the bitmap might turn out very small, depending on the resolution of your printer. The bitmap might have to be stretched to look right. If you need to stretch the bitmap, use the StretchDraw() method instead of Draw().

Summary

In some cases printing support is built into a particular component, and in those cases printing is incredibly easy. In other cases you have to roll up your sleeves and go to work with the TPrinter class. Even at those times, though, printing is nothing to fear.

Workshop

The Workshop contains quiz questions to help you solidify your understanding of the material covered and exercises to provide you with experience in using what you have learned.

Q&A

Q I just want basic output of a large, multiline edit control in my application. What's the easiest way?

A The easiest way is to use a RichEdit component and use its Print() method to print the contents of the component.

Q I see that there is a Handle property for the Printer object and also a Handle property for the Canvas property of the Printer object. What's the difference?

A In this case there is no difference. If you are calling a Windows API function that requires the printer device context handle, you can use either Printer()->Handle or Printer()->Canvas->Handle.

Quiz

1. How do you access the printer in a C++Builder application?
2. What method do you call to begin printing with the TPrinter class?
3. What method of TPrinter do you call when you want to start a new page when printing?
4. How do you print a bitmap?

Answers

1. You access printers through the `Printer()` function. This function returns a pointer to the global `TPrinter` object.

2. To begin printing, call the `BeginDoc()` function.

3. To start a new page, call the `NewPage()` function.

4. To print a bitmap, call the `Draw()` or `StretchDraw()` function of the printer's `Canvas`.

Exercise

1. Create a new application. Place a `RichEdit` and a `Button` component on the form. Write code to print the contents of the `RichEdit` when the button is clicked.

Hour 23

Using the Debugger

A major feature of the C++Builder IDE is the integrated debugger. The debugger enables you to easily set breakpoints, watch variables, inspect objects, and do much more. Using the debugger, you can quickly find out what is happening (or not happening) with your program as it runs. A good debugger is vital to efficient program development.

The IDE debugger provides several features and tools to help you in your debugging chores. The following are discussed in this hour:

- Debugger menu items
- Using breakpoints
- Inspecting variables with the Watch List
- Stepping through code

Why use the debugger? The quick answer is that the debugger helps you find bugs in your program. But the debugging process isn't just for finding and fixing bugs—it is a development tool as well. As important as debugging is, many programmers don't take the time to learn how to use all the features of the IDE debugger. As a result, they cost themselves time and money, not to mention the frustration caused by a bug that is difficult to find.

You begin a debugging session by starting up the program under the debugger. You automatically use the debugger when you click the Run button on the toolbar. You can also choose Run, Run from the main menu or press F9 on the keyboard.

The Debugging Menu Items

Before we get into the details of the debugger, let's review the menu items that pertain to the debugger. Some of these menu items are on the main menu under Run, and others are on the Code Editor context menu. Table 23.1 lists the Code Editor context menu items specific to the debugger, along with their descriptions. These menu items are subitems under the Code Editor's Debug menu item.

TABLE 23.1 CODE EDITOR CONTEXT MENU DEBUGGING ITEMS

Menu Item	Shortcut	Description
Toggle Breakpoint	F5	Toggles a breakpoint on or off for the current line in the Code Editor.
Run to Cursor	F4	Starts the program (if necessary) and runs it until the line in the editor window containing the cursor is reached.
Goto Address	None	Enables you to specify an address in the program at which program execution will resume.
Evaluate/Modify	None	Enables you to view and/or modify a variable at runtime.
Add Watch at Cursor	Ctrl+F5	Adds the variable under the cursor to the Watch List.
View CPU	None	Displays the CPU window.

The Run item on the main menu has several selections that pertain to running programs under the debugger. The Run menu items enable you to start a program under the debugger, to terminate a program running under the debugger, and to specify command-line parameters for your program, to name just a few functions. Some items found here are duplicated on the Code Editor context menu. Table 23.2 shows the Run menu items that control debugging operations.

TABLE 23.2 THE RUN MENU'S DEBUGGING ITEMS

Menu Item	Shortcut	Description
Run	F9	Compiles the program (if needed) and then runs the program under the control of the IDE debugger. Same as the Run toolbar button.

Menu Item	Shortcut	Description
Parameters	None	Enables you to enter command-line parameters for your program and to assign a host application when debugging a DLL.
Step Over	F8	Executes the source code line at the execution point and pauses at the next source code line.
Trace Into	F7	Traces into the function at the execution point.
Trace to Next Source Line	Shift+F7	Causes the execution point to move to the next line in the program's source code.
Run to Cursor	F4	Runs the program and pauses when program execution reaches the current line in the source code.
Run Until Return	Shift+F8	Executes the current function and stops program execution at the line immediately following the line that called the function. This feature is basically a "step out of function" action.
Show Execution Point	None	Displays the program execution point in the Code Editor (for lines with source code) or the CPU view (if no source code is available). Scrolls the source code window if necessary. Only works when program execution is paused.
Program Pause	None	Pauses program execution on the next machine instruction. Displays either the Code Editor or the CPU view.
Program Reset	Ctrl+F2	Closes down the program and returns to the C++Builder IDE.
Evaluate/Modify	Ctrl+F7	Displays the Evaluate/Modify dialog box.
Add Watch	Ctrl+F5	Displays the Watch Properties dialog box.
Add Breakpoint	None	Contains a submenu that allows you to set a Source Breakpoint, Address Breakpoint, or a Module Load Breakpoint.

23

You will use these menu items a lot when you are debugging your programs. You should also become familiar with the various keyboard shortcuts for the debugging operations.

Now let's take a look at breakpoints and how to use them in your program.

Setting and Clearing Breakpoints

When you run your program from the C++Builder IDE, it runs at full speed, stopping only where you have set breakpoints.

 A *breakpoint* is a marker that tells the debugger to pause program execution when that place in the program is reached.

> Throughout this chapter I refer to colors that indicate a particular debugger feature or state. The colors I refer to assume that you are using the default color settings for the IDE.

To set a breakpoint, click in the editor window's gutter to the left of the line on which you want to pause program execution (the gutter is the gray margin along the Code Editor window's left edge). The breakpoint icon (a red circle) appears in the gutter, and the entire line is highlighted in red. To clear the breakpoint, click on the breakpoint icon and the breakpoint is removed. You can also press F5 or choose Toggle Breakpoint from the Code Editor context menu to toggle a breakpoint on or off.

> A breakpoint can be set only on a line that generates actual code. Breakpoints are not valid if set on blank lines, comment lines, or declaration lines. You are not prevented from setting a breakpoint on these types of lines, but the debugger warns you if you do. Attempting to set a breakpoint on any of the following lines will produce an invalid breakpoint warning:
>
> ```
> // this is a comment followed by a blank line
> ```
>
> ```
> int x;  // a declaration
> ```
>
> Breakpoints can be set on return statements or on the right brace of a function.

If you set a breakpoint on an invalid line, the Code Editor displays the breakpoint in green and the breakpoint icon in the gutter has a yellow X on it. This only happens when you run the program because the debugger validates breakpoints on each run. An invalid breakpoint looks like any other breakpoint until you click the Run button.

When the program is run under the debugger, it behaves as it normally would—until a breakpoint is hit, that is. When a breakpoint is hit, the IDE is brought to the top and the breakpoint line is highlighted in the source code. The line where the program has stopped is highlighted in red.

NEW TERM The *execution point* indicates the line that will be executed next in your source code.

> In Windows 98 the IDE doesn't come to the top when a breakpoint is hit. Instead, the IDE's task bar icon will flash. You must click on the task bar icon to bring the IDE to the top if you are running Windows 98.

23

As you step through the program, the execution point is highlighted in blue, and the editor window gutter displays a green arrow glyph. Understand that the line highlighted in blue has not yet been executed but will be when program execution resumes. Figure 23.1 shows the Code Editor window during a debugging session.

FIGURE 23.1

The Code Editor window shows breakpoints, the execution point, and gutter glyphs when debugging.

Blue dots in the gutter show compiled lines of code

A breakpoint line is displayed in red

The breakpoint icon in the gutter indicates a breakpoint

The arrow icon in the gutter shows the current execution point

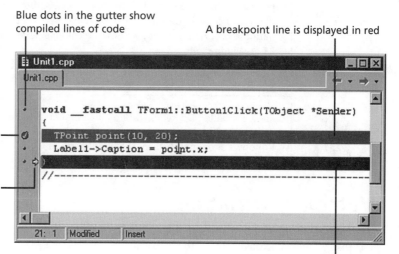

```
void __fastcall TForm1::Button1Click(TObject *Sender)
{
    TPoint point(10, 20);
    Label1->Caption = point.x;
}
//------------------------------------------------
```

The current execution point line is displayed in blue

> The current execution point is highlighted in blue unless the line containing the execution point contains a breakpoint. In that case the line is highlighted in red. The green arrow glyph in the gutter is the most accurate indication of the execution point because it is present regardless of the line's highlighting color.

When you stop at a breakpoint, you can view variables, view the call stack, browse symbols, or step through your code. After you have inspected any variables and objects, you can resume normal program execution by clicking the Run button. Your application will again run normally until the next breakpoint is encountered.

It's common to detect coding errors in your program after you have stopped at a breakpoint. If you change your source code in the middle of a debugging session and then choose Run to resume program execution, the IDE prompts you with a message box asking whether you want to rebuild the source code. If you choose Yes, the current process is terminated, the source code is recompiled, and the program is restarted.

The problem with this approach is that your program doesn't get a chance to close normally, and any resources currently in use might not be freed properly, which could result in memory leaks. Although 32-bit Windows handles resource leaks better than 16-bit Windows, it is still advisable to terminate the program normally and then recompile, especially if using Windows 95 or Windows 98.

The C++Builder IDE keeps track of the breakpoints you have set in the Breakpoint List window. To view the breakpoint list, choose View, Debug Windows, Breakpoints from the main menu.

Watching Variables

So what do you do when you stop at a breakpoint? Usually you stop at a breakpoint to inspect the value of one or more variables. You might want to ensure that a particular variable has the value you think it should, or you might not have any idea what a variable's value is and simply want to find out.

The function of the Watch List is basic: It enables you to inspect the values of variables. Programmers often overlook this simple but essential feature because they don't take the time to learn how to fully use the debugger. To display the Watch List, you can choose View, Debug Windows, Watches from the main menu or press Ctrl+Alt+W to display it. You can add as many variables to the Watch List as you like, but for performance reasons you should remove any unused Watch List items. Figure 23.2 shows the Watch List during a debugging session.

FIGURE 23.2

The Watch List showing the value of program variables.

The variable name is displayed in the Watch List followed by its value. How the variable value is displayed is determined by the variable's data type and the current display settings for that watch item.

ToolTip Expression Evaluation

The debugger and Code Editor have a nice feature that makes checking the value of a variable easy. This feature, the ToolTip expression evaluator, is on by default, so you don't have to do anything special to use it. If you want, you can turn off the ToolTip evaluator via the Code Insight page of the Environment Options dialog box.

So what is ToolTip expression evaluation (besides hard to say)? It works like this: After you have stopped at a breakpoint, you place the editing cursor over a variable, and a ToolTip window pops up, showing the variable's current value. This makes it easy to quickly inspect variables. Just place your cursor over a variable and wait a half second or so.

The ToolTip evaluator has different displays for different variable types. For regular data members (`int`, `char`, `long`, and so on) the actual value of the variable is displayed. For dynamically created objects (an instance of a class, for example) the ToolTip evaluator shows the memory location of the object. In the case of `AnsiString` variables, the ToolTip evaluator is smart enough to show the contents of the string. For structures the ToolTip evaluator shows all the structure elements. Figure 23.3 shows the ToolTip expression evaluator inspecting a structure's contents.

FIGURE 23.3

ToolTips are great for displaying the value of a variable.

23

Sometimes the ToolTip evaluator acts as if it's not working properly. If, for example, you place the editing cursor over a variable that is out of scope, no ToolTip appears. The ToolTip evaluator has nothing to show for that particular variable, so it doesn't display anything.

The ToolTip expression evaluator is a great feature, so don't forget to use it.

The Watch List Context Menu

As with every other C++Builder window discussed so far, the Watch List has its own context menu. (You'd be disappointed if it didn't, right?) Table 23.3 lists the Watch List context menu items and their descriptions.

TABLE 23.3   THE WATCH LIST CONTEXT MENU

Menu Item	Description
Edit Watch	Enables you to edit the watch item with the Watch Properties dialog box.
Add Watch	Adds a new item to the Watch List.
Enable Watch	Enables the watch item.
Disable Watch	Disables the watch item.
Delete Watch	Removes the watch item from the Watch List.
Enable All Watches	Enables all items in the Watch List.
Disable All Watches	Disables all items in the Watch List.
Delete All Watches	Deletes all items in the Watch List.
Stay on Top	Forces the Watch List to the top of all other windows in the IDE.
Dockable	Enables or disables docking of the watch window.

Both the Edit Watch and Add Watch context menu items invoke the Watch Properties dialog box. The Watch Properties dialog box allows you to change the watch variable and to choose the method used to display the variable's data.

Dock the Watch List to the bottom of the Code Editor so it is always in view when debugging. For example, when you drag the Watch List over the bottom edge of the Code Editor, the drag rectangle snaps into place. When you release the mouse, the Watch List attaches itself to the Code Editor window.

Adding Variables to the Watch List

You can add variables to the Watch List in several ways. The quickest is to click the variable name in the editor window and then select Debug, Add Watch at Cursor from the Code Editor context menu or press Ctrl+F5. The watch item is immediately added to the Watch List. You can then edit the watch item to change the display properties, if needed.

To add a variable to the watch without first locating it in the source file, choose Run, Add Watch from the main menu. When the Watch Properties dialog box comes up, enter the name of the variable you want to add to the Watch List and click OK.

Using the Watch List

When a breakpoint is hit, the Watch List displays the current value of any variables that have been added to the Watch List. If the Watch List isn't currently open, you can choose View, Debug Windows, Watches from the main menu or press Ctrl+Alt+W to display it.

Under certain circumstances, a message is displayed next to the variable instead of the variable's value. If, for instance, a variable is out of scope or not found, the Watch List displays Undefined symbol 'x' next to the variable name. If the program isn't running or isn't stopped at a breakpoint, the Watch List displays [process not accessible] for all watch items. A disabled watch item will have <disabled> next to it. Other messages can be displayed, depending on the current state of the application or the current state of a particular variable.

You might on occasion see Variable 'x' Has Been Optimized and Is Not Available in the Watch List. This is one of the minor disadvantages to having an optimizing compiler. If you need to inspect variables that are subject to optimization, declare the variable with the volatile keyword. Declaring a variable with the volatile keyword looks like this:

```
volatile int x = 20;
```

The volatile keyword tells the compiler not to use CPU registers for storing the variable's data. This prevents the variable from being optimized. However, you should be aware that allowing the compiler to use register variables results in faster code execution, so you should remove the volatile modifier after debugging a particular section of code.

The Watch List is a simple but vital tool in debugging applications. To illustrate the use of the Watch List, perform this exercise:

1. Create a new application and place a button on the form. Change the button's Name property to WatchBtn and its Caption to Watch Test. Change the form's Name property to DebugMain and the Caption property to whatever you like.

2. Double-click the button to display its OnClick handler in the Code Editor. Enter the following code at the cursor:

```
String s;
int x = Width;
s = String(x);
int y = Height;
x *= y;
s = String(x);
x /= y;
s = String(x);
Width = x;
Height = y;
```

3. Save the project. Name the unit DbgMain and the project DebugTst.

4. Set a breakpoint on the second code line from step 2. Run the program.

5. Click the Watch Test button. The debugger stops at the breakpoint.

6. Add watches for the variables s, x, and y. (Initially the variables x and y will contain random values, but don't worry about that.)

7. Arrange the Watch List and Code Editor so that you can see both. The best way to accomplish that is to dock the Watch List to the bottom of the Code Editor.

8. Switch focus to the Code Editor and press F8 to execute the next line of code. That line is executed, and the execution point moves to the next line. The variable x now shows a valid value (y still shows a random value).

9. Continue to step through the program by pressing F8. Watch the results of the variables in the Watch List.

10. When the execution point gets to the last line in the function, click the Run button on the toolbar to continue running the program.

11. Click the Watch Test button as many times as you want to get a feel for how the Watch List works. Experiment with different watch settings each time through.

The code in this example obtains the values for the form's Width and Height properties, performs some calculations, and then sets the Width and Height back to where they were when you started. In the end nothing changes, but there is a good reason for assigning values to the Width and Height properties at the end of the function.

If you don't actually do something with the variables x and y, you can't inspect them because the compiler will optimize them and they won't be available to watch.

Essentially, the compiler can look ahead, see that the variables are never used, and just discard them. Putting the variables to use at the end of the function avoids having them optimized away by the compiler.

Stepping Through Your Code

Stepping through code is one of the most basic debugging operations. Before we begin this section, I'll say a few words about the symbols that appear in the Code Editor gutter during a debugging session. In the section "Setting and Clearing Breakpoints," I told you that a red circle appears in the gutter when you set a breakpoint on a code line. I also said that a green arrow glyph indicates the execution point when you are stepping through code. One thing I didn't mention, though, is the little blue dots that appear in the gutter next to certain code lines. These dots indicate lines in your source code that actually generate assembly code. Figure 23.4 shows the Code Editor with the debugger stopped at a breakpoint. It shows the small dots that indicate generated code, the arrow glyph indicating the execution point, and the breakpoint glyph as well. The check mark on the breakpoint glyph indicates that the breakpoint was checked and was determined to be a valid breakpoint.

FIGURE 23.4

The Code Editor showing gutter symbols.

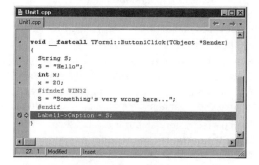

Take a closer look at Figure 23.4. Notice that the small dots only appear next to certain code lines. Lines without the dots don't generate any code. Take this line, for instance:

```
int x;
```

Why doesn't this line generate code? It is because this line is simply a declaration and does not generate any compiled code.

If you had optimizations turned on (Project Options dialog, Compiler page), the line that reads x = 20 would not generate code either. When optimizations are on, the compiler looks ahead and sees that the variable x is never used, so it completely ignores all references to that variable.

Okay, back to stepping through code. When you stop at a breakpoint, you can do many things to determine what is going on with your code. For example, you can set up variables to watch in the Watch List or view the call stack. You can also step through your code to watch what happens to your variables and objects as each code line is executed. As you continue to step through your code, you will see that the line in your source code to be executed next is highlighted in blue. If you have the Watch List window open, it is updated as each code line is executed. Any changes to variables are immediately visible in the watch window.

Seemingly odd things happen when the Optimize for Speed compiler option is turned on. When the compiler optimizes code, it rearranges your source code using mysterious means about which mere mortals can only speculate. Your source code isn't rearranged per se, but the resulting assembly code might not exactly match the source code in your source file. The end result is a program that runs faster, and that, of course, is a good thing.

This benefit does come at a cost, however. When you step through your code, the execution point might not proceed sequentially from line to line as you expect. Rather, the execution point might appear to jump around in your source and even land on a single line of code multiple times.

This is all perfectly normal, but it can be disconcerting when you are learning to use the debugger. If you prefer to see the execution point proceed sequentially through your code, turn off optimizations while debugging. Turn optimizations back on again for your final builds. Remember that when you change optimization settings, you need to do a Build All for all modules to be rebuilt using the new settings.

The IDE debugger has two primary stepping commands to aid in your debugging operations: Step Over and Trace Into. Step Over means to execute the next line in the source code and pause on the line immediately following. Step Over is sort of a misnomer. The name indicates that you can step over a source line and the line won't be executed. That isn't the case, however. Step Over means that the current line will be executed and any functions which that source line calls will be run at full speed.

For instance, let's say you have set a breakpoint at a line that calls another function in your program. When you tell the debugger to step over the function, the debugger executes the function and stops on the next line. (Contrast this with how Trace Into works, which you'll learn about in a minute, and it will make more sense.) To use Step Over to step through your program, you can either press F8 or choose Run, Step Over from the main menu.

23

> As you step through various source code units in your program, the Code Editor automatically loads and displays the needed source units if they are not already open.

The Trace Into command enables you to trace into any functions that are encountered as you step through your code. Rather than execute the function and return to the next line as Step Over does, Trace Into places the execution point on the first source code line in the function being called. You can then step line by line through that function using Step Over or Trace Into as necessary. The keyboard shortcut for Trace Into is F7.

After you have inspected variables and done whatever debugging you need to do, you can again run the program at full speed by clicking the Run button. The program will function normally until the next breakpoint is encountered.

> When you are stepping through a function, the execution point will eventually get to the right brace. If the function you are stepping through returns control to Windows when it finishes, pressing F8 when on the right brace exits the function and returns control to the program being debugged. There is no obvious indication that the program is no longer paused because the IDE still has focus. This behavior can be confusing the first few times you encounter it unless you are aware of what has happened. To switch back to your program, just activate it as you would any other program (click its glyph on the Windows taskbar or use Alt+Tab).

As I said, stepping through your code is a basic debugging technique, but it is one that you will use constantly while debugging. Of all the keyboard shortcuts available to you in C++Builder, F7 (Trace Into), F8 (Step Over), and F9 (Run) should definitely be in your arsenal.

On some systems the debugger might take a long time between steps when single-stepping through code. To help alleviate this problem, make sure that you don't have any more than the minimum number of variables in the Watch List.

A big factor in debugger speed is the amount of system RAM. RAM is cheap, so you might consider adding more memory to your system if the debugger is too slow for you and if the preceding suggestions don't increase speed.

If you are running C++Builder on Windows 9x, use the Program Reset option sparingly. In some cases using Program Reset to kill an application can crash Windows 9x. Not all Windows 9x systems behave the same way, so you might not experience this problem. Windows NT doesn't suffer from this problem, so you can use Program Reset more liberally under Windows NT. Personally, I only use Program Reset if the application I am debugging locks up.

Summary

Debugging is a never-ending task. Debugging means more than just tracking down a bug in your program. Savvy programmers learn to use the debugger from the outset of a new project. The debugger is a development tool as well as a bug-finding tool. After this hour, you should have at least a basic understanding of how to use the debugger. You will still have to spend a lot of time actually using the debugger before you are proficient at it, but you now have a place to start.

Workshop

The Workshop contains quiz questions to help you solidify your understanding of the material covered and exercises to provide you with experience in using what you have learned.

Q&A

Q My program used to run at regular speed when I ran it from the IDE. Now it's as slow as molasses in January. Why is that?

A More than likely you have too many variables in the Watch List. Remove any unused variables in the Watch List, especially any that are not currently in scope.

Q **I'm stepping through my code and I get to a function in my program that I want to debug. When I press F8, the execution point jumps right over the function. How do I get into that function?**

A When the execution point is on the line where the function is called, press F7 (`Trace Into`) instead of F8. Now you can step through the function a line at a time.

Quiz

1. How do you set a breakpoint on a particular code line?
2. What is an invalid breakpoint?
3. What's the quickest way to add a variable to the Watch List?
4. How do you trace into a function call when stepping with the debugger?

Answers

1. To set a breakpoint, click in the gutter (the left margin) of that code line. You can also press F5 or choose Debug, Toggle Breakpoint from the Code Editor context menu.
2. An invalid breakpoint is a breakpoint that is inadvertently set on a source code line that generates no compiled code.
3. To quickly add a variable to the Watch List, click on the variable and type Ctrl+F5.
4. Use the Trace Into option (F7 on the keyboard) to trace into a function when debugging.

Exercises

1. Load the `DebugTst` program you created earlier in this hour. Place a breakpoint in the `WatchBtnClick()` function. Add the `s` and `x` variables to the Watch List. Add each variable to the Watch List four times. Edit each of the watches with the Watch Properties dialog (double-click the variable in the Watch List) and change the display options. Run the program and step through the function to see the effects in the Watch List.
2. Load any program and switch to the Code Editor. Place the cursor on any code line and choose the Debug, Run to Cursor item from the Code Editor context menu. Experiment with the program until the breakpoint is hit.

HOUR **24**

New Features in C++Builder 4

This final hour covers features that are new to C++Builder 4. One major new feature is the docking support for both the Integrated Development Environment's (IDE) windows and for Visual Component Library (VCL) components. Two new Code Editor features, Code Completion and Code Parameters, greatly enhance programmer productivity. C++Builder 4 also adds a few components not found in previous versions of C++Builder.

Dockable IDE Windows

A new feature in C++Builder 4 is dockable windows.

 A *dockable window* is a window that can be dragged from its current location (using the mouse) and docked to one of the IDE's dock sites.

 A *dock site* is a specific location in the IDE where a dockable window can be docked. The IDE has several dock sites.

Just about every window in C++Builder is dockable. This includes the Project Manager, the Object Inspector, the Watch List window, the Message window, and on and on. In fact, there are very few windows in C++Builder that are not dockable.

Am I enamored with dockable windows just for the sake of dockable windows alone? Not in the least. I don't even bother with dockable windows in most Windows programs I own. In the C++Builder IDE, however, dockable windows make me more productive and that's why I like them.

Dock Sites

You can't talk dockable windows without talking dock sites. Sure, you can undock a window and drag it around on the screen, dropping it wherever you want. That just makes for a bunch of scattered windows all over your screen, though. In order for dockable windows to make sense, you must have a place to dock them. In the C++Builder IDE that usually means the Code Editor window.

The Code Editor has three dock sites. One dock site is along the left side of the Code Editor window. The second dock site is along the bottom of the Code Editor window. The default C++Builder configuration places the Message window in the bottom dock site (although you don't see the Message window unless there are messages to display). The third Code Editor dock site is along the left edge of the Code Editor window. These three dock sites are really all you need to fully customize the IDE.

There is one other type of dock site that I want to mention. If you have a tool window open (such as the Project Manager), you can dock another tool window to it. This enables two or more C++Builder windows to be hosted within the same tool window. For example, the Project Manager and Object Inspector could both be docked in the same floating tool window. A floating tool window has five dock sites: right, left, top, bottom, and center.

When you dock a window to the center of a tool window, the tool window becomes a tabbed window. Each tab in the window contains the title of the window that tab represents. I realize that doesn't make a lot of sense, so in the following section I show you how to dock two tool windows together.

Experimenting with Dockable Windows

Rather than trying to put the relationships between the various windows into words, I think an exercise is in order. This exercise doesn't take long and should prove very enlightening. Here goes:

1. Create a new application and switch to the Code Editor.
2. Display the Project Manager (View, Project Manager from the main menu).

3. Drag the project manager over the Code Editor's left edge. When your mouse pointer reaches the left edge of the Code Editor, the drag rectangle pops into place. Let go of the mouse and the Project Manager is docked to the Code Editor.

4. To undock the Project Manager again, click and drag the grip at the top of the Project Manager window. Drag the Project Manager to the middle of the Code Editor and let go of the mouse. The Project Manager again becomes a floating tool window.

5. Now drag the Project Manager to the bottom of the Code Editor. When your mouse pointer reaches the bottom edge of the Code Editor window, the drag rectangle snaps into place and is as wide as the Code Editor. Let go of the mouse button. The Project Manager is docked to the Code Editor's bottom dock site. Notice that the drag grip is vertical when the Project Manager is docked to the bottom dock site.

This exercise is simple but gives you an idea of what you can do with dockable windows at the most basic level. The next exercise is a little more interesting. Perform these steps:

1. Undock the Project Manager and move it to the right. Drop it anywhere on the right side of the Code Editor.

2. Size the Project Manager window so that it is roughly square.

3. Drag the Object Inspector over the Project Manager window. When the drag rectangle snaps into place in the center of the Project Manager window, release the mouse button. The floating tool window should now look similar to Figure 24.1. Notice that the floating tool window has become a tabbed window and has the title Project Manager, Object Inspector. You can click on either of the two tabs to see the Project Manager or the Object Inspector.

FIGURE 24.1

The Object Inspector and Project Manager docked together in a tool window.

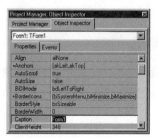

4. Drag the tool window back to the left side of the Code Editor and dock it there. Now you have both the Object Inspector and the Project Manager docked where you can get to them easily whenever you want them.

Are you starting to get the picture? You can have as many tool windows as you want in one tabbed window. Let's do one more exercise along the same lines. Often you want the debugger Watch List window in view while you are debugging. I will show you how you can keep the Watch List window handy at all times. Perform these steps:

1. Right-click on the Code Editor and choose Message View from the Code Editor context menu. The message window appears in the Code Editor's bottom dock site.

2. Choose View, Debug Windows, Watches from the main menu. The Watch List window is displayed as a floating tool window.

3. Drag the Watch List window over the Message window and dock it to the center of the Message window. Two tabs appear in the dock site: Messages and Watch List.

4. Make the dock site taller by dragging the sizing bar between the dock site and the Code Editor window.

Now you can click on the Watch List tab at the bottom of the Code Editor any time you want to view your watches. The Message window takes care of itself because it will come and go in the tabbed window any time there are messages to display. Figure 24.2 shows the IDE after performing the last exercise.

FIGURE 24.2

Four tool windows docked to the Code Editor.

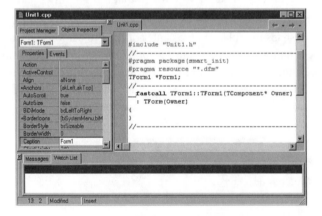

No Docking, Please

Sometimes you don't want a particular window to be dockable. As nice as dockable windows are, sometimes it's hard to find a location to place a window when you don't want it docked. It seems like anywhere you try to put the window it wants to dock to something. The good news is that you can shut off the docking capability of any tool window.

Each of the dockable tool windows has a menu item at the bottom of its context menu called Dockable. If Dockable is checked, the window is dockable. If Dockable is not checked, the window is not dockable and you can place it anywhere in the IDE.

The dockable windows in the C++Builder IDE are a great feature. You can arrange the tool windows you use most often in any way you want. You no longer have to go hunting for a Project Manager, Watch List, or Object Inspector hidden under other windows. The window you are looking for is just a couple of mouse clicks away.

Docking Support for VCL Components

Another aspect of docking in C++Builder is the VCL's docking support. Dockable toolbars are common in many Windows programs, so I'll illustrate this feature using a dockable toolbar.

 The docking features discussed in this section apply to any windowed control, not just to toolbars.

24

Making a toolbar dockable requires two steps:

1. Set the DragKind property to dkDock.

2. Set the DragMode property to dmAutomatic.

After you set these two properties, you can drag your toolbar around the screen. Dragging the toolbar around the screen doesn't get you very much, though. In order for dockable toolbars to make sense, you have to have a target for the drop part of the drag-and-drop equation.

Dock Sites

A dockable toolbar needs to have a place to dock. As Roger Waters said, "Any fool knows a dog needs a home." Home for a dockable toolbar is a *dock site*. A dock site is any windowed component that has its DockSite property set to True. Components that are typically used as dock sites are TCoolBar, TControlBar, TPageScroller, TPanel, and TPageControl. There are other controls that have a DockSite property, but those controls are less likely to be used as dock sites.

An exercise helps illustrate the use of dock sites. Follow these steps:

1. Drop a CoolBar component on a blank form (it's on the Win32 tab). Set its DockSite property to True.

2. Drop a ToolBar on the CoolBar. Set the toolbar's DragKind property to dkDock and its DragMode property to dmAutomatic. Create a few buttons on the toolbar so that you can better see the toolbar.

3. Place a second CoolBar on the form. Change its Align property to alBottom and its DockSite property to True.

4. Place a third CoolBar on the form. Change its Align property to alLeft and its DockSite property to True. Size the CoolBar so that its width is 40 pixels or so.

Now run the program. Drag the toolbar from dock site to dock site. Notice how the toolbar changes its orientation when you drag it to the coolbar on the left side of the form.

Let's experiment some more. Set each of the CoolBar components' AutoSize properties to True. This causes each CoolBar to change its size based on the controls it contains. Now run the program again and move the toolbar to the individual dock sites. Notice that each coolbar is nearly invisible until the toolbar is docked to the site. Then the coolbar expands to contain the toolbar.

Floating Windows

VCL components that support docking can be made floating windows. A toolbar, for example, can be made into a floating toolbox by simply dragging the toolbar off its dock site and dropping it anywhere (anywhere other than another dock site, that is). The toolbar becomes a floating window. You can specify the type of window that should host the floating dock site by setting the FloatingDockSiteClass property to the name of the class you want to act as the parent to the floating toolbar. For example, suppose that you design a form that has all the characteristics you want for a custom floating toolbox, and that the form is called MyToolBox. In that case, you could cause this form to be the host for a floating toolbar with the following code:

```
ToolBar->FloatingDockSiteClass = __classid(TMyToolBox);
```

When the toolbar is undocked and the mouse button is released, C++Builder automatically creates an instance of the TMyToolBox class and places the toolbar in the form for that class. To dock the floating toolbox again, simply drop it on any dock site. To make a dock site accept a floating toolbox, you must respond to the OnDockOver and OnDockDrop events for the dock site. In the OnDockDrop event handler, call the ManualDock method of the toolbar to cause the toolbar to dock.

The floating toolbox form can be a regular form, but you must be sure to add this line of code to the form's OnCreate event handler:

```
Visible = true;
```

Without this line the form will never be visible and the toolbar will simply disappear when you undock it from its dock site.

Code Editor Features

The Code Editor contains two new features that can greatly enhance your productivity as a programmer.

Code Parameters

The Code Parameters feature of the Code Editor displays a ToolTip that prompts you with the needed parameters of a VCL method or Windows API function. With hundreds of VCL methods and Windows API functions, there is virtually no way to remember every function's parameters. The Code Parameters feature saves you time by showing you the parameters of a method as you type. For example, let's say you are calling the SetBounds method. When you type the opening parentheses, a hint window pops up as shown in Figure 24.3.

24

FIGURE 24.3

Code Parameters displayed as a ToolTip in the Code Editor.

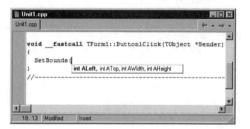

As you can see in Figure 24.3, each parameter is listed in the ToolTip. The parameter you need to type next is displayed in bold. As you type a parameter, the next parameter is displayed in bold. This continues until you type all the method's parameters. After you have typed all the required parameters, the Code Parameters ToolTip disappears. The Code Parameters options are set on the Code Insight page of the Environment Options dialog box. I'll discuss that page later in the section "Code Insight Options."

> The first time you implement Code Parameters in a new application it will take a few seconds for the ToolTip to be displayed. The delay is because C++Builder has to compile the application before it can display the Code Parameters ToolTip. Subsequent Code Parameters operations will be quicker.

Sometimes the Code Parameters ToolTip window disappears before you are finished with it. For example, if you move the cursor off the line you are typing, the ToolTip window disappears. To display the Code Parameters window again, press Ctrl+Shift+Spacebar.

Code Completion

Code Completion is another Code Editor feature that can save you development time. Type a class variable name followed by the membership operator and the Code Editor displays a list box with all that class's properties and methods. If, for example, you have a memo component called Memo, you will type

Memo->

and pause for a moment. A list box pops up as shown in Figure 24.4.

FIGURE 24.4

Code Completion displaying the properties and methods of TMemo.

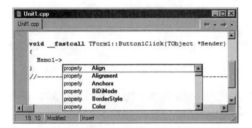

When you see the list box, you can select an item from the list in one of two ways. One way is to locate a property or method in the list box using the mouse or the keyboard and press Enter. The property or method will be inserted into your code. Alternatively, you can type the first few letters of the property or method you want to insert into your code. As you type, C++Builder searches the list of properties and methods for a match and highlights the item in the list that most closely matches the text you are typing.

When you see the property or method you want, press the Enter key and the property or method is inserted into your code. If you don't want to use the Code Completion list box, you can press the Esc key on the keyboard and the Code Completion list box disappears. To invoke the Code Completion list box manually, press Ctrl+Spacebar.

Code Completion saves you time by providing a list of properties and methods from which to choose. It has the added benefit of providing perfect spelling and capitalization of property and method names. Just choose the property or method you want, press the Enter key, and C++Builder inserts the identifier in your code.

Code Insight Options

Code Insight options are set on the Code Insight page of the Environment Options dialog. Figure 24.5 shows the Code Insight page.

FIGURE 24.5

The Code Insight page of the Environment Options dialog.

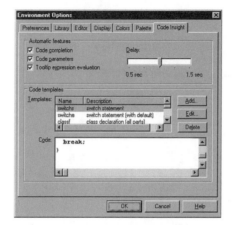

24

The Automatic features section allows you to turn automatic display of each Code Insight feature on or off. When automatic invocation of a feature is off, you can still invoke that feature manually using the keystrokes discussed earlier. You might want to turn off automatic invocation of these features if you have a slow computer or are short on system RAM. The Delay trackbar is used to control the amount of time the IDE waits before invoking a Code Insight feature.

The Code templates section allows you to add, delete, or edit code templates. Code templates were discussed in Hour 20 in the section "Code Templates."

New Bookmark Menu Items

The Code Editor context menu now contains two pop-up menus for setting bookmarks and going to bookmarks. The Toggle Bookmarks pop-up menu allows you to set a bookmark. The Goto Bookmarks pop-up menu allows you to return to a bookmark you had previously set. I prefer to use the keyboard shortcuts to set and go to bookmarks. However, if you prefer to use the mouse, these menu items are just what the doctor ordered.

Package Manager

The C++Builder Package Manager makes creating, editing, and installing component packages easier than it was in C++Builder 3. Figure 24.6 shows the Package Manager window.

FIGURE 24.6

*The Package Manager
makes working with
packages easy.*

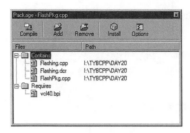

Any components you write must go into a package (writing components is an advanced topic, so I don't cover it in this book). The Package Manger allows you to easily add and remove units in a package. Simply click the Add or Remove buttons on the toolbar. You can also right-click the Package Manager window and choose Add to add a unit, or Remove File to remove a unit. The Compile button builds the package. The Install button will install the package to the C++Builder Component palette (provided the package is a design-time package). The Options button displays the Project Options dialog, so you can set the options for the package (package description, runtime or design-time package, version information, and so on).

New VCL Components

Several new components have been added to the Visual Component Library in C++Builder 4. I won't cover these new components in detail, but I'll mention each so you have an idea what these components do.

TActionList and TAction

The TActionList class provides a convenient way of performing command enabling. *Command enabling* is the process of enabling or disabling buttons depending on current conditions. For example, there's not much point of having the Cut or Copy button or menu item enabled for a text editor when no text is currently selected. Likewise, if there is no text in the Clipboard, the Paste button should be disabled.

TActionList, the non-visual component that manages actions, is found on the Standard tab of the Component palette. TActionList, as its name implies, contains a list of TAction objects. You create an action and then assign that action to any controls that need to be enabled or disabled based on that action. By controls I mean menu items, toolbar buttons, context menu items, and so on.

Let's take the Edit, Cut menu item, for example. You could have at least three objects associated with this particular task:

- A main menu item
- A toolbar button
- A pop-up menu item

You create actions with the ActionList Editor. To invoke the ActionList Editor, double click the ActionList component on your form. Given the Edit, Cut example, you would create an action for Cut called, say, CutAction. Then, using the Object Inspector, you assign CutAction to the Action property of each of the objects that correspond to the cut operation (toolbar buttons and menus, for example). At runtime, when you need to enable the Cut option, you can do so with just one line of code:

```
CutAction->Enabled = true;
```

This will enable all components with their Action properties set to CutAction. Disabling the Cut items is as simple as assigning False to the Enabled property of the action. The OnUpdate event of TAction and TActionList provides a convenient place to put your command-enabling code.

24

TControlBar

The TControlBar component is very similar to the Win32 TCoolBar component. TControlBar is provided as an alternative to the coolbar because the coolbar's operation can vary based on the version of Windows your users have installed. By using a TControlBar where you would normally use a TCoolBar, you can be assured that your application behaves properly, regardless of the version of Windows that the target machine is using.

TMonthCalendar

The TMonthCalendar component encapsulates the Win32 calendar component. It can be used to allow your users to visually select a date. Read the Date property to determine the date that the user selected.

New VCL Properties

Many new properties have been added to the base VCL components. I won't attempt to cover every new property, but instead will focus on the more interesting new properties.

Docking Properties

Some of the new properties deal with docking support for VCL components as discussed in the section "Docking Support for VCL Components." The docking support properties include DockSite, DragKind, and DragMode.

Constraints

The Constraints property can be used to set a form's maximum and minimum size. To see how the Constraints property works, perform this exercise:

1. Start a new application.

2. Double-click the Constraints property in the Object Inspector to see the constraint properties.

3. Set the MaxHeight, MaxWidth, MinHeight, and MinWidth properties to 300, 400, 100, and 200, respectively.

Run the application and size the main window. You will find that the form size is limited to the constraints you set in the Constraints property.

Anchor

The Anchor property can be used to force components on a form to retain their position relative to the form when it is resized. Too see how the Anchor property works, perform these steps:

1. Start a new application and place a button component in the lower-right corner of the form.

2. Select the button component and double-click the Anchors property to expand it.

3. Set the akLeft and akTop properties to False.

4. Set the akRight and akBottom properties to True.

Run the program and resize the main window. Notice that the button retains its position relative to the lower-right corner of the form as you resize the window.

Bitmaps for Menus

You can easily add bitmaps to menus in C++Builder 4. It's as easy as setting the menu's Images property to an image list and setting the ImageIndex property of each menu item. To illustrate, let's add images to the ScratchPad program's menu. Perform these steps:

1. Open the ScratchPad project.

2. Click on the MainMenu component and change its Images property to ImageList1 (select it from the drop-down list).

3. Double-click the MainMenu component to invoke the Menu Designer.

4. Click on the File, New menu item and change its ImageIndex property to 0 (the first image in the list).

5. Click on the Open menu item and change its `ImageIndex` to 1.

6. Set the Edit menu's Cut, Copy, and Paste items' `ImageIndex` property to 2, 3, and 4, respectively.

7. Click on the Help, About menu item. Change its `ImageIndex` property to 5.

8. Close the Menu Designer and run the program.

When the program runs, click on the File menu. You should see images next to the New and Open menu items. Check the Edit and Help menus, too. Each menu item for which you set the `ImageIndex` should have a bitmap next to it. Note that the menu bitmaps do not show in the Menu Designer at design time, but will show at runtime.

C++ Language Features

24

The C++ language standard is now official. After several years, the standards committee has finally determined what the C++ language rules are. Prior to this time there was only the proposed standard. Dealing with a proposed standard made it difficult for compiler vendors to implement C++ language features because they were constantly trying to hit a moving target. Now that the standard is defined, compiler makers can bring their compilers in line with the standard. To this end, C++Builder 4 implements many new C++ language features. Most of these features come in the form of additional support for template classes. Templates are an advanced topic and not something I can cover in this book. For more information on C++ templates I would suggest *C++Builder 4 Unleashed* by Sams Publishing, ISBN 0-672-31510-6. If you are interested in the new C++ language features implemented in C++Builder 4, see the "New Compiler Features" topic in the Cbuilder4\Help\BCB4NEW.HLP help file.

Project Options Enhancements

The most notable of the new project options features is the ability to specify the output directories for the intermediate and final files that C++Builder produces as it builds projects. I covered these directories in Hour 19 in the section "Output Directories." Refer to that chapter for additional details on how C++Builder uses the intermediate and final output directories.

Summary

As with every new C++Builder release, C++Builder 4 provides many new features. The new features in C++Builder 4 include enhancements to the IDE itself and to the VCL. Be sure to read the BCB4NEW.HLP file for a complete list of new features.

Workshop

The Workshop contains quiz questions to help you solidify your understanding of the material covered and exercises to provide you with experience in using what you have learned.

Q&A

Q I'm trying to position one of the IDE windows off to the side of the Code Editor. Every time I try, however, the window wants to dock to the Code Editor. How do I prevent the window from docking?

A Right-click on the window and turn the Dockable option off.

Q I'm trying to create a dockable toolbar. I have created the dock sites but I cannot drag my toolbar. What have I done wrong?

A More than likely you forgot to set the toolbar's DragKind property to dkDock and the DragMode property to dmAutomatic.

Quiz

1. Name two components that can be used as dock sites.

2. How can you make the Watch List window always visible during debugging sessions?

3. What property is used to set the maximum and minimum size of a form?

4. How do you invoke Code Parameters manually?

Answers

1. Components that can be dock sites include TCoolBar, TControlBar, TPanel, TForm, and TPageControl. Other components can be dock sites, too, but these are the components you are most likely to use as dock sites.

2. To make the Watch List window always visible during debugging, dock it to the Code Editor window.

3. The Constraints property is used to control a form's size at runtime.

4. To invoke Code Parameters manually, press Ctrl+Shift+Spacebar.

Exercises

1. Experiment with docking various IDE windows to the dock sites on the Code Editor.

2. Open the ScratchPad program. Make its toolbar dockable.

APPENDIX A

Installing C++Builder 4

To begin the installation process for C++Builder, place the book's CD in your CD-ROM drive. The C++Builder installation program will automatically run. (If the installation program does not auto-run, browse to the CD drive with Windows Explorer and double-click INSTALL.EXE.) The C++Builder installation program's main screen contains three options:

- Install C++Builder
- Browse CD
- Register Now

Click on C++Builder on the right side of the install program's main window to begin installing C++Builder. When you do, the C++Builder Setup will run. The first few screens of the Setup program contain general information and copyright notices like you see in most install programs. Click the Next or Yes button (depending on the screen) to continue. After clicking the Next button a few times you will get to the Setup Type screen. This screen allows you to choose from one of three setup options as shown in Figure A.1.

FIGURE A.1

*The C++Builder 4
Setup Options screen.*

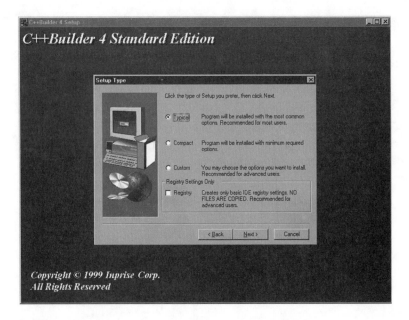

The following are the setup option types:

- Typical—Unless you want to specifically select the options to install, you should leave this radio button selected. The Typical option installs the files required by the average user. This option requires about 120MB of hard disk space.

- Compact—This option installs the minimum number of files on your hard drive, but might require you to keep the CD-ROM in your CD drive in order to fully use C++Builder. This option requires about 90MB of hard disk space.

- Custom—The Custom option allows you to select specific options to install. Until you become more familiar with C++Builder, you should probably let C++Builder Setup determine which files to install. The amount of disk space required for a custom install varies with the options you have selected. If you choose this option you can select specific options to install, such as the Help files, utilities, sample programs, and image files (bitmaps for buttons and splash screens).

After selecting the setup type, press Next to continue. The next screen, Select Component Directories, allows you to specify the directories where C++Builder will be installed. The Program Files directory is where the C++Builder main program files will be placed by default. You can select a different directory (or folder) if you want by clicking the Browse button and specifying the new location.

The Shared Files directory is where files common to all Inprise products will be installed. If you already have, or later buy, Borland Delphi, for example, both Delphi and C++Builder will use the files in the Shared Files directories, thus saving hard disk space. Shared files include images (bitmaps for buttons, splash screens, icons, and so on) and the Windows API help files. The Shared Files directory is not displayed on this screen if you earlier chose the Compact setup option. Click Next to accept the default directories or modify the directories as desired before clicking Next.

Next you are shown the Select Program Folder screen. Click Next to continue or type a new name for the folder name; then click Next. At this point the Start Copying Files screen is displayed. This screen shows you the options you have chosen. This is the final step before actual installation begins. You can still click the Back button to change installation options. If you are ready to install C++Builder, click the Install button.

C++Builder Setup installs the files from the CD-ROM to your hard drive. At the end of the install, you will be prompted to restart your computer. It is highly recommended that you restart at this time.

Running C++Builder

After you have installed C++Builder, you run the program by clicking the Windows Start button, and then choosing Programs, Borland C++Builder 4, C++Builder 4.

You might elect to place a shortcut to C++Builder on your desktop. To place a shortcut on your desktop, start Windows Explorer and navigate to the CBuilder4\Bin directory. Locate the file called BCB.EXE, click and drag it, and drop it on your desktop. Windows creates a shortcut to the C++Builder main program. You can now start C++Builder by simply double-clicking the shortcut icon on your desktop.

Registering Your Copy of C++Builder

You should register your copy of C++Builder as soon as possible. As I said earlier, the install screen has a Register Now link. Clicking this link begins the registration process. Your Web browser will be started and you can follow the links to the Inprise registration pages.

A

Registering your copy of C++Builder provides these benefits:

- Access to the latest C++Builder 4 information
- Special product offerings
- Access to Inprise Online Discussion Forums

If you register right away, you might be eligible for a free software product. See the Inprise Web site for more information.

INDEX

E

T

Other Related Titles

Sams Teach Yourself Borland Delphi 4 in 21 Days
Kent Reisdorph
ISBN: 0-672-31286-7
$39.99 US/$59.95 CAN

C++Builder 4 Unleashed
Kent Reisdorph
Charlie Calvert
ISBN: 0-672-31510-6
$59.99 US/$89.95 CAN

JBuilder3 Unleashed
Neal Ford
Ed Weber
ISBN: 0-672-31548-3
$49.99 US/$74.95 CAN

The Waite Group's C++ How-To
Jan Walter, et. al
ISBN: 1-57169-159-6
$39.99 US/$59.95 CAN

Sams Teach Yourself Linux Programming in 24 Hours
Warren Gay
ISBN: 0-672-31582-3
$24.99 US/$37.95 CAN

The Waite Group's Object-Oriented Programming in C++, Third Edition
Robert Lafore
ISBN: 1-57169-160-X
$34.99 US/$52.95 CAN

Sams Teach Yourself Data Structures and Algorithms in 24 Hours
Robert Lafore
ISBN: 0-672-31633-1
$24.99 US/$37.95 CAN

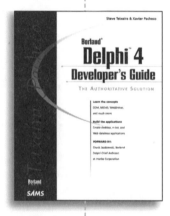

Borland Delphi 4 Developer's Guide
Xavier Pacheco
Steve Teixeira
ISBN: 0-672-31284-0
$59.99 US/$89.95 CAN

Charlie Calvert's Delphi 4 Unleashed
Charlie Calvert
ISBN: 0-672-31285-9
$49.99 US/$74.95 CAN

SAMS

www.samspublishing.com

All prices are subject to change.

What's on the Disc

The companion CD-ROM contains all the author's source code and some third-party software products.

Windows 95, Windows 98, and Windows NT 4 Installation Instructions

1. Insert the CD-ROM disc into your CD-ROM drive.
2. From the desktop, double-click the My Computer icon.
3. Double-click the icon representing your CD-ROM drive.
4. Double-click the icon titled START.EXE to run the installation program.
5. Follow the onscreen instructions to finish the installation.

If Windows 95, Windows 98, or Windows NT 4 is installed on your computer and you have the AutoPlay feature enabled, the START.EXE program starts automatically whenever you insert the disc into your CD-ROM drive.

Inprise Corporation

TRIAL EDITION SOFTWARE

License Statement

YOUR USE OF THE TRIAL EDITION SOFTWARE DISTRIBUTED WITH THIS LICENSE IS SUBJECT TO ALL OF THE TERMS AND CONDITIONS OF THIS LICENSE STATEMENT. IF YOU DO NOT AGREE TO ALL OF THE TERMS AND CONDITIONS OF THIS STATEMENT, DO NOT USE THE SOFTWARE.

1. This Software is protected by copyright law and international copyright treaty. Therefore, you must treat this Software just like a book, except that you may copy it onto a computer to be used and you may make archive copies of the Software for the sole purpose of backing up the Software and protecting your investment from loss. Your use of this software is limited to evaluation and trial use purposes only.

FURTHER, THIS SOFTWARE MAY CONTAIN A TIME-OUT FEATURE THAT DISABLES ITS OPERATION AFTER A CERTAIN PERIOD OF TIME. A TEXT FILE DELIVERED WITH THE SOFTWARE WILL STATE THE TIME PERIOD AND/OR SPECIFIC DATE ("EVALUATION PERIOD") ON WHICH THE SOFTWARE WILL EXPIRE. Though Inprise does not offer technical support for the Software, we welcome your feedback.

If the Software is an Inprise development tool, you can write and compile applications for your own personal use on the computer on which you have installed the Software, but you do not have a right to distribute or otherwise share those applications or any files of the Software which may be required to support those applications. APPLICATIONS THAT YOU CREATE MAY REQUIRE THE SOFTWARE IN ORDER TO RUN. UPON EXPIRATION OF THE EVALUATION PERIOD, THOSE APPLICATIONS MAY NO LONGER RUN. You should therefore take precautions to avoid any loss of data that might result.

2. INPRISE MAKES NO REPRESENTATIONS ABOUT THE SUITABILITY OF THIS SOFTWARE OR ABOUT ANY CONTENT OR INFORMATION MADE ACCESSIBLE BY THE SOFTWARE, FOR ANY PURPOSE. THE SOFTWARE IS PROVIDED 'AS IS' WITHOUT EXPRESS OR IMPLIED WARRANTIES, INCLUDING WARRANTIES OF MERCHANTABILITY AND FITNESS FOR A PARTICULAR PURPOSE OR NONINFRINGEMENT. THIS SOFTWARE IS PROVIDED GRATUITOUSLY AND, ACCORDINGLY, INPRISE SHALL NOT BE LIABLE UNDER ANY THEORY FOR ANY DAMAGES SUFFERED BY YOU OR ANY USER OF THE SOFTWARE. INPRISE WILL NOT SUPPORT THIS SOFTWARE AND IS UNDER NO OBLIGATION TO ISSUE UPDATES TO THIS SOFTWARE.

3. While Inprise intends to distribute (or may have already distributed) a commercial release of the Software, Inprise reserves the right at any time to not release a commercial release of the Software or, if released, to alter prices, features, specifications, capabilities, functions, licensing terms, release dates, general availability or other characteristics of the commercial release.

4. Title, ownership rights, and intellectual property rights in and to the Software shall remain in Inprise and/or its suppliers. You agree to abide by the copyright law and all other applicable laws of the United States including, but not limited to, export control laws. You acknowledge that the Software in source code form remains a confidential trade secret of Inprise and/or its suppliers and therefore you agree not to modify the Software or attempt to decipher, decompile, disassemble or reverse engineer the Software, except to the extent applicable laws specifically prohibit such restriction.

5. Upon expiration of the Evaluation Period, you agree to destroy or erase the Software, and to not re-install a new copy of the Software. This statement shall be governed by and construed in accordance with the laws of the State of California and, as to matters affecting copyrights, trademarks and patents, by U.S. federal law. This statement sets forth the entire agreement between you and Inprise.

6. Use, duplication or disclosure by the Government is subject to restrictions set forth in subparagraphs (a) through (d) of the Commercial Computer-Restricted Rights clause at FAR 52.227-19 when applicable, or in subparagraph (c) (1) (ii) of the Rights in Technical Data and Computer Software clause at DFARS 252.227-7013, and in similar clauses in the NASA AR Supplement. Contractor/manufacturer is Inprise Corporation, 100 Enterprise Way, Scotts Valley, CA 95066.

7. You may not download or otherwise export or reexport the Software or any underlying information or technology except in full compliance with all United States and other applicable laws and regulations. In particular, but without limitation, none of the Software or underlying information or technology may be downloaded or otherwise exported or reexported (i) into (or to a national or resident of) Cuba, Haiti, Iraq, Libya, Yugoslavia, North Korea, Iran, or Syria or (ii) to anyone on the US Treasury Department's list of Specially Designated Nationals or the US Commerce Department's Table of Deny Orders. By downloading the Software, you are agreeing to the foregoing and you are representing and warranting that you are not located in, under control of, or a national or resident of any such country or on any such list.

8. INPRISE OR ITS SUPPLIERS SHALL NOT BE LIABLE FOR (a) INCIDENTAL, CONSEQUENTIAL, SPECIAL OR INDIRECT DAMAGES OF ANY SORT, WHETHER ARISING IN TORT, CONTRACT OR OTHERWISE, EVEN IF INPRISE HAS BEEN INFORMED OF THE POSSIBILITY OF SUCH DAMAGES, OR (b) FOR ANY CLAIM BY ANY OTHER PARTY. THIS LIMITATION OF LIABILITY SHALL NOT APPLY TO LIABILITY FOR DEATH OR PERSONAL INJURY TO THE EXTENT APPLICABLE LAW PROHIBITS SUCH LIMITATION. FURTHERMORE, SOME STATES DO NOT ALLOW THE EXCLUSION OR LIMITATION OF INCIDENTAL OR CONSEQUENTIAL DAMAGES, SO THIS LIMITATION AND EXCLUSION MAY NOT APPLY TO YOU.

9. HIGH RISK ACTIVITIES. The Software is not fault-tolerant and is not designed, manufactured or intended for use or resale as on-line control equipment in hazardous environments requiring fail-safe performance, such as in the operation of nuclear facilities, aircraft navigation or communication systems, air traffic control, direct life support machines, or weapons systems, in which the failure of the Software could lead directly to death, personal injury, or severe physical or environmental damage ("High Risk Activities"). Inprise and its suppliers specifically disclaim any express or implied warranty of fitness for High Risk Activities.